STUDIES
IN MODERN HISTORY

STUDIES
IN MODERN HISTORY

BY

G. P. GOOCH, D.Litt., F.B.A.

Essay Index Reprint Series

BOOKS FOR LIBRARIES PRESS

FREEPORT, NEW YORK

First Published 1931
Reprinted 1968

LIBRARY OF CONGRESS CATALOG CARD NUMBER:

68-16934

PRINTED IN THE UNITED STATES OF AMERICA

PREFACE

MOST of the pieces in this volume have appeared before, though not all in their present form. ' Baron von Holstein' expands a sketch contributed to the *Cambridge Historical Journal* in 1923. ' The Study of the French Revolution' appeared in 1920 in the series entitled *Helps to Students of History*, and has been brought up to date. ' The Political Background of Goethe's Life' was delivered as an address to the English Goethe Society in 1926, and was published in its *Transactions*. ' Germany's Debt to the French Revolution' is reprinted from the *Quarterly Review* of January, 1919. ' German Political Ideas,' an address to the Sociological Society, was published in the *Contemporary Review* of June, 1915, was reprinted as a brochure, and has received a few trifling additions. ' The Study of Bismarck' is new, though a few passages have been taken from an article entitled ' The Rise and Fall of the German Empire' in the *Quarterly Review* of October, 1919. ' German Historical Studies since the War' was written for the German number of the *Times Literary Supplement* of April 18, 1929, and has been brought up to date. ' The Cambridge Chair of Modern History' has grown out of a paper read at the International Historical Congress in London in 1913. ' The Study of Foreign Affairs,' the Presidential Address to the Social and Political Education League in 1921, was published in the

Contemporary Review, reprinted as a brochure, and has been largely rewritten. 'Historical Novels' in its original form was an address to the National Home Reading Union, and was published in the *Journal* of the Union. I desire to express my gratitude to the editors and publishers who have most kindly granted permission for the use of old material.

G. P. G.

August, 1931.

CONTENTS

STUDIES IN
MODERN HISTORY

BARON VON HOLSTEIN

THOUGH historians are still waiting for Holstein's papers,[1] enough material has accumulated since his death in 1909 to attempt a sketch of the man who had the largest share in the shaping of German foreign policy from the fall of Bismarck in 1890 till his own enforced retirement in 1906. During his lifetime his name was scarcely known even to his countrymen. The brilliant sketch published immediately after his death by Maximilian Harden, the friend of his closing years, revealed him to a wider circle ; and directly the war was over the Memoirs of Otto Hammann and Baron von Eckardstein threw a flood of light on the *Éminence Grise* of modern Germany, who, like Père Joseph, loved to work in the dark and preferred the reality to the pomp of power. In the following years the publication of *Die Grosse Politik* enabled historians to reconstruct his policy from his own memoranda and to estimate his relations with his colleagues and chiefs. Still later, the outlines of the picture were filled in from the testimony of Waldersee, Eulenburg, Bülow and a host of other actors on the Bismarckian and post-Bismarckian stage. To-day the Mystery Man of the Wilhelmstrasse, the *Reichsjesuit*, as he was called by some of his enemies, is familiar by name to all the world.

---

[1] Holstein left his papers to the widow of his friend Geheimrat von Lebbin, who handed them over to Paul von Schwabach, head of Bleichröder's bank. See Schwabach, *Aus meinen Akten*, 446–8.

I

Baron Friedrich von Holstein, a member of an old Mecklenburg family, was born at Schwedt in the Mark of Brandenburg in 1837. He was educated in a *Realgymnasium* at Cologne, where he passed his leaving examination at the exceptionally early age of sixteen. His ambition, like that of Treitschke, was to become a soldier, but his parents insisted on his studying Law. His youth was darkened by the loss of his father in a fire, a tragedy which he witnessed with his own eyes.[1] After leaving the University of Berlin he spent four years as an official at the City Court of the Prussian capital. The shy young lawyer was introduced into the society of the capital by his dashing friend Schlieffen, who was destined to become Chief of the Staff.[2]

In 1860, at the age of twenty-three, he changed his course and decided to enter the diplomatic service. He was attached on probation to the Prussian Embassy at Petrograd, where Bismarck had been stationed for more than a year. 'A fortnight ago,' wrote Kurd von Schlözer on January 16, 1861, 'Baron Holstein came to us as Attaché, twenty-three years old, speaks French and English fluently, a good lad, many prejudices, very young and unobservant, will have to unlearn a good deal, but is zealous and not stupid.'[3] Two months later Bismarck wrote to his sister that he was very satisfied with Holstein's work, and was trying to train him for social life. Thus began an intimate association of thirty years with the founder of the German Empire, who presented him to Nesselrode with the words 'A future diplomat!' In June of the same year Bismarck wrote that he had the makings of a very good and industrious worker.[4] In 1862 he reported on the

---

[1] Theodor Wolff, *Das Vorspiel*, 76.
[2] Lancken, *Meine Dreissig Dienstjahre*, 58.
[3] Kurd von Schlözer, *Petersbürger Briefe*, 187–8.
[4] Poschinger, *Bismarck-Portefeuille*, V. 25.

young Attaché to Bernstorff, the Prussian Minister of
Foreign Affairs.[1] 'In addition to very good natural
gifts he has shown himself an earnest and indefatigable
worker, and in a short time he has made himself so fully
acquainted with his professional duties that he has been
of real service in the transaction of business. His
academic training is complete, and he is equally master
of French, English and Italian. At first he lacked
savoir faire. But here too he revealed the same capacity
to learn as he had displayed in his official tasks, and he
ended by winning a recognised place in all the circles
which he frequented. I therefore recommend to Your
Excellency a young man who promises to be extremely
useful in the diplomatic service.' A less flattering
comment on his sojourn in Petrograd is the caustic
observation of Nesselrode or some other Russian
diplomatist quoted twenty years later by Lothar Bucher
to Busch : 'Ce jeune homme sait une foule de choses,
mais il n'est pas capable de faire une seule.'[2] Returning to Berlin in 1863 for his final examination, which
he passed with distinction, he was sent on a mission to
the Allied troops in the Danish war of 1864 where,
though a civilian, he displayed conspicuous bravery
before the lines of Duppel. His next post was
London, whence he was transferred after a few months
to Rio de Janeiro, and then to Washington. He
left America in 1867 and served for brief terms in
Stuttgart, Florence and Copenhagen ; but of the
experiences of these formative years we know practically
nothing.

When war broke out in 1870 Bismarck despatched
the young Legationsrat on a mission to Italy. He met
Mazzini in Florence, and pointed out that a victorious
France would never allow the occupation of Rome.
Mazzini promised to find a way of keeping Visconti-
Venosta, the Foreign Minister, from indiscretions. In
October of the same year Holstein was introduced to

---

[1] Sass, *Preussische Jahrbücher*, March, 1930, 232–4.
[2] May 12, 1882. Busch's *Bismarck*, III. 49.

the young Bernhard von Bülow by Herbert Bismarck with the words : 'Our truest friend.'[1] He had accompanied the Chancellor's sons to England in the previous year and was liked by all the family.[2] At the opening of 1871 the Chancellor summoned him to join the Foreign Office Staff at Versailles. 'The Bureau has been re-inforced by two officials,' wrote Busch in his diary on January 6, 1871, one of whom was Holstein.[3] Three days later the diarist observes that he has turned out to be 'exceedingly amiable, hard-working and helpful.'[4] The German Boswell records several conversations at the Chancellor's table in the next few weeks in which Holstein took a minor part ; but there is no suggestion at this stage of such un-questioning discipleship as that which secured for Busch and Lothar Bucher a privileged position in the entourage of the Man of Destiny. On the other hand his capacity for clear and cogent statement was of value in drafting the memoranda and correspondence which preceded and followed the surrender of the beleaguered city ; and he retained as a memento the inkpot and pen with which the preliminary peace of February 26 was signed. When the struggle was ended and the Chancellor returned home, he was attached to General von Fabrice, the Governor-General of the occupied zone, at Soisy. Paris was now in the hands of the Commune, and General Cluseret promptly approached the German authorities. Bismarck instructed Fabrice to reply that he would listen to any overtures and forward them to Berlin. Holstein received a visit from Cluseret, who proposed an arrangement with the Commune, to be followed by German mediation between it and the French Government at Versailles. Fabrice reported the proposals to Berlin ; but the Chancellor had only wished to explore the situation, and made no response

[1] Bülow, *Denkwürdigkeiten*, IV. 160, 178.
[2] *Johanna von Bismarck, Ein Lebensbild in Briefen*, 200.
[3] Busch, I. 437.
[4] *Ib.* I. 445.

to the advances of the Communists, who were quickly suppressed by the iron hand of Galliffet.[1]

Bismarck's close association with Holstein at Versailles had confirmed his favourable opinion of his abilities, and he decided that he should be attached to the German Embassy at Paris. Count Waldersee, who had been Military Attaché in 1870, returned in June, 1871, as Chargé d'Affaires, and took over Holstein as Second Secretary from the *personnel* of General von Fabrice.[2] 'He was a very restless spirit, very vain and lacking in thoroughness,' he wrote on nearer acquaintance.[3] 'Despite his immense zeal and his desire to do everything, he really accomplished nothing. But he wrote and spoke French admirably, and therefore was very useful to me, and was often employed in tasks outside the Embassy.' The two men, both greedy for power, were destined to co-operation and conflict during the decades that lay ahead.

The position of the first Ambassador of the German Empire in the capital of its defeated rival was bound to be difficult, and the Chancellor displayed less than his usual acumen in transferring Count Harry Arnim from Rome. His ability was beyond question, but his views as to the policy to be pursued towards France differed radically from those of his chief. A few weeks after his appointment an entry in Busch's diary suggests that the Wilhelmstrasse was dissatisfied.[4] 'Bucher tells me that Arnim has shown great want of skill in negotiating the agreement relating to the Customs of Alsace-Lorraine. He is incapable, and so are his subordinates. Holstein is otherwise quite an able man, but he has no real knowledge of State affairs.' The Chancellor, however, was soon to find the latter's services of particular value. While the official German policy was to uphold the Republic on the ground that it was unlikely to find

---

[1] Busch, II. 59–61, and *Die Grosse Politik*, I. 34, note.
[2] *Waldersee in seinem militärischen Wirken*, I. 386, June 15, 1871.
[3] *Denkwürdigkeiten*, I. 156.
[4] Busch, II. 117, September 22, 1871.

allies in a monarchical Europe, the Ambassador openly favoured the Royalists ; and it was useful to learn from a man on the spot what game he was playing. The feud was embittered by Bismarck's conviction that Arnim, who had powerful friends at Court, was intriguing to succeed him as Chancellor.

In 1874 the Ambassador was transferred from Paris to Constantinople. His successor, Prince Hohenlohe, received instructions from Berlin in which reference was made to earlier communications from the Wilhelmstrasse. Search was made for the documents, but in vain, and Bismarck asked Arnim if he had removed them by mistake. Arnim coolly replied that he had taken them with him because they dealt with ecclesiastical questions, and concerned, *inter alia*, Cardinal Hohenlohe, adding that he wished his successor not to see the documents relating to his brother. When the Chancellor peremptorily ordered their restoration to the Paris Embassy, Arnim defiantly retorted that he regarded them as his personal property. Bismarck hereupon summoned the offender before a Court on the charge of removing documents belonging to the State. The offender was condemned to three months' imprisonment, fled to Switzerland, and died in exile, a broken man.

In this *cause célèbre*, in which the Chancellor was not only vindicating the authority of the State but striking down a dangerous rival, Holstein was the principal witness.[1] Arnim's advocate informed the Court that he did not accuse Holstein of spying, but that the Second Secretary had sent reports to the Wilhelmstrasse, without the knowledge of his Chief, which envenomed the conflict. Holstein replied that he had never addressed, nor been invited to address, reports to the Chancellor or his entourage. At first, he added, he and all the members of the Paris Embassy had greatly admired the Count. Indeed when he was at Berlin in the spring of 1872, at

---

[1] The documents are printed in *Der Arnim'sche Process*. Arnim's apologia, *Pro Nihilo*, charges Holstein with reporting confidential conversations, 12–14 (English translation). An authoritative work on Arnim is much needed.

a moment when the Chancellor was credited with the intention of resigning, he had observed that there could not be a better successor than Arnim. After returning to Paris in the autumn of 1872 from a visit to Varzin, he had found that the opinions of the Ambassador differed widely from those of the Chancellor, who had promised Thiers his support to any Government which made and carried out the peace. Thiers had done so ; yet Arnim desired a change of regime. ' I opposed his view, but I soon realised that it was his fixed idea. His proceedings raised the question which of the two men was to rule the Empire. For fourteen years I had been in close relations with the Chancellor. I wrote my impressions to several friends. Later I spoke to Arnim, and told him that I wished to change my post. He saw no reason for such a step ; but the interview made me feel that he had not behaved very well. This impression was confirmed when I learned that his relations with the Chancellor were very strained. Arnim has accused me of being the cause of all the trouble. That charge is answered by the documents themselves. From January, 1873, my social relations with him ceased completely. In the autumn of 1873 I learned at Berlin that there was open war. Everybody talked of it. My position between the two was impossible. I wished for a change, but friends agreed that I should seem to be shirking a difficult task.'

Holstein's conduct on this occasion was variously judged at the time. The trial naturally aroused keen interest in France ; and, in his Introduction to a French translation of the evidence, Valfrey defends him against the charge of dishonourable conduct, and argues that he showed himself an open adversary.[1] In his own country, on the other hand, his attitude was generally condemned. ' I remember the scene in Court when Holstein gave evidence against Arnim,' writes Baron von Eckardstein. ' I recall the excitement when it appeared that, at Bismarck's orders, he had systematically spied on his

[1] *Le Procès d'Arnim.*

Chief.'[1]   His action, echoes Prince Alexander Hohenlohe, always remained a blot on his character, and made
him an embittered recluse.[2]   Henceforth he was the
Judas of German politics.   He was cut by his friends
and for the rest of his life he suffered from persecution
mania.   The man of the world who loved society and
pretty women lived like a hermit in an unfashionable
quarter of Berlin, taking solitary holidays and seeking
consolation for the worm that gnawed at his heart in the
favour of the Chancellor and the unsleeping struggle
for power.   ' The Bismarcks have branded me on the
forehead like a galley slave,' he complained to a friend,
' and therewith they hold me fast.'[3]

Holstein remained at Paris for two years after the
eviction of Arnim, and his conduct during the reign of
the second Ambassador to the Republic confirmed in
some measure the unfavourable impression produced by
his record under the first.   Princess Hohenlohe, records
her son Alexander, who was then a boy, used to complain that when she and her daughters walked out they
were often followed by him.   They received friendly
warnings from certain members of the French official
world against the practices of the Secretary, who—whatever he may have done under Arnim—now corresponded
direct with the Chancellor.   Prince Alexander adds that,
though his mother retained her profound distrust and
antipathy to the end of her life, Holstein won the confidence of his father, in whose diary he occasionally
appears.   ' I met a Prussian Legationsrat von Holstein,'
he wrote on December 8, 1870, ' who told me a great
deal about his sport on the American prairies.'[4]   On
succeeding to the Paris Embassy in 1874 he records
dinners and visits to the theatre with his subordinate ;
and on December 18, 1875, while on a visit to Bismarck,
he notes the decision that Holstein is to be First
Secretary.[5]   Twenty years later the two men were

[1] *Erinnerungen*, I. 22–3.   [2] *Aus meinem Leben*, ch. 12.
[3] Theodor Wolff, *Das Vorspiel*, 77.
[4] *Denkwürdigkeiten*, I. 33.   [5] *Ib.* I. 177.

to renew their association in even more responsible positions.

In 1876, after five instructive years at Paris, Holstein was recalled to the Wilhelmstrasse, where he was to labour for thirty eventful years. 'The faithful Fritz,' as he was called in the Bismarck household, had proved himself an ardent disciple of the Chancellor, who rewarded him with his confidence and shared with him many of his secrets. In 1876 the elder Bülow informed his son Bernhard that he had intended to send him to the Embassy in Paris, but that the plan had been frustrated by Holstein.[1] 'Who is Holstein?' asked the young diplomat. 'I hardly know him.' 'Who is Holstein?' repeated the Foreign Secretary. 'That is not so easy to answer. He came as a raw attaché to Bismarck in St. Petersburg. Since then he has been to our great man what Père Joseph was to Richelieu.' He added that Holstein made him feel uncomfortable and that he had warned Bismarck. The Prince replied that he must have some one whom he could thoroughly trust. When Bülow rejoined that the Chancellor could trust him too, he received the reply : Yes, but only for the good things. Sometimes I must do evil things in this evil world. *A corsaire corsaire et demi.* ' Holstein is a corsair, ready for anything. Besides his capacity for dirty business he is an outstanding political brain. He has doubtless opposed your appointment to Paris because you might have learned more of his intrigues against Arnim than he would like.' The *ipsissima verba* cannot be guaranteed after so many years ; but the conversation as served up in the *Memoirs* of the ex-Chancellor may well represent the attitude of his father and Bismarck at the time. In October, 1877, Busch records a visit to Varzin, when Holstein was the only other visitor.[2] On the latter's return to the Wilhelmstrasse after a sojourn of five weeks with the Chancellor, he reported his chief's views and plans to Lucius von

[1] Bülow, *Denkwürdigkeiten*, IV. 386–7.
[2] Busch, II. 317, 319.

Ballhausen.[1] Though Holstein was an official of the Foreign Office, it is clear from this conversation that Bismarck was in the habit of discussing internal and Parliamentary questions with his trusted subordinate as well as foreign affairs.[2]

As one of the Secretaries of the Berlin Congress in 1878 Holstein appears in the familiar official picture painted by Anton von Werner to commemorate the makers of the treaty. His perfect mastery of English and French made him a useful satellite, and he had the pleasure of introducing to the Chancellor the incomparable Blowitz, whom he had learned to know at Paris. He was rewarded by the French Government with one of the lower grades of the Legion of Honour ; but the drudgery of the Secretariat was by no means to the taste of a man who had seen so much of the world. He was one day to become the greatest worker in the Wilhelmstrasse, but the time had not arrived when power should sweeten and justify unsleeping toil.

He proved himself useless, complains his colleague Radowitz in his Memoirs.[3] 'In the first meetings for drawing up the protocols, he made himself so objectionable by his uncalled for observations, and contributed so little to the work, that we at once saw it was impossible to get through our heavy task, for which every minute was of importance, if he were to remain. Henceforth he devoted himself to the foreign journalists, which was his *métier*. Steady, thorough work bored him. During the Congress he did as good as nothing, but he tried to have his finger in every pie. He never forgave me for evicting him, and began his embittered campaign against me, which, when he became so powerful, had a fatal influence on my career.' Radowitz is a hostile witness ; but he was one of the best brains in the service, and his testimony cannot be ignored.

---

[1] Lucius von Ballhausen, *Erinnerungen*, 114–5.
[2] During the same autumn he had conversations with Crispi both before and after his visit to the Chancellor at Gastein. See Crispi's *Memoirs*, II. 41–6.
[3] *Aufzeichnungen und Erinnerungen*, II. 23.

Holstein was *persona gratissima* with the Bismarcks, and Herbert had joined him in complaining to the Chancellor of the conduct of the other members of the Secretariat. Without waiting to read the protocol which Radowitz and his French colleague, Comte de Möuy, had drawn up, Bismarck sharply exhorted him to greater accuracy. The protocol was none the less approved and Radowitz explained the situation to Bülow, the Foreign Minister, who secured the removal of Holstein.[1] It was, however, a Pyrrhic victory, and Radowitz soon tasted the fruits of his implacable hostility. Soon after the Congress Holstein tried to poison the younger Bülow against his enemy and through him to influence the Foreign Secretary.[2] In the winter of 1879 the Prince was led to believe that Radowitz had intrigued against him during his last illness, and aspired to the post of Foreign Minister under a new Chancellor.[3] In February, 1880, the suspicious Dictator called for a report on his activities ; but the individual selected for this duty happened to be a friend of Radowitz and told him what was in the wind. It was obvious to both that the preposterous story had reached the Chancellor through Holstein, who had been alone with him in Varzin during the autumn and winter ; and they had little doubt that that unscrupulous official had invented as well as reported the legend. Holstein, adds Radowitz, possessed not only the ear of the Prince, who believed in his utter devotion, but the confidence of the Princess, whose influence in personal matters was not to be despised. No proof of Radowitz's disloyalty was forthcoming ; but a difficult situation was ended by keeping him abroad.

Holstein stood close to his master during the critical weeks of August and September 1879 when a decision was taken which affected European history for forty

[1] *Aufzeichnungen und Erinnerungen*, II. 42.
[2] Bülow, *Denkwürdigkeiten*, IV. 452-5. According to Bülow the quarrel arose because Radowitz received a higher Order than Holstein ; but Radowitz is here a better witness.
[3] Radowitz, II. 117-9.

years. While Bismarck was wrestling with the unwillingness of the Emperor to approve an Austro-
German defensive alliance against the growing Russian
menace, Holstein, whom the Chancellor had taken with
him to Gastein, suggested that Hohenlohe's mediation
should be invoked. The Ambassador, then on leave,
was summoned by telegraph and was met by Holstein,
who explained the situation. Hohenlohe was quickly
converted to the need for an alliance and was despatched
to convert the harassed ruler.[1] No sooner was the Dual
Alliance signed and ratified than Bülow, the Foreign
Minister, died. On October 28, 1879, Hohenlohe's
diary records a discussion at the Wilhelmstrasse in which
he was pressed from several quarters to take up the
burden.[2] Next day he journeyed to Varzin, where he
found Holstein, who strongly urged him to accept the
post if he received the offer. When Bismarck proposed
his appointment, he explained that the salary was too
low for his needs, but volunteered for the following
summer, while the Chancellor was away. The zeal
with which Holstein urged the nomination was an
additional cause of resentment to Princess Hohenlohe,
who feared that the work would be too much for her
husband's strength. Her apprehensions were fulfilled ;
and Count Hatzfeldt, whom Bismarck described as the
best horse in Germany's diplomatic stable, and who was
a *persona grata* with Holstein, became Secretary for
Foreign Affairs.

II

In 1880 Holstein, hitherto a Legationsrat, was
appointed a Vortragender Rat, or what we should call
an Assistant Under-Secretary, and held the post for
the next twenty-six years. Prince Bülow has expressed
the opinion in his *Memoirs* [3] that he never exercised a
greater influence than in the second half of the Bismarck

[1] Hohenlohe, *Denkwürdigkeiten*, II. 274.   [2] *Ib.* II. 278–80.
[3] *Denkwürdigkeiten*, II. 112–3.

era. ' His power at that time in regard to questions of
personnel was very far-reaching, his position almost
impregnable owing to the absolute confidence reposed
in him by the great Chancellor, and to the intimate
friendship with Herbert. Especially since the death in
1879 of my father, who by his old and trustful relations
to Prince Bismarck and his tranquil clarity was a useful
counterweight, Holstein came more and more into the
foreground. My father did not love him ; they were
utterly different natures.' Nobody would agree that
Holstein's influence reached highwater mark at this
period ; but certainly none of his colleagues enjoyed so
much of the confidence of Hatzfeldt, who appointed
him *interim* Under-Secretary in the summer of 1882, to
the disgust of Lothar Bucher and the disturbance of the
harmony that had hitherto prevailed in the Political
Department.[1] The work of the Foreign Office was
complicated by the fact that the Dictator was often
away for months at a time, and even the faithful Lothar
Bucher was tempted to grumble. ' Bucher complains
that he occupies himself too much with the press,' wrote
Busch in his diary, October 25, 1881.[2] ' Instructions
arrive from Varzin almost daily. No one in the office
understands them—neither the sons, nor Holstein, who
is a mere bungler.' Bucher returned to his theme a
fortnight later.[3] The press campaign had been very
foolishly conducted. ' We have no less than four
Secretaries—Busch, the real one, who is good ; Herbert
at Varzin ; Rantzau and Holstein here. These know
nothing and can do nothing properly. None of them
reads the papers or knows what is going on, and if the
Chief gives violent instructions they are carried out with
still greater violence.' Bucher's growing dislike of
Holstein is reflected in an entry in Busch's diary two
years later.[4] ' He has recently developed, owing to his
ambition, into a very dangerous intriguer. He tells

---

[1] Poschinger, *Stunden bei Bismarck*, 72.
[2] III. 9. [3] *Ib.* III. 13.
[4] *Ib.* III. 112, November 19, 1883.

Hatzfeldt everything he hears.' In the following year Bucher again complained of the shocking way in which business was conducted in the Foreign Office by Hatzfeldt and Holstein, with the latter of whom he had ceased to exchange salutations.[1]

In 1885 an important change occurred in the Wilhelmstrasse. The Chancellor was dissatisfied with Münster's handling of the colonial negotiations with England, complaining that his representations to Lord Granville had been lacking in vigour. Münster was therefore transferred to Paris, and was succeeded in London by Hatzfeldt, while Herbert Bismarck was installed as Foreign Secretary. Herbert, observed Lothar Bucher to Busch, had selected Holstein as Under-Secretary, and would probably get his way, though the Chancellor had another candidate in view.[2] Herbert had made up the differences between his mother and Holstein. If the latter were appointed, added Bucher, he would retire. The new Foreign Secretary failed to carry his point, for Berchem was appointed ; but he worked in full harmony with Holstein, who had known him since childhood, and who acted as his chief adviser when the Chancellor was away. Herbert assigned to his old friend the room next to his own, and he retained his strategic position till his retirement twenty years later. He was still *persona gratissima* to the Chancellor, and Dryander records that he was specially skilled in persuading his Chief to talk about the dramatic incidents of his life.[3]

Holstein's ex-chief Waldersee, now Quarter-Master-General, records in his diary that he was in constant touch with the Foreign Office, chiefly through Holstein ; and he now began to realise both the lofty position to which his old subordinate had climbed and the curious twist in his mind.[4] It was easy to work with Hatzfeldt, Herbert and Berchem. ' It was otherwise with

[1] Busch, III. 118, September 23, 1884.
[2] *Ib.* III. 146.   [3] Dryander, *Erinnerungen*, 165.
[4] *Waldersee in seinem militärischen Wirken*, II. 31-3.

Holstein. One always had to reckon with his suspicions and sudden resentments. But I was well acquainted with the eccentric from 1871, and enjoyed what was for him a very high degree of his confidence. I must say too that till Bismarck's departure he was always the same, and took interest in me, apparently, like Berchem, regarding me as a candidate for the Chancellorship. I very often went to him and he occasionally visited me. He was at that time very communicative, gave me everything to read that could interest me, so that I obtained a considerable insight into the diplomatic situation.' The confidence of the Chancellor was still unshaken. In 1885 Klemens Busch, the Under-Secretary, asked for a post abroad. ' You cannot get on with my son ?' inquired Bismarck. Busch replied that he could not get on with Holstein. ' There I cannot help you,' was the rejoinder ; ' I must have somebody on whom I can absolutely rely.' [1]

In 1886, when William I was in his ninetieth year, Waldersee records unblushing Bismarckian attempts to obtain control of his heir. ' To maintain the monopoly of the future Emperor,' he wrote on April 2, ' everyone is to be removed who might possess or attain power, and discreditable means are employed. One of the worst of the agents turns out to be Holstein. He is clever enough to keep out of the limelight, so that many people scarcely know of his existence.' [2] In November he records a fresh attempt to remove someone from the entourage of the Crown Prince. ' The driving force behind Rado-linski is again Holstein, this evil spirit of last winter. He has such a bad conscience that he avoids me since the spring. I have discovered that it was he who talked scandal to the Crown Prince and Princess about me ; and he actually painted me as an evil counsellor of Prince William, the same prince before whom he cringes and

[1] Bülow, IV. 623.
[2] Waldersee, I. 286. Eulenburg asserts, on the authority of the Bismarcks, that Holstein urged the Chancellor to have the Crown Prince Frederick poisoned. But this was doubtless nothing more than a grim joke. Haller, *Eulenburg*, 383.

whom he always tells how much he reverences him.
With the Crown Prince he pretends to be a champion
of the Battenberg marriage, though he knows quite well
that Bismarck will never give his consent.'[1]   Though
Waldersee had taken the measure of Holstein, he preferred even a temporary and uncertain friendship to a
perilous enmity.   ' To-day I was in the Foreign Office,'
he wrote on May 31, 1887, ' and established friendly
relations with Holstein.   Third parties seemed to have
an interest in this reconciliation and maintain that there
were misunderstandings.   That is quite possible.   So
I came forward gladly and had the impression that he
was immensely relieved.'[2]   In the following March he
records a dinner with Holstein, ' with whom I am quite
on the old footing.   I hear from several quarters that
he is really exerting himself in my interest.'[3]   For the
next year or two Waldersee was in high favour, and his
correspondence contains long and intimate letters written
by his political mentor.

Numerous portraits of Holstein have been painted
by friends and foes, but all agree in their emphasis on
his extensive knowledge, his brain power, and his morbid
temperament.   He was the first of the higher officials
to arrive at the Foreign Office and the last to leave.   No
one could now complain that he eschewed drudgery.
He read every document and report, could explain the
history and present position of any negotiations, and
possessed an uncanny acquaintance with the private
affairs of the *personnel* of the diplomatic service.   Yet
the greatest worker in the Wilhelmstrasse was more
of a liability than an asset.   Schweinitz, the veteran
German Ambassador in St. Petersburg, records a visit
to the Wilhelmstrasse in the autumn of 1887.[4]   ' This
eccentric, who compelled my respect when in 1864
before Duppel he assisted the wounded in the front
ranks and who still does much good in secret, has a
spiteful character, allows himself to be influenced by

[1] *Denkwürdigkeiten*, I. 304.   [2] *Ib.* I. 327.
[3] *Ib.* I. 365, March 3, 1888.   [4] *Erinnerungen*, II. 349.

personal dislikes, and makes mischief, without it being known, by his odious press methods. He has a remarkable brain, but the spirit and character of a hunchback. He perfectly understands the great dangers into which we have fallen through our over-subtle and yet often brutal policy. He explained so clearly and coolly all that may happen that I left with an uncomfortable feeling.' If Raschdau is to be believed, Holstein talked better than he wrote, for his drafts required the most careful revision.[1]

It was about this time that Prince William, in the course of his apprenticeship, was allowed to work in the Wilhelmstrasse, of which the Chancellor, for his guidance, described the *personnel*. 'When he came to Holstein, relates the fallen ruler in his *Memoirs*, 'it seemed to me that a warning sounded through his words. As I became more intimate in the Bismarck circle, Holstein was discussed with greater frankness. He was very clever, very industrious, immensely vain, full of mistrust, dominated by fancies, a good hater and therefore a dangerous man. Bismarck called him the man with the hyæna eyes, whom I should be wise to avoid. The sharp criticism of later years was already ripening.'[2] According to Raschdau, a colleague in the Political Department, the intimacy of earlier years had now ceased, and he does not remember him being asked to draft any document of importance.[3]

Holstein was in fact, though not in name, second in importance to the Foreign Secretary, and he now took an active part in discussions of high policy. The renewal of the Triple Alliance in 1887 involved a good deal of friction, owing to the extent of Italy's demands and Austria's unwillingness to concede them. No such repugnance was felt by Bismarck, whose fear of simultaneous attack by the France of Boulanger and the

---

[1] Brauer, Marcks and Müller, *Erinnerungen an Bismarck*, 30.

[2] *Ereignisse und Gestalten*, 6. The reference to the hyæna eyes is not so bad as it sounds, for Holstein had almost completely lost the use of one eye in a shooting accident. He was sometimes called Polyphemus.

[3] *Süddeutsche Monatshefte*, March, 1931, 390.

Russia of Katkoff disposed him to accept almost any proposals from Rome and to urge their acceptance at Vienna. When Prince Reuss reported his unsatisfactory conversations with Kalnoky, Holstein expressed to the Austrian Ambassador, Count Széchenyi, his concern at the ' not easily comprehensible decision ' of his chief.[1] What would become of Austria, he asked, if she failed to settle the Bulgarian question with Russia and at the same time lost her Italian ally ? To the Ambassador's rejoinder that no reliance could be placed on the Italians, he replied that it was a question, not of a permanent alliance, but of acquiring a paid corps of auxiliaries, like the mercenaries of the Middle Ages. To dispel Kalnoky's fears that Italy might demand southern Tirol in return for support in an Austro-Russian war, he consulted the Italian Ambassador, who authorised him to declare that Italy had no such idea.   On the other hand, added Holstein, it might be impossible to prevent Italy establishing herself in Albania.   A few days later he referred angrily to Italy's demands for *pourboire*, but once more urged the necessity of yielding.   Not, however, till Bismarck threw his whole weight into the scale of surrender did the stubborn Kalnoky purchase the continuation of Italy's support at her own high price. On the other hand Holstein considered the Chancellor too subservient in regard to Russia, encouraged Austria to sharp measures and used the press to suggest a danger in Galicia ; nor did he approve the Russophil policy in the case of the Battenberg marriage.[2]   It was the first overt sign of an ominous independence.

The accession of William II in 1888 changed nothing for the moment, and indeed the death of the liberal Emperor Frederick removed a menace for the Chancellor and his friends.   Yet shrewd observers began to ask whether the old gladiator was as invulnerable as he

[1] Pribram, *The Secret Treaties of Austria-Hungary*, II. 69–75.

[2] Waldersee, *Denkwürdigkeiten*, I. 340, December 12, 1887, and Bülow, IV. 607. Bülow believes that his hostility to Russia was due to his lack of social success in St. Petersburg as a young man ; but this is fanciful.

believed. 'At the Emperor's accession,' wrote
Waldersee in his diary in July, 1889, 'I prophesied to
Holstein and others that he would not for long put up
with Bismarck ; but no one believed me. In the late
summer they began to see it, and henceforward the rats
gradually left the ship. One of the first to go was
Holstein. Eulenburg and Kiderlen soon followed.'[1]
We cannot tell when Holstein began to regard the fall
of the Chancellor as a probability, and it is not certain
how far he worked for a change before the catastrophe
was in sight. That he played for his own hand is clear
enough ; but for one in so exposed a position it was
dangerous to risk high stakes. Bismarck's second son,
Bill, had never trusted him ;[2] Herbert no longer treated
him with the old consideration ; and the Chancellor
was no longer his oracle. 'He is an egotist to his
finger-tips,' complained Holstein. Yet it was not his
habit to burn his boats till the necessity arose, for his
chair in the Wilhelmstrasse was all that he had in the
world.

  'As a Bismarckian,' wrote Holstein to Waldersee in
August, 1889, 'I ought to desire an unfavourable result to
the elections, for the more difficult the internal situation
becomes, the more indispensable is the Chancellor.'[3]
A remarkable letter to Bötticher, dated January 7, 1890,
advising him on a forthcoming visit to Friedrichsruh to
dissuade the Prince from his projected declaration against
the ruler's plans on social reform, points in the same
direction.[4] Otherwise, he argued, the Chancellor would
lose the election, find himself more isolated than at any
time since 1866, and provide the Emperor with an
opportunity of getting rid of him. It would therefore
be best for himself and the nation if he were to compromise, or at any rate not to be directly antagonistic.
'Holstein,' testifies Maximilian Harden, a friend of
both in later years, 'declared a hundred times that he

[1] Waldersee, II. 56, July 7.   [2] Bülow, IV. 453-4.
[3] Waldersee, *Briefwechsel*, I. 317.
[4] Eppstein, *Bismarcks Entlassung*, 35-6.

had neither worked nor wished for Bismarck's overthrow.' When he saw the sapping and mining he urged Herbert to hurry his father to Berlin to avert the explosion. But the Prince came too late. When the young ruler complained of the Chancellor's "lectures" in the presence of others, Holstein wrote to Herbert from a sick-bed to say that the Prince could tell the Emperor anything he liked in private, but not before the Ministers.[1]

There is, however, evidence to show that Holstein was not so loyal as these quotations might suggest. In the winter of 1887-8 he told a friend of the Emperor, whom he asked to lunch at his favourite restaurant, that Bismarck was losing his memory and getting too old for work.[2] In the autumn of 1889 Bülow found him preoccupied and sharply critical of the Russophil Policy of his chief.[3] Moreover he had quarrelled with Rantzau, and in consequence no longer visited his wife or his mother-in-law, Princess Bismarck. ' Your brother Adolf, the Adjutant and friend of the young Emperor,' asked Holstein as they parted, ' is for Bismarck ? ' ' Certainly,' replied Bülow, ' and he would regard his retirement as a grave misfortune.' Holstein's disappointed face wore an almost diabolical expression, and he turned away without a word. It was clear to Bülow that he had already turned his back on Bismarck. Yet he concealed the change from his chief so cleverly that on the following day Herbert Bismarck exclaimed at a lunch party : ' Holstein is true as gold. Whoever asperses him will have to deal with me.' No wonder he was often called the mole, for he worked in the dark.

Holstein was a dangerous foe because he possessed so much compromising knowledge. ' Bismarck only shews the Emperor despatches which reflect his policy,' wrote Waldersee in his diary on January 2, 1890, ' and his agents hardly dare to send in anything which has not been ordered. Nothing from foreign papers respecting

---

[1] Harden, *Köpfe*, I. 101.
[2] Sidney Whitman, *German Memories*, 230-1.
[3] Bülow, IV. 627.

the real opinion in Russia may be shewn.' The diarist adds that he learned this from Holstein, who had often invited him to transmit news to the monarch.[1] Holstein himself told Lucanus, the Emperor's Political Secretary, that the Chancellor withheld certain documents ; and Bülow assures us that the alarming reports from the German Consul, which Bismarck had kept from the Kaiser, and which were brought to his notice by Waldersee, were supplied by Holstein.[2] It was obvious that a breach was at hand, and Holstein would have been untrue to himself had he not joined the winning side in good time ; for if Bismarck were to leave the stage he might virtually control the Wilhelmstrasse. It was true that the Iron Chancellor had made his career, but it was no less a fact that he had ruined his happiness. Holstein was not a forgiving nature, and he never forgave him. As a young man with his way to make in the world, he had sacrificed himself at his master's orders : he had now to think of himself. Harden tells us that Holstein tried to persuade Herbert Bismarck to retain the Foreign Office as the Emperor desired, when the Prince left Office ;[3] but this may mean very little, for Herbert's resolve to stand and fall with his father was known to his intimates. After the Ides of March Holstein had no further dealings with the Bismarckian *Fronde*, and firmly linked his fortune with the new regime. ' When Herbert gave a farewell dinner to the officials of the Foreign Office,' wrote Lothar Bucher to Busch on July 10, ' Holstein, Lindau, Kayser and Raschdau declined the invitation. All four owed everything to the Prince.'[4]

The Chancellor could hardly expect all his old staff to resign in sympathy, but his heart was filled with angry suspicions. In some cases he saw conspirators where clearer eyes saw only loyal and grieving friends, such as the blameless Bötticher, who is held up to obloquy in the third volume of his apologia. His

---

[1] II. 85.
[2] Bülow, IV. 637.
[3] Harden, *Köpfe*, I. 101-2.
[4] Busch, III. 341.

condemnation of Holstein had much more justification.
When Princess Bismarck observed that he had for some
time avoided their house, her husband bitterly rejoined :
' Yes, he always had a good *flair* (*Er hat immer eine feine
Nase gehabt*).' ' He was rather Arnim's disciple than
mine,' observed Bismarck later to Harden ; ' he is only
useful for work below ground, and he has spots on the
inner iris.' [1]   On another occasion he added : ' Extremely useful in the second and third position, but
dangerous in command.' [2]

Sharp condemnation of Holstein's conduct at the
time of the Chancellor crisis comes from his old enemy
Radowitz, who happened to be in Berlin and visited the
Wilhelmstrasse on April 2.   ' Berchem does not seem
likely to stay long,' he wrote.[3] ' How should he ? The
real political control will be in Holstein's hands, as he is
long and intimately acquainted with Caprivi.   At any
rate he has been in touch with him for some time, since
he noticed that the Bismarck regime was nearing its end.
The change occurred just at the right time for him.
His personal position in the Office had deteriorated so
much in the last months that there would probably
have been a crash.   He had quarrelled with Rantzau,
the son-in-law of Bismarck, and ceased to speak to him,
and he was at enmity with Lothar Bucher.   Quicker
than anyone in the Foreign Office he has deserted and
repudiated the Bismarckian banner.   Young Attachés
who worked under him are astonished at the satisfaction
with which he speaks of the change and at the lack of
piety with which he criticises the Prince.   That is the
man in whom the Bismarck family believed as " the truest
of the true," and by whom they allowed themselves to be
influenced against everyone who stood in his path.
I hear today that he is the only official to whom the
Prince did not say goodbye on leaving the office.   Indeed
he kept out of the way.   Now he remains as the *Spiritus*

---

[1] Harden, *Köpfe*, I. 127.
[2] Nowak, *Das dritte deutsche Kaiserreich*, I. 149.
[3] *Aufzeichnungen und Erinnerungen*, II. 326-7.

Rector for the new men. Caprivi told me that he had
the fullest confidence in Holstein and would have to
trust to his great experience, and Marschall will be clever
enough to enter into partnership. Kiderlen is already,
as I could see, quite his amanuensis. During my present visit I have not seen Holstein himself. Berchem
warned me against him and described him as semi-
irresponsible when personal antipathies arise, such as
exist in my case.'

Eulenburg's verdict is no less severe. Holstein, he
declares, till now a house-dog on Bismarck's chain, had
played a sort of whist with a dummy hand against
Bismarck and his son.[1] ' Who was the dummy ? The
Emperor. If the Bismarcks lost, the Emperor was his
partner. If the Bismarcks won, then it was only a game.
In any case he knew that Bismarck passionately opposed
the idea of a Congress. His opposition to Herbert was
known to me before ; now he secretly turned against
the Chancellor. For he thought he could play his part
in the Foreign Office better without Bismarck—if his
enemy Waldersee were not his successor—and he succeeded in eliminating him. I believe that Machiavelli
himself could have taken lessons from his crafty dealings
at that time. He always assumed the airs of an old
Prussian official, but he was at heart a democrat. In
this connection he often betrayed himself to me. A
nature like his could only be revolutionary.' His clever
manœuvres extorted Eulenburg's reluctant admiration.[2]
' That Holstein, the inseparable companion of the
Bismarcks and the confidant of Bötticher in the burning
issues between Kaiser and Chancellor, was not included
in the list of the arch " traitors " shows his extraordinary
skill. I cannot explain his secret thoughts in the days
of the catastrophe. But I cannot help thinking that he
had perhaps a larger share in Bismarck's suspicions of
Bötticher than is generally known, in other words, that
he sacrificed his friend Bötticher to save himself. For
it is always a riddle to me that Holstein, who had

[1] Eulenburg, *Aus 50 Jahren*, 244-5.　　　　[2] *Ib.* 253.

such a large part in the quarrel between Bismarck and
William II, was not more hated by the former.' The
heart of Herbert Bismarck, on the other hand, was
filled with passionate anger, and Bülow roundly accuses
Holstein of stabbing the Prince in the back.[1]

III

William II had selected Caprivi as his second
Chancellor before he parted with the first ; but the
choice of a Foreign Minister to succeed Herbert
Bismarck proved more difficult. Holstein was widely
expected to receive the appointment ; but he shirked
the post partly because he felt unequal to the Parliamentary and social duties which it involved, [2] and he
always preferred the reality to the show of power. On
the other hand he was largely responsible for the selection
which was made. According to Julius von Eckardt,
he vetoed the appointment of two diplomats on the
ground that he could not work with them.[3] ' Holstein
and Berchem,' wrote Hohenlohe in his diary on March 27,
1890, ' have proposed Marschall von Bieberstein, after
Alvensleben declined.'[4]   Marschall was the representative of Baden in the Bundesrath, and the Grand Duke
Frederick recommended him as a good speaker and an
expert in economic questions. He was certainly a great
lawyer ; but Bismarck contemptuously described him
as the *Ministre étranger aux affaires*.

No sooner had the Bismarcks left office than a
momentous decision was taken which angered them
against the man whom they rightly regarded as its
principal author. Holstein had approved almost every
important move of Bismarck on the European chess-
board down to 1887 ; but the reinsurance treaty con-

---

[1] *Denkwürdigkeiten*, I. 498.
[2] Waldersee, *Briefwechsel*, I. 351, and H. von Rath, ' Erinnerungen an
Holstein,' *Deutsche Revue*, October, 1909.
[3] *Aus den Tagen Bismarcks Kampf gegen Caprivi*, 1–9.
[4] *Denkwürdigkeiten*, II. 466.

cluded with Russia in that year made him feel that the master-builder was losing his sureness of touch. Austria and Russia were on such bad terms in consequence of the prolonged Bulgarian crisis that a second renewal of the *Dreikaiserbund* of 1881 was out of the question, and Bismarck therefore determined to save what he could from the wreck. His desire to inform Francis Joseph of what he had done was frustrated by the Tsar, and in Holstein's eyes the dangers involved in a precarious secrecy outweighed the value of Russia's promise of neutrality in the event of a French attack. ' Nothing tangible is to be expected from it,' he observed, ' and if it leaks out we are blamed as false fellows.' When Bismarck fell, the consent of the Emperor to the renewal of the treaty for another three years when it expired on June 13 had been obtained ; and so anxious was its author that his handiwork should endure that his son's continuance in office for a day or two longer was attributed by Holstein to his desire to renew the treaty before handing over the reins. But the power of the Bismarck dynasty was at an end.

The day after the fall of his father Herbert Bismarck asked for the papers, and was told that they were in Holstein's room. For Holstein, without the knowledge of his official chief, laid them before Caprivi, Marschall and Schweinitz, the Ambassador in St. Petersburg, who happened to be in Berlin. Herbert turned his steps thither, and an angry scene ensued. The opinion of Berchem, the Under-Secretary, and the Assistant-Secretaries, who discussed the question with Caprivi, was unanimous against renewal ; and Schweinitz, who had supported its conclusion in 1887, was converted by a sight of the treaty with Roumania signed in 1883 of which he had been unaware. ' As the treaty contradicts other treaties,' argued Holstein in a letter to a friend on March 27, ' our good name would depend on Russia's discretion. But Russia's interest is to be indiscreet ; for directly it became known our other friends would leave us. Then we should be compelled to look to Russia alone, and she would make her own conditions as to our further relations.'[1]   Caprivi accordingly advised the Kaiser to let it drop, explaining in his simple way that the relationship was ' too complicated ' ; for Bismarck could juggle with three balls at a time, while he himself could only manage two.

Alexander III took the news calmly, but Giers, his Foreign Minister, was deeply distressed, and pleaded for its continuance even if in an attenuated form.   The Assistant-Secretaries in the Foreign Office were now asked to record their opinion.   Holstein's Memorandum, dated May 20,[2] maintains that the modifications proposed by Giers were useless, since the objections to the pact were fundamental.   ' The mere fact that a secret treaty exists between us and Russia would have a devastating effect on our relations with Austria, Roumania and Italy.   Italy, in particular, by the text of the German-Italian treaty, has the right to be informed by us of our arrangements and those of other Powers in all questions relating to the Aegean and the Ottoman coasts and islands.   But everything which can arouse suspicion against Germany's policy would operate with special force at the present moment, since many of Prince Bismarck's recent utterances are calculated to unsettle our allies.   Only a public agreement with Russia could be considered, so that our allies might convince themselves that neither we nor Russia intended to abridge treaty rights.'   The Austrophil Marschall expressed his entire agreement with the Memorandum ; Kiderlen and Raschdau, the other Assistant-Secretaries, drew up Memoranda on similar lines, and Prince Reuss, the German Ambassador in Vienna, volunteered his opinion that the slightest suspicion of German sincerity would lead to the permanent alienation of Austria.   Schweinitz, on the other hand, desired to meet Giers half-way.   Thus in face of the almost unanimous opinion of the official

[1] Eckardstein, *Erinnerungen*, III. 18–9.
[2] *Die Grosse Politik*, VII. 22–3.   For a subsequent Memorandum written in 1904, *ib*. 48–9.

authorities the secret treaty was regretfully allowed by the Kaiser to lapse.[1]

Holstein divided the responsibility for this disastrous step with his colleagues and official superiors ; but his advice weighed heavily in the scales, and the larger part of the almost universal condemnation now meted out to its authors is visited on his head. Russia, it is true, had already begun to move towards France ; but nothing irrevocable had occurred, and the pro-German Giers was almost pathetically anxious to avert the cutting of the wires. The argument that the treaty was incompatible with loyalty to Austria was repudiated by its author, who was so little ashamed of his handiwork that he revealed the secret in 1896 ; but this was a matter of opinion. The fact remains that its termination, as Bülow sorrowfully declares, led automatically to the Franco-Russian alliance ; and when Russia was once tied to France it proved impossible to restore full contact with St. Petersburg, despite the later attempts at Björko and Potsdam and the confidential correspondence of Willy and Nicky. Had German policy under ' the new course ' been conducted with greater skill, the dangers inherent in the decision of 1890 might have been mini-mised ; but the subsequent alienation of Great Britain, and the surrender of the control of Balkan policy into the hands of the Ballplatz,. led straight to the entangle-ment of a weakened Germany in the Austro-Russian quarrel which it had been Bismarck's aim and achieve-ment to avert.

For this decision Bismarck held Holstein chiefly responsible ; for Caprivi and Marschall were novices and the Emperor a reluctant convert. ' The men in Berlin have no experience or knowledge of statecraft,' he complained ; ' I am afraid the Privy Councillors

[1] The documents are collected in *Die Grosse Politik*, VII. ch. 44. For careful discussions of the incident and of Holstein's share in it, see Otto Becker, *Das Französisch-Russische Bündnis*, ch. 1, and Appendix IX; and Frankenberg, *Die Nichterneuerung des deutsch-russichen Rückversicherungsvertrages*, 33–9. Holstein remarked later to Hammann that it would have been dangerous to leave the secret in Bismarck's keeping ; Hammann, *Der neue Kurs*, 33.

have it all their own way.'[1]   The new position held by
Holstein, and the animosity with which his old patron
had come to regard him, are reflected in a letter from
his enemy Lothar Bucher to Busch from Varzin on
October 14, 1890, six months after the catastrophe.[2]
'Holstein, whom for ten years nobody took seriously,
now does everything.   He not only slanders the Prince,
which he did twelve months ago, but also abuses
Herbert, who, with inconceivable blindness, had supported him to the last.'   If it was not strictly true that
Holstein now 'did everything,' 'the great Geheimrat,'
as he was called, was at any rate henceforward the oracle
of the Wilhelmstrasse, where nobody approached him
in knowledge of the *Arcana Imperii*, and where he
discharged the duties of Under-Secretary when that
official was on holiday.   'The figure of Holstein,'
reported a member of the Austrian Embassy in
September, 'comes more and more into the foreground.
There is only one opinion in the Foreign Office,—that
he is its life and soul.   No important political decision
is taken till his opinion has been asked by His Majesty
or the Chancellor.'[3]   'Caprivi and Marschall,' declares
Bülow with the lofty contempt of the expert for the
amateur, 'who had no conception of the international
chess-board or the technique of diplomacy and not even
the necessary knowledge of languages, clung to him
like drowning men to a safety belt.'[4]   Count Berchem,
the Under-Secretary, remained for a time under the new
regime ; but when he found that Holstein was usurping
his position as chief adviser to the Foreign Secretary, he
resigned, and made way for Rotenhan, a more pliable
successor.   'Berchem thinks Holstein has got rid of
him,' wrote Waldersee in his diary on May 30, 1890,
'in order to rule without a rival.   Certainly Marschall is
a friend of Holstein and depends greatly on his advice.'[5]

---

[1] *Süddeutsche Monatshefte*, March, 1931, 379.   [2] Busch, III. 343.
[3] Otto Becker, *Das Französisch-Russische Bündnis*, 307.
[4] Bülow, *Denkwürdigkeiten*, II. 112.
[5] Waldersee, *Denkwürdigkeiten*, II. 129.

Holstein now began to practise the methods which were to disfigure the later years of his official life. When Eckardstein entered the Foreign Office in 1891 he discovered to his amazement that he withheld copies of important dispatches from German diplomatic representatives abroad whom he disliked. ' Behind cool and reserved forms,' wrote Julius von Eckardt at this period,[1] ' there was a hidden passion. The veil of melancholy gave a special charm, and he was a good talker when he was in the mood. But he was thought dangerous because he was believed to be implacable. For fourteen months he cut me owing to an unfounded accusation. Then it was explained, and he was friendly again.' He adds that Caprivi feared both Holstein and Kiderlen-Wächter, who stood next to him in influence, but that he felt them both to be indispensable. Hohenlohe, indeed, described Holstein as ' the diplomatic chart of the Foreign Office.' Unfortunately he possessed knowledge without understanding.

We owe a vivid picture of the Mystery Man at this period to Otto Hammann, who was appointed by Caprivi to direct the Press Department of the Foreign Office. ' I was a complete stranger to the Great Unknown. On crossing the threshold of this uncanny master of the deepest secrets I felt like the pupil in *Faust*. Like all who approached him, I knew I was in the presence of a man of outstanding gifts. His masterly manner of conducting the conversation and of clothing his thought in striking language commanded respect for his capacities. A powerful will and a warning Take care ! seemed written on his face, with its Roman nose and darkly glittering deep-set eyes. Despite the friendliness with which he welcomed the novice, I carried away the feeling—perhaps in consequence of what I had already heard about him—that there was something abnormal and morbid about the man.'[2] One of his colleagues remarked that if he wanted to reach Madrid

---

[1] *Aus den Tagen Bismarcks Kampf gegen Caprivi*, 1–9.
[2] *Der neue Kurs*, 57–8.

from Berlin he would go round by Jerusalem. He was never photographed, belonged to no club, and only visited in a few houses where he was sure that he would not meet strangers. When Sir Rennell Rodd, then on the staff of the British Embassy, rallied him on his unsociable ways, he replied that the service of the State had spoiled him as a human being.[1] It was typical of his misanthropy that he carried a loaded revolver. His best quality was his sturdy independence. ' The better I came to know the political world of Berlin,' writes Chirol, the *Times* correspondent, ' the more I respected him for the possession of sterling qualities that grew exceedingly rare during William II's reign.' [2]

Like an oriental despot Holstein had favourites whose rise was as rapid as their fall. He had inherited a modest fortune, which was used up in secret kindly actions and which his petty speculations on the Bourse failed to replenish.[3] A privileged young diplomat or secretary would receive what he called *le droit de la porte*,—the right to enter his room unannounced. This concession, however, might at any moment be withdrawn, for no one was so ready to take offence. Two servants who stood before the door would break the news to the astonished visitor that the Baron was unable to receive him, and no explanation was given. In one case a daily and confidential intercourse of two years was suddenly ended because ' the monster' discovered that his *protégé* had lunched with Herbert Bismarck twice in a single week. Though he recognised his ex-disciple, he never spoke to him again. Another victim, young Count Pourtalès, who also possessed *le droit de la porte*, found the way barred one day by the lackeys, and the Baron cut him ever afterwards.[4]

Holstein was inflexibly determined to gather all the threads of foreign policy into his hands. ' A conflict

---

[1] ' Der Staatsdienst hat mich als Mensch verdorben.'   Sir Rennell Rodd, *Social and Diplomatic Memories*, I. 135.

[2] *Fifty Years*, 269.

[3] See *Berliner Tageblatt*, December 16, 17, 24, 1925.

[4] Nowak, *Das dritte deutsche Kaiserreich*, I. 155-7.

with Caprivi is approaching,' wrote Waldersee, now
Moltke's successor as Chief of the Staff, in his diary in
August, 1890.[1] ' I have long tried to raise the position
of the Military Attachés. The Emperor agrees to
make them independent of the Minister. Caprivi gives
orders to the contrary, and instructs them never to
discuss politics in their reports, though they are cleverer
than almost all the diplomats. There is only one
opinion,—that Caprivi had been egged on by Holstein
and that the whole *coup* is directed against myself. I
have often defended Holstein and have given him my
confidence. If this is really his doing it would be an
infamy. It would be not only evil but frivolous, for he
has delivered himself into my hands owing to my knowledge of his double game with the Bismarcks.' Holstein,
added Waldersee in a note of a later date, had in 1889
and 1890 often asked him to procure direct and purely
political reports to show to the Emperor, not only in
regard to Russia, but in reference to a dispute with
Switzerland. ' He asked me to tell the Emperor that
Bismarck's policy was mistaken, and supplied me with
the necessary material. Thus he intrigued against his
direct superior and betrayed him, and yet he had the
face to say I carried on a forbidden correspondence
with the Military Attachés.' Waldersee complained to
Marschall, who replied that the whole affair was due to
the rancour of Holstein against Major Engelbrecht,
whom he could not bear, though the point was directed
against the Chief of the Staff.[2] Waldersee next
appealed to Caprivi, who complained of secret correspondence behind his back, but explained that he needed
his services for the present. The dispute dragged on
throughout the autumn. ' Holstein is ill because he
cannot get Engelbrecht moved from Rome,' wrote
Waldersee at the end of the year.[3] ' I said I did not
like the *rôle* he made us play,—he pulls the strings and

---

[1] *Denkwürdegkeiten*, II. 136, August 10.
[2] *Ib*. II. 139, August 13.
[3] *Ib*. II. 170, December 22.

we had to dance.'   A month later Waldersee had lost his post. Holstein had begun to avoid him in the summer of 1890, and now confided his satisfaction to a friend. ' Well, that *was* a job to get rid of him, as he was so in with the Kaiser.' [1]

Waldersee had warned the Emperor that Holstein was intriguing against the Chancellor ; but Eulenburg stood up for his friend, and neither the ruler nor Caprivi took any notice of the charge.[2]   The Chancellor, how-ever, was quite aware of Holstein's peculiarities. ' I criticised the way the business of the Foreign Office was transacted,' wrote Schweinitz after a talk with Caprivi in 1892 ; ' a personage not quite right in the head had too much influence.[3] Caprivi replies that he knows very well Holstein has the grave fault of being swayed by personal prejudices, but it was impossible to do without him. The Chancellor in his great modesty realises that he does not possess the technique of diplomacy, and neither he nor Marschall nor Rotenhan has the power or will to replace these people by more capable men. Thus the real direction of our policy falls into the hands of the only official who combines the tradition of the office and the knowledge of the machine, for he served thirty years under Bismarck and was honoured for a time with his confidence, and he was also used for secret and not always quite savoury affairs, especially in regard to the press. He never wished to shine, asked nothing for himself, neither high posts nor decorations, and has many excellent qualities ; but he has personal rancours—not only against me—and allows them too much influence in his actions.'

Among his victims was the Bismarckian Schlözer, who lost his post as Ambassador at Rome in 1892.[4] Waldersee noted in his diary in August, 1892, that Holstein wished to keep Caprivi at all costs as a

---

[1] *Denkwürdigkeiten*, II. 195.

[2] Gradenwitz, *Bismarcks letzter Kampf*, 174–6, quoting a report of the Baden Minister in Berlin.

[3] Schweinitz, *Denkwürdigkeiten*, II. 443.

[4] Kurd von Schlözer, *Letzte Römische Briefe*, 175, 179, 183–4.

guarantee of the continuance of his power ; but he felt himself under no obligation of loyalty to his in-experienced chief. Bismarck had withheld despatches from the three Emperors or presented them in garbled form, and Holstein copied the evil precedent of secret diplomacy. For instance, he instructed Eulenburg, the Prussian Minister in Munich, to communicate the report of a conversation between the Chancellor and the Bavarian Minister in an altered form, and actually ordered him in advance how to reply.[1] This was too much for Eulenburg. ' Directly a situation boils up Holstein goes absolutely mad. The suggestion that I should report what Crailsheim ought to have said is grotesque. The letter can be kept as a curiosity.' A month later Holstein instructed his friend what to tell the Emperor about a letter which had not arrived. In 1894 he suggested that Eulenburg should limit the scope of his official despatches and communicate every-thing of importance in private letters to himself. ' So the Chancellor is to be eliminated ! ' noted Eulenburg in disgust. ' If poor Caprivi saw this note, Holstein's days would be numbered. But as—I had almost said unfortunately—we cannot do without him, I shall take no notice of the hint and shall not show the note to the good Caprivi. My God, what a comedy ! '[2] On the other hand, Holstein was shrewd enough to know with whom he could or could not afford to quarrel. ' He rules in the Foreign Office,' notes Waldersee in his diary in the summer of 1892, ' and he has divided up the business with Kiderlen, with whom he has to reckon on account of his relations with the Emperor.'[3] The Swabian Bismarck, as Friedrich Naumann called him, was still in high favour at Court, and he was a man who, if he were to be attacked, was certain to hit back. More-over in 1896 he was to leave Berlin for appointments abroad.

Though Holstein was supreme in the Foreign Office

[1] Haller, *Eulenburg*, 166.   [2] *Ib.* 166.
[3] *Denkwürdigkeiten,* II. 245, June 12.

he was continually haunted by the possibility of a reconciliation between Bismarck and the Emperor, which the German people ardently desired. 'Caprivi and Holstein and perhaps some of the small fry of the Foreign Office alone oppose it,' wrote Waldersee in his diary in June, 1892.[1] The journey of the Prince to Vienna to attend the marriage of his son Herbert gave the Chancellor the opportunity of breaking down the frail bridge which many good patriots were endeavouring to build. Francis Joseph was bluntly asked not to receive him, and the German Embassy was forbidden to take part in the ceremony, a deplorable error of taste and policy. The counter-attacks of the Bismarckian press on Caprivi and his henchmen were unceasing, and the fallen Chancellor indulged in bitter comments on his old *protégé*. 'Holstein,' he remarked to Poschinger at Varzin in October, 1892, 'is now one-eyed.[2] But among the blind men of the Foreign Office the one-eyed man is King.' Holstein, he added, had displayed exceptional elasticity at the time that the officials were changing over from the Bismarckian to the new regime. 'He was useful in drafting French documents; but as man and character—well, you know him as well as I. I hear that he has quarrelled with all his colleagues, and that Raschdau declines to take orders from him. He has only one friend—Radolin.'

To his horror Holstein found himself one day in the limelight for the first time since the Arnim trial. At the end of 1893, *Kladderadatsch*, a comic journal of Bismarckian sympathies, began a campaign against the trio, Geheimrat von Austernfreund, Geheimrat von Spätzle, and Graf Troubadour.[3] The former was described as a sly old fox who preferred the backstairs and never mentioned the Arnim trial. The allusions were obvious : the names stood for Holstein, Kiderlen

[1] II. 247, June 26.

[2] Bismarck, *Gesammelte Werke*, IX. 255-7. Holstein was at this time suffering from eye trouble.

[3] Hammann, *Der neue Kurs*, 58-66. (The Oyster-lover, the Sparrow, and Count Troubadour).

and Eulenburg. ' I believe they do not wholly trust one another,' commented Waldersee in his diary, ' but they stick together because it pays them.' [1] For weeks the trio figured prominently in the paper, forming the theme of satirical verses and caricatures. After this careful preparation the readers were presented with an apologue, entitled ' Three Men in a Fiery Oven.' ' There was once a King, who had many faithful servants. But three of them, whose names were Insinuans, Intrigans and Calumnians, were deceitful, and accused several of his most faithful servants, so that they were turned out of the palace. Then a plain man arose and had the three evildoers cast into a fiery oven.' Holstein, who hated the publicity as much as the attack, brooded over the problem ' Who is behind it ? ', and Hammann heard that he had sent his seconds to Herbert Bismarck. Emissaries from the Foreign Office were despatched to the editor and the publisher of the paper, but in vain. The *Zukunft* reminded its readers that Holstein had betrayed Arnim and discredited himself in the eyes of the world. ' But will the Emperor open his eyes ? No, because that would be to confess his own short-sightedness.' The scandal was now the talk of the town. Kiderlen challenged a member of the editorial staff, and wounded his opponent. Holstein, who was a good shot and had fought a duel in Washington for the sake of a lady, challenged Count Henckel von Donnersmarck, ' since the attitude of the *Berliner Neueste Nachrichten* suggests that he is privy to the attacks.' The Count declined to fight, as there was no ground for the suspicion. The attacks came to an end, and in 1898 the angry Holstein accepted the assurances of Count Henckel. The prime mover in the campaign was an official of the Foreign Office ; but the secret was only revealed thirty years later.[2]

Marschall, like Caprivi, started as an amateur in

---

[1] *Denkwürdigkeiten*, II. 300, December 23.
[2] Jäckh, *Kiderlen-Wächter*, I. 98. The official was Geheimer Legationsrat von Bothmer, of the Legal Department of the Foreign Office.

foreign affairs, and there was a widespread belief that neither of them would retain his place for any length of time.   On January 13, 1893, Hohenlohe noted in his diary a conversation with Eulenburg, who declared that Holstein and Kiderlen desired him to become Foreign Minister if Bötticher were to resign the Home Office, to which Marschall would, they believed, be gladly transferred.[1]   Eulenburg, however, had no desire for the post, and felt unequal to it ; and he asked Hohenlohe to discuss with Holstein the succession to Marschall and to convert him from the plan of proposing him.   Hohenlohe promised to try, but did not think Holstein would change his view.

Hohenlohe had exchanged the Paris Embassy in 1884 for the office of Statthalter of Alsace-Lorraine ; but he continued his practice of discussing the political situation with his old friend whenever he visited Berlin. ' I talked with Holstein,' he records on December 14, 1893, ' about the attacks of the Bismarckian press on the New Course and its foreign policy.[2]   He replied by enlarging on Bismarck's mistakes—the Berlin Congress, the prevention of a conflict between England and Russia in Afghanistan, and his whole policy towards Russia.   His last plan to leave Austria in the lurch would have made us so contemptible that we should have been isolated and become dependent on Russia.' Passing to another subject, Holstein informed his visitor that the Chancellor and the Foreign Office were disturbed by the activities of Crispi, whose actions were beyond prediction.   It was therefore necessary to send a clever Ambassador to watch the situation in Rome, and Bülow was proposed for the task.

At the opening of 1894 Caprivi's position had become insecure, for his commercial treaties angered the Agrarians, who shuddered at the lower duties on Russian corn.   Moreover the outward reconciliation of Potsdam and Friedrichsruh increased the *malaise*. ' Bismarck will come and thank the Kaiser for his present

---

[1] II. 497.   [2] *Ib.* II. 507.

of wine and the congratulations on his recovery,' wrote
Hohenlohe in his diary on January 22, 1894.[1] 'My
friends in the Foreign Office are afraid he may suggest
a new Chancellor. Holstein thinks I ought to advise
the Kaiser to summon me also if he receives Bismarck.
That I should not do ; but, if opportunity offered, I
would advise him to have a witness. If a Bismarck
regime returned, I should have to make room for one
of his friends at Strassburg.' Bismarck's visit to Berlin
on January 26, which roused Holstein to fury, gave
heartfelt pleasure to the German people ; but politics
were avoided, and the incident did nothing either to
solve or to complicate the problems of succession which
were agitating the Wilhelmstrasse. An interesting
letter from General von Stosch to Bennigsen, dated
July 3, 1894, proves that William II had already
resolved to change his principal adviser.[2] 'The
Emperor has told a friend, " Caprivi is useful to me,
but not sympathetic. He lacks imagination, and does
not understand me when I tell him of my wider thoughts.
I shall choose as his successor a younger man, who is
nearer to me ; and he shall be exclusively my man." '
Stosch added that the monarch was believed to be
thinking of Eulenburg, and, if he refused the post, of
Bülow.

IV

Caprivi left office in the autumn of 1894 without
regrets. He had never coveted the post, and he had
lost the confidence of the Emperor and the Conservatives. Moreover he had long mistrusted Holstein,
whose room he described as 'that poison shop ' ; and
Holstein was ready· for a change.[3] Hohenlohe, who
had wished for the office in 1890, accepted it without

[1] Ib. II. 509.
[2] Oncken, Bennigsen, II. 591–2.
[3] Holstein's tortuous course is discussed in Zechlin, Staatsstreichpläne
Bismarcks und Wilhelm II, Part II, Die Entlassung Caprivis.

enthusiasm in 1894, when he was seventy-five years old. Holstein, on the other hand, was eager to have his old chief installed in the Wilhelmstrasse, not only because they were on intimate terms but because a weary Titan would be unlikely to challenge his authority. ' My mother,' writes Prince Alexander Hohenlohe, ' tried to prevent my father becoming Chancellor, as he was too old.[1] But Holstein, seeing that the days of Caprivi were numbered, worked for his fall, and wished for a Chancellor who would allow him to continue his rôle. He believed that my father would do so, and worked hard to secure him. One day my father received a telegram from the Emperor : " Come to Potsdam ; important Imperial interests concerned " ; and it was only during his journey that he learned from a newspaper of the fall of Caprivi. He intended to refuse the offer ; but Holstein travelled to meet him at Leipzig and persuaded him to accept. My mother wired the Empress to help him to escape the burden on the ground of health ; but the Empress replied " The Prince sacrifices himself for Kaiser and Reich." ' Prince Alexander adds that his father soon regretted his decision ; and the third Chancellor's diary, even in the meagre form in which we know it, suggests some of the difficulties, personal as well as political, that confronted him.

' At the end of the Caprivi era,' writes William II in his *Memoirs*, ' Holstein, the *soi-disant* representative of the Bismarck tradition, began to become powerful, and manifested an indisposition to work with me. The Foreign Office thought it must carry on Bismarck's policy alone.' [2]   No steps, however, were taken to diminish his influence, and the change of Chancellor brought no excessive jubilation in Bismarckian circles. ' It is good Caprivi is gone,' wrote the faithful Conservative Kardorff to Herbert on November 21, 1894 ; ' but if Hohenlohe is only chosen to keep the place warm for Eulenburg and if Marschall and Holstein

[1] *Aus meinem Leben*, ch. 12.   [2] *Ereignisse und Gestalten*, 51.

continue to direct foreign policy, and Bötticher and
Berlepsch to protect the Socialists, there is still much
to be done before things improve.' [1]   Shortly after his
appointment Hohenlohe, to the horror of Holstein, paid
a visit of courtesy to Friedrichsruh, and was amicably
received by his host, who proceeded to give him some
advice. 'If you do not at once get rid of Bötticher,
Marschall and Holstein, they will intrigue you out of
office as they did me.' [2]   The forecast was not fulfilled,
for Hohenlohe was on his guard. He treated Holstein
with invariable courtesy, but he never shared the blind
confidence which the first Chancellor had entertained
for twenty years.

The two outstanding events of Hohenlohe's Chancellorship were the ill-judged interventions in the
Far East and in South Africa. Hohenlohe was rightly
anxious to restore the intimacy which had been impaired
by the lapse of the secret treaty of 1887, and he believed
that support of Russia's ambitions in the Far East was
the best way to regain her favours. Moreover the
arrangement which allowed her to swallow Port Arthur
at her own convenience was accompanied by the Tsar's
assent in advance to a German settlement at Kiao-Chau.
The belief, however, that Russia could be won back
without far greater concessions was unfounded, and the
failure to estimate the strength or to foresee the resentment of Japan was a glaring failure of statesmanship.
'We shall remember,' observed a Japanese statesman as
he bowed to necessity in 1895 ; and his countrymen
were to prove in 1914 that they had not forgotten.
Hohenlohe's chief aim was to restore the wire to Petrograd, Marschall's to develop German trade in the Far
East. Holstein supported the policy, as he explained
in a letter to Chirol,[3] on the ground that it was desirable
to prevent the consecration of the Franco-Russian
Alliance by joint salvos of artillery ; for while Japan
might possibly resist a summons from Russia and France,

<hr>

[1] Thimme, 'Bismarck und Kardorff,' *Deutsche Revue*, May, 1917.
[2] *Ib.* June, 1917.   [3] Chirol, *Fifty Years*, 191.

she would obey a command backed by Germany as well.
His second motive was to encourage Russia to expand
in the Far East and thus weaken Pan-Slav ambitions in
Europe.   The treaty for the lease of Tsing-tau in its
final form was drawn up by Holstein and Tirpitz.[1]
Though plausible arguments were adduced for the
policy of intervention, the alienation of Japan was
scarcely less a blunder than the momentous decision of
1890.

Next in importance in the field of foreign affairs
to the lapse of the secret treaty with Russia was the
Emperor's telegram to Kruger, the full story of which
was revealed, not in *Die Grosse Politik*, but in an article
by Thimme based on the diaries of Marschall and
Admiral von Senden and other new material.[2]   That
Holstein played no leading part in the hazardous game
was already known, but the extent to which he was involved remained a mystery till it was partially cleared
up by Thimme's researches.   A memorandum drawn up
at the time, explaining his objections to the telegram and
his refusal to initial the document, was seen by an official
of the Foreign Office in 1908, but has not been found
or at any rate published.   According to Eckardstein,
Holstein wrote to Hatzfeldt in March, 1896 : ' It was
unfortunately impossible for me to prevent the Kruger
telegram.   The Secretary of State, worked up by the
Colonial enthusiasts, was set on it, and I could not alter
it.'[3]   No such letter, however, has been found among
Hatzfeldt's papers.

We learn from Marschall's diary that on January 3,
1896, after hearing the Kaiser's wild proposals of a
Protectorate over the Transvaal and the despatch of
troops, the Foreign Secretary proposed a telegram of
congratulation to the President.   The widow of Kayser,
the Director of the Colonial Department, on the other

---

[1] Tirpitz, *Memoirs*, I. 76.
[2] ' Die Krüger Depesche,' in *Europäische Gespräche*, May, 1924.   Cp.
Meinecke, *Geschichte des deutsch-englischen Bündnisproblems*, ch. 5.
[3] Eckardstein, *Erinnerungen*, I. 277.

hand, asserts that her husband, who was called in when agreement proved impossible, proposed a telegram, and on the acceptance of the idea made the first draft, which was sharpened and promptly despatched. According to von dem Bussche Holstein was asked by Marschall during an interval in the discussion to come and take part, but declined, not so much because he disapproved Marschall's attitude but because he wished to avoid confronting the Emperor. It appears that he then returned from the Chancellor's palace, where the discussion was held, to the Foreign Office. According to Mumm von Schwarzenstein, an eye-witness, he was horrified when Marschall entered his room shortly afterwards with the fateful telegram in his hands, and implored him not to send it. The Foreign Minister explained that this was the price of holding back the Emperor from something worse. If Holstein in truth declined to take part in the discussion, he had no right to blame the decision which was reached in his absence, and he deserves Meinecke's censure of 'the cowardly policy of the ante-chamber.' For it was not the telegram in itself but its sharp wording which aroused in equal measure the enthusiasm of the German people and the resentment of the British Empire. Bismarck immediately fastened on the mistake in phraseology, and it may be plausibly argued that but for Holstein's reluctance to meeting the Emperor face to face, the telegram might have assumed a different form. The monarch's attempt in his *Memoirs* to shelter himself behind 'the insistence of Hohenlohe, the powerful personality of Marschall, and the siren voice of Holstein,' can deceive nobody;[1] for his letter to the Tsar, written within a few hours of the despatch of the telegram, breathes the same spirit of angry excitement, and we now know that the ruler was held back, not spurred on, by his official advisers. Eckardstein's suggestion that Holstein had a finger in the pie is worth nothing, for he gives no evidence and was not in Berlin at the time. On the other hand, are

[1] *Ereignisse und Gestalten*, 68–9.

we to assume that he was a mere onlooker ? That the Chancellor and Marschall did not seek his advice in a matter of first-class importance seems to Johannes Haller so improbable that he suggests that the master of stratagems allowed the error to be committed in order to diminish the prestige and therefore the power of William II.[1] Thus the historian still cries aloud for more light.

Though Holstein was in no wise responsible for the manufacture of the high explosive, he was in agreement with the general policy by which it was inspired, and must therefore shoulder some portion of the blame for the evil that it wrought. Chirol had never seen him so worked up against British policy as in the autumn of 1895, and he was full of mysterious hints as to the danger of incurring Germany's enmity.[2] The object of Hohenlohe, Marschall and Holstein was not to change the whole orientation by a union of Continental Powers against Great Britain, but to frighten her by the spectre of a coalition into climbing down in the Transvaal and to force her into the arms of the Triple Alliance. The idea of a Continental league appears for the first time in official Germany in a Memorandum of Holstein, dated December 30, 1895.[3] He desired to use Italy's resentment of British policy in Abyssinia to enable Germany and Italy jointly to co-operate with the Franco-Russian group, thus preventing Italy from leaving the Triple Alliance and bringing the advantages of closer relations with it sharply before the statesmen in Downing Street. His exclusion of the Egyptian question from the discussion shews that his idea of a League was a means not an end. Thus his policy at the height of the Transvaal crisis was to hold the Triplice together and to make Great Britain more friendly to it, but, if that proved impossible, to combine with the Franco-Russian group. After discussing the price and terms of an arrangement with France and Russia, he concludes that England will

[1] Haller, *Eulenburg*, 190–1.   [2] Chirol, *Fifty Years*, 278–9.
[3] *Die Grosse Politik*, XI. 67–9.

see the necessity of a *rapprochement* with the Triplice when she realises that it is not at her beck and call. On January 1, 1906, in a letter to Hatzfeldt, he spoke of the desirability of giving England a lesson—the very phrase used by Marschall a few days later to Chirol, the correspondent of the *Times*.

Though Holstein disapproved of the wording of the telegram, he was in no apologetic mood in a conversation with Chirol on January 8 which he reported to Hatzfeldt.[1] He earnestly hoped that the direct negotiations between the Transvaal and England would succeed. If not, the matter would go much further. Germany could not accept a *diminutio capitis*. Russia had hinted that she would not neglect the unique opportunity to play off Germany against England. France would also have to come in, despite Alsace-Lorraine, because otherwise Germany would cut her out at St. Petersburg, and the German-Russian group would constitute a standing threat to France against which the British fleet would be of no avail. For these reasons he believed in a satisfactory solution. The suspicion of a German seizure of Lorenzo Marquez was absurd, as it would drive France on to the English side on account of Madagascar. The recent policy of England made her a useless factor. Whether the Transvaal experience would suffice to open her eyes to the need of a continental attachment was very doubtful. Holstein added that he thought the Transvaal would suggest a discussion by the Powers if the direct negotiations broke down. It was important for peace that England should not go so far with her naval demonstrations as to enable the German Admiralty to secure a partial mobilisation. ' We agree in thinking that the destruction of England's position as a Great Power would be a doubtful blessing for Germany,' he telegraphed to Hatzfeldt on January 10.[2] ' So let us be glad if the matter ends, as it seems likely to do, with a little diplomatic success for Germany and a little political lesson for England.' Holstein misunderstood

[1] *Die Grosse Politik*, XI. 41-2.   [2] *Ib.* XI. 48-9.

the British nation in believing that it could be coerced into the orbit of the Triple Alliance by threats and challenges, but he had no desire to push things to extremes.   Hammann records a conversation of the time in which he spoke of the dangers of estrangement from Great Britain, and declared that South Africa was not worth a war.   His attitude was well understood in the British Embassy.   'He certainly did not like it,' reported Spring Rice on January 11 in reference to the Kruger telegram ; but he added in April that 'the underground inspirer of the Foreign Office is using all his influence against us.'[1]   In six short years he had done as much as any of his countrymen to alienate the goodwill of Russia, Japan and the British Empire.

A striking portrait of Holstein in the middle nineties has been drawn by Prince Alexander Hohenlohe, who acted as Private Secretary to the Chancellor.[2]   'He was one of the greatest personages in the Empire, before whom many an Ambassador grown grey in the service of the State trembled, and on whose whim depended the fate of many officials, not only of the diplomatic service but of the internal administration, and by whose decisions the tendency of the whole foreign policy of Germany was determined.   He possessed diabolical skill in discovering the weaknesses or the private secrets of people and using his knowledge to make them his tools.   He was incredibly autocratic.   When he went for his month's holiday he did not as a rule leave his address.   On one occasion the Foreign Minister asked for an important document, and received the reply, "The Baron has locked it up, and you cannot have it."   The Minister did not dare to remonstrate with his subordinate.   When German diplomatists were in Berlin he would often let them wait for days, and some he never received at all.   I know some Ambassadors who for years were never admitted to his presence, owing to some personal pique.   As my father's secretary it was often

[1] Gwynn, *Letters and Friendships of Cecil Spring Rice*, I. 185, 204.
[2] *Aus meinem Leben*, ch. 12.

necessary for me to see him. Once, without giving any
reason, he refused to see me for several days. My
father, much inconvenienced thereby, inquired as to the
reason. " Because he said, ' *I should advise you*,' " was
the reply, which seemed to him disrespectful. My
father persuaded him to see me again.'

Despite his suspicious nature, Prince Alexander
enjoyed his talks with the man who held all the threads
in his hand. ' From twelve to one daily a little gathering was held in Holstein's room. The Berlin Correspondents of the *Frankfurter* and *Kölnische Zeitung* were
often there, with Kiderlen-Wächter, Hammann, Pourtalès,
or Marschall. Foreign and domestic questions were
discussed, and Holstein often gave directions to the
journalists. His morbid fear of personal attacks in
the press made him decline office, though my father
repeatedly offered it. He only accepted the title
Excellenz reluctantly at the end of the nineties, long after
it was due. He had a passion for power and a horror
of the appearance of it. He was like a spider, sitting
in a dark corner and watching its victims. He had
learned from his great master to hate implacably. Yet
I have rarely noticed such fascination in a glance, and
I have had to defend myself against his magnetic power.'
He was almost invisible. ' I worked for decades by
his side,' testifies Wermuth, the Minister of Finance ;
' only once did I see him, and I never spoke to
him.' When the Crown Prince asked Richthofen
to introduce him to Holstein, the Foreign Secretary
replied : ' Your Royal Highness asks the impossible.
If we enter his room by one door, he will escape by
the other.' [1]

In his unresting struggle for power Holstein, like
Bismarck, refused to regard any obstacle as insurmountable. When Engelbrecht, the Military Attaché
in Rome, who was honoured by his special hatred, complained of him to the Emperor at the opening of 1894,
he received the reply : ' I know him well ; he is a good

[1] Wermuth, *Ein Beamtenleben*, 192–3.

honourable fellow.'[1]   In reality William II hardly
knew him at all.   He met him for the first time in 1894,
liked him, and gave him his portrait ;[2] but he had no
notion of the vast extent and sinister nature of his
influence, still less of the opinion which he had formed
of him.   The publication by Johannes Haller of Eulenburg's fascinating correspondence in 1924 revealed that
Holstein, already almost undisputed master of the
Foreign Office, flew at still higher game.[3]   That the
Emperor was dangerously impulsive and unbalanced was
known to every German ; but it was rather his power
than his policy which prompted the spider of the Wilhelmstrasse to attempt to draw him also into his all-
devouring web.

For a few years Holstein loved Eulenburg as much
as his withered heart could love anybody.   There was
no warmer admirer of his poetical gifts, and Eulenburg's
children talked of ' the good uncle ' who provided them
with sweets.[4]   Moreover the assistance of the Emperor's
most intimate friend might be of service in the highest
circles.   But Holstein was a jealous lover, and when he
broke with any one he expected his friends to share his
fanatical animosity.   He was angry that Eulenburg had
not attempted to prevent Bismarck's visit to Berlin and
indeed actually approved it.   Bismarck's return to the
Wilhelmstrasse was not to be feared, but Herbert in the
Foreign Office would from Holstein's point of view be
equally fatal.   That the Emperor, like Eulenburg, had
a mind and will of his own infuriated him.   When Count
Henckel declined the challenge in the *Kladderadatsch*
affair Holstein begged his friend to urge the Emperor
to press the Count to risk his life.   ' This time, my dear
friend, I am really counting on your friendship.   If His

---

[1] Waldersee, *Denkwürdigkeiten*, II. 303, January 5, 1894.
[2] Otto Becker, *Das Französisch-Russische Bündnis*, 43.
[3] Haller, *Eulenburg*, 164–222.
[4] Muschler, *Eulenburg*, 388.   In his interesting obituary notice in the
Times, May 10, 1909, Chirol describes him as the most kindly and generous
of men, though extremely sensitive and prone to take offence where none was
meant.

Majesty does nothing against Henckel, he will thereby join the side of my enemies.' To this insane suggestion Eulenburg replied by advising him not to threaten any one else, lest people should think him a fool ; yet he was alarmed at the prospect that the ruler might be added to the black list of his foes. 'The danger has arisen that he will hate His Majesty if he does not come out against Henckel. And such a hatred would create a very serious situation.' That he was prevented from fighting an innocent man was an offence for which he could forgive neither the Kaiser nor Eulenburg. He had never been among the admirers of the young ruler, and his letters to Eulenburg had been sharply critical. When Hohenlohe became Chancellor Eulenburg felt it his duty to warn him that Holstein was working through the press for the removal of Lucanus, August Eulenburg and other high functionaries who had incurred his displeasure. Moreover the feud with Friedrichsruh burned as fiercely as ever. 'The attitude towards Bismarck, in which I support Hohenlohe, infuriates Holstein,' reported Eulenburg to Bülow. 'He can only love or hate. There is no middle course for our friend.' He was soon to find terrible confirmation of this judgment in his own unhappy fate.

Hohenlohe, who had spent his life in high politics, was far less dependent on his officials than the amateur Caprivi, and Holstein feared that the Kaiser and his new Chancellor might occasionally go their own way. His tortured spirit now began to cavil at the system of personal government which he compared to *opera bouffe*. On December 2, 1894, Eulenburg, while confessing his own opinion that the time was ripe for a Parliamentary ruler, remonstrated with Holstein for resenting the exercise of the Emperor's constitutional privileges. His correspondent rejoined that he did not grudge him his prerogatives, but that behind the façade of personal rule he espied the spectre of Bismarck. Thus William II was put on the black list because the public feud with Bismarck had closed ; and Eulenburg was trounced for going over to the 'Court-Conservatives' because he remained a friend of the monarch. His own days at the Foreign Office, remarked Holstein plaintively, were numbered, and Hohenlohe would not last long. The Emperor's private correspondence with the new Tsar was an added grievance, for he resented any move on the international chess-board of which he was unaware and which he was unable in some degree to control. The growing hostility of the virtual head of the Foreign Office to the monarch filled Eulenburg with apprehension. 'Holstein is beside himself,' he wrote to Bülow in November, 1895. 'He is no longer omnipotent. In our present difficult situation we cannot possibly do without his genius, but the Emperor's impulsive ways may easily lead to incidents.' That William II was a potential danger they both agreed ; but while the one sought salvation in the influence of wise and unselfish counsellors, the other attempted to put spokes in his wheel. Holstein endeavoured to separate Hohenlohe from his master, not in order to overthow him, but in the belief that the Chancellor should assert his authority, while remaining of course subject to the ultimate control of his nominal subordinate.

At the end of 1895 Bülow wrote to Eulenburg : 'I not only admire the energy and genius of Holstein, but he has become very dear to me. Many would not understand that, but you can. I love his tragic nature. I would never turn my back on him. I wish to help him. But it makes it very difficult for us that he loses all self-control if his system is or seems to be threatened. You fear that his dealings may lead to the break-up of the Hohenlohe-Marschall regime which you desire to maintain. You could perhaps give Hohenlohe a hint. But do not forget that the latter has been in the closest intimacy for twenty-two years, regards him as his surest support, and inclines rather to his view of a Parliamentary bureaucracy than to our old Prussian royalism.' Like most other people, Bülow was to like Holstein less when he knew him better.

Eulenburg, perhaps the only man who ever loved William II, did his utmost to avert an explosion by argument and remonstrance. ' When through Bismarck's retirement the control of foreign policy passed into your hands,' he wrote to Holstein in February, 1896, ' you, who are born to rule, found the Emperor in your way, since he developed contrary to your wishes and expectations. That must lead to differences. I have confidence in his shining gifts and in the lofty idealism which will win through—the confidence that you lack. We both serve him, I with love, you without.' Holstein replied that it was true that he felt himself *de facto* Director of the Political Department of the Foreign Office. His differences with the Emperor were in respect of method, not of policy. He had once shared the hope that he would learn from life. ' Today the hope is much weaker. I fear that if the experiences are to have any effect they will have to be of a rough character, experiences in which the whole people will be involved.' Eulenburg was increasingly alarmed at the growing hostility of such a powerful and unscrupulous foe. ' I am horrified,' he wrote to Bülow in March, 1896, in reference to the cabal against the Emperer ; ' they stick at nothing.' The group, he added, consisted of Holstein, Marschall and Bronsart, whose tactics were to provoke difficulties in order to range the Chancellor against the ruler, and thus to confront the latter with a massed opposition before which he would have to give way.

Hohenlohe knew what was going on, and Eulenburg's conversations with him and the Emperor had established full harmony between them. ' The Holstein system,' he concluded, ' feels itself threatened by Hohenlohe's pliability and my mediation.' The Chancellor expressed his gratitude. ' The dream of Holstein's heart,' wrote Eulenburg in 1902, ' was a tame Emperor living away from Berlin, affixing his signature to documents, with Hohenlohe and Marschall bending obediently before his will. Yet it was not I alone who felt his great diplomatic talent to be indispensable. He must be taken care of in the interest of the Emperor and the Government, as one takes care of an ill-tempered and even dangerous sporting dog for the sake of his excellent scent.' Holstein's position, in fact, seemed impregnable. 'He is in complete control of the Office,' reported Monts to Bülow in March, 1896.[1] 'His capacity for work arouses admiration. Unfortunately his nerviness and touchiness grow on him.' He suffered under the coldness of the Emperor, added Monts ; but so long as he and Hohenlohe held the reins of foreign policy firmly in their hands, things would go fairly well despite the occasional escapades of the monarch.

V

The burly Marschall, nicknamed by Kiderlen the Hippopotamus, was not a man to make friends, and the Emperor, who had never cared for him, had grown to detest the sound of his name. His approaching fall was freely canvassed in 1896, and it was thought likely that the aged Hohenlohe would go too. Holstein shivered at the prospect of a change which might shake him out of the saddle, and he was terrified lest Botho Eulenburg, over whom he had no influence, should be the next Chancellor. 'You know that I go if Hohenlohe and Marschall go,' he wrote to Philip Eulenburg early in 1897. A middle way was found in the relegation of Marschall to Constantinople, the retention of Hohenlohe, and the appointment of Bülow. Early in 1895 Eulenburg had written to the Emperor : 'Bernhard is the most valuable official Your Majesty possesses, the predestined Chancellor of the future.' At the end of the same year William II was repeating the fateful words : 'He and no other shall be the future Chancellor. He shall be my Bismarck.' [2] Eulenburg was prompted not only by personal friendship, but by the conviction that Bülow alone could put an end to an intolerable situation

---

[1] Bülow, *Denkwürdigkeiten*, I. 38–9.   [2] Haller, *Eulenburg*, 225.

in the Wilhelmstrasse and give the lonely monarch the
support that he needed.   In April, 1897, the Emperor
spoke of Holstein as ' an old man for whom I have broken
many a lance ; full of brains and full of hallucinations,
who sometimes makes the Wilhelmstrasse even madder
than it is already.'   But he never knew how Holstein
used to speak of him.   In a letter to Bülow of June 1,
1897, the disgusted Eulenburg describes an evening in
Holstein's room in the Foreign Office, when Kiderlen,
who was half drunk, and Holstein denounced the ruler,
the latter remarking that he must be treated as the child
or the fool that he was.   The time was certainly ripe for
a new broom, and Bismarck among others welcomed the
change.   ' He will be better than Marschall,' he observed ; ' Holstein's influence at any rate will diminish.' [1]

On his way from Rome to Kiel, where he was to meet
his master, Bülow broke the journey at Berlin.   He
found an emotional letter from Holstein, beseeching him
to speak to no one in or out of the Foreign Office and to
keep his hands free till they had had a talk.   ' I found
him in a rather uncertain mood,' writes the Prince,
' in his celebrated room adjoining that of the Foreign
Minister, on whom he used to burst at any moment, to
the great distress of the latter's peace of mind and nerves.[2]
He would have preferred to keep Marschall in office, in
view of the commanding influence he exerted over him.
That his position was badly damaged increased Holstein's
penchant for the Minister, because he thereby became
more dependent.   Yet he preferred me to other possible
successors.   He made a clever remark that Kiderlen was
impossible.   " The Foreign Office puts up with Holstein
or at worst with Kiderlen, but Kiderlen and Holstein
together would be too much."   I soon discovered that
what he feared was the re-emergence of Berchem or the
return to Herbert Bismarck, who, since his break with
the house of Bismarck, appeared to him in sleepless
nights as a nightmare with his angry colossus of a father

[1] Bismarck, *Gesammelte Werke*, IX. 474, August 8, 1897.
[2] *Denkwürdigkeiten*, I. 6–7.

behind him.   While on the one hand he besought me
not to give the Emperor a blank refusal, on the other he
pictured the Foreign Office, the relations of the Ministers
to one another, and the life in Berlin as a veritable Inferno.
That was intended to make me anxious and uncertain at
the start and thus to enhance my dependence on the
great Geheimrat who under Hohenlohe, under Caprivi
and through his old and powerful influence on Herbert,
even in the last years of the Bismarck era, was the determining influence in the Foreign Office.'   Bülow adds
that, though Holstein and Kiderlen had often intrigued,
they were, despite their failings, primarily concerned
with the welfare of the country.   ' Holstein was a stiff
Prussian.   The idea that Prussia and Germany might
lose their position and be damaged or misused by other
Powers stirred him to the depths of his being.   It could
truly be said of him that zeal for our House consumed
him, indeed often destroyed his sense of realities, and his
watchfulness turned into an excess of mistrust.   Kiderlen
was to Holstein like Sancho Panza to Don Quixote.'

The father of the new Foreign Secretary had said to
Holstein many years earlier, ' Look after my eldest son
when I am gone.'[1]   When, however, on the fall of
the Bismarcks, Bülow was mentioned for the post of
Foreign Secretary, Holstein declared that in that event
he would resign.   He secured the promotion of Bülow
from Bucharest to Rome in 1893 despite the opposition
of Marschall ;[2] but he had no wish to see him in the
Wilhelmstrasse.   When he learned of the Emperor's
prophecy at the end of 1895, he tried to stave off the day
of its fulfilment.   To become Foreign Secretary, he
told Bülow, would damage his chances of the Chancellorship, for Foreign Secretaries were not promoted.   The
new Minister was aware that his advent was a blow to
the man who had held the rudder for seven years ; and
Herbert Bismarck, with whom he maintained friendly
relations, repeatedly warned him against the malice and
knavery of the man whom in Friedrichsruh they called

---

[1] Bülow doubts the story, IV. 547.   [2] Ib. IV. 650.

the slow-worm. 'There were worse plans in the Foreign Office last winter than we imagined,' wrote Bülow to Eulenburg a few weeks after his appointment.[1] 'The chief group, Holstein, Kiderlen, Pourtalès, display a bad conscience and great apprehension. Holstein is sentimental ("For twenty years I have felt like a father to you"), Kiderlen is like an earwig, Pourtalès like a submissive Attaché. Of course the group has not yet lost the hope of regaining control. Their ideal is Hermann Hatzfeldt (Duke of Trachenberg) as Chancellor and Kiderlen as Foreign Secretary, with His Majesty to be treated as a minor.' Eulenburg, who knew the undercurrents of Berlin infinitely better than his friend, exhorted him to show his teeth when necessary. 'Good nature does not carry one far in the Wilhelmstrasse. Even the monster of the labyrinth begins to cringe at your feet.' Holstein knew a clever man when he saw him, and in October he reported to Kiderlen that Bülow was threading his way very skilfully among the thorns.[2]

Strong in the support of his impressionable master, the new Minister proceeded to assert himself. 'I must get into my hands the *personnel*, the press and the political police,' he observed to Hammann.[3] He knew, adds the head of the Press Department, that the first of these objects would involve friction with the Baron; and when in 1898 he made the changes which he deemed necessary, Holstein stayed away from the office for two months in the sulks. In the summer of that year the monarch expressed his delight to Eulenburg. 'The rule of the Privy Counsellors is over. Who speaks now of Herr von Holstein? He occupies the position which he ought to occupy. When his foes tell me he had better go, I rejoin: "Is he still taking the lead?" Since Bülow has had the reins in his hands no one knows the names of his Counsellors, so there is no need to trouble about them.'[4]

[1] Haller, *Eulenburg*, 240.   [2] Jäckh, *Kiderlen*, I. 169.
[3] Hammann, *Zur Vorgeschichte des Weltkrieges*, 4-5.
[4] Haller, *Eulenburg*, 240.

The Emperor was far too sanguine, for ' the Monster '
was scotched but not killed.   Hohenlohe warned Bülow
on his appointment that ' dangerous and evil counsels
usually come from Holstein,'[1] and in truth the game of
intrigue never ceased for a day.   No sooner was the new
Minister installed than he received a collection of the
Emperor's *marginalia* on Waldersee, of which ' traitor '
was one of the mildest expressions ; for he feared that
Bülow might become too friendly with the ex-Chief of the
Staff, who, though temporarily out of favour at Court, was
not to be despised.[2]   His maxim was *Divide et Impera*.
At the end of his life Bülow confessed that Holstein
was never sympathetic to him ; but he added that his
wide personal contacts, his knowledge, his great experience,
his quickness of apprehension, his resolution and, last but
not least, his cunning and his unscrupulousness made
him one of the most powerful personages in the State.

A fresh revelation of an abnormal mind was afforded
by the death of Bismarck in the summer of 1898, which
brought immense relief to his apostate pupil.   The
temptation to give a parting kick at the dead lion was
irresistible.   ' With fevered zeal,' writes Bülow, ' he
tried to persuade me that Bismarck's death had provoked no emotion, still less sorrow.[3]   He quoted
Talleyrand's odious remark on the death of the great
Napoleon : *Ce n'est pas un événement, c'est à peine une
nouvelle.* He complained of the Under-Secretary
Richthofen, who had succeeded Rotenhan in 1897, for
hoisting the flag on the Foreign Office at half-mast.
This demonstration of grief, he argued, would displease
the liberal *bourgeoisie* and still more the working classes,
and, worst of all, would incur the wrath of His Majesty.
In his blind yet petty animosity the old Geheimrat, who
had stood closer to the great Bismarck for over thirty
years than most other people, seemed to me like a
malignant wolf who ought to be behind bars and not
roaming at large.'   The new Foreign Minister, how-

[1] Bülow, *Denkwürdigkeiten*, II. 113.   [2] *Ib*. I. 363.
[3] *Ib*. I. 229.

ever, was as incapable of caging the wild animal as his predecessors. Holstein's influence, he declares, was not so great during his term of office as in the preceding decades ; [1] but this judgment is not confirmed by those who saw them working together. He told Raschdau, who complained of Holstein's intrigues, that he hoped to get rid of him within three months ; but nothing more was heard of the bold intention.[2]

Bülow became aware of the difficulties of his task in the first diplomatic problem by which he was faced. The seizure of Kiao-Chau, while ostensibly the result of the murder of German missionaries, was in reality the fulfilment of a secret deal with the Tsar ; but it came as a shock to the uninitiated world. The handling of a delicate situation was complicated by the gymnastics of Holstein. ' Less positive than negative, more destructive than constructive,' complains Bülow in relating the incident, ' he felt himself more indispensable the less secure were his superiors.[3] From this point of view the Emperor's friendly feeling towards me disquieted him. The idea occurred to him to spur on the Chancellor in the Eastern question and to hold back the Foreign Minister. While he depicted all the dangers of the enterprise in excited private telegrams, he egged on Prince Hohenlohe to take a bold and confident line with the Emperor. I saw through his game, and was much too convinced of the wisdom of my policy to be caught ; and Prince Hohenlohe was too much of a gentleman and too old to lend himself to such intrigues. On this and on many later occasions Holstein resembled a watchdog who guards the house against robbers, but with whom one can never be sure that he will not bite his master in the legs.'

Holstein had received permission from Bismarck to correspond direct with the diplomatic representatives of Germany through private telegrams which were not

---

[1] Bülow, *Denkwürdigkeiten*, I. 112.
[2] *Süddeutsche Monatshefte*, March, 1931, 390.
[3] Bülow, *Denkwürdigkeiten*, I. 186–7.

entered in the file, and not always shown to the Chancellor or the Foreign Minister. It was a dangerous precedent, but the privilege once granted could not be withdrawn. Like Louis XV he carried on a secret diplomacy of his own. He corresponded incessantly with Hatzfeldt in London, Radolin in St. Petersburg, Eulenburg in Vienna, Monts in Munich and Rome, while among the younger generation Eckardstein was the most favoured. If certain members of the diplomatic service were thus singled out for confidence and collaboration, others were punished or ignored. Radowitz had never been forgiven for his conduct in 1878. ' I do not know whom Holstein hates most, the French or me,' complained Münster, the veteran Ambassador at Paris, to Eckardstein in 1898 ; ' in recent months he has kept me without information except what directly concerns Paris. How he can take the responsibility of leaving me utterly uninformed in this important post, simply from personal pique, he must reconcile with his conscience if he has one. It is good that Hatzfeldt at any rate is in touch with this unfathomable eccentric.' When Raschdau, his colleague in the Political Department, was given a diplomatic post at Weimar in 1894 because he found Holstein intolerable, the latter revenged himself by cutting off the usual supply of despatches. Despite the protests of the old Grand Duke, who had long enjoyed the privilege of reading them, and despite the intervention of Marschall and Hohenlohe, the boycott continued, and the disgusted Raschdau left the diplomatic service in 1897.[1]

The animosities of the misanthrope were not confined to his own countrymen. ' Your Goluchowski is a sheep,' he wrote to Eulenburg in 1897. The Austro-Hungarian Foreign Minister was well aware of these sentiments, for the two men had been Secretaries of Legation in Paris in the early seventies. Goluchowski had shown his sense of social superiority, and Holstein never forgave

[1] The correspondence was published by Raschdau, ' Zum Kapitel Holstein,' in *Deutsche Rundschau*, December, 1924.

personal humiliations. At the end of 1898 the expulsion
of some Austrian subjects from Posen provoked loud
resentment in Austria, and he proceeded to launch an
attack on the Ballplatz. ' The inspirer of this campaign,'
wrote the distracted Eulenburg in February, 1899, ' is
our friend Holstein, who is slowly turning his back on me
since I stick up for Goluchowski, because he is the only
guarantee that Austria does not throw herself into the
arms of Russia.[1] If His Majesty and Bernhard Bülow
did not listen to me, we should soon be confronted by
a Franco-Russo-Austrian alliance. The whole Triplice
rests for the moment on Goluchowski, the Schratt and
myself. It is maddening when Holstein carries a personal vendetta into politics.' The tension was relieved
by a change of Ministry in Austria, but the uneasy
friendship of Eulenburg and Holstein was at an end.
The latter ceased to write, and when the Ambassador
visited Berlin he was ' not at home.' ' I was deeply
sorry,' comments the Prince ; ' though he was half crazy,
he was a lonely, unhappy nature; and my sympathy with
him is great. The cause of the change was not only his
partial exclusion by Bülow, but also my political " failure "
in relation to Goluchowski. I put the interests of the
Fatherland above his whims.' Two years later, when
the enmity of ' the monster ' assumed new forms,
Eulenburg poured out his heart to Bülow. ' When
I think that I have done him nothing but good, that
I helped him whenever I could, that I have suffered
much on his account—and now this enmity, this hatred !
It is wholly inexplicable. I shall never lift a finger
against him, because I am sorry for him and despite
everything I cannot forget what we were to each other.'
Holstein's feud with Goluchowski continued, and Eulenburg's retirement from Vienna and from public life in
1902 was due not merely to growing ill-health, resulting
from years of overwork, but to the unceasing friction
with the Wilhelmstrasse.

When Bülow followed Hohenlohe as Chancellor in

[1] Haller, *Eulenburg*, 262-6.

1900 he vainly pressed Holstein to accept the post which he vacated ; but under Richthofen the power of ' the monster ' automatically increased.   ' In one of my first talks,' writes the Emperor of his new Chancellor,[1] ' I cautioned him against Holstein.   He was endowed with great ability and a phenomenal memory.   He could make or mar the career of all the young diplomats.   At times he was the *Spiritus Rector* both of the Foreign Office and of foreign policy.   The worst of it was that he evaded all official responsibility.   He preferred to work in the dark.   He declined every responsible post, though many were open to him.   For long I tried in vain to make his acquaintance.   I invited him to meals, but he declined every time.   Only once did he condescend to dine with me in the Foreign Office, where he appeared in morning coat and explained that he had no dress suit.   His memoranda, though clever, were often as ambiguous as the Delphic oracle.   This powerful influence, often exerted behind the back of the officials, seemed to me dangerous.   It often happened, especially in the Richthofen era, that when I advised a foreign Ambassador to discuss a question with the Foreign Secretary I received the reply " J'en parlerai avec mon ami Holstein."   Thus he controlled a large part of foreign policy.   He listened to the Chancellor ; but what the Kaiser thought or said was a matter of indifference to him.   If success was achieved it was claimed by the Foreign Office, if not, it was put down to the impulsive young ruler.   For long he seemed to Bülow indispensable, but at length the pressure that this sinister man exerted on everyone became intolerable.'

' From month to month I watch the dependence of Bülow on Holstein with ever growing apprehension,' wrote Eulenburg in May, 1902 ; and after his fall he confessed that he had never dreamed that Bülow could become so terribly dependent on Holstein, who had a rope round his neck.   The recovery of power was observed by everybody.   ' I do not understand how Bülow

[1] *Ereignisse und Gestalten*, 83-5.

allows it,' noted Waldersee in his diary at the end of 1901, in reference to a press campaign against himself and the Emperor.[1] ' It is a subject of general comment that he keeps his place under Bülow, when one imagined he would promptly dismiss him. I think the Emperor supports him—the reason I cannot entrust to paper.' According to Arthur Zimmermann, Holstein used to stay away when Bülow opposed his suggestions, and Princess Bülow was despatched to his home to entice him back.[2] Bülow could not fail to be aware of his deficiencies, and he complained of the unsteadiness of his nerves, of which the breakdown of the tripartite rule in Samoa in 1899 provided one of the earliest examples. When the news arrived that British and American cruisers had bombarded Apia and that German colonists had been arrested, Bülow, who was in his Flottbek home, hurried to Berlin. ' Holstein was at the station to tell me in great but, as I thought, forced excitement, that the only possible way of getting out of this disagreeable situation was for me to resign after such a blow. I quietly replied to the incorrigible eccentric that I found his solution rather attractive. If I were to go I should recommend as my successor Prince Herbert Bismarck. Holstein, who, since 1890, feared the Bismarck family as the devil fears holy water, at once took a calmer view of the situation.'[3] It was with such an egotistical and neurotic counsellor at his elbow that the new Foreign Minister was condemned to undertake negotiations of the most delicate character with Great Britain, Russia and France in turn.

VI

The cardinal problem of Bülow's twelve years of office was the relation between Germany and Great Britain. The anger created by the Kruger telegram, though never forgotten, was softened by Germany's steady

---

[1] *Denkwürdigkeiten*, III. 171.
[2] *Süddeutsche Monatshefte*, March, 1931, 391.
[3] Bülow, *Denkwürdigkeiten*, I. 282–3.

support in Egypt, which was all the more welcome at a
time when our relations with France in Africa and with
Russia in the Far East were ominously strained. The
agitating experiences of the year 1898, which opened
with the seizure of Port Arthur and closed with the
Fashoda crisis, raised the question whether the traditional
policy of splendid isolation provided the necessary
security. The new orientation found a vigorous exponent in Chamberlain, who expressed his opinion
of France and Russia with his usual unreserve, and
suggested a working partnership with Germany and the
United States. The latter, as might have been foreseen,
had no stomach for European entanglements, and anything in the nature of an alliance with the latter was at
the moment out of the question ; for Salisbury and the
majority of his colleagues saw no reason for abandoning
the policy of the free hand, and Germany was unwilling
to compromise her friendly relations with Russia by a
close association with her hated rival. The approaches
of Chamberlain, though approved by some of his colleagues, never amounted to a substantial offer ; for it is
the prerogative of the Prime Minister or the Foreign
Secretary, not of the Colonial Secretary, to declare and
carry out the policy of the British Government. That the
discussions of 1898 so vividly described in Eckardstein's
Memoirs were academic is suggested by the fact that
they left no trace in the archives of the British Foreign
Office. They were, however, symptomatic of a distinct
atmospheric change, and what Chamberlain thought
today his countrymen might think tomorrow.

Though an alliance was impossible, a *rapprochement*
with Germany was the obvious course for British statesmanship at a time when war with France and Russia
was by no means impossible. The secret treaty signed
in August, 1898, which divided the Portuguese colonies
into British and German spheres of influence, registered
the high-water-mark of cordial co-operation. The ensuing negotiations with regard to Samoa proved much
more difficult, and the stubbornness of the British

Premier aroused intense resentment in Berlin. Holstein had no craving for a large-scale diplomatic partnership and was filled with distrust of Salisbury ; but he was eager for regional agreements. ' Could not Salisbury be side-tracked by some of his colleagues in the questions which concern us ? ' he telegraphed to Hatzfeldt on February 24, 1899.[1] ' Chamberlain must have realised the gain to England in prestige, independence and power by the relatively unimportant Portuguese agreement. He must be clever enough to see that similar special agreements would bring further strength. This inquiry is purely on my own. You alone can say if direct inter-course with Chamberlain would do more harm than good. Another question. Cecil Rhodes wishes to come to Berlin. Is he a man with whom one could discuss the policy of compensations in the grand style ? In other words, is his influence strong enough to push through an agreed settlement against the *vis inertiae* of Salisbury ? Would he have a say in Moroccan questions ? Would he consider the surrender of Zanzi-bar in return for railway and other concessions on the mainland ? Would his influence tell in the Samoa question ? ' To this hail of questions the Ambassador replied that it would be dangerous to go behind Salis-bury's back, and that the Prime Minister had no present intention to make special agreements with Germany. The influence of Rhodes, he added, must not be over-estimated since the Raid. A few weeks later, when the Samoa problem seemed as far as ever from solution, Hatzfeldt reported to his friend that Salisbury's earlier sympathy for Germany had ended, mainly for personal reasons. Under these circumstances it would be best neither to run after England nor to make binding agree-ments with other Powers which would prevent an under-standing with the English if they came to their senses.

On receiving Hatzfeldt's rather depressing letter Holstein drew up one of the comprehensive Memoranda in which from time to time he crystallised his thoughts

[1] *Die Grosse Politik,* XIV. 580–3.

as his telescope swept the ever-changing horizon.[1]
' Today France cannot reach an agreement with England
because the objects of compensation would not suffice
to satisfy Russia,—to say nothing of Germany, who would
not be content merely to look on during the partition of
the globe.'   Harmonious relations between Russia and
Germany, he added, were a vital interest of both, but
there was no need for a binding agreement with a point
against another state which would thereby become an
opponent.   ' The dangers which threaten us from Russia
are too remote to compel us to bind ourselves to her
natural antagonists.'   France remained irreconcilable.
' But the possibility cannot be excluded that Germany,
Russia and France, in the press of events, may one day
form a League whose first article would be the mutual
guarantee of their territories.   Till then Russia and
Germany will continue their present policy without any
treaty agreement, namely the maintenance or peaceful
modification of the situation.   In this we are nearer to
Russia than is Russia, despite her alliance, to France.
For the supreme aim of France is unattainable by peaceful
means.'   With such confidence in the moderation of
Russia, Holstein saw no reason to jeopardise her goodwill
by serious flirtations with her principal rival.   Her
ambitions and commitments in the Far East necessitated
caution in Europe, and her agreement with Austria in
1897 had put the Balkan question into cold storage for
a time.   There was, therefore, he believed, no need
to abandon what Bülow always described as the independence of German policy.   He was equally hostile
to the ideas which were discussed at the Hague Conference during the summer of 1899.   ' Arbitration,' he
wrote, ' is all right for small states and small questions,
not for large states and large questions.' [2]

The outbreak of the Boer War in October, 1899,
weakened the bargaining power of Great Britain, and
with Chamberlain's potent aid the dragging dispute over

[1] *Die Grosse Politik*, XIV. 534–8.
[2] Memorandum of May 8, 1899.   *Die Grosse Politik*, XV. 188–9.

Samoa was settled by the division of the islands between
Germany and the United States. If Eckardstein is to
be believed, Holstein remarked on the eve of the South
African conflict that it was naïve of him to imagine that
England would risk a war, since the other Powers would
intervene. When the storm broke he feared that Great
Britain in her extremity would offer a bait which Germany
might be tempted to swallow. The Emperor's visit to
England in November, the first since the Kruger telegram, was a welcome sign that the barometer was rising ;
but Holstein's suspicious brain dwelt more on the pitfalls
than on the advantages of the visit. ' Avoid all political
conversations, especially with Salisbury, and treat him
with cool courtesy,' he wrote in a characteristic Memorandum for the Emperor which was approved by Hatzfeldt and Hohenlohe.[1] ' Be equally reserved but warmer
in tone with Chamberlain, who will doubtless press for
an agreement pointed against Russia. Say that you will
carefully consider the proposal, but display no enthusiasm,
and thus his offer will increase. Accept nothing positive,
and reveal no plans.'

Holstein knew nothing of England and the English,
and Lascelles, the British Ambassador, never saw him
till he had held his post for several years ; but as Bülow
very truly points out, he was never an Anglophobe.
' He was not anti-British but pro-British, hotly, almost
passionately as was his wont.[2] Though a Pomeranian
Junker by birth, he was as anti-Russian as any Liberal.
He was against accepting Chamberlain's proposals without firm obligations and guarantees, but he long cherished
the hope that such guarantees would be forthcoming
some day.' The whole Foreign Office, adds Bülow,—
Holstein, Richthofen and Mühlberg—were, like Hohenlohe himself, quite ready for a treaty with England if
only the indispensable pledges were given. ' On our
side everything was done to procure them.' Bülow did
not believe, as Holstein used sometimes to suspect, that
Chamberlain never seriously intended closer relations,

---

[1] Bülow, *Denkwürdigkeiten*, I. 311-3. [2] *Ib*. i. 326-7.

but only talked of them in order to make the French and Russians pliable, and to compromise Germany in the eyes of the latter. ' In my view he attempted to bind us at the moment when that course suited him, convinced that with a change in the situation he would easily escape from his promises.'[1]

The fruits of the visit of the Emperor and his Foreign Minister were disappointing. Salisbury had lost his wife and kept out of the way. Chamberlain's speech at Leicester, which he believed—wrongly, according to Bülow—to embody his visitor's ideas no less than his own, received a chilly response from the German Foreign Minister, who was convinced that public opinion, inflamed by detestation of the Boer War, would tolerate no intimacy with Great Britain. Bülow's *douche* was quickly followed by the seizure of German ships wrongfully suspected of carrying contraband to the Boers, which led to peremptory demands in Downing Street and smoothed the way for the Second Navy Bill. ' If England does not release the steamers and give us satisfaction or arbitration,' telegraphed Holstein to Hatzfeldt on January 7, 1900, ' a continental group will at once arise, primarily to consider the principles of sea-law.[2] As they are only waiting for Germany, the grouping could be effected in a few days. That would be the first step in a direction which Germany regrets to choose, but the blindness of the English statesmen leaves us no choice.' The flower which Chamberlain had sown and watered had withered away.

The second and far more important chapter of the negotiations for an Anglo-German partnership begins in January, 1901.[3] During a visit to Chatsworth, the country home of the Duke of Devonshire, Baron Eckardstein was assured by Chamberlain that for him

---

[1] Bülow, *Denkwürdigkeiten*, I. 331.

[2] *Die Grosse Politik*, XV. 457.

[3] The documents quoted and summarised in the following pages are taken from *Die Grosse Politik*, XVII. ch. 109 ; Eckardstein, *Erinnerungen*, Vol. II. ; and *British Documents on the Origins of the War*, ed. Gooch and Temperley, II. ch. 10. Cp. Hammann, *Zur Vorgeschichte des Weltkrieges*, ch. 5.

and his friends in the Cabinet the time of 'splendid isolation' was over ; that the choice lay between the Dual and the Triple Alliance ; that, unlike some of his colleagues, he would prefer the former ; and that the first step should be a secret Moroccan agreement between England and Germany on the basis of previous discussions.   The matter should be taken up when Salisbury left for the Riviera and the details discussed with Lansdowne and himself.   So long as he felt convinced that a lasting co-operation with Germany was possible, he would stoutly resist the idea of an arrangement with Russia.   If, however, it appeared that such co-operation was impracticable, he would turn to Russia, despite the high price England would have to pay, perhaps involving China and the Persian Gulf.   These declarations, except as regards Morocco, were to be regarded for the present as purely academic.

On the same day that this significant news was telegraphed to Berlin, Hatzfeldt, the invalid Ambassador, sent one of his innumerable private wires to Holstein. Chamberlain's utterances, he observed, confirmed his old opinion that England would come to them when she felt the need of support.   'You and I agree that the idea of an alliance is premature.   Chamberlain seems to share this opinion, and to wish to lead up to the later definitive understanding by a special pact concerning Morocco. That we can accept.'   Holstein, who travelled through life in blinkers, was in no way impressed either by the prospect of a deal with Great Britain or by the warning that she might turn her eyes elsewhere.   'The whole threat of disarming the enmity of Russia and France by yielding in China and the Persian Gulf,' he telegraphed to Eckardstein, 'is utter nonsense.   In the first place France does not get enough out of it.   Neither for this nor any other concession would she be induced to hand over Tangier and therewith the Straits of Gibraltar to England.   If England made large concessions in territory and spheres of influence to Russia and France, she would whet their appetite and make the struggle for

existence inevitable, even were it to be postponed :
a weakened England against strengthened foes. A
broader treaty with England is almost unthinkable for
us, since it would almost certainly involve a danger of
war. For this immense risk a corresponding payment
will be forthcoming only when England forms a more
correct, that is to say more modest, estimate of her
achievements and of the friendship of America. Salisbury's words to Hatzfeldt : " You ask too much for
your friendship " still hold good. This and the ill-
treatment of Germany, which under Salisbury has become
a habit, must be forgotten on both sides so as to make
a fresh start. Meanwhile Kitchener is applying Salisbury's methods in the treatment of Germans in South
Africa.' [1]   Holstein spoke in the same sense to Richthofen, his nominal superior, who wrote to the Chancellor
on February 5 : ' Let England come to us. The spectre
of a Russo-English alliance appears to me, after numerous
conversations with Holstein, nothing but a spectre.' [2]
Thus the Wilhelmstrasse was of one mind. Its pundits
were blind to the signs of the times, repeating like
parrots that they had merely to wait till England was
compelled to accept their terms.

Three weeks after Chamberlain's unofficial conversations at Chatsworth, the question of Anglo-German
co-operation was officially raised by the Foreign Secretary.
In view of the rumours of a Manchurian agreement
between Russia and China, reported Eckardstein on
February 7, Lansdowne had informed him that Great

---

[1] A shorter telegram to Metternich, who was attached to the Emperor
during his visit to England on the occasion of the Queen's illness, reiterated his
standpoint. ' I am particularly suspicious of the present ardent wooing by
Chamberlain & Co., because the threatened understanding with Russia and
France is such an utter fraud. By yielding England would postpone the
struggle for existence for a year or two, but make it all the more certain, since
her foes would be strengthened and England weakened in power and prestige.
We can wait : time is on our side. A sensible agreement with England, that is
one which pays a fair price for the almost certain risk of war, is only to be
expected when the feeling of insecurity becomes more general in England than
it is today.'

[2] Bülow, *Denkwürdigkeiten*, I. 512.

Britain and Japan intended to protest to China, and inquired whether Germany would join in holding Russia in check. Two days later Holstein telegraphed to the Chancellor in Homburg his draft of a reply to the British inquiry. Germany could not involve herself in so sharp an antagonism to Russia on account of Manchuria, but would be ready to declare : ' We desire the preservation of the peace of the world, as we wish to live in peace ourselves. If this proves impossible we intend to remain neutral ; but we cannot foresee the extent and development of a conflict once begun, nor what tasks the preservation of an equilibrium may impose upon us.' This declaration, added Holstein, should limit the area of the war and indeed render it impossible ; and he hoped that England would be content with it. ' I agree with your proposals,' replied Bülow ; ' I hope indeed they will satisfy England, for, in view of the present acute anti-English feeling in Germany, too far-reaching demands for our support of English interests in China would render a subsequent understanding with England on a broad basis far more difficult.'

On February 11 Holstein explained his views in greater detail in an illuminating telegram to Eckardstein. ' You and I have often discussed the question of a German-English alliance. Such an alliance, in which each party deals with a single aggressor and the *casus foederis* only arises when there is more than one foe, has many attractions for the thoughtful statesman, but would unfortunately be in direct conflict with German opinion to-day. The systematic campaign against England, which began after Bismarck's retirement, is largely due to the intolerable personality of Salisbury, whose antipathy to the German Emperor and sympathy for France have shaped English policy during the last decade. This policy revealed itself as brutal and untrustworthy. The Chancellor, who has most to suffer from attacks, will not be inclined to divert them in even greater strength against the Emperor, which would certainly occur if a German-English alliance were now

to be made.   It would then be said that England gets
the advantages at our expense, but would as usual slip
out of her obligations.   This conviction, which is
shared by 99 per cent. of the German people, could not
be altered by assurances but only by facts, if the German-
English defensive treaty, apart from a fully-secured
reciprocity, carried with it direct advantages, not mere
promises.   I begin a new paragraph in order to emphasise
that the offer of an alliance cannot proceed from Germany.
For firstly I do not believe that England will make
acceptable concessions so long as Salisbury has a say,
and I think it unworthy of a Great Power again to be
told : You ask too much for your friendship.   And
secondly, after all our experiences with Salisbury, he
could quite well inform St. Petersburg of our offer and
its conditions and ask : What do you offer ?   England's
position, owing to Japanese co-operation and the certainty
of the neutrality of the Triple Alliance, is exceptionally
good, and can only become worse.   Thus an alliance
with Germany is unnecessary for the attainment of her
present aims.   The people could only be convinced by
positive facts that a German-English Treaty did not
subserve English purposes.'

On March 18 a momentous conversation took place
between Lansdowne and Eckardstein.   According to
the latter the Foreign Minister observed that he was
considering the possibility of a long-term defensive
alliance between England and Germany, which he
believed that several of his most influential colleagues
would approve.[1]   According to Lansdowne's report, on
the other hand, the suggestion was made not by himself
but by his visitor.[2]   The latter believed that the German
Government, while averse from an agreement entered
into solely with reference to the present situation in China,
would entertain favourably the idea of an understanding of a more durable and extended character which he
contemplated might be described as a purely defensive
alliance between the two Powers, directed solely against

[1] *Die Grosse Politik*, XVII. 41–2.   [2] Gooch and Temperley, II. 60–1.

France and Russia. So long as Germany and England were attacked by one only of the other two Powers, the Alliance would not operate ; but if either Germany or England had to defend itself against both France and Russia, Germany would have to help England, or England Germany, as the case might be. After replying that the project was very novel and far-reaching and would require careful examination, the Foreign Minister proceeded to indicate some of the difficulties. ' Baron Eckardstein was careful to assure me that his suggestion was not made under instructions,' concluded the report, ' but I feel no doubt that he has been desired to sound me.'

Which of these rival versions are we to believe ? There should be little difficulty in answering the question. Lansdowne was not only a man of spotless integrity and wide experience, but he was bound by every obligation of honour and precedent to provide the Cabinet with an accurate account of a conversation of such high significance. Eckardstein's report, on the other hand, was conveyed in the form of a private telegram to Holstein, who in a letter of March 17, which reached him on March 19, sent a precise injunction : ' I expressly forbid you the slightest mention of an alliance. The moment, if it ever comes, has not yet arrived.' [1] How then, it may be asked, could Eckardstein venture to make such a proposal without permission ? The probable explanation is that the ardent Anglophil, the husband of an English wife and with a good position in society, was deeply convinced not only of the desirability but of the possibility of such a pact and was eager to reap the credit of it were it to be achieved. Moreover he confesses that on March 16, when he was the guest of the Foreign Minister, he had given his host a broad hint to come forward with an offer of alliance, remarking : ' If there were a defensive alliance covering all eventualities, Germany would of course be in a position to localise a war between Russia and Japan by influencing France.' This passage, he adds, was omitted from his

[1] Eckardstein, II. 279.

telegram to Holstein lest he should denounce him for going too far.[1]   Holstein, in fact, was an impossible chief, and his letters and telegrams were the despair of his correspondents. 'I have often begun important negotiations at his order,' complains Eckardstein, 'and then been instructed to break them off as soon as the other party was ready for agreement.   Directly negotiations began to go smoothly, he became suspicious.'

Bülow replied on March 20 that the defensive arrangement which he believed Lansdowne to have proposed appealed to the German Government, which must however first consult its allies.   Meanwhile it would be well for England to approach Austria, though not Italy.   If Goluchowski approved, Germany would be ready for negotiations, and perhaps Japan might be drawn in.   In a conversation on March 22 [2] Lansdowne is stated to have made some informal inquiries as to the nature and scope of a defensive alliance, to which the German representative was instructed to return informal replies.   The best plan, he was to say, would be for England to connect herself with the Triple Alliance ; the *casus foederis* would arise in the case of two or more enemies ; and the pact must be public.   Japan, who pursued a policy of expansion, would find no advantage in a purely defensive alliance, but might be glad to get into good company.

The position of Japan presented grave difficulties to the Wilhelmstrasse ; for it was generally known that before very long she might be at war with Russia, with whom Germany was determined not to quarrel.   'Japan, who pursues an acquisitive policy,' wrote Holstein on March 27,[3] 'is a compromising comrade for Germany, who wishes to keep on terms with Russia.   Even the fact that we were discussing common action with Japan would be taken by Russia as a sign that we wish to change from a purely defensive to an aggressive policy.   It

[1] Eckardstein, II. 280.
[2] There is no record of this conversation in the British Foreign Office.
[3] *Die Grosse Politik*, XVI. 350–1.

would be quite different if England would some day affiliate herself with the Triple Alliance, and if Japan could be brought in as an appendage of England. In that case England, who stands essentially on the defensive in Asia and Europe, would act as a make-weight against Japanese effervescence ; and, if not, the new group would be so strong that the sentiments of other Powers towards us would be of less consequence than they are today. We have told Japan that we have no political arrangements with Russia, and therefore that we should remain neutral in a Russo-Japanese conflict and thereby in all probability secure the neutrality of France. Beyond that we cannot go.' Bülow expressed his gratitude for ' this masterly Memorandum with which he agreed in every point.' The possibility, in fact, of a struggle for the hegemony of the Far East seemed an additional reason for extreme circumspection in dealing with Great Britain.

On March 29 Lansdowne told Eckardstein that as Salisbury was ill he could not say much ; that his colleagues were apprehensive of the vague and far-reaching arrangement suggested ; and that it would be desirable to know for instance what would happen if Japan were at war with Russia and threatened by France. Eckardstein replied that as Salisbury was ill and the temper of the Reichstag irritable, it would be best to defer the discussion till after Easter. During this interval the Wilhelmstrasse, conscious of the difficulties arising from the unpopularity of Great Britain, became ever more convinced that a purely Anglo-German arrangement was impracticable. In a telegram of April 14 from Richthofen, drafted by Holstein, Hatzfeldt was instructed to explain to Lansdowne, in case he recurred to the subject, that the foes of the Triple Alliance were trying to turn Austria against Germany by attributing to her plans of partition after the death of Francis Joseph. ' This suspicion can best be dispelled when it is seen that a leading *rôle* in the formation of the projected alliance is assigned by Germany to Austria. That is why we lay so much weight on Vienna being in some measure the centre of the negotiations.'

In proposing to substitute the Triple Alliance for Germany as a bargaining and contracting unit, the Wilhelmstrasse had overshot the mark. According to Eckardstein,[1] Lansdowne informed him on May 15 that he and some of his colleagues would welcome a defensive alliance with Germany. He had seen the Prime Minister, who approved the principle of mutual support against two or more assailants, but not of complicating the issue by the inclusion of Germany and Italy. If the matter was to advance further both sides must now put their ideas on paper, though the drafts would still be of an academic character. Since no report of this interview has been found in the British archives, we may be allowed to doubt how far Eckardstein was correct in his account of the conversation, particularly with regard to the attitude of Salisbury.

On May 23 Lansdowne discussed the alliance question for the first time with the Ambassador himself, who, though old and ill, retained his mental alertness. When the Foreign Secretary pointed out the difficulties and uncertainties involved in joining the Triple Alliance, Hatzfeldt replied that an alliance with Germany alone was impossible. He stressed the dangers of isolation, and argued that Great Britain would be wise to join one or other of the two European groups. If she tried Russia she would have to pay a high price. If nothing came of these discussions, Germany might be driven to remove the friction with Russia by a deal. The conversation did nothing to bridge the gulf, and Lansdowne wrote to Eckardstein that it in no way diminished his desire for the memorandum which he had been promised. The memorandum, however, was never sent, for the Wilhelmstrasse intervened. ' I am suspicious of putting anything on paper at the present moment,' wired Holstein to his friend. ' When the first written document in the

---

[1] Though the telegram bears Hatzfeldt's signature, the interview took place between Eckardstein and Lansdowne.

alliance question leaves our hands, the first formal suggestion of an alliance comes from us—exactly what we wish
to avoid. To decide on the principle whether an attack
on the Triple Alliance should raise the *casus foederis* for
England the English require nothing in writing. When
England has expressed herself on the principle, written
notes, for instance on the meaning of the word Attack,
can be exchanged. Till then, in my opinion, we should
give nothing in writing.'

The failure to provide the memorandum was of little
importance, for on the very day on which Holstein was
warning Hatzfeldt of its perils, Salisbury condemned
the whole project root and branch.[1] ' It would hardly
be wise to incur novel and most onerous obligations in
order to guard against a danger in whose existence we
have no historical reason for believing.' Moreover, it
was impossible to promise aid, since the British Government could only wage a war supported by public opinion
at the time. Holstein had proved right in his unvarying
scepticism with regard to the Prime Minister, and
Eckardstein, despite his boasted acquaintance with
British statesmen, had deceived himself. Whatever life
there had been in the plan was trampled out of it by
Salisbury's uncompromising sentences.

On June 14 Holstein discussed the deeper issues of
Anglo-German relations in one of the most elaborate of
his memoranda. Salisbury's reply to Bismarck's celebrated letter of 1887, he declares, was regarded by the
Chancellor as a refusal of his advances. British policy,
indeed, rested on the conviction that a continental struggle
was inevitable, and that Great Britain would profit by
a struggle in which she took no part. In other words it
was the business of other Powers to pull the chestnuts
out of the fire for her. ' This catspaw theory, which
has gradually become a fetish for a certain school of English
politicians, is beyond doubt the cause of the universal
hatred of England today. No one likes being duped,
and the people of the Continent have gradually reached

[1] Gooch and Temperley, II. 68–9.

the conviction that England is out to dupe them.   Salisbury has carried out this policy more openly than any of
his predecessors.'   Turning to the project of an alliance
he reiterates the familiar arguments.   ' If we assume the
immense burden and responsibility of defending the
British Empire with all its colonies against all comers,
the Triple Alliance must be regarded as a whole, just like
the British Empire,—so that for instance an attack on
Austria or Italy by two or more Powers would call not
only the members of the Triplice but also England into
the field.   An alliance of England with Germany alone
would make the position of the latter worse instead of
better.   For since the contents of the treaty would be
published, her opponents will know that if they attack
Austria, and Germany goes to her assistance, England
will take no part.   But the inclination to fight with
Germany would be greatly enhanced when it was known
that in certain eventualities she is pledged to support
Great Britain.   At present we feel strong enough not
to hurry in the search for support.   Moreover we believe
that the current of events will probably one day bring
Germany and England together.   In times of excitement
we have avoided building dams which would impede
the flow of the stream, and we will retain our freedom
as long as we can.   Neither Yunnan nor Morocco are
important enough for us to risk a war or seek support.'

The opposition of Salisbury and the refusal of the
German Government to supply a written draft combined
with the ill-health of Hatzfeldt to defer further discussion
till the autumn.   When, however, the summer holidays
were over neither Metternich, the new Ambassador, nor
Eckardstein reverted to the subject.   Lansdowne agreed
with the Prime Minister that to join the Triple Alliance
was out of the question ; but he was less satisfied with
the policy of isolation than his chief, and was ready for
a limited Anglo-German understanding without pledges
of military support.[1]   Even this appeared to Salisbury
to be full of risks and to carry with it no compensating

[1] Gooch and Temperley, II. 79–80.

advantage. But what was too much for the British Premier was too little for the German Government, as Metternich frankly explained to Lansdowne in their first and last interview on the subject.[1] If a defensive alliance between the British Empire and the Triple Alliance were ruled out in London, no minor proposal would be considered at Berlin. Thus the conversations which began on March 18 ended on December 19, never to be renewed.

The failure of the discussions of an Anglo-German partnership caused Holstein no pangs, for he neither initiated them nor believed in their success. Eugen Fischer was in error in arguing that Holstein's Great No [2] had ruined a promising prospect ; for the Wilhelmstrasse was agreed that the Triple Alliance must be treated as a unit, and Salisbury's consent was never won even to an Anglo-German defensive alliance or to a declaratory pact. No British offer of an alliance was refused, for no official offer had been made. In a conversation with Chirol on October 31, the first since the crisis of the Kruger telegram, Holstein explained his position to his old friend.[3] ' I wished to avoid treating the alliance question as actual. Firstly I did not believe that Salisbury would wish to change his catspaw policy, though every one saw through it. Secondly, there was no reason for Germany to seek support, for our position had greatly improved in recent years. The German and Russian Emperors were convinced of each other's peaceful intentions, but I was one of those who felt that the tendency of the time would gradually bring together Germany and England, perhaps after I am gone. This view is shared by the Emperor and the Chancellor.

---

[1] Gooch and Temperley, II. 3.

[2] Eugen Fischer's volume, *Holsteins Grosses Nein*, is partially vitiated by his confidence in the testimony of Eckardstein.

[3] *Fifty Years*, 288–97. Chirol's statement that he visited Berlin at the pressing invitation of Holstein is contradicted by Rosen (*Oriental Memories*, 176–80). This interview, he declares, was sought by Chirol, not by Holstein, who at first refused to receive him, and only yielded to the representations of Mühlberg, the Under-Secretary.

The alliance question, in my opinion, could not be seriously discussed so long as Salisbury was at the helm. All that could be done was to leave the future open.'

On the following day Holstein drew up a memorandum on what he intended to say when he saw Chirol again. 'Luckily Germany can wait ; for with the paralysing influence of Salisbury nothing serious can be done.' Bülow approved the memorandum, and added : 'We must display neither restlessness nor impatience but allow hope to glitter on the horizon. In that hope lies the safest guarantee against the capitulation of the English to Russia.' The two men had been in agreement throughout. If there had been a spark of vitality left in the project of an alliance, it would have been extinguished by the sharp exchanges between Chamberlain and Bülow at the end of the year in regard to the conduct of British troops in South Africa and German troops in the campaign of 1870. A violent attack on the Colonial Minister was launched in the German press, and Holstein explained the situation to Chirol : *Wir haben unseren Korb bekommen und wir danken dafür.*[1] That expressive message may serve as the end of a confused chapter of diplomatic history. Even Chamberlain had had enough.

On January 3, 1902, Holstein wrote a friendly New Year's letter to Chirol containing a few final reflections on the discussions of the past year. Since Salisbury was known not to share Chamberlain's views, he declared, the German representatives in London were instructed not to broach the subject but simply to receive any overtures. These directions had been followed except in one isolated case in the summer of 1901, when ' poor Hatzfeldt in an access of nervous over-excitement appears to have summoned Lord Lansdowne to come to terms then and there.' Hatzfeldt was thereupon disavowed and recalled. 'I was therefore somewhat surprised to hear about a week ago that Lascelles had

[1] 'Our offer of marriage has been rejected, and we are conveying our thanks.' Chirol, *Fifty Years*, 297.

informed the Chancellor that the British Government considered the present time unfavourable for further discussion of an Anglo-German agreement. Why not have let the matter rest since nobody—to my knowledge at least—had urged it ? '

Whether the statesmen of Germany might have made better use of the friendly sentiments of Chamberlain and Lansdowne, during the years of anxiety when we had South Africa on our hands, will long remain a subject of debate.[1] It seems clear that the importance of British friendship in a divided Europe was insufficiently recognised at Berlin, and that no sustained attempt to achieve it was made. Yet there is no ground for the wholesale condemnation that has been meted out to them by certain critics. Even if Salisbury had been ready to meet them half way, the weakness of Russia had not yet been revealed on the Manchurian battle-fields, and the contingent estrangement of the Colossus might well seem a needless as well as a formidable risk. The failure of the discussions of 1901 left no scars in Downing Street, where they were never taken very seriously. What angered British citizens was not the breakdown of the negotiations, of which they never heard, but the unbridled hostility displayed during the South African war. The hot resentment might gradually have cooled, as it had cooled with regard to the Kruger telegram ; but, before the mellowing influence of time had begun to act, German policy in Morocco and on the high seas chose a path which banished all hope of genuine reconciliation. In a word a valuable opportunity for some sort of *rapprochement* had been missed ;

---

[1] The best recent discussions are Willy Becker's *Fürst Bülow und England,* which, broadly speaking, follows in the path of Eckardstein and Fischer, and Gerhard Ritter's *Die Legende von der verschmähten Freundschaft Englands,* the argument of which is summarised in its title. Cp. Brandenburg, *From Bismarck to the World War,* chs. 5 and 7, and Meinecke, *Geschichte des Deutsch-englischen Bündnisproblems, 1890–1901.* On the appearance of Vol. II. of the *British Documents on the Origins of the War,* edited by Gooch and Temperley, Meinecke surveyed the problem afresh in an article *Zur Geschichte der deutsch-englischen Bündnisverhandlung von 1901,* in *Am Webstuhl der Zeit, Festschrif für Delbrück.*

but the breach between the nations took place not in 1901 but in 1905 and the darkening years which followed.

VII

While Great Britain and Germany were drifting ever further apart, a vigorous but clumsy attempt was made to restore the wire to St. Petersburg which had been rashly cut in 1890. The approaching struggle in the Far East rendered the attitude of Germany of the first importance to Russia, and busy brains in the Wilhelm-strasse began to assess the benefits which might be granted and received. In a closely argued memorandum dated January 16, 1904, on the eve of the war, Holstein discussed the price which his country might exact for her support.[1] ' The Far Eastern policy of Russia,' he concluded, ' is in acute antagonism to that of Japan, America and England, while her Balkan policy, in its attempt to secure the latch-key of the Mediterranean, infringes the interests not only of England, France and Italy, but also of Austria-Hungary and of Roumania. It is not improbable that, if Russia becomes involved in hostilities over one of these two questions, the Powers interested in the other will use the opportunity for a simultaneous attack. Russia must therefore reckon with the possibility that all the Great Powers, with the single exception of Germany, may make a concentric attack either by arms or diplomatic pressure. Thus Germany is the only Power to which she can turn for help. An entente between Russia and England is outside the sphere of practical politics for many grave reasons, especially the Russophobe attitude of America. Germany must therefore weigh the question whether and on what conditions she would join Russia against her foes. What would be the possible gain and the possible risk ? This can only be answered after obtaining military and naval opinion.'

[1] *Die Grosse Politik*, XIX. 37.

The Japanese victories on sea and land, and the friction with Great Britain arising from the seizure by Russia of her merchantmen, had enhanced the value of German friendship when the Dogger Bank outrage brought an alliance for the first time within sight.[1] Two days later, on October 24, Holstein was discussing an agreement with the Russian Ambassador, and a telegram from Willy to Nicky suggested that, in view of a possible joint protest from the Japanese and British Governments against the coaling of the Russian fleet, Russia, Germany and France should combine. The angry Tsar warmly approved such an arrangement ' to abolish Anglo-Japanese arrogance and insolence,' and invited William II to draft it.[2] The Chancellor forwarded the draft of a defensive treaty to the Emperor ; but after further negotiations, conducted by the ruler in letters and telegrams drafted by Bülow and Holstein, the project foundered when Russia very naturally insisted that France must be informed before an agreement was signed.

The annihilation of the Russian fleet at Tsushima brought peace within sight, and encouraged the German Government to renew the offer of an agreement on the occasion of a meeting between the two monarchs in Finnish waters. In the preparations for the historic conference, and in the discussions which followed the signing of the Björko pact, Holstein's part was at least as important as that of the Chancellor, who deferentially

---

[1] *Die Grosse Politik*, XIX. 303, note.

[2] On October 31 a meeting was held at the Chancellor's residence which Tirpitz has described in his *Memoirs* (i. 166–9). Holstein, at the instigation of the Kaiser, advocated the offer of an alliance to Russia, adding that the two countries should press France to join the coalition. After some observations from Schlieffen, the Chief of the Staff, the Admiral and Richthofen criticised the proposal and argued that Holstein's psychological calculations were mistaken. Pointing a pistol at her head, argued Tirpitz, would not persuade France to mobilise her army for German aims, while a Russian alliance would increase the danger of a war with England, in which Germany would have to pay the bill, since her fleet was in its infancy. Holstein, records Tirpitz, stoutly defended his plan ; and Tirpitz renewed his opposition in a letter to Richthofen, arguing that the true policy was to gain time in which to build a fleet.

sought his advice at every step of the way.   There is no
chapter in Holstein's long reign at the Foreign Office in
which, to judge by the published documents,[1] his influence was so marked.   Indeed parts of the correspondence reveal the Chancellor, who had begun his summer
residence at Norderney, as the pupil, and the old Privy
Councillor as the master.

On July 20, 1905, Bülow telegraphed to Holstein
that the Tsar had accepted the Kaiser's offer of a visit,
and that the latter wished for a copy of the defensive
alliance proposed in the previous autumn.   No one, he
added, must know of the coming interview, which, he
believed, would be useful.   ' Telegraph me above all
what you advise me to suggest to His Majesty in forwarding the text.   I believe your inventive mind will
know how to pick out the threads which may be of use
to us.'   Support for Russia in the peace negotiations,
he concluded, was out of the question ; but it would be
advantageous if the Tsar could be so far won over that
Witte and Lamsdorff on the conclusion of peace would
be unable at once to engineer a Russo-Franco-British
Entente.   In forwarding the draft Holstein expressed
a doubt whether the Emperor should be advised to renew
the question of an alliance, since the sentiments of the
Tsar were unknown.   Moreover, Lamsdorff would use
the German suggestion and the Russian refusal to the
detriment of Germany, according to his habit.   On the
other hand, if the adhesion of Germany to the Franco-
Russian alliance brought Russia no direct military advantage in the Far East, the moral effect when the new
grouping became known would be calculated to reduce
Japanese demands very greatly.   This indeed was the
chief argument for Russia attaching Germany, not
England, to the Dual Alliance, and in consequence the
treaty would have to be published and must contain no
secret articles.   On the same day, after further consideration, he despatched a second telegram : ' If it is
possible to stop His Majesty taking the initiative, I think

[1] *Die Grosse Politik*, XIX. ch. 138.

it would be better. He should wait till the other party, even though in quite general terms, displays a wish for co-operation.' Meanwhile, as he added on the following day, the Emperor should renew his advice to the Tsar to grant a Constitution, since, if he did not do so, the Russian press was sure to attribute it to the Kaiser's advice.

The conclusion of an agreement had been frustrated in 1904 by Russia's obligations to France, and the Chancellor sought Holstein's advice on this difficult matter. ' Shall I telegraph His Majesty that we cannot allow Russia to inform France and invite her to join before Russia has bound herself to us ? ' The demand that Russia must agree with Germany before she negotiated for the adhesion of France, replied Holstein, was out of date, for the Rouvier Cabinet would be less hostile than Delcassé ; and Russia today was more dependent on France than six months ago, and therefore would not take a step of such importance without French consent. Moreover, Rouvier, Lamsdorff and Witte might say to the Tsar : 'Had we not better align ourselves with England rather than Germany ? ' The only advantage of association with Germany was that it would improve Russian prospects in the peace negotiations, whereas England would only be of use on their termination. The Tsar would probably merely promise to consider the question and would then telegraph from St. Petersburg to decline. It was therefore most important that the Emperor should wait for the Tsar to begin, since a Russian refusal would damage Russo-German relations. In commenting on the Chancellor's suggestions to the Emperor Holstein advised some additional bait for the hook. If Germany joined the Dual Alliance, he should tell the Tsar, she would always side with Russia, who would thus have her way, whereas England as the third party would always go with France, especially in the Near East. England was working for an Anglo-Franco-Russo-Japanese grouping, and Russia needed Germany if the equilibrium was to be preserved.

The Björko pact was signed on board the *Hohenzollern*

on July 24, though not in the expected form. ' Do you think that the addition *en Europe*,' wired the horrified Chancellor to Holstein when he heard the news, ' renders the treaty useless ? If so, shall I refuse my signature and thus cancel the treaty ? Or would it even thus be valuable as loosening the Dual Alliance ? ' Its value, replied Holstein, was greatly diminished. The interpolation would be very welcome to Russia, who, in the event of an Anglo-German war, would not need to attack India. In Europe Russia would not be able to help Germany for years on account of the state of her fleet, whereas Germany was bound to attack England if Russia moved through Persia towards the Indian ocean and was in consequence attacked by England. It would be fruitless, however, to ask Lamsdorff to remove words which were so useful to Russia and so detrimental to German interests, but the Emperor might mention it at his next meeting with the Tsar. ' The only positive advantage is that Russia cannot join the Quadruple group, and the circle round Germany cannot close. That is something.'

When the Emperor defended his handiwork, the Chancellor explained that England was afraid of a Russian attack on India, and that, if that fear were removed, she was more likely to attack Germany. Bülow, indeed, took the matter more tragically than Holstein, and suggested that the Tsar should be invited to promise that Russia should fight on the whole line, despite the limiting words. Holstein stuck to his guns. Lamsdorff, he rejoined, would decline, and things would only be made worse. It was premature to urge an alteration till Lamsdorff's real view of the treaty was known. Moreover, the treaty was of use as a symbol of the Tsar's sentiments and as a possible instrument of pressure on France. The 100 per cent. pact had been reduced to 50 per cent., but the 50 per cent. remained. After an emotional interlude caused by the Chancellor's offer of resignation, the Emperor was brought to see the error of his ways, and desired to suggest a change in a telegram to the Tsar. But Holstein was still immovable. ' If we propose to alter the text, Lamsdorff will also insist on changes, and we may lose the whole treaty. Use your whole authority to prevent any suggestion of a change and indeed any discussion of the treaty. Remember that Lamsdorff is eager for an opportunity to water it down in its bearing on France. Do not give him that opportunity.' Holstein was right, for an approach to the Foreign Minister would have been useless. He had not been consulted by his master, and when he saw the document he pointed out that it was incompatible with the Dual Alliance. Witte lent his powerful aid, the Tsar was converted, and the house of cards toppled down. The addition of the words *en Europe*, which had caused such a flutter at Norderney, was of no real importance, for the project was doomed from its birth. The difficulty which had prevented success in 1904 proved insurmountable in 1905, for since 1891 Russia was no longer a free agent in her dealings with Berlin. An effective Russo-German partnership was equally impossible with or without France. It was a deep personal disappointment to William II, who had seen for a moment the mirage of a stabilised monarchical Europe under the control of himself and the Tsar. Holstein's expectations had been more modest, and the *débâcle* confirmed his opinion that it would have been wiser to leave the initiative to Russia. With the end of the war in the Far East her need for German support disappeared, the main obstacle to Anglo-Russian friendship was removed, and the road was clear for the creation of the Triple Entente.

VIII

The last chapter of Holstein's official career is headed Morocco, where, as far back as 1900, he foretold an international crisis.[1] ' Like you,' he wrote to Bülow

---

[1] The latest, fullest and fairest account is by Eugene N. Anderson, *The First Moroccan Crisis, 1904-6*. For the French side, in addition to the official publications, see G. Saint-René Taillandier, *Les Origines du Maroc Français, Récit d'une Mission* (1901-6).

on August 24, ' I greatly fear the Morocco question will flare up one day.   We must reckon with the fact that Salisbury may have to sacrifice to the French not Tangier indeed but the whole of the interior to the Atlantic, in order to make them pliable in other quarters such as China, or in the hope that a French advance on the Atlantic would make Germany attack her.   I really do not know if we could accept that and if we should not take a strong diplomatic step in Paris, either asking France's intentions or proposing an agreement on Morocco,—the latter a fairly hopeless prospect.   We shall not be able to wait too long with this move, for the longer the French Government is committed to action, the more difficult it will be for her to retreat.   Her answer will of course depend on the relations of France and Germany to other countries, especially England, at that moment.   Relations with England are just now more important than ever, and I would give a good deal if Salisbury's rule came to an end.'

The failure of the attempt to secure some kind of Anglo-German agreement was logically followed first by a *détente* and later by an *entente* with France.   Eckardstein reported in 1902 that he had seen Chamberlain and Paul Cambon in close conversation and had caught the fateful words Egypt and Morocco ; but Holstein was blind to the obvious trend of events.   On the occasion of King Edward's visit to Paris in the spring of 1903 the Russian Ambassador in Berlin told the Emperor that he feared that Delcassé would swing over to England at the cost of Russia and Germany.   ' Osten-Sacken's fear of Delcassé is so exaggerated,' telegraphed Holstein to the Chancellor on March 30, ' that I regard it as a pose.[1]   Delcassé has English sympathies, and has probably often shown the Russians that he is not disposed to let them use him against England.   But the Franco-English alliance is music of the future.   This idea will only become practical politics when the *Revanche* idea has passed away.   So long as it lasts, France needs

---

[1] *Die Grosse Politik,* XVII. 573, note.

the backing of Russia, for only Russia, not England, could call halt to an invading German army.' That France might win the friendship of Great Britain without sacrificing Russian support had not crossed his mind. The spectacular triumph of the King's visit set the world talking, and on May 10 Eckardstein, now a free-lance, wrote to the Chancellor that France and England were working for a solution of all their difficulties, and that a new Triple Alliance was in process of formation.[1] The shrewd warning fell on deaf ears. ' Eckardstein is till now alone in his view of the eventuality of a Franco-Anglo-Russian grouping,' wrote Bülow to the German Ambassador in St. Petersburg on May 13. ' I see no reasons so far to concur in his view.' The cheers in the streets of Paris modified the ideas of Holstein as little as those of his chief. According to Eckardstein he declared that it was naïve to believe in the possibility of a Moroccan agreement between England and France. When it came a year later he accepted the new situation with the same outward tranquillity as Bülow ; but by the end of 1904 dark clouds were gathering in the sky, and the growth of German naval power was beginning to fret British nerves.

On December 26, 1904, Holstein discussed Anglo-German relations with the British Ambassador.[2] The alarm at the possible action of the German fleet, he argued, was absurd, whereas the British press had long carried on a regular campaign, of which the Government could not disapprove since it did nothing to check it. The newspapers had created a situation in which the nation might be involved in war by any untoward incident, though he personally shared Metternich's opinion that England had no intention of attacking Germany. Holstein, like most men of the older generation, was much more interested in maintaining the strength of the army than in the development of sea-power, and he described the Chancellor's policy of building a formidable fleet

[1] *Die Grosse Politik*, XVII. 567–70.
[2] Gooch and Temperley, III. 58–9.

without a collision with England as an attempt to square the circle.[1] Yet though he was more alive than his chief to the dangers of the naval programme, he had no hesitation in advising a risky policy in defence of German claims in Morocco at a time when Anglo-German relations were becoming strained.

Germany had a good legal case in Morocco, and the action of France at the end of 1904 suggested that her treaty rights were in jeopardy. The first warning came in January, 1905, from Kühlmann, the Chargé d'Affaires in Tangier, who ominously remarked that his country was in no way bound by the Anglo-French agreement of the previous year. A more pointed and public protest seemed to the Wilhelmstrasse to be required, and it was decided that the Emperor should visit Tangier on his Easter cruise in the Mediterranean and stiffen the backbone of the Sultan. According to Hammann the idea of the demonstration emanated from Holstein ; but it was approved by the Chancellor and forced on the reluctant ruler. The two men must therefore share the responsibility for a step which required to be thought out to the last detail. By an extraordinary oversight the Imperial tourist was not provided before starting with an agreed text in which every word had been weighed. The Emperor's two speeches, writes Bülow in his *Memoirs*, were sharper than he intended— a result which he foolishly ascribes to the excitement of a rough landing and an unruly steed. The effect upon the highly-strung Holstein was to produce hemorrhage of the stomach, the first manifestation of the illness of which he died four years later.[2]

The challenge to French policy so stridently proclaimed at Tangier was followed by the Sultan's invitation to a Conference of the signatories of the Treaty of Madrid in 1880. What seemed to the Wilhelmstrasse, who suggested it, the obvious way out of a dangerous situation appeared to Delcassé as a summons to a humili-

---

[1] Bülow, I. 431.

[2] Holstein told Schwabach that the reading of the speeches made him ill and compelled him to take to his bed. Schwabach, *Aus meinen Akten*, 336.

ating surrender. Moreover he believed that Germany
had no real grievance and no intention of going to war if
the invitation were declined. But had he any grounds
for the conviction that Germany's peremptory tones were
merely bluff ? There was certainly a difference of opinion
in the Foreign Office. Eckardstein quotes King Edward's
angry remark : ' Of course we know already from
Lascelles that this infernal mischief-maker Holstein is
at the bottom of the whole affair.'[1] Hammann declares
a note drawn up by Holstein for the semi-official organ
at the beginning of April, 1905, to have been a summons
to war, and he therefore substituted a milder version of
his own. The document has not been found in the
Archives ; but the surviving papers do not indicate that
Holstein was bellicose at this stage, and he was angry at
its suppression. ' Why did not my programme for the
press, approved by the Chancellor, appear in the *Norddeutsche Allgemeine Zeitung* yesterday ? ' he wrote in a
memorandum of April 3. ' It was not at all sharp.
Yesterday's article was in direct contrast, as it merely
complained that Delcassé had not invited us to share in
the negotiations. That makes us look ridiculous, as if
we are sulking. If France now proposes separate
negotiations, we must reply " Only a general Conference
of Treaty Powers,"—else we shall be considered as greedy
as France. We should therefore say, if possible today :
" Germany will not take part in any separate agreement
in which the Morocco Government and all the Treaty
Powers do not share." Our position will only be clear
and impregnable when this is the common property of
the press. By our present attitude to the public we run
the risk of seeming afraid and therefore may easily be
compelled to take all the stronger action.'[2]

[1] *Erinnerungen*, III. 122. Von der Lancken (*Meine Dreissig Dienstjahre*,
57–60) suggests that Holstein's attitude was partly determined by that of his
old friend Schlieffen, Chief of the Staff, who, convinced that Germany would
some day have to fight for her life, desired to seize the opportunity of the Russo-
Japanese war for a reckoning with France. For Schlieffen's views during the
Moroccan crisis, see Hugo Rochs, *Schlieffen*, 43–4, 49–50.
[2] *Die Grosse Politik*, XX. 297–301. Cp. Hammann, *Zur Vorgeschichte des
Weltkrieges*, 136.

Hammann replied on the same day with a vigorous counter-attack. ' Till now our rule with the press was : We go direct to Fez, not *via* Paris. Now it is to be : We go neither to Paris nor to Fez, but to a Conference. The proposed repudiation of any separate agreement contradicts the announcement of the Emperor and the Chancellor that we negotiate direct with the Sultan. If this new idea goes out officially without the most careful preparation of the press, public opinion will be confused. The people much more than the press is opposed to a serious conflict with France and England about Morocco. We should therefore avoid everything which would diminish the confidence in the steadiness and coolness of German policy. If we nail our colours to a Conference in the official press, we must see it through, else the Chancellor would get a slap in the face.' To this closing reflection Bülow appended the words : ' Quite right.'

During the anxious weeks between the invitation to a Conference and the fall of Delcassé, Rouvier, who was determined to keep his country out of war, began to take the reins into his own hands. On May 1 Schwabach, the head of Bleichröder's bank, was visited by an acquaintance named Betzold, a German residing in Paris, who informed him that the French Premier intended to dismiss Delcassé, and asked him to arrange for an interview with Holstein.[1] Holstein, who had known Betzold in his Paris days, agreed to receive him, and pointed out that in the previous year it would have been easy to reach a direct agreement between Paris and Berlin, but that, having at last been compelled to take a stand on the treaty rights of the Powers, it would be difficult for Germany to change her programme. Holstein proceeded to accuse Delcassé of hostility and untruthfulness, and added that the only explanation of his conduct, now that Russia was temporarily out of action, was the encouragement of England. In suggesting that the *tempo* of the negotiations should be slowed down and that Delcassé should be removed he was

---

[1] Schwabach, *Aus meinen Akten*, 290–2.

forcing an open door, for Betzold replied that Rouvier entirely shared his view of the Foreign Minister.[1]

Rouvier's secret message in reference to Delcassé enabled Bülow and Holstein to go ahead without fear of war, since they knew that his fall was desired by his chief no less than by themselves. The news of his resignation in June was received with delight in the Wilhelmstrasse, and the Chancellor blossomed into a Prince. But at this moment a slip of the Emperor reduced the dimensions of the victory.[2] Overjoyed at the fall of the obnoxious Minister, the impulsive Monarch remarked to General Lacroix, who was representing France at the wedding of the Crown Prince, that all would now be well, that he had never cared about Morocco, and that he did not grudge it to the French. This Imperial impromptu complicated the task of the Wilhelmstrasse throughout the long negotiations that ensued. 'While we, in the sweat of our brow,' wrote Holstein despondingly to Bülow some months later, 'are fighting for a settlement of the Morocco question securing our economic and political interests, His Majesty had long given way. The French knew it, but our public did not, and therefore could not understand why the French Government was weak and yielding before the return of General Lacroix, but firm and self-confident afterwards. The French held a direct acceptance from the Emperor.'

The satisfaction in Germany at the fall of Delcassé was qualified by the rumour that Great Britain had offered France armed support in the event of war. The statement, though devoid of foundation, was believed both in Paris and Berlin, and the assumed revelation of British hostility was a grave addition to the anxieties of the German Government. On June 10, four days after the resignation of the French Minister, the British Ambassador had earnest conversations with Bülow and

[1] *Die Grosse Politik*, XX. 257–9. According to Eckardstein, Betzold carried away the impression that Holstein was determined on war. *Erinnerungen*, III. 114.

[2] Bülow, II. 123.

Holstein.[1] If anyone had told him two years ago,
declared the latter, that a war between England and
Germany was within the bounds of possibility, he would
have laughed ; but now things had reached such a point
that it could no longer be considered impossible.   What
explanation could be given of the offer to conclude
an offensive and defensive alliance with France against
Germany ? When Lascelles replied, as he had replied to
the Chancellor a few minutes earlier, that he did not
believe the story, Holstein rejoined that he feared there
could be no doubt of its accuracy.   He did not apprehend
any immediate danger, and the Moroccan question would
not lead to any serious complications. Germany's
action had been most considerate and conciliatory. She
desired no territory and no special privileges, merely
commercial opportunity for all.   The legend of a British
offer of military support was promptly and emphatically
denied by Lansdowne ; but as it was reiterated by
Delcassé and his friends, German statesmen could
hardly be expected to disbelieve it.

Holstein's attitude at this moment was explained in
a revealing conversation with Chirol.[2] ' His object,'
relates the latter, ' was to show me that no more on
this occasion than on any other in the course of his
long career had his policy been inspired by hostility to
England.   As it was a *conditio sine qua non* of German
security to keep France isolated, Germany was bound to
take the earliest opportunity to drive a wedge into the
Entente before it had time to consolidate. That his
policy had in this respect failed and would continue to
fail he flatly refused to believe.   It had, he said, succeeded in Paris since the French had already sacrificed
Delcassé, who had signed the Anglo-French agreement ;
and England would very soon realise that she could never
rely on the French. He was especially bitter against
' the Admirals ' who were exploiting the Emperor's
mania for ships to drive Germany into a policy of naval
expansion which could only be carried out at the expense

[1] Gooch and Temperley, III. 80–2.   [2] Chirol, *Fifty Years*, 300–1.

of her land forces, and, worse still, at the risk of collision with England. He went very near to admitting that a war with France would not have been unwelcome to him, if only because it would have served to bring the Emperor back to the bed-rock of Germany's continental position in Europe from his dangerous vision of her future lying on the seas.'

A fresh disappointment arose when it was discovered that the French Premier was not his own master. Rouvier, telegraphed Holstein to Radolin on June 28, was counter-working the Conference without wishing to do so.[1] ' I do not understand why France shirks the Conference where she is sure to find more support than Germany if Germany was bent—as she is not—on systematic opposition. On the contrary our plan is to use the opportunity to prepare the way for better relations. This is much more practicable in a Conference than in negotiations *à trois*, where the third party is an Oriental. It is easier for Germany to make concessions to France in a Conference than direct.' Radolin showed the telegram to Jean Depuy, who agreed with every word and promised to explain to Rouvier the gravity of the situation. A private letter of the same date (June 28) to the *Kölnische Zeitung* also shews Holstein in a conciliatory mood. ' I consider the danger of war at the present moment to be extremely small. It will be still smaller if our firmness is realised. Please keep this summary of the situation secret, and spare French susceptibilities, and do not give the chauvinistic press (which is to be found rather in England than in France) the excuse of talking of the violence of the German press. If calmly and politely but firmly handled, the French will eventually realise that nobody benefits from the economic paralysis but the English neighbour.'

After wearisome negotiations a preliminary agreement with France was reached on September 28. The Conference was accepted, and the three principles of the integrity of Morocco, the independence of the Sultan,

---

[1] *Die Grosse Politik*, XX. 490–3.

and the economic equality of the Powers were recognised
as its basis.   This arrangement left over the vital question
of the control of the police in the ports which, as both
sides well understood, was to dominate the Conference.
French policy would obviously depend in large measure
on the attitude of Great Britain ; and on January 3, 1906,
Sir Edward Grey reiterated to the German Ambassador
the informal warning, which Lansdowne had given in
the previous year, that British opinion might demand
intervention if France were to be attacked.[1]   The
Wilhelmstrasse naturally desired further light on this
weighty matter, and on January 12 the British Ambassador visited Holstein at the invitation of the latter.[2]
France, declared Holstein, sought a mandate for the
organisation of the police in Morocco, which Germany
would strenuously resist.   There was a danger that
France, dissatisfied with the results of the Conference,
and relying on the support of England in anything she
might do, might seek to create a *fait accompli* by invading
Morocco.   The Sultan would appeal to the Emperor,
and war would result.   What would England do ?   The
danger would be averted if the British Government
hinted that in such a case public opinion in England
would probably refuse military aid.   Lascelles rejoined
that the danger of a French invasion of Morocco seemed
very remote.   Holstein's suggestion was forwarded to
Sir Francis Bertie, who replied that he was convinced
that France would not invade Morocco, and that any
such hint to the French Government would shake its
confidence in the British Government.   The Ambassador was accordingly instructed to tell Holstein that
the British Government could not deprecate any action
on the part of France which came within the terms of
the agreement of 1904.

The anxious reflections suggested to Holstein by
the British reply were embodied in a memorandum of
January 18.[3]   ' The outcome of the Conference depends

[1] Gooch and Temperley, III. 209.   [2] *Ib*. III. 222–5.
[3] *Die Grosse Politik*, XXI. 96–7.

on the method in which England supports France. The Anglo-French agreement of April, 1904, only stipulates diplomatic support. But Lord Lansdowne told Count Metternich that in the event of a Franco-German war it would be difficult to prevent the English people giving military aid. Will England be content with fulfilling her treaty obligations, or will she cover the French flank with her armed hand in the conquest of Morocco and the ensuing complications ? That would mean that England, after receiving compensation for her sacrifice, joins France in forcing the other Treaty States to yield without similar compensation. Who is then the attacking party ? If England confines herself to her diplomatic *rôle*, France will follow a quiet policy, and the Conference will end in peace with honour for all parties. But if she holds out the prospect of armed support, one cannot foretell whether France will resist the temptation once more to turn the world upside down. There are some sections who are dissatisfied with the situation today and therefore desire such a catastrophe ; but I do not think that the game is worth the candle for England, Germany or even France.'

The first month of the Conference at Algeciras, which opened on January 16, 1906, revealed the gulf that separated the protagonists, and indicated that Germany could rely on Austria alone. Baron de Courcel, ex-Ambassador to Berlin, visited the Wilhelmstrasse on his way home from representing France at the burial of King Christian in Copenhagen, and had three important interviews with Bülow and Holstein on the Moroccan crisis.[1] The latter urged the internationalisation of the police for four or five years, after which Germany and France could, without a new Conference, make a fresh agreement, and Germany might perhaps hand over Morocco to France in return for concessions elsewhere. The Emperor, he added, would never demand any part of Moroccan territory. Courcel

[1] *Die Grosse Politik*, XXI. 206–9. Cp. Tardieu, *La Conférence d'Algéciras*, 241–6.

had no great opinion of the value of Morocco, but feared that Germany might drive a wedge between France and England. Of the second interview we know nothing. In the third Holstein declared that, in recognition of her privileged position, France might have exclusive control of one port. All others would be controlled by several states, including Germany and France, each state providing an equal number of officers. As compensation for the privilege given to France, Germany must insist on the principle of equality in the Bank, though there also France might perhaps have a slight advantage. Courcel replied that the proposals were not inacceptable, but that it was not for him to decide. *Je suis arrivé à Berlin comme Ambassadeur de France, je pars comme Ambassadeur d'Allemagne.*

Summing up his impressions of the Courcel mission Holstein revealed the governing principle of his Moroccan policy. ' The *rapprochement* with England began directly after Fashoda, when the French saw that they could achieve nothing in opposition to England. In the same way the French will only begin to entertain the idea of a *rapprochement* with Germany when they see that the friendship of England—which since the last elections can only be Platonic—does not suffice to obtain Germany's consent to the French occupation of Morocco, but that Germany wishes to be loved for her own sake.' Holstein had no preference for war, for he believed that France could be brought by steady pressure to recognise German rights. It was a tragic miscalculation ; for at Fashoda France had stood alone, and at Algeciras she was surrounded by friends. Moreover the British elections did not alter the policy of Downing Street by a hairsbreadth.

A week later, on March 1, General Swaine, who had been on friendly terms with Holstein during his residence in Berlin as Military Attaché, found him incensed against Delcassé and Révoil.[1] He regretted that Nicolson's

---

[1] Gooch and Temperley, III. 280. Révoil was the chief French representative.

instructions at Algeciras were blindly to support France instead of forming with his American, Austrian and Italian colleagues a Court of Arbitration to seek some means of satisfying both sides. He believed the Conference would end satisfactorily, but if not, and even if Germany were alone, this would not mean war. France would not attack Germany, and Germany would certainly not attack France. Germany, however, had been much pained at the time of the Anglo-French Convention to be regarded as a negligible quantity, and no Great Power would consent to be thus treated. During the whole conversation, concluded General Swaine, there was a vein of bitterness in the Baron's manner, like a microbe trying to sting ; but this was always his way.

So far there is no documentary evidence that Holstein differed from the Chancellor or that he was set on violent courses ; but Hammann complains that for months no one in the Foreign Office knew what he was after, and the Chancellor now took frequent counsel with Hammann and Mühlberg.[1] The isolation of Germany became increasingly apparent. Austria indeed stood by her side, though without the slightest enthusiasm. The open defection of Italy was the surprise of the Conference, which knew nothing of the Tripoli-Morocco agreement of 1900 ; and Russia and England found one another in their joint support of France. In the background Roosevelt worked manfully for compromise, and cautioned Germany not to press France too hard. On March 12, accordingly, the German Government accepted in principle a compromise on the control of the police proposed by Austria.[2] Holstein, whose policy was based on the conviction that France would not fight, was staggered by the decision. He took no further part in the negotiations, and, according to Harden, never again spoke of Morocco to the Chancellor.

There is nothing in *Die Grosse Politik* to suggest anything beyond a legitimate difference of opinion on

[1] Hammann, *Zur Vorgeschichte des Weltkrieges*, 148–51.
[2] *Die Grosse Politik*, XXI. 276–8.

a vital issue between the responsible statesman and his principal adviser. Both men were playing with fire, but the Chancellor drew back before a conflagration occurred. Bülow, however, complains in his spiteful *Memoirs*, written twenty years later, that his old associate had not been playing the game. The situation, he declares, was complicated by Holstein's relations with the Ambassador in Paris.[1] He had known Radolin since they were fellow students at Bonn, and had persuaded Bülow, against his better judgment, to transfer him from St. Petersburg to Paris in 1900 as Münster's successor. ' I have never asked you for anything,' he pleaded, ' but to-day I have an urgent wish. I have only one really good friend and that is Radolin. Get him appointed to Paris, if not for his sake, then for mine. As I want neither promotion nor Orders nor any of the honours which most people covet, do this at any rate for my friend.' His wish was fulfilled ; but when the Morocco crisis arose the Chancellor regretted his decision. For the Ambassador, he complains, looked rather to his patron, who corresponded with him by private cipher, than to the Chancellor, whose instructions were delayed, evaded or incorrectly carried out. But Bülow is a very untrustworthy witness, and Holstein emphatically repudiated the charge of disloyalty after his fall.

According to Bülow, who is often more picturesque than convincing, the end of Holstein's official career was due not to the increased activity of the Chancellor nor to political disagreement, but to the accident of a ministerial change. Richthofen, who had succeeded Bülow as Foreign Minister in 1900, had been treated throughout as a cipher by his nominal subordinate. Holstein's official career was nearly ship-wrecked in 1904 by a particularly gross abuse of his position.[2] The

---

[1] *Denkwürdigkeiten*, I. 496–7. Radolin stoutly maintained in Paris that Holstein was pacifically inclined. Tardieu, *La Conférence d'Algéciras*, 74 note and 163 note.

[2] Hammann, *Zur Vorgeschichte des Weltkrieges*, 127–9, and *Bilder aus der letzten Kaiserzeit*, 29–34.

Emperor's toast at the dinner to King Edward at the forthcoming Kiel regatta was drafted as usual in the Foreign Office ; but on this occasion Holstein not only drafted but despatched it before it was approved by the Foreign Secretary. When Richthofen entered Holstein's room and asked to see the draft, he was informed that it had been sent off. When the Minister told Holstein what he thought of him, Holstein urged his dismissal on the ground of laziness. The audacious request was refused by Bülow, who commissioned Hammann and Mühlberg, the Under-Secretary, to secure the withdrawal of the resignation he had sent in. The two men grudgingly resumed official co-operation, but the Minister remained a mere figurehead. Their relations are suggested in an anecdote of Eckardstein. When the ex-diplomatist explained the danger of the Morocco situation to Bebel on a visit to Berlin, Richthofen warned him to leave the capital, lest the angry Holstein should arrest him. For in these latter days he was known in the Foreign Office as ' the mad hyena.' [1]

When the blameless but impotent Richthofen died of a stroke in January, 1906, Bülow sought a successor who was *persona grata* to the Emperor and not too strongly disapproved by Holstein.[2] The choice fell on Tschirschky, whom Holstein warmly approved, not for his personal qualities, but because he was a friend of his favourite Radolin. The honeymoon, however, was brief. For many years Holstein had enjoyed the privilege of entering the room of the Minister unannounced. These sudden invasions proved too much for Tschirschky, who locked the door. This was bad enough, but worse was to follow. When the old Geheimrat entered from the corridor with a bundle of documents under his arm, Tschirschky coolly invited him to lay them on the table and to wait till he was called. After ruling for sixteen years he was not content to serve. An official letter of resignation was despatched on April 3, accompanied by a private letter to the Chan-

[1] Haller, *Die Aera Bülow*, 35.   [2] Bülow, II. 214-5.

cellor.[1] ' The Foreign Office is too small for Tschirschky and myself. Please accept my request to resign. It is best for my dignity and peace of mind to make an end.' According to Eulenberg it was the fifteenth time that he had played this Bismarckian card, according to Holstein himself the fourth. ' He was convinced,' writes Bülow, who knew his habit of bluff, ' that I should prevent the acceptance of his resignation ' ; but the old campaigner had not allowed for the chapter of accidents. On April 5 the Chancellor, worn out by the Moroccan crisis, fainted at the close of a speech in the Reichstag.

On the same day the British Ambassador, who had received a note from Holstein stating that he had sent in his resignation on April 3, visited him at his request in the Foreign Office.[2]   Lascelles found him in a state of great agitation, as he had just heard of the Chancellor's seizure. ' He said that he had asked me to call on him in order to speak to me about his resignation, which was now definitive. On two previous occasions he had offered his resignation, on account of his disapproval of the manner in which the business of the Press Bureau was conducted, but was induced to withdraw it at the urgent request of Prince Bülow, who had assured him of his support. I had no doubt seen the recent attacks on him in the press, one of which had been directly inspired by a high official in the diplomatic service. This alone would not have induced him to resign ; but he had received information, which he could not doubt, that the Emperor had been assured that the British Government regarded him as the one obstacle to the establishment of friendly relations between England and Germany.

' I said that he had astonished me very greatly. I had always understood that he had desired a friendly understanding between our two countries, although we might have had considerable differences of opinion on certain points and perhaps on the methods of bringing

---

[1] See Holstein's account in *Die Zukunft*, October 18, 1907.
[2] Gooch and Temperley, III. 332-4.   Lascelles to Grey, April 5, 1906.

it about, but I never doubted the sincerity of his wish for
the maintenance of peace between the two countries.
Herr von Holstein said that he was inclined to believe
that the information given to the Emperor had been
invented, but His Majesty seemed to believe it, and
would probably have dismissed him before long.   There
could be no doubt that the Emperor desired a friendly
understanding with England.   So far his attempts to
bring one about had not been successful, and he required
a scapegoat, which he had now found.   I said I understood that in the position which Herr von Holstein held,
it was only natural that he should have made some
enemies, who were jealous of the influence he possessed.
To this he replied that his influence had been very greatly
exaggerated.   It was true that he was consulted on all
important matters of foreign policy, but he was in the
position of the man whose advice was sometimes taken,
sometimes rejected, and sometimes partly taken.   His
influence therefore could not be considered as very great,
but such as it was it had no doubt created jealousies
which had been employed with great effect against him.
He was now sixty-nine years old.   His eyesight was failing.   He had done his work, at least, his work was now
finished, and in any case it could not have continued much
longer ; but it was hard that he should be misrepresented
as an obstacle to a friendly understanding with England,
when the cardinal point of his policy had been that a war
between the two countries would be the greatest calamity
that could happen to either.   It would be a satisfaction
to him in his retirement if he could think that his sovereign
should some day know that he had been misrepresented,
and he would be gratified, if the opportunity should arise,
that I should tell His Majesty that in my opinion he
ought not to be considered as an enemy of England.' [1]

[1] In a minute on this despatch Sir Eyre Crowe wrote : ' Herr von Holstein
has not, I think, been a friend to this country. . . . It is not unjust that he
should now pay the penalty of having persistently failed to appreciate the
position which England really occupies in the world (so long as she is strong).'
    Sir Eric Barrington wrote : ' Herr von Holstein is modest with regard to
the influence he exercised, but members of the German Embassy here have

A minute of April 9 by Eyre Crowe on this interesting despatch concluded with the words : ' Meanwhile his resignation does not appear as yet to have been accepted. There is many a slip. . . .' Holstein's fate, however, had already been decided ; for on the morning of April 5 Tschirschky informed William II of his request to resign. According to Hammann the Emperor congratulated the Foreign Minister, and the matter was officially concluded on April 16.[1]   The victim believed that he had been sacrificed while the ailing Chancellor was unconscious of events ; for it seemed unthinkable that his old chief should desert him.   He had been living, however, in a fool's paradise, and Bülow's *Memoirs* reveal what he thought of the ' incorrigible intriguer.' Two years earlier, wearied by the unceasing feuds between Holstein and the staff of the Foreign Office, the Chancellor had told him that unless there was peace he would be regretfully compelled to dispense with his services.[2] Holstein immediately informed the Emperor of the warning through his friend Radolin, and at their next meeting the Chancellor was greeted with the words : ' I tell you, Bernhard, you must leave my good old Holstein alone.   He was the only man who stood by me loyally in my fight against Bismarck.'   The Emperor, however, who, like Bülow, wished to untie the Moroccan knot instead of cutting it, was now ready and indeed eager for the change.   When shortly afterwards the Chancellor was dilating on the incapacity of the Foreign Minister, the monarch interrupted him : ' I must beg you, dear Bernhard, to leave Tschirschky alone.   He was the only man who stood loyally by my side in my struggle against the diabolical [3] Holstein.'   The Monster had at last reaped what he had sown, for he was now without a single friend.

On mentioning Holstein's name in conversation always assured me that no matter who was Foreign Minister at Berlin, the policy was invariably his.'

[1] *Die Grosse Politik*, XXI. 338–9, note. The resignation was announced on April 18.

[2] *Denkwürdigkeiten*, II. 216.   [3] Höllensohn.

with William II at Homburg in August, 1906,[1] Lascelles was astonished at the outburst of indignation which it evoked. ' His Majesty said that he was a most dangerous man. He had, no doubt, great ability, but the influence he exercised over the German Foreign Office was a most pernicious one. Had Herr von Holstein had his way the Algeciras Conference would have broken down, and His Majesty himself had been obliged to intervene strenuously to prevent instructions being sent to the German representatives which would at once have brought the Conference to an end.' It was clear, commented the British Ambassador, that Holstein was made the scapegoat for the failure of German diplomacy. In the following spring the Emperor's wrath was still hot. ' Herr von Holstein,' he minuted on a despatch describing Tardieu's history of the Algeciras Conference,[2] ' so altered my very definite instructions and arrangements with the Chancellor that finally the opposite was done. He has again and again stirred up and injected the poison against France, and so worked on the Chancellor that to my intense astonishment he asked me on several occasions whether I wished for war with France, whereas my instructions were clear : The Algeciras Conference is to be the stepping stone of the beginning of the agreement between France and Germany.'[3]

The Foreign Minister was the prime mover in the eviction of Holstein ; but what was Bülow's part in the catastrophe ? ' He had laid his plans carefully,' writes the Prince ; ' but it had not occurred to him that I should fall ill, and by doctor's orders be beyond the reach of interviews and documents at the very moment at which his letter came into the hands of his enemy Tschirschky, who used the favourable opportunity to butcher him in cold blood.'[4] This was the version which Holstein believed[5] and which rendered possible their continued

[1] Gooch and Temperley, III. 365–6.
[2] *Die Grosse Politik*, XXI. 566–7.
[3] The last sentence is in English.   [4] Bülow, II. 215.
[5] ' Briefe des Geheimrats von Holstein,' *Süddeutsche Monatshefte*, March, 1919.

intercourse ; but it is none the less disingenuous and incorrect. In January the Chancellor yielded to his demand to be made Director of the Political Department ; but he had told the exasperated Hammann that he would part with him when the Conference was over.[1] Moreover we learn from *Die Grosse Politik* that in informing the Emperor of the letter on April 5 Tschirschky was acting in agreement with Bülow ; and when the matter was formally dealt with on April 16 it was again with his knowledge.[2] For on April 14 Karl Ulrich von Bülow wrote to Tschirschky : ' I beg to inform Your Excellency that yesterday my brother requested me to ask Your Excellency to settle the affair of Herr von Holstein orally with His Majesty.' The Chancellor was pulling the strings all the time, and never lifted a finger to save his old subordinate, as indeed William II revealed in his *Memoirs*.[3] We cannot blame him ; for Hammann testifies that the struggle with Holstein undermined his health even more than the Morocco crisis itself. His fall was hailed with delight in Paris, where the *Journal des Débats* described him as the most dangerous enemy of France since Bismarck ; and no tears were shed in the Wilhelmstrasse over the disappearance of the autocrat whose capricious sway had already lasted far too long.

IX

Holstein received brilliants of the First Class of the Red Eagle for his services in the Morocco negotiations ; but the acceptance of his resignation filled him with the same incredulous rage that had maddened Bismarck sixteen years earlier, and he glared angrily round for the snake in the grass. The enmity of Tschirschky and Hammann was notorious, and he knew that the Emperor

---

[1] The fullest account of the events which led to his resignation is in Hammann, *Bilder aus der letzten Kaiserzeit*, 29–39.

[2] *Die Grosse Politik*, XXI. 338–9. This confirms Hammann's statements.

[3] *Ereignisse und Gestalten*, 86.

was not his friend ; but having determined without the slightest reason that Eulenburg, who had lived in retirement since 1902, was the chief offender, he wrote him a furious letter.[1] 'My eviction, which has been your goal for many years, is at last attained, and the low attacks on me have your approval.' He added that for certain reasons Eulenburg was a man whom it was best to avoid. The Prince read the letter with horror, hurried off to Berlin, sent a challenge to his tormentor, and reported to the Foreign Office. Tschirschky and the Under-Secretary Mühlberg, anxious to avoid a scandal, sent Geheimrat Kriege to tell Holstein that he must withdraw, and the infuriated old man was persuaded to sign the following apology : ' Since Prince Eulenburg has declared on his word of honour that he had nothing to do with my dismissal or the press attacks, I withdraw the wounding expressions in my letter of May 1.' Eulenburg had in fact learned of the resignation from the Emperor himself, who explained that it was impossible to keep him and that he was now quite mad.

The Prince knew his old associate well enough to feel sure that his apology was not a capitulation, and he foretold that the implacable eccentric would revenge himself in his own way. He had not long to wait, for on August 17 the *Zukunft* published a letter of Holstein defending himself against criticisms of his Moroccan policy, denying the assertion that he had controlled affairs since the fall of Bismarck, and attributing his resignation to departmental differences. The *rapprochement* of the two men who had long hated each other filled the Prince with dark foreboding. ' I consider the Holstein-Harden alliance an ominous affair, and not I alone,' he wrote. ' Whoever knows these conspirators shares my opinion. What will the pair brew ? ' On November 24 the *Zukunft*, in a flamboyant article entitled ' Dies Irae,' denounced some of the closest associates of the Emperor

---

[1] Eulenburg's side of the story is told in Haller, *Eulenburg*, 313–63, and Muschler, *Philipp zu Eulenburg*, 605–61.

—'the Liebenberg Round Table'—as political mischief-makers and as a coterie in which spiritualism, faith-healing and other morbid tendencies were rife. A fortnight later Harden wrote that he would hesitate three times before declaring that any man was an intimate of Eulenburg. Finally, on April 27, 1907, Harden openly charged the Prince with sexual abnormalities. Harden assures us that none of his ammunition was supplied by Holstein, who merely rejoiced at the downfall of his enemy ; [1] but Eulenburg himself and Bülow found his hand in the plot, and they used to call him the weasel, as he never desisted till he had cleared out the hen-roost.

' I am wholly innocent,' wrote Eulenburg to Bülow, ' but I am afraid of false testimony as Holstein would not stick at 10,000 Marks if he could find a good witness.' There is no need to describe the Harden and Eulenburg trials, for Holstein remained in the background. Kuno Moltke emerged unscathed ; but as an unfortunate breakdown of the Prince's health prevented the completion of his trial for perjury, friends and foes alike continued to assert his innocence or guilt. After an exhaustive examination of the evidence the editor of his papers, Professor Johannes Haller, pronounces him a deeply injured man who bore his unmerited sufferings with Christian resignation ; and his judgment is confirmed by Muschler, who has been over the same ground. Only one of Harden's witnesses could be taken seriously ; but the evidence of the fisherman of the Starnberger See left an abiding impression on the public mind, all the more since there had been gossip of the sort for many years. The poisoned arrows had found their mark. Eulenburg's scutcheon was tarnished and the Emperor's prestige impaired. Europe rang with stories of the decadent camarilla at Berlin, and William II cancelled

[1] For Harden's side of the controversy, see his ' Holstein ' in *Köpfe*, Vol. I. and his ' Eulenburg ' in *Köpfe*, Vol. III. For Holstein's share in a seemingly compromising document in the Foreign Office see Muschler, 465–8, 512, and Haller, 323–4. Eulenburg's biographers have no doubt that Holstein supplied Harden with material.

the most cherished friendship of his life. Bülow
acidly suggests that if Holstein's death-bed, like that of
Richard III, was haunted by the ghosts of his victims,
the spectre of Eulenburg was in the van.

A series of private letters to the editor of a South
German paper during the spring of 1906 mirrors the
state of mind of the fallen demigod.[1] The first letter,
dated April 23, complained of the belief that he was for
war with France. 'I am too much of a Royalist to say
that His Majesty employed these rumours as a pretext;
but that I had long been out of favour you know as well
as I.' The chief author of his fall, he suggests, was
Hammann, head of the Press Bureau, which he compares
to a swollen liver. 'I shall not start a press campaign,
partly in order not to damage the Chancellor. His
position is not improved by my departure, which was
forced through while he was ill.' Writing again on
May 13, Holstein thanks the editor for his support,—
almost the only aid he received. In an interesting
passage he adds that the Moroccan question was not
dangerous, for France would not have fought. First to
threaten and then to climb down was a strategy that
could lead to no good result, and German policy had
suffered from a failure of nerve. A third letter, written
a fortnight later, finds confirmation of his judgment in
the aggressive attitude of the French press,—the first
manifestation of such a spirit since 1870. The surrender
of Germany, he feared, would encourage France to put
forward impossible demands, even perhaps for a revision
of the Treaty of Frankfurt. From these interesting
letters we see that his resignation was due at least as
much to a divergence of opinion on a fundamental
question of policy as to personal friction within the office.

The end of Holstein's official career was not the
termination of his political influence, as was commonly
believed at the time, for he remained in close touch with
Bülow till the day of his death. In 1907 the British
Ambassador reported that the two men were on the best

[1] The letters were published in the *Süddeutsche Monatshefte*, March, 1919.

of terms and met frequently at the Chancellor's house, whereas the door of the Foreign Office was closed to him.[1] The Chancellor explained to his friends that he continued to see him because he knew too much and might reveal State secrets, and secondly because as a gentleman he could not cut a man with whom he had been associated for thirty or forty years.[2]   Hammann was convinced that Bülow's sole motive was to avert the betrayal of diplomatic secrets. A very different explanation, offered by Professor Johannes Haller after the Prince's death, asserts that the old Geheimrat had procured copies of letters compromising the reputation of Princess Bülow in her earlier years ; and Raschdau, the last survivor of the Bismarckian Foreign Office, had received confidences from Holstein which, he declares, compromised the Chancellor himself.[3]   Whatever were the reasons for their continued association, Bülow kept him fully informed of the progress of events and freely sought his advice. When Haussmann complained in the Reichstag on December 10, 1908, that Holstein had played the *rôle* of 'a little Delcassé,' and had been in the habit of requiring German diplomatists to correct their despatches, the Chancellor threw his shield over his old subordinate.[4] He had grown grey in long and arduous service under four Chancellors, declared Bülow. He was a man of strong and watchful patriotism, who had defended German interests for a generation ; and his exceptional industry, outstanding political capacity and independent character had won the respect of all who knew him. It was a handsome testimonial, though not exactly the whole truth.

On the occasion of the visit of British journalists to Germany in the summer of 1907, Mr. Alfred Spender, Editor of the *Westminster Gazette*, called on the Chan-

---

[1] Gooch and Temperley, III. 333, note. According to Hans von Flotow he arrived in the dark and was admitted through a special door, the servants being pledged to secrecy, *Süddeutsche Monatshefte*, March, 1931, 399.

[2] *Denkwürdigkeiten*, III. 48–9.

[3] *Süddeutsche Monatshefte*, March, 1931, 390.

[4] Bülow, *Reden*, III. 164.

cellor in his official residence.[1]   At the end of the
conversation Bülow remarked : ' Come along, I must
introduce you to Holstein,' who was sitting in an adjoining room,—a stout, elderly man of rather forbidding
appearance, who spoke perfect English without a trace
of German accent.   Bülow introduced his visitor as ' the
editor of one of the friendly papers.'   ' Pardon me,
Prince,' came the sharp reply, ' one of the relatively
friendly papers.'   ' He seemed beside himself with anger,
and was about to display an intimate knowledge of a
certain article I had written on the Morocco question
nearly two years previously, when the Prince turned the
conversation to English books and literature.   Holstein
then recovered his temper, and quoted Kipling with
much admiration.   Then, as he seemed to be getting
back to Morocco, the Prince said he must go and dress.'
When Mr. Spender reported the adventure to Count
Metternich, the Ambassador bluntly exclaimed that it
was impossible ; and Benckendorff, the Russian Ambassador, was almost equally sceptical.   The unbroken
intimacy with the Chancellor is confirmed by the biography of Kiderlen, with whom Holstein remained on
excellent terms till his death.   It was natural that he
should denounce the doings of Tschirschky, whom the
Emperor, he bitterly observed, loved for his pliability ;
but the confidence of the highest official in the land was
a compensation for the hostility of a mediocre Minister.
' Aehrenthal's visit has made a good impression,' he wrote
to Kiderlen in May, 1907 ; ' Bülow told me all about it.'
The Chancellor, he added, had talked to him the last
two Mondays for two hours on each occasion.[2]

In the autumn of 1907 Holstein addressed his
countrymen in his own name.   In a letter published in
the *Zukunft* of October 18, after thanking the editor for
defending him against attacks on his Moroccan policy,
he declared himself compelled to correct the misstatements which the Foreign Office had done nothing to

[1] Spender, *Life, Politics and Journalism*, I. 210–1.
[2] Jäckh, *Kiderlen*, I. 225.

rectify.[1]   He denied that his resignation was due to
difference of opinion with Tschirschky, for nothing was
or could be settled without the concurrence of the
Chancellor, who maintained personal control throughout
the negotiations.   He was unaware of any difference
with Bülow until ' the change of front ' on March 12,
after which he ceased to take any part in Moroccan
affairs.   ' That I ever pursued other aims in Morocco
than his or employed methods not approved by him is
an invention.'   The statement may be true in the sense
that Bülow on some occasions yielded to his arguments
without being fully convinced ; but the fact remains
that the Chancellor at last found himself compelled to
seize the rudder lest the ship should be steered straight
into the tornado of war.   After his fall Holstein always
endeavoured to minimise his influence.   ' For those
who know the inside of our foreign policy,' he wrote to
Harden, ' the assumption that I decided everything does
not need refutation.   For instance, everyone knows that
I had no share in the steps which critics regard as the
causes of the Anglo-French treaty of 1904, the Kruger
telegram, the Bagdad railway and the anti-English
speeches in the Reichstag.'   It is true enough that
neither Holstein nor anyone else had been in sole
command since the fall of Bismarck ; yet no other pilot
had so large a share in determining the course of the ship.

The three main international problems of Holstein's
closing years were the naval rivalry with Great Britain,
the Bosnian crisis and the Morocco problem.   In
regard to the first his record was consistently good,
though he had never seen fit to throw his whole weight
against the short-sighted Tirpitz policy.   On one
occasion he urged Schwabach to introduce a resolution
in the Berlin Chamber of Commerce condemning
excessive ship-building ;[2] but as a rule he contented
himself with grumbling.   The fleet, testifies Harden,

---

[1] The letter was summarised in a despatch from Sir F. Lascelles, October 23,
1907.   Gooch and Temperley, III. 332–3, note.

[2] Schwabach, *Aus meinen Akten*, 442–3.

was the bitterest anxiety of his closing years. ' Navy fever,' wrote Holstein to a friend in December, 1907, ' rages in Germany.[1] This dangerous illness is nourished by the needless fear of an English attack. It produces three bad results,—in domestic policy through the activities of the Navy League, in finance by the endless expenditure, and in foreign policy by the mistrust that this arming provokes. England sees in it a threat which binds her to the side of France. And it is impossible, however we tax ourselves, to build a fleet equal to those of England and France in combination. The Liberal Ministry will not draw the logical conclusion from the menace which is universally recognised, but the Conservatives will do so. Many members of the Reichstag condemn the Navy fever, but nobody will take the responsibility of opposing the demand for ships. If one resists the fever one is denounced as unpatriotic ; but in a few years the correctness of my view will be recognised. We must expose the lying phrase that every new vessel increases the power of the Reich ; for every new ship causes England to build two.'

Holstein had always been anti-Russian, and when the Bosnian crisis broke over Europe like a tropical thunderstorm, his position was clear. From the lonely farmhouse in the Harz, where as usual he was spending his summer holiday, he at once wrote to the Chancellor urging him to support the annexation even though he had not approved it. In the British demand for a Conference he detected an attempt to break up the Austro-German alliance. Austria, he declared, would regard it as a deadly insult to be placed in the dock, and, if Germany consented, the friendship would be at an end. ' If we hold fast, the object of the whole *Einkreisungspolitik* is frustrated.' The news leaked out that he was trying to regain influence, and his ' unofficial councils ' were criticised in the Reichstag, but the Chancellor undertook his defence.[2]

[1] Hermann von Rath, ' Erinnerungen au Holstein,' in *Deutsche Revue*, October, 1909, 17–18.　　　　[2] December 10, 1908.

On October 19, 1908, Chirol had a long conversation with his friend, and was struck by the tone of authority in which he surveyed German policy.[1] 'Had he been Foreign Minister he could not have spoken with more assurance. He was probably conscious of the impression he was making on me, for as we parted he said : " Of course I no longer speak as a responsible official, but I need not tell you that I still know perfectly well what I am talking about." ' After fighting the old battles of the Kruger telegram and the Tangier visit he passed to the two burning issues of the time. He had always been opposed to excessive naval expansion, he explained, not only because it would lead to ruinous competition but because it might involve the neglect of the army, which was a matter of life and death. He added that Bülow would strive against any further expansion and indeed make a Cabinet question of it. He went on to complain that he was tarred with the brush of Anglophobia, and that probably nothing he could say would destroy that legend. Passing to the Bosnian crisis he urged that Austria could not safely have postponed action. 'We might have used our good offices in Vienna had we been consulted, but as usual we were not consulted. You must not be under any misapprehension. We are not going to desert our ally.' The conversation ended with a warning against the danger of irritating Austria ; ' because, remember, there we come in too. I do not want to say too much about our Emperor, and it is not for me to pose as his champion. He is only too much inclined to blow hot and cold, and his bark is worse than his bite. He too will never go to war if he can help it. But there are two things he could not help going to war about : if France were to give any open provocation, or if Austria was threatened.' His last words to his visitor were that the Emperor would either die in a madhouse or destroy the German Empire.[2]

---

[1] Gooch and Temperley, VI. 158–61. His position was well understood in Downing Street.

[2] This item comes not from the report to the Foreign Office but from *Fifty Years*, 301.

Holstein had constantly urged the Chancellor to summon Kiderlen from Bucharest to the Wilhelmstrasse ; for Schön, who succeeded Tschirschky in 1907, was unequal to his task.   He was delighted that his old colleague was appointed acting minister in November, 1908, when the Bosnian crisis was at its height.   The two men were in close contact during the five months of Schön's absence through illness.   One of Kiderlen's first visits was to Holstein's flat, and his letters to Fräulein Kypke show that he found time for several more.[1] Advancing years had in no way diminished the feverish interest with which the old war-horse watched the swaying fortunes of the campaign.   'I had a very excited express letter from Fritz, whom the Emperor's New Year's language has robbed of his sleep,' wrote Kiderlen on January 10, 1909, in referring to the Imperial comments on Schlieffen's famous article on Germany's military prospects.[2]   'I am glad to have been, for he was visibly relieved when I came, and repeatedly said that he could talk things out with me and could only be reassured about public affairs if he had talked them over with me.   Recently he became so excited that he thought the Chancellor ought to threaten to resign.   He had already drawn up an eight page letter of resignation for him which he read to me.   I talked him out of it.   But I fear he is ill.'

Holstein warmly applauded the Chancellor's handling of the Bosnian crisis, and was ever ready with advice. Indeed Hans von Flotow, at that time an official in the Foreign Office and later Ambassador at Rome, declares that the whole policy was his.[3]   He denounced the pro-Turk sentiment of the Foreign Office and ironically suggested that the gentlemen of the Wilhelmstrasse should all wear a fez.   In an undated letter of November, 1908, he congratulated Bülow on his passive attitude, urging him to declare that Bosnia was an Austrian

[1] Jäckh, *Kiderlen*, II. 2.
[2] Jäckh, II. 21.
[3] *Süddeutsche Monatshefte*, March, 1931, 399.

domestic question. England, he added, seemed to be making a last attempt to bring about a Turco-Bulgar war, which could easily be prevented by a reference to the Hague Court. 'Perhaps you will discuss with Kiderlen whether Rosenberg should speak to the Prince in this sense, if he is consulted, as is probable.' In the following month the Chancellor explained to Monts, the German Ambassador in Rome, the importance of keeping Aehrenthal in office, and for this purpose Austria should not be frightened by emphasising the Italian danger. 'If there was too much talk of Italian faithlessness it would confirm the tendency of Vienna to immobilise a needlessly large force on the Italian frontier, which, in the event of a war with Russia, would be a disadvantage to Germany as well as to Austria. I have discussed these questions fully with Holstein, Kiderlen and Jagow, and the military aspect with Moltke ; all of them absolutely agree to this course.' With Bülow and Kiderlen in office, a first-class European crisis in full swing, and his counsel continually in demand, the last winter of Holstein's life was the happiest time of his failing years. He frequented one or two houses where he knew that he would not meet strangers, particularly that of Frau von Lebbin, a clever and elderly Jewess, to whom he bequeathed his papers. Paul von Schwabach, the well-informed head of Bleichröder's bank, wrote him long and interesting letters about high politics.[1] He delighted in the friendship of Harden, who describes him as a kindly old man of simple tastes, fond of children and an admirable talker. Though he loved good literature, the conversation never strayed far from foreign affairs. Of domestic politics, parties, finance, economics, administration, he knew nothing.

While the Bosnian crisis was dragging its weary length, Berlin and Paris sought and found a *modus vivendi* in Morocco. In an interview published in the *Matin* in May, 1908, Holstein declared that his advice about Morocco had never been asked or given since his

[1] Paul von Schwabach, *Aus meinen Akten*, 147–51.

resignation ;[1] but it is an eloquent testimony to the persistence of his influence that the Chancellor did not decide on the final step before he had secured the approval of his friend, now near his death. For this purpose he chose von der Lancken, who had carried on the negotiations in Paris and was a *persona grata* with the old recluse.[2] To ensure the secrecy of the consultation the mission was arranged through Stemrich, the Under-Secretary, to whom the envoy was bidden to report. Bülow might well feel a little apprehensive, for Holstein had always scouted the notion of a *rapprochement* with France, and Morocco was the chief cause of his fall. When, however, von der Lancken explained the situation he was astonished to find that he was forcing an open door, since the old expert had himself discovered the error of his ways. ' You are surprised to find so little opposition,' he remarked quietly to his visitor. ' I must confess that things have gone differently from what I intended and wished. We made a mistake in 1905 in working for a conference. I had already realised my mistake in believing that England would never associate herself with the Franco-Russian alliance. When this danger loomed up I felt we must break the ring, even at the risk of war, before it closed on us. Hence the Emperor's visit to Tangier. But there again I was wrong in my reading of the leading actors. I ought to have known that Prince Bülow would find it difficult, and His Majesty impossible, to decide for war.' He added that with Russia fighting in the Far East, England weakened by the Boer war, and France distracted by internal controversies, it would have been an easy matter. Thus the error lay not in the policy but in the failure to carry it out. Now that the whole situation had changed a Moroccan deal was the best course. The Franco-German agreement of February 9, 1909, however, which thus received a blessing from an unexpected

---

[1] Summarised in a report from its Berlin correspondent in the *Times*, May 27, 1908.
[2] Von der Lancken, *Meine Dreissig Dienstjahre*, 54–7.

quarter, merely brought a temporary *détente*, for the mischief of 1905–6 was too deep-seated to be undone. On October 11, 1909, Pichon, the French Foreign Minister, expressed the opinion to Mumm von Schwarzenstein, the German Ambassador in Tokio, that Holstein's morbid distrust had been largely responsible for the misunderstanding between the two countries.[1]

No one in Germany felt keener satisfaction than Holstein when in March, 1909, Izvolsky bowed to what the Wilhelmstrasse described as a friendly service, but what the victim declared to the British Ambassador to be a diplomatic ultimatum. Though signed by the Chancellor, the decisive despatch was suggested and drafted by Kiderlen, who journeyed to the Grossbeerenstrasse to receive the congratulations of his old friend.[2] 'Fritz, who is still in bed with phlebitis,' he reported on March 29, 'said he admired my cheek[3] in daring to inflict this humiliation on Izvolsky, especially as I had no one behind me.' It was the last gleam of sunshine for the man who had watched Bismarck make the alliance of 1879, and to whom that partnership had always remained the impregnable rock of German policy.

When the end was in sight the Chancellor paid his last visit to the modest home of his old associate.[4] The dying man was in bed with high fever, but he had prepared himself for the interview by a strong injection. His first question was whether Bülow would remain in office, to which the Chancellor rejoined that it did not depend on himself alone. Visibly excited and in the most emphatic tone he proceeded to argue that, in view of the foreign situation, it was his duty to remain with or without the confidence of the Emperor, whether or not the finance bill was passed. Bülow retorted that he must decline to accept laws or measures which he disapproved. 'You must remain, I tell you, you must remain !' retorted the old man, whose words poured

---

[1] *Die Grosse Politik*, XXXIX. 287.
[2] Jäckh, *Kiderlen*, II. 29.   [3] Frechheit.
[4] Bülow, *Denkwürdigkeiten*, II. 466–8.

forth in a torrent. 'Who except you can steer our ship
with such an impulsive Emperor, with an unpolitical
people and with a Reichstag immature as a child in
foreign affairs ? Stay on at any rate four or five years.
You have handled the Bosnian crisis with brilliant
success ; and at the same time you have established
better relations with Russia than at any time since
Bismarck. You must remain ! Even your enemy
Maximilian Harden says so. You ought at any rate to
have time to reach a naval agreement with England.
Then they may get rid of you. Till then you are indispensable.' As he left the room the Chancellor heard
the husky voice : *Bleiben ! Bleiben !* Bülow's fate,
though Holstein did not know it, had been sealed by the
Daily Telegraph incident ; but he was spared the pain
of seeing the pilot dropped. Among the mourners at
the grave no one displayed more signs of grief than the
Chancellor himself.[1]

The eyes of the dying man were fixed to the last on
the European chessboard over which he had brooded for
half a century. Three weeks before the end on May 8,
1909, a telegram was sent at his wish by the Under-
Secretary to the Chancellor in Venice, urging the addition
of a sentence in the instructions to Metternich to prevent
the raising of the subject of capture at sea leading to
an increase of friction between the two nations.[2] For
thirty years his aim had been the maintenance of the
Austrian alliance and the benevolent neutrality of Great
Britain. But the first was of limited utility if the
smouldering wrath of the Russian people was its price,
and a condition of the second was a *détente* with France.
The various factors of the European situation were so
closely interlocked that an error in judgment on one vital
issue vitiated the whole scheme. The main diplomatic
event of the first decade of the twentieth century was the
birth of the Triple Entente, in the possibility of which
Holstein had obstinately refused to believe but which he

[1] *Süddeutsche Monatshefte*, March, 1931, 391.
[2] *Die Grosse Politik*, XXVIII. 156-7, note.

had nevertheless done as much as any other man to provoke.

Holstein's career was a misfortune to his country. No one ever doubted his patriotism, and he was wholly free from the Byzantinism of official circles ; but the sixteen years of his veiled dictatorship witnessed the dissipation of the Bismarckian heritage and left Germany without a friend except Austria, whose strength was ebbing as the tide of nationalism rose. He combined an incomparable knowledge of detail with a pathetic inability to forecast the trend of events or to measure the effect of his policy on the decisions of other Governments. His colleagues were agreed that he was not quite right in the head ; but if some excuse for his vagaries be sought in his pathological temperament, it was a costly error on the part of his superiors to allow a Civil Servant to win and retain the position which he abused. Future generations, observed Count Lerchenfeld, the veteran Bavarian Minister at Berlin, would fail to understand that a people of sixty millions allowed itself to be led and misled by a lunatic.[1] If it was true, as Eulenburg declared, that he possessed the biggest brain since Bismarck, it was equally true, to borrow a witty phrase of Donna Laura Minghetti, the mother of Princess Bülow, that it was for men like him that the Bastille had been built. No one trusted him, for he shunned the light and loved devious ways. From the fall of the Iron Chancellor to the outbreak of the Great War the foreign policy of Germany lacked unity of control ; and the moral of Holstein's underground activities, unique in the annals of modern history, is that power and public responsibility should reside in the same hands.[2]

[1] Wermuth, *Ein Beamtenleben*, 192-3.

[2] Hohenlohe's *Denkwürdigkeiten der Reichskanzlerzeit*, which appeared too late to be utilised in the text, shows Holstein to have acted as an adviser in domestic as well as foreign affairs.

THE STUDY OF THE FRENCH
REVOLUTION

THE French Revolution is the most important event in the life of modern Europe. Herder compared it to the Reformation and the rise of Christianity ; and it deserves to be ranked with those two great movements in history, because, like them, it destroyed the landmarks of the world in which generations of men had passed their lives, because it was a movement towards a completer humanity, and because it too was a religion, with its doctrines, its apostles, and its martyrs. It brought on the stage of human affairs forces which have moulded the actions of men ever since, and have taken a permanent place among the formative influences of civilisation. As Christianity taught that man was a spiritual being, and the Reformation proclaimed that no barrier should stand between the soul and God, so the Revolution asserted the equality of men, and declared each one of them, regardless of birth, colour, or creed, to be possessed of inalienable rights.

The universal significance of the event was recognised both by those who took part in it and by those who watched it from afar. The orators on the Seine were fully conscious that the eyes of the world were upon them. 'Your laws will be the laws of Europe if you are worthy of them,' declared Mirabeau to the Constituent Assembly ; 'the Revolution will make the round of the globe.' 'When France has a cold,' remarked Metternich bitterly, 'all Europe sneezes.' 'Whoever regards this Revolution as exclusively French,' echoed

Mallet du Pan, ' is incapable of pronouncing judgment upon it.' ' The French Revolution,' wrote Gentz in 1794, ' is one of those events which belong to the whole human race. It is of such dimensions that it is hardly permissible to occupy oneself with any subordinate interest, of such magnitude that posterity will eagerly inquire how contemporaries of every country thought and felt about it, how they argued and how they acted.' Friends and foes of the ' principles of '89 ' were at one in emphasising the power of its appeal ; and men like Burke and Tom Paine, Immanuel Kant and Joseph de Maistre, who agreed in nothing else, were convinced that the problems it raised concerned humanity as a whole. The books in which the causes, events, and results of the Revolution have been narrated and discussed are beyond computation. Brief surveys of the more important among the earlier contributions to our knowledge are given in an appendix to Lord Acton's *Lectures on the French Revolution* and in Chapter XIII of *History and Historians in the Nineteenth Century* by G. P. Gooch.

I

Travellers and publicists of the eighteenth century foresaw the Revolution, and historians of every school have sought its roots in the generations and, indeed, the centuries which preceded it. Louis Blanc declared that no man could date its beginning, since all nations had contributed to produce it. ' All the revolts of the past unite and lose themselves in it, like rivers in the sea. It is the glory of France to have performed the work of the human race at the price of her own blood.' The socialist historian commences his long-winded narrative with Hus ; but this is to pile a needless burden on our backs. We must, however, at the outset form a clear conception of the life of the French people and the methods of government under the monarchical system elaborated by Henri IV, Richelieu, and Louis XIV. This may be obtained from the later volumes of Lavisse's

co-operative *Histoire de France*, or, if a simpler presentation is needed, from A. J. Grant's serviceable work *The
French Monarchy, 1483–1789*.

The real nature of the *Ancien Régime* in the last
century of its existence was revealed to the modern
world by Tocqueville's *L'Ancien Régime et la Révolution*,
published in 1855. The author described his work as
a study, not a history ; but it threw more light on the
coming of the Revolution than any of the histories that
had appeared, and inaugurated the era of scientific
inquiry. The Revolution itself had exerted such a
fascination that it had occurred to no one to ascertain
its relation to the regime which it superseded. Realising
the necessity of exploring the provincial archives,
Tocqueville made a prolonged stay at Tours, where he
found a complete collection of the records and correspondence of the Intendants. He pursued his researches in
his native Normandy and in Languedoc, studying the
decrees of the Provincial Parliaments and the registers
of the parishes, and thus gradually acquiring a clear conception of the classes of society, the nature and extent
of feudal rights, the central and local administration.
His results were as unexpected as they were irrefutable.
' As I advanced I was surprised to find at every moment
traits which meet us in France today. I discovered
a mass of sentiments and habits which I had thought
were the offspring of the Revolution.' The centralised
administration of the nineteenth century proved to be
an inheritance from the *Ancien Régime*. France had
been subject to three governments :. the King and his
ministers, working through the Intendants ; the feudal
powers and jurisdictions ; and finally the Provincial
institutions. Of these the first were by far the strongest;
the feudal powers were weak ; and the Provincial
institutions were ghosts of their former selves except
in Brittany and Languedoc. Feudalism as a political
system, aristocracy as a political force, had disappeared ;
but the feudal privileges that remained appeared all the
more odious because the system of which they formed

a part was dead. ' Some good people have endeavoured to rehabilitate the *Ancien Régime*. I judge it by the sentiments it inspired in those who lived under it and destroyed it. I see that all through the Revolution, cruel as it was, hatred of the old regime outweighed all other hates, and that during the perilous vicissitudes of the last sixty years the fear of its return has outweighed all other fears. That is enough for me.' The verdict is the more impressive since the writer was neither a radical nor a socialist, but a moderate liberal.

Tocqueville, declared Scherer, accomplished for the Revolution what Lyell had done for the history of the globe. He destroyed the cataclysmic theory and substituted the slow action of secular causes. Where men had seen a radical contradiction between the monarchy and the Revolution, he saw a logical continuation. The *Ancien Régime* was strongly centralised : the Revolution still further centralised administration. The *Ancien Régime* had destroyed the greater part of feudalism : the Revolution destroyed the rest. The driving-force of the Revolution was equality of rights ; and it was equality before the law which the monarchy had been striving to establish in its long struggle with feudalism. The fruitful researches of Tocqueville have inspired two generations of students to reconstruct the administrative machinery and the social life of eighteenth-century France. Of special importance are the writings of Albert Babeau on the province, the town, and the village. Arthur Young's well-known *Travels in France in 1787– 1789*, which should be read in the excellent edition of Miss Constantia Maxwell, reminds us that conditions varied from province to province.

The Revolution was due to the union of concrete grievances, which were actually worse in many parts of the Continent, with an intellectual ferment which made the France of Louis XV and XVI the leader of European thought. John Morley's celebrated studies of Voltaire, Rousseau, Diderot and the Encyclopaedists paint a vivid picture of the group of men who taught the French bourgeoisie to think, to criticise, and to rebel. Sorel's little volume on Montesquieu and Higgs' study of the Physiocrats, the dominant school of economists, are equally indispensable. Rocquain's *L'Esprit Révolutionnaire avant la Révolution*, Kingsley Martin's *French Liberal Thought in the Eighteenth Century*, and Roustan's *Pioneers of the French Revolution* are also useful. No one should miss the brilliant if somewhat uncritical survey of the life and atmosphere of France in Taine's *Ancien Régime*, or the long and admirable chapter entitled ' Causes of the French Revolution ' in the sixth volume of Lecky's *History of England in the Eighteenth Century*.

The reign of Louis XVI is best studied in the ninth volume of Lavisse. The most satisfying account of the attempts to avert a revolution by reform is provided in Ségur's *Au Couchant de la Monarchie*, one of the classics of French historical literature. The first volume deals with Turgot, whose noble aims during two years' tenure of office are gratefully recognised, but whose hasty methods are condemned. The second portrays the five years' rule of his successor, Necker, who wisely aimed at less sweeping changes, but whose sincere endeavours to render France solvent were shipwrecked on the heavy expenses of the American war. The commanding figure of Turgot was revealed to English readers by John Morley, whose essay in the second volume of his *Miscellanies* still retains its appeal.

II

The critical study of the French Revolution is just half a century old, and only two of the histories written before that date require our notice. Mignet's concise and lucid narrative, published in 1824, is still worth reading, for it was the first book to present the Revolution as the story of a connected series of events, organically related to the periods which preceded and followed it. Instead of closing with Thermidor, or the establishment of the Directory, or Brumaire, as most historians have done, he brings the narrative down to the fall of Napoleon, thus expounding the story of twenty-five years as a single drama of disturbance. The printed material at his disposal was very limited in extent ; but many of the actors were still alive and he made good use of what he was told. Mignet was in general sympathy with the Revolution ; but he was the least emotional of men, and his cool narrative, translated into many languages, was a boon to readers for a couple of generations.

Carlyle's immortal work, published in 1837, which should be read in C. R. Fletcher's or Holland Rose's edition, revealed the greatest event in modern history to the English-speaking world. By a supreme effort of creative imagination he succeeded in rendering the vision as real to his readers as to himself. If Mignet's book may be compared to a lecture, that of Carlyle may be described as a dramatic performance. The storming of the Bastille, the oath in the Tennis Court, the women's raid on Versailles, the Fête of the Federation, the flight to Varennes, the trial and death of the King, the Girondins and Danton, the moving tragedy of Charlotte Corday, the fall of Robespierre—these pageants we carry with us through life. No writer except Michelet has approached him in the power of rendering the atmosphere of hope and horror, of tense passion and animal fury. No less remarkable is his insight into the character of the leading actors. Though misconceiving the Girondins, like other writers before Biré, he drew portraits of Louis and Marie Antoinette, Mirabeau and Lafayette, Danton, Robespierre, and Marat, which require little correction.

The deficiencies of the epic are as conspicuous as its merits. Carlyle's knowledge of the period was extremely limited. The relations of France with Europe are neglected, and the provinces are forgotten. He conceived the Revolution as purely destructive, a huge bonfire of feudal lumber. That it inherited many principles and tendencies of the *Ancien Régime*, that constructive work of a permanent character was accomplished, that its two main watchwords, equality and the

sovereignty of the people, were to mould the thought
and action of the nineteenth century, was unknown to
him.   His book is less a history than a series of *tableaux
vivants*, less an explanation of events than an evocation
of the past.   His success frightened British historians
off the field ; and it was not till half a century later that
Morse Stephens summarised for English readers the
researches of French scholars.   The greatest novelty of
his learned and valuable book, which breathes an ardent
sympathy with the revolutionists, was that he traced the
course of the Revolution in the provinces ; but after
bringing his story down to 1793 he migrated to the
United States, and the third volume never appeared.
To this day we possess no detailed history written by
a single British hand.   The best introductory sketch in
English is Miss Bradby's *Short History of the French
Revolution, 1789-1795.*

With the exception of Sybel, whose work will be
noticed later, the middle decades of the century contributed little of importance to any understanding of the
Revolution.   The forty volumes of the *Histoire Parla-
mentaire de la Révolution Française, ou Journal des
Assemblées Nationales, 1789-1815*, edited by Buchez
and Roux, contain material not accessible elsewhere and
are useful for reference.   Thiers' prolix narrative is the
fruit of much less research than his later work on the
Consulate and Empire.   The voluminous record of
Louis Blanc is the work of a man who employed history
to illustrate his political convictions.   Michelet's seven
volumes were superior to anything written in France
since Mignet, and they embodied material which
perished when the Hôtel de Ville was burned by the
Communists in 1871 ; but the author was a bundle of
nerves, and the book was part of a campaign against the
Ancien Régime to which he devoted the second half of
his life.   The shorter work of his friend Quinet was
rather a philosophical dissertation than a historical survey.
During the Second Empire it was natural that attention
should be focussed on Napoleon ; and it was not till the

establishment of the Third Republic that the Revolution became the most favoured and the most fruitful field of French historical research.

The most resounding attack since the days of Burke was delivered by Taine. While his volume on the *Ancien Régime* had won general approval for its literary brilliance and its relatively balanced attitude, its successor aroused enthusiasm in royalist and clerical circles and indignation among Radical Republicans. He brushes aside the traditional distinction between the principles of 1789 and the principles of 1793. On being asked when the Terror began, Malouet replied, ' On July 14, 1789.' Taine shared his opinion. The ' Golden Dawn ' never existed ; moderate men were never at the helm ; sound principles never prevailed ; bloodshed and rapine began at once. It was more than a revolution : it was a dissolution. The Revolution was in essence, he declares, a transfer of property. ' That is its permanent force, its primary motive, its historical meaning.' He had discovered a good deal of evidence in the archives on the burning of *châteaux* in the summer of 1789, but his picture of France rushing headlong into anarchy is a gross exaggeration. The *Ancien Régime* fell in thousands of villages without bloodshed or disturbance.

No less partisan were the second and third volumes, devoted to the Jacobins, whom he depicts as crazy doctrinaires, thirsting for blood and revelling in destruction. Taine's Jacobins are mere figments of the imagination of a sensitive philosopher who had lived through the Commune. He charges them with blindness to the facts around them ; but he himself is blind to the most important influences which shaped their course. He depicts them as the children of Rousseau, learning nothing and forgetting nothing, whereas they were all monarchists in the early years of the Revolution. The Emigrés on the Rhine, the ceaseless intrigues of the Court with foreign Powers, the flight to Varennes, the hostile armies massed on the frontier a few days' march from the capital, the savage threats of the Brunswick

Manifesto, the rebellion in the Vendée—these tremendous facts, without which the Terror is unintelligible, are left virtually unnoticed.   Many of the acts of the Constituent, the Legislative, and the Convention were hideously cruel and tragically unwise ; but definite reasons can be assigned for them independently of any philosophy. We should bear continually in mind the warning of Acton : ' The Revolution will never be intelligibly known to us till we discover its conformity to the common law, and recognise that it is not utterly singular and exceptional, that other scenes have been as horrible as these, and many men as bad.'   Taine's slipshod methods of research have been criticised as sharply as his judgment of men and events.   In his *Taine, historien de la Révolution Française* Aulard endeavoured to prove that the book is virtually worthless for the purposes of history ; but Cochin, in *La Crise de l'histoire révolutionnaire*, replied to the attack.   Taine may still be read with profit by advanced students as an antidote to the hardly less uncritical pæans which the great upheaval continues to inspire.

Taine wrote under the impact of the shattering events of 1870–1, and his volumes were primarily missiles in his campaign against radical democracy. The work of his friend Albert Sorel, on the other hand, which was begun a few years later, is as dispassionate as any history of controversial events can be.   *L'Europe et la Révolution Française* presents a panorama of the conflict between the new France and the old Europe from 1789 to 1815 ; but the three volumes devoted to Napoleon are of smaller value than the five which deal with the Revolution.   His object was to exhibit the Revolution, which appeared to some as the subversion and to others as the regeneration of the world, as the natural result of the history of France and of Europe. While Tocqueville had found the model of its internal policy in the reigns of Louis XIV and Louis XV, Sorel announced that in their foreign policy the revolutionists were equally the direct heirs of the monarchy.   In his

monumental *Geschichte der Revolutionszeit 1789-1800*
Sybel had been the first to connect the Revolution with
the main stream of European history, and to elucidate
the Polish and other factors which determined the policy
of Prussia, Austria and Russia during its course. But
Sorel, writing a generation later, enjoyed the advantage
of access to a mass of new material, and his book was
the first satisfactory study of the Revolution in its
international bearings.

After devoting a preliminary volume to an analysis
of the political methods and ideas of the eighteenth
century and to describing the decrepitude of France and
of feudal Europe, Sorel traces the atmospheric change
from the noble principles with which the leaders set out.
He does not scoff at the Declaration of the Rights of Man,
but he contests its practical value. He is fair to the
Emigrés, distinguishing the early intransigents, who in
their blind hatred endeavoured to arm Europe against
their fatherland, from the later victims of persecution
who fled for their lives. . He comprehends the sentiments
of the Court, while censuring its policy. Like Sybel he
ascribes the more immediate responsibility for the war
to the chauvinism of the Girondins, though the explosive
forces of the Revolution and the old instinct for ' the
natural frontiers ' of the Rhine and the Alps prepared
the way. Yet his sympathies are with his countrymen,
for the integrity of the national territory and the maintenance of the priceless achievements of the Revolution
were at stake. He recognises the intimate connection
between the danger on the frontier and the worst excesses
in Paris, but makes no attempt to palliate them. Rejecting Taine's wholesale indictment, he returns to the
sensible tradition of supporting the principles of 1789
and condemning the Terror. The lights and shadows
are evenly distributed. ' Taine,' wrote Hanotaux, who
was the friend of both, ' only sees blood dropping from
the scaffold ; Sorel sees it spread over the battlefield to
save the country and to fertilise Europe.' Though his
pages often throw light on the fate of individuals and the

struggles of parties, his real theme is France as a Great Power. 'Instead of investigating the human interior,' writes Acton, ' he is on the lookout across the Alps and beyond the Rhine, writing, as it were, from the point of view of the Foreign Office. He is at his best when his pawns are diplomatists. In the process of home politics and the development of political ideas he does not surpass those who went before him.' Mathiez complains that he never understood democracy. Even in the vast field of foreign affairs he does not always tread with equal sureness, and his dealings with British policy fall below his high standard.

During the interval which separated the earlier and the later portions of Sorel's *magnum opus* the first critical and comprehensive survey of the Revolution was presented in the eighth volume of the *Histoire Générale* edited by Lavisse and Rambaud. In accordance with the scheme of the work, it is the revolutionary era which forms its theme ; but France occupies as of right the centre of the stage, and the chapters in which Aulard outlines the history of the critical years are its most valuable feature. Though Aulard was still to work for decades at his subject and to publish a vast number of monographs, he never again attempted a narrative of the opening years. His chapters are a landmark in the study of the Revolution as the first authoritative sketch by a scholar who derived much of his knowledge directly from the archives.

While Sorel was calling attention to the international aspects of the Revolution, two men of rare ability were busy on the history of parties and ideas. The *Histoire Socialiste, 1789-1900,* a co-operative illustrated history of modern France in eleven volumes from the Socialist point of view, began to appear in 1901. The first four volumes were contributed by the editor Jaurès—philosopher, statesman, orator, historian—who found time in his crowded life to obtain a singularly wide knowledge of the printed materials and the press of the revolutionary era. The didactic purpose of the book is proclaimed in

the title, and its bias is as unabashed as that of Taine.
It is, however, of enduring value as the first large-scale
attempt to penetrate behind the political screen and to
understand the economic and social aspects of the
mighty struggle.   It should be read in the eight-volume
edition of 1922–4, revised by Mathiez, who however has
deliberately done little more than correct mistakes and
misprints.   ' Tout ce qu'a écrit cet évocateur prodigieux
est sacré,' writes his admiring friend, who explains that
the author as an actor on the public stage was peculiarly
fitted to revive the emotions of the revolutionaries.   He
adds that all previous histories were political, and that
Jaurès first presented an economic and social picture of
the crisis which was the cradle of the modern world.
' The bourgeoisie had tried to make people believe that
it was only a political revolution.   The proletariat will
now know that it was a revolution of property, a social
revolution.'

The note of the work is struck in the Introduction
and reverberates through its three thousand pages.
' The key to the French Revolution is the passage from
the bourgeois oligarchy to social democracy.'   He begins
with a vivid picture of the country in 1789, making full
use of the *Cahiers*, and devotes three volumes to the
Constituent and Legislative Assemblies ; but he is less
interested in the fall of the *Ancien Régime* than in the rise
of the Fourth Estate.   Socialism is part of democracy, he
argues, since it desires to organise the sovereignty of the
whole community in the economic as well as in the
political sphere ; and socialism flows from the Revolution, as he notes ' with passionate joy.'   Jaurès was a
humane man, and he deplores the violence which accompanied the change ; but his heart is filled with gratitude
as he contemplates the epic of emancipation.   His
journey ends at Thermidor, and in taking leave of the
actors he gratefully summarises their achievements.
' They affirmed the idea of democracy in all its amplitude.
They displayed to the world the first example of a great
country governing itself and saving itself with the strength

of a whole people. And they gave to France and the world such a prodigious urge towards liberty that, despite reaction and eclipse, it has come to stay.' The student who reaches Jaurès after a long course of reading in political histories and monographs will be surprised to find how much his conception of the Revolution is deepened and enlarged by the work of this gifted amateur. Not the least novel feature of the work is the fifth volume, which is devoted to the effect of the Revolution on German and English thought. If Jaurès is too big a mouthful to swallow, a briefer socialist presentation of the drama may be found in Prince Kropotkin's volume *The Great French Revolution*, in which the wisdom and virtue of the Fourth Estate are exalted at the expense of the selfish bourgeoisie.

No man, alive or dead, has done so much to discover and to expound the history of the Revolution in all its length and depth and breadth as Aulard, for whom a Chair of the History of the French Revolution was founded in 1886 by the Municipal Council of Paris. His chief narrative work, *The Political History of the French Revolution*, published in 1902,[1] bears the subtitle, *Origins and Development of Democracy and the Republic*, and makes no pretence to offer a history of France between 1789 and 1795. He merely glances at the events of the first three years, and has little to say of the Court, finance, economic conditions, diplomacy and war. His theme is the evolution and application of the two governing principles of the Revolution—equality and the sovereignty of the people. The most striking novelty of the book is the demonstration of the relative conservatism of the men of 1789 and of the late appearance of the republican idea. No one of note except Brissot and Condorcet asked for a republic till the autumn of 1790, and the Legislative Assembly was as monarchical as the Constituent. The Monarchy was overthrown not by republicans but by the blunders and intrigues of its champions.

[1] English translation in four volumes.

Aulard's second main thesis is that the Terror was due, not to the domination of abstract ideas, but to the necessity of repelling the invading armies and of safe-guarding the precious reforms already achieved. The men who believed in the principles of 1789 and were determined to uphold them acted as they might have been expected to act. The Jacobins were the custodians of the Revolution and of the national territory, and against their savagery must be set the supreme achievement that they saved their country from the return of the *Ancien Régime* and from conquest and spoliation by foreign armies. 'I am a respectful and grateful son of the Revolution which has emancipated humanity and science,' writes the historian, who stands for the militant radicalism and anti-clericalism characteristic of France at the turn of the century. His hero is Danton, the man of iron will and swift decision ; but the real guide of the Revolution was the people itself. After the decisive constitutional victories of 1789 a rift began between the bourgeoisie and the masses ; and it was owing to the latter that the Revolution did not stop short with political changes but undertook the championship of the peasant and the artisan. Aulard's book is written with a mastery of the sources that no historian had ever approached, and he renders the evolution of the drama thoroughly intel-ligible ; but he lacks literary charm and he is a frank partisan. His dislike of monarchy, feudalism and the Church is only equalled by his gratitude to their destroyers, and no other competent writer had come so near justifying the Terror as a patriotic necessity.

Two years after the appearance of Aulard's epoch-making work the eighth volume of the *Cambridge Modern History* presented English readers with the first critical and comprehensive survey of the revolutionary era. The narrative of the Constituent, the Legislative and the National Assemblies is provided by Professor F. C. Montague, our leading specialist since the migration of Morse Stephens, and Moreton Macdonald. Among the most useful chapters in the volume are those on finance by Professor Henry Higgs, and the masterly treatment of law by Professor Paul Viollet. Such co-operative works embody the results of the latest research, of which only the specialist can be fully aware ; but a movement of such complexity and significance as the Reformation and the Revolution demands also synthetic treatment by scholars who can stand a little way back and can see the wood as well as the trees.

Lord Acton's *Lectures on the French Revolution*, delivered at Cambridge at the close of the century but not published till 1910, offers the best philosophic survey of the stupendous movement and of the derivation and significance of the ideas by which it was inspired. The opening lecture on 'The Heralds of Revolution' is remarkable for the prominence assigned to Fénelon, 'the first man who saw through the majestic hypocrisy of the Court and knew that France was on the road to ruin.' The second, on 'The Influence of America,' is the most novel and valuable in the book. Acton proceeds to ascribe the failure of the moderate reformers mainly to the intrigues of the Court with foreign Powers ; for, though the King began as the convinced advocate of reform, he was surrounded by evil advisers, the worst of whom was the Queen. Of the Declaration of the Rights of Man he speaks with the enthusiasm of a Liberal idealist. 'It is the triumphant proclamation of the doctrine that human obligations are not all assignable to contract or to interest or to force. This single page of print outweighs libraries and is stronger than all the armies of Napoleon.' It had, however, one cardinal fault ; it sacrificed liberty to equality, and the absolutism of the King was succeeded by the absolutism of the Assembly. The attack on the Church, represented by the Civil Constitution of the Clergy, was a needless and fatal blunder, and turned the monarch as well as the minor clergy into conscientious enemies of the Revolution. The Constituent Assembly was better than the Legislative, and the Legislative was superior to the Convention. The reign of violence began when the danger on the frontier became acute and ended when it was removed. A despotic executive was inevitable, and the Girondins went down before the Jacobins, who were worse men and cared still less for liberty, but who knew how to defend the fatherland. Despite its horrors and its crimes, the Revolution was a great effort towards the emancipation of the common man.

If Acton's lectures are the most suggestive English survey of the course and meaning of the movement, Madelin's *La Révolution*, published in 1911 as a volume in Funck-Brentano's *Histoire de France racontée à tous*, is the safest French guide. It is indeed still the best introduction for the student of the decade 1789–1799 that exists in any language. If a student had time for only a single volume on the great upheaval, he would be wise to select this admirable work. To study the level pages of Madelin, who proudly describes himself as a pupil of Sorel, after reading Carlyle or Michelet or Taine is to measure the sensational advance that has taken place in our knowledge and interpretation of forces, persons and events. Written in a spirit of cool detachment, distinguished by the usual French clarity of arrangement and furnished with useful bibliographies, the work is as useful to the advanced student as to the humble apprentice. He approached his theme, he tells us, without any preconceived idea, and he claims that he has rendered justice to all. He quotes with warm approval the protest of Vandal against a view of the Revolution dear to a certain type of politician. ' Loin d'être un bloc, la Révolution est peut-être le phénomène le plus complexe qui ait existé. C'est un phénomène le plus essentiellement multiple dans ses causes, dans ses éléments, dans ses mouvements, dans ses conséquences.' A later and more popular volume by Madelin, of which the translation bears the title *The Revolutionaries*, forms a portrait gallery of the leading actors in the drama, and may be regarded as an appendix to the earlier work. It is one of the glories of French scholarship that, after a century of bitter polemics, it has at last become possible to discuss the Revolution as dispassionately as the fall of the Roman Empire.

The lofty standard of impartiality set by Madelin was followed in the co-operative *Histoire de France contemporaine*, edited by Lavisse in continuation of the *Histoire de France* which brought the story to 1789. The first volume, covering the three opening years of the Revolution, was written by Sagnac, long distinguished as one of the leading authorities on the period. There are none of the thrills which attracted our fathers and grandfathers, and indeed there is more analysis than narrative in these tranquil pages. He calmly assesses the strength and weakness of the Declaration of the Rights of Man, which was full of dangers and omissions yet none the less embodied a new religion. The march to Versailles left the King popular, and, given skill and courage, the game was not yet lost. The Constituent Assembly is credited not only with ' an infinite love of the public good,' but with a mass of useful reforms. The war of 1792 was inevitable sooner or later, for Europe could hardly tolerate a proselytising France. The author's general sympathy with the Revolution does not prevent him from denouncing the horrors which dishonoured the people, from the taking of the Bastille to the September Massacres and the Terror. In the second volume, continuing the record to Brumaire, Pariset attempts to do justice both to Danton and Robespierre who, though they personified different policies, were both patriots. After the downfall of the Girondins in the summer of 1793, he declares, two policies were possible, represented respectively by the two chief Jacobin leaders. Danton desired to reconstitute patriotic unity. Despite his failings, his vision was lofty and humane, and he had no wish to identify the Revolution with a few of the elect. Robespierre, on the other hand, sincerely believed that reconciliation with Royalists and Moderates would compromise not only the Revolution but the safety of France. No one can make the Directory interesting, but Pariset does his best. The illustrations form an important feature in these handsome quartos, and the full bibliographical notes are beyond all praise.

The three little volumes summarising the history of the Revolution published by Mathiez in 1922, 1924 and 1927, and gathered into a single stout volume in the English translation, differ in several respects from the works of Madelin, Sagnac and Pariset. In the first place the curtain falls on Thermidor. In the second, there are no bibliographies and scarcely any notes, since the book, as he explains in the Preface, is intended for the general reader. He adds, however, that it is based on many authorities, some of them unpublished ; and indeed nobody would challenge the erudition of the scholar who since the death of Aulard is unquestionably the chief authority on the Revolution, and whose knowledge of the Convention even Aulard never surpassed. But the most striking difference from his immediate predecessors is the fact that he has a hero. Aulard's admiration for Danton is known to all the world, but the partiality of Mathiez for Robespierre is more paradoxical. The two great specialists resemble one another in their contempt for the comfortable bourgeoisie ; but while the one was a radical the other is a socialist, and their paths diverge widely when they come to weigh the merits of the rival Jacobin chiefs.

Danton, we are told, was the hired agent of the Royalists, and morality was his weak point. Robespierre, on the other hand, as Louis Blanc had argued long before, was not only a man of unselfish character but the champion of the weak and the unfortunate, who strove not merely for political liberty but for social justice. He desired to abolish primogeniture and to impose restrictions on inheritance, but he was never a communist. His ideal was not to abolish property but to prevent its abuse. The Girondins were chained to the bourgeois mentality, regarding the populace as unfit for power and the rights of property as sacrosanct. The Jacobins represented the humbler classes ; but the

venial Danton lived in style, while his incorruptible
rival had no thought but the interest of the Revolution.
A great democrat and a great patriot, he raised the
Republic from the abyss.   The Jacobins were indeed a
minority ; but a dictatorship was inevitable and so was
the Terror. ' They slew that they might not be slain.'
France accepted the Terror as the condition of victory
—and the victory was won.   While other historians,
sickened by the fumes of blood, greet Thermidor with
a cheer, Mathiez wrings his hands over the disappearance
of the man who laboured to overthrow the selfish rule of
wealth. ' The levelling Republic of his dreams, without
rich or poor, received its death-blow.   In the person of
Robespierre they had slain the democratic Republic for
a century.'   As in a well-constructed drama the author
rings down the curtain on the death of the hero.   There
can be no question as to the interest of this remarkable
book by the founder of the *Société des Études Robespierristes*, and the editor of its organ, *Annales Historiques de la
Révolution Française* ; but it represents a reversion to
the type of polemical narrative from which historians
are gradually emancipating themselves.

One more synthetic work calls for mention before
we press on to the monographs. *La Révolution Française* by Lefebvre, Guyot and Sagnac, published in 1930,
forms the thirteenth volume of the *Histoire Générale*
edited by Halphen and Sagnac.   In other words, like
the *Cambridge Modern History* and the *Histoire Générale*,
it deals with the life of Europe as a whole as well as
with France. Lefebvre, one of the leading authorities on
the social history of the time, covers the years 1789–
1795 ; Guyot returns to his familiar theme of the
Directory, devoting much more attention to foreign
policy than to domestic events ; and Sagnac adds two
thoughtful chapters on the constructive work of the
Revolution and its influence on European civilisation.
All three admire the Revolution as a powerful and
enduring impulse to the construction of a better social
order throughout the world, and Lefebvre explains the

Terror as a war measure. In the unending dispute between the partisans of Danton and Robespierre he occupies a middle position, recognising the venality of the one and the comparative disinterestedness of the other, though without sharing the enthusiasm of Aulard and Mathiez for their respective champions. The full bibliographical notes scattered freely throughout the book are of special value to advanced students of the revolutionary era in Europe.

III

Most of the best work on the Revolution is stored in a vast array of monographs and biographies, to a few of which attention may be directed. In *La France d'après les cahiers de 1789* Champion briefly and clearly summarises the astonishingly moderate demands for reform put forward in the first half of 1789 by the people of France. In recent years a lively controversy has arisen as to the derivation of the Declaration of the Rights of Man, the articles of which, with an elaborate commentary, are printed by Eugène Blum in *La Déclaration des droits de l'homme et du citoyen*. The Heidelberg jurist Jellinek argued in his booklet, *Die Erklärung der Menschenrechte*, of which French and American translations exist, that the Declaration would not have been drawn up but for the example of America, and pointed out that many formulas were borrowed from the constitutions of the separate States. Émile Boutmy replied in an article in *Les Annales de l'École libre des sciences politiques* (reprinted in his *Études politiques*) that the resemblances were mainly external, and that the Declaration arose from the needs and traditions of France and the atmosphere of the *Aufklärung*. The subject has been exhaustively discussed in Wilhelm Rees' *Die Erklärung der Menschen- und Bürgerrechte von 1789*, which leans rather to Boutmy than to Jellinek. The ' ideas of 1789 ' are analysed at length by Redslob in *Die Staatstheorien der Französischen Nationalversammlung von 1789*, and by Karl Löwenstein in *Volk und Parlament nach der Staatstheorie der französischen Nationalversammlung von 1789*. Champion's *J. J. Rousseau et la République Française* discusses the relation of his teaching to the different phases of the movement, and warmly defends him from the charge of being the spiritual father of the Terrorists. Hedwig Hintze's *Staatseinheit und Föderalismus im alten Frankreich und in der Revolution* traces with power and learning the progressive triumph of centralised bureaucracy over provincialism and federal theory in a survey which extends from the *Ancien Régime* to the fall of the Girondins.

The two years of the Constituent Assembly should be studied with the aid of Wickham Legg's *Select Documents illustrating the History of the French Revolution* ; Morse Stephens' *The Principal Speeches of the Statesmen and Orators of the French Revolution* ; and Aulard, *Les Orateurs de la . Constituante*. Barthou's *Mirabeau* gives a good short account of the great orator ; but the standard Life is by Alfred Stern, Professor of History at Zurich, of whose work there is a French translation. Clapham's *Life of the Abbé Sieyès* admirably portrays the cold-blooded theorist who was mainly responsible for the Declaration of the Rights of Man. Lanzac de Laborie's *Mounier* narrates the fruitless efforts of the moderate reformers at the very outset to secure the adoption of something like the British Constitution. Miss Bradby's *Life of Barnave*, the most imposing contribution to the history of the Revolution made by a British scholar since Morse Stephens, not only revives the attractive figure of the young lawyer but describes the growth of parties and analyses in detail the political, ecclesiastical, and colonial problems they had to face. In *La Révolution Française et le régime féodal* Aulard describes the feudal regime as it survived under Louis XVI, and traces the successive stages in the liquidation of feudal rights. The tragic episode of the flight to Varennes can be studied in Lenotre's *Le Drame de Varennes*.

'It had only one fault left to commit,' declared Taine in concluding his account of the Constituent Assembly, 'and this it committed by resolving that none of its members should find a place in its successor.' The Constitution of 1791, which it had taken the Constituent two years to elaborate, and which Louis XVI was compelled to accept, retained a shadow king and entrusted power to an Assembly of new and untried men. The Legislative Assembly was inferior in ability and character to its predecessor, and it was dominated by the Girondins. The eloquence of Vergniaud, the fascination of Madame Roland, and the tragic fate of the leaders won the sympathy of their contemporaries and captivated the historians of the first half of the nineteenth century. They were depicted in Lamartine's forgotten rhapsody as high-souled idealists, who went down before the assault of the men of blood and iron ; but further study has shattered this alluring portrait. In *La Légende des Girondins* the royalist Biré reminded his readers that they were for the most part as ready for violent courses as the Jacobins, that they desired a war which Robespierre and other Jacobin leaders were anxious to avoid, and that the majority for the execution of the King was secured by their votes. Sybel and Sorel emphasised their responsibility for the declaration of war in the spring of 1792, and Aulard argued that nothing but the rigid centralisation which they opposed enabled the Jacobins to keep the invaders at bay and to frustrate the counter-revolution. The partisan character of the *Memoires* of Madame Roland, once so popular, is now fully recognised, and her voluminous correspondence, published at intervals in recent years, clearly reveals her faults of mind and temper. The latest of her many biographers is Mme Clemenceau-Jacquemaire. Brissot, the leader of the party at the height of their power, has found a highly competent American interpreter in Miss Ellery, and the rather shadowy figure of Vergniaud may be studied in the biography of Lintilhac. Cahen's *Condorcet et la Révolution Française* depicts the boldest thinker of his party and his time in France. On the political philosophy of the Girondins there is a sharp division between Aulard and Mathiez, the former maintaining that they merely differed from the Jacobins in their championship of the provinces against Paris, the latter arguing that they represented the well-to-do bourgeoisie, while the Jacobins stood for the working-classes. A concise discussion of the origins of the struggle between France and the old Europe is given in Clapham's *Causes of the War of 1792*; and Ranke's *Ursprung und Beginn der Revolutionskriege*, old though it is, retains its value. Frédéric Masson's *Le Département des Affaires Étrangères, 1787–1804* is a mine of information on the conduct of foreign affairs. Important speeches are given in Aulard, *Les Orateurs de la Législative et de la Convention*.

The Legislative Assembly, like the Constituent, was theoretically monarchical in sentiment ; but during the first half of 1792 republicanism made rapid advances. Brunswick's invasion and brutal Manifesto swept away the Monarchy, provoked the September Massacres, brought Danton into power, and substituted the radical Convention, elected on a wide franchise, for the timid and rather colourless Legislative Assembly. The fall of the throne may be studied in Mathiez' little book *Le Dix Août*. For the next two years domestic politics were dominated by the war, which opened badly for France, took a more favourable turn with the cannonade at Valmy and the retreat of Brunswick, passed through a highly critical phase in 1793, and in 1794 scored victories in Belgium and on the Rhine which removed all immediate fear of invasion or defeat. The story of the titanic efforts of the young Republic to vanquish a world in arms has been told with admirable impartiality in the eleven small volumes of Chuquet's *Guerres de la Révolution*, based on the archives of the War Office ; and a brief summary of the campaigns by an expert is given in Belloc's little volume *The French Revolution* in the Home University Library.

For the Terror we must continue to consult the eight volumes of Mortimer-Ternaux' unfinished *Histoire de la Terreur*, which contains extracts from materials now lost. Danton must be studied in Madelin's biography, which in its psychological insight, its serene impartiality and its literary skill it is a delight to read. We see a coarse, full-blooded creature of impulse, born for action, a force rather than a brain, venal but not wholly degraded, who overthrew the Monarchy and approved the September Massacres, but who deplored the Terror as a system. Danton, declares Madelin, was an opportunist in the best sense of the word, and therefore ten times more of a statesman than Robespierre the unbending dogmatist. In 1792 he was the man of the moment, despite his atrocious faults, and it is his glory that he saved his country.

No satisfactory biography of Robespierre exists ; but no student of the Revolution can ignore the series of polemical works in which Mathiez has striven to rescue the reputation and exalt the statesmanship of his hero, —the *Études Robespierristes*, *Autour de Robespierre*, *Robespierre Terroriste*, *Autour de Danton*, *Danton et la Paix* and, most recently, *Girondins et Montagnards*. Mathiez presents to us ' not an imaginary Robespierre, but the real man, a just and clear-sighted statesman who lived but for the good of his country.' His private character, we are told, was stainless. Though he supported the Terror as a means to the attainment of social justice and was inexorable for enemies of his country, he was a moderating influence and saved—or tried to save— some innocent lives. He was never a Dictator and Fouquier-Tinville was not his obedient tool. Danton was removed, not because he was a rival, but because he was a traitor to France and to the Revolution,—a bad man and a bad Frenchman. Robespierre was one of the greatest orators who ever lived, ranking with Pericles, Demosthenes and Cicero, and towering above Danton and Gambetta. ' There was a time when Robespierre and democracy were synonymous. It will return.' Meanwhile 'la légende Dantonienne,' created by Michelet, Robinet and Aulard, must be demolished by the exposure of his utter selfishness, his shameless venality, his defeatism, and his shady friends. The reader soon wearies of these rhapsodies, which have made no notable converts ; but he dare not neglect them, for they embody a mass of new material discovered by the indefatigable researches of the greatest living authority on the Convention. *Robespierre's Rise and Fall*, by Lenotre, paints a vivid picture of the personal life of the famous Terrorist and of the Duplay family who gave him a home.

There is no wholly satisfactory life of Marat ; but the American scholar Gottschalk has given us a careful biographical sketch in which special attention is devoted to the political ideas of the man who declared in terrible words ' I am the anger of the people,' and who laboured more effectively than any of his contemporaries to render the proletariat class-conscious. Camille Desmoulins, the most powerful of Jacobin journalists after Marat, found a competent biographer in Jules Claretie. The second volume of Moncure Conway's *Life of Thomas Paine* describes the activities of the only Anglo-Saxon member of the Convention, who owed his election to *The Rights of Man*, the most effective of the replies to Burke. The tragic end of the King and Queen is described with great power in Belloc's *Life of Marie Antoinette*, the best of his biographies. A flood of light is thrown on the whole history of the activity of the Convention in Paris and the provinces and of the revolution of Thermidor by the first volume of Madelin's *Fouché*, the most valuable biography of the revolutionary era. The story of national defence is illustrated by Lévy-Schneider's *Jean-Bon Saint-André*. Nesta Webster's *Chevalier de Boufflers* is among the best of the numberless books which describe the life of the upper classes before and during the Revolution.

While only the expert will read the twenty-six volumes of Aulard's *Recueil des actes du Comité du Salut Public*, it aids us to visualise the methods by which France was governed during the Convention if we open its pages at random, watch its members at work in Paris, and read a few reports from the Representatives on Mission in the provinces. Of smaller bulk but of no less importance are the six volumes, entitled *La Société des Jacobins*, commenced by Aulard simultaneously with the *Recueil*, and covering the five years from the foundation of the Jacobin Club in 1789 till its existence was terminated after Thermidor by Fouché locking the door. With the record of the debates before us we learn that the famous club, far from being from the first the haunt of wild men, began with a monarchist atmosphere, and reflected rather than caused the change as public opinion drifted towards republicanism. During the Convention the debates in the club were often of greater importance than those in the Assembly, as the rival leaders rehearsed their parts and tested their strength before the decisive struggle and the operative vote. A third documentary source of the utmost value is the great collection *Les Actes de la Commune de Paris pendant la Révolution*, edited by Lacroix. A brief but useful account of the Commune is given in Alger's *Paris in 1789–1794*, Chapter III. The registers of the wards have been utilised in Mellié's valuable work *Les Sections de Paris pendant la Révolution Française*, and are summarised in Alger's *Paris*, Chapter IV. As a result of these publications we dare no longer confine ourselves to the main stream of history in the three Assemblies, but must follow the tributaries that flow in from the political clubs and the Municipality. It is in such contemporary records, not in the tendentious memoirs written in many cases long after the events described, that the changing phases of the Revolution must be traced.

The last year of the Convention, after the revolution of Thermidor, and the four years of the Directory which succeeded it, have attracted neither the public nor the historian. Mathiez' substantial monograph *La Réaction Thermidorienne* naturally denounces the men who overthrew Robespierre, but is indispensable for the dying Convention whose leaders, according to him, made politics their trade. The fever of the Revolution is over, and the personal interest begins to shift to Bonaparte and his campaigns. It is impossible to make a hero of the shady Barras or the icy Sieyès ; and the work of Carnot, the organiser of victory, continued to be done behind the scenes. Neither Barras nor Carnot has found a competent biographer, but the first volume of Lacour-Gayet's life of Talleyrand shews the ex-Bishop at work in diplomacy. Sciout's comprehensive work, *Le Directoire*, which first utilised the documents in the National Archives, is now in parts out of date. Foreign relations are surveyed in Sorel's fifth volume and more recently in Guyot's enormous monograph, *Le Directoire et la paix de l'Europe*, which supplements and in part corrects Sorel. Deville's *Thermidor et le Directoire*, the fifth volume of the *Histoire Socialiste* edited by Jaurès, devotes special attention to economic factors. A dazzling picture of the political, economic, and social anarchy under the Directory is painted in the first volume of Vandal's masterpiece *L'Avènement de Bonaparte*. Bonaparte's early life may be studied in the two standard biographies of Holland Rose and Fournier, and in more detail in Chuquet's volumes *La Jeunesse de Napoléon*. The *Recueil des Actes du Directoire Exécutif*, edited by Debidour, of which only four volumes were published, and Aulard's vast collection of material, *Paris pendant la Réaction Thermidorienne et sous le Directoire*, are indispensable to the advanced student.

If we are to understand the course and the scope of the Revolution we must extend our vision beyond the sphere of mere politics. A useful collection of essays entitled *L'Œuvre sociale de la Révolution*, edited by Émile Faguet, briefly summarises the problems of the army, education, the clergy, socialism, and the land. Legislation is admirably surveyed in Sagnac's *La Législation civile de la Révolution Française 1789–1804 : Essai d'histoire sociale*, and in Cahen et Guyot, *L'Œuvre législative de la Révolution.* The vital problem of finance was fully analysed for the first time in Stourm's *Les Finances de l'ancien régime et de la Révolution,* and has been explored more recently in Gomel's *Histoire financière de l'Assemblée Constituante,* and *Histoire financière de la Législative et de la Convention.* In *La Vie chère et le mouvement social sous la Terreur,* one of the most valuable of his many books, Mathiez has explored the fluctuation of prices, inflation, monopolies, taxation, requisitions and restrictions.

Religious life during the decade of upheaval has attracted authors of different schools. The best summary in English, though published half a century ago, is contained in Jervis's *The Gallican Church and the Revolution* ; but much material has subsequently come to light. La Gorce, the eminent historian of the Second Empire, has completed a monumental *Histoire religieuse de la Révolution Française* from the standpoint of Catholic Royalism, which carries the story down to the Concordat, in five volumes. In his *Études sur l'histoire religieuse de la Révolution Française* Gazier has shown, with the aid of Bishop Grégoire's papers, that the churches were only shut from the end of 1793 to the beginning of 1795, when Notre-Dame was reopened for worship, and the dying Convention retreated from the extreme anti-clericalism of its prime. France was ripe for the Concordat in 1795 ; but the Directory renewed the persecution. Aulard's instructive little book *Le Christianisme et la Révolution Française,* published in 1925, records the author's discovery—contrary to his earlier impression—that there was not much more faith in the villages than in the towns. The lower clergy approved the beginnings of the Revolution and no one dreamed in 1789 of attacking religion, which the *Constitution Civile* left intact. If, however, the Terror and its anti-clerical policy had continued very much longer, Aulard believes that Catholicism and even Christianity might have been completely uprooted. He has described part of the conflict in more detail in *Le Culte de la raison et le culte de l'Être suprême.* Mathiez has defended the Civil Constitution of the Clergy in his important work *Rome et le clergé français sous la Constituante*, and thrown light on the curious movement associated with the name of Larevellière-Lépeaux in his great monograph, *La Théophilanthropie et le culte décadaire 1796–1801*. He has discussed other aspects of the religious history of the years 1789–1802 in *Les Origines des Cultes Révolutionnaires*, and in the two volumes of essays entitled *Contributions à l'histoire religieuse de la Révolution Française* and *La Révolution et l'Église*, which sympathetically records the efforts to ' nationalise Catholicism.'

The literature of the end of the eighteenth century is described by specialists in the great co-operative *Histoire littéraire de la France*, edited by Petit de Julleville. An entertaining picture of social life is painted in the volumes of Edmond and Jules de Goncourt, *Histoire de la société française pendant la Révolution et le Directoire*, which may be supplemented by E. F. Henderson's *Symbol and Satire in the French Revolution*. Alger's *Paris in 1789–1794* adds some interesting traits. Lenotre's essays collected in the six volumes of *Vieilles Maisons, Vieux papiers*, and his many monographs, among them *Paris in the Revolution, The Guillotine and its Servants, The Tribunal of the Terror*, are as scholarly as they are readable. Approaches to socialism are described in André Lichtenberger's *Le Socialisme et la Révolution Française*, and in Laski's suggestive brochure *The Socialist Tradition in the French Revolution*, which attempts to do justice to Babeuf.

In addition to the larger works of Aulard already mentioned, the Professor collected his essays and lectures into volumes published at intervals with the title *Études et Leçons sur la Révolution Française*. Every article from his busy pen repays study ; but among the most interesting items of the long procession are the numerous studies of Danton and the survey of the foreign policy of the Convention in the third volume. Many of the *Études et Leçons* are reprinted from the review *La Révolution Française*, founded in 1881 and conducted by Aulard and his pupils. A rival periodical, *La Revue de la Révolution*, created in 1883 to receive the contributions and to spread the views of Catholic royalists, expired in 1889. A new and more formidable rival emerged in 1908 with the *Annales Historiques de la Révolution Française*, in which Mathiez and his pupils defend the cause of Robespierre, while unceasingly enriching our knowledge of the period.

One of the outstanding features of recent research has been the study of social and economic conditions, the early stages of which were described in Boissonade's booklet, *Les Études relatives à l'histoire économique de la Révolution Française*, published in 1906. An Economic Commission, created by the State in 1904 at the instigation of Jaurès, undertook the publication of the *Cahiers*, which when complete will form a small library. The six volumes printed at the end of the Second Empire neglected the documents of the villages, which are more valuable than the ambitious efforts of the three Estates, often drawn up by lawyers and in many cases copied from models with a few local additions. The publication of the proceedings of the Committees of the Assemblies on agriculture and commerce, feudal rights, mendicity, and food supply, unlocks an aspect of the time of which the political historians knew practically nothing. Students who desire to consult the French archives will find the technical guidance which they require in Pierre Caron's *Manuel pratique pour l'étude de la Révolution Française*. The Revolution in the provinces and the cities has a literature of its own so vast that it is impossible even to glance at it in a brief survey.

IV

In a triple sense the French Revolution belongs to European history. It grew out of conditions which were in large measure common to other countries ; its course closely affected and was continuously modified by the policy of almost every State in Europe ; and finally its influence on the institutions and ideas of the Old World was deep and enduring. The student must therefore travel beyond the meridian of Paris and view its repercussions on the life and thought of other members of the European family. It is the conspicuous merit of Sybel and Sorel to have established the vital connection of the internal and external policy of France with that of the rulers of the great European States. The Émigrés, for instance, belong as much to European as to French history, as we may learn from Ernest Daudet's classical *Histoire de l'Émigration*, Lady Blennerhassett's monumental biography of Madame de Staël, Bernard Mallet's delightful Life of his grandfather Mallet du Pan, and Baldensperger's *Le Mouvement des Idées dans l'Émigration Française*. The relevant volumes of the *Cambridge Modern History* and of the *Histoire Générale* should lie on our table. The best brief English survey of the relations of France and Europe is to be found in Morse Stephens' *Revolutionary Europe, 1789–1815*. The gradual crumbling of feudalism on the Continent is traced through half a century in Doniol's *La Révolution Française et la Féodalité*.

The countries most interested in and most affected by the eruption of the French volcano were Great Britain and Germany, in both of which the opening scenes of the drama were welcomed with general enthusiasm. The best introduction to its political effects on the former is P. A. Brown's *The French Revolution in English History*, which tells the story of the Radical movements and societies with the help of new material. The same large theme is instructively discussed by Laprade, *England and the French Revolution, 1789–1798* ; W. P. Hall, *British Radicalism, 1791–1797* ; Veitch, *The Genesis of Parliamentary Reform* ; Kent, *The English Radicals* ; Brinton, *The English Jacobins* ; and Meikle, *Scotland and the French Revolution*. The later volumes of Lecky's *Ireland in the Eighteenth Century*, Litton Falkiner's *Studies in Irish History and Biography*, and Guillon, *La France et l'Irlande pendant la Révolution*, give the Irish side of the

drama.   John Morley's two separate volumes on Burke
should be followed by the study of the *Reflections on the
Revolution in France* and the *Letters on a Regicide Peace* in
the excellent edition of E. J. Payne.   Lord Rosebery's
Pitt should be mastered before approaching Holland
Rose's standard biography or Felix Salomon's impressive torso.   André Lebon's *L'Angleterre et l'émigration
française, 1794–1801,* describes our futile negotiations
with the Émigrés.   Alger's *Englishmen in the French
Revolution* follows the footsteps of a number of British
enthusiasts to Paris.   The fertilising influence on
literature may be studied in Dowden's delightful
lectures *The French Revolution and English Literature* ;
Cestre's *La Révolution Française et les poètes anglais* ;
Brailsford's *Shelley, Godwin and their Circle* ; and Legouis's
La Jeunesse de Wordsworth, which utilises the new
material relating to the poet's French romance.

The effect of the Revolution on the mind and institutions of Germany was far greater than on England.
While in the latter the reform movement in its widest
sense was thrown back by a generation, in the former the
ideas of 1789 and the impetuous onset of the French
armies swept away the worst abuses of feudalism, and
overthrew the Holy Roman Empire with its antiquated
system.   A full account of the repercussion of the
Revolution on the mind of Germany, on the institutions
of the Empire, and on individual German States is given
in Gooch's *Germany and the German Revolution.*   Certain
aspects of the same subject are treated in Wenck's
scholarly volumes *Deutschland vor Hundert Jahren,* and
in Alfred Stern's *Der Einfluss der französischen Revolution
auf das deutsche Geistesleben,* which includes German
Switzerland in its scope.   Bavaria is studied in Ludwig
Männer's *Bayern vor und in der französischen Revolution,*
and German enthusiasts figure largely in Mathiez' *La
Révolution et les Étrangers.*   The political history of the
revolutionary era is related with admirable impartiality in
Heigel's standard *Deutsche Geschichte, 1786–1806,* which
supersedes Häusser's narrative of the same period and

supplements the tendencious work of Sybel. A brief but brilliant sketch of Germany before and during the Revolution is provided in the first half of the first volume of Treitschke's *History of Germany in the Nineteenth Century.* Martin Philippson's *Geschichte des preussischen Staatswesens vom Tode Friedrichs des Grossen,* covering the reign of Frederick William II, though faulty in scholarship, is of value for its new material. Ernst von Meier's *Preussen und die französische Révolution* analyses the influence of French ideas on the reformers of Prussia, contesting their importance in the case of Stein, in opposition to Max Lehmann, and admitting it in the case of Hardenberg. On the other hand the significance of the ideas of the Revolution for Prussia is stoutly maintained in Cavaignac's *La Formation de la Prusse contemporaine.* Rambaud's *Les Français sur le Rhin* and Sagnac's *Le Rhin français pendant la Révolution et l'Empire* describe the conquest of the left bank and the reforms introduced during the twenty years of French occupation. Some interesting utterances are collected in Raif's *Die Urteile der Deutschen über die französische Nationalität im Zeitalter der Revolution ünd der deutschen Erhebung.*

The political history of the revolutionary era in Italy is most authoritatively related in Franchetti's *Storia d'Italia, 1789–1799.* Hazard's learned monograph, *La Révolution Française et les lettres italiennes, 1789–1815,* describes the effect on literature and thought. Giglioli's *Naples in 1799* (written in English) reconstructs the fascinating and tragic story of the short-lived Neapolitan Republic, modelled on that of France. For Spain we may consult Baumgarten's *Geschichte Spaniens während der französischen Revolution* ; for Belgium, Lanzac de Laborie's *La Belgique sous la domination française,* and Engerand's *L'Opinion publique dans les Provinces Rhénanes et en Belgique, 1789–1815* ; for Holland, Legrand's *La Révolution Française en Hollande* ; for Russia, Larivière's *Catherine II et la Révolution Française,* mainly based on extracts from the correspondence of the Empress, with a valuable Introduction by Rambaud. Bernard Faÿ's

L'Esprit Révolutionnaire en France et aux États Unis, a brilliant study of the intellectual relations of thinkers and reformers on both sides of the Atlantic between 1770 and 1800, based largely on a study of the press, is, in the author's words, ' a story of love.' Hazen's *American Opinion on the French Revolution* sketches the attitude of Jefferson, Gouverneur Morris, the American Minister to France, and Monroe ; the brief and fruitless mission of the French Minister Genet in 1793 to drag the United States into war ; the democratic societies ; and the evidence of contemporary literature.

V

The influence of the Revolution on the ideas, the policy, and the institutions of France has moulded the history of the succeeding century. Almost every writer and politician who has attempted to guide his countrymen has been compelled to define his attitude to the greatest event in the life of his country. Some typical judgments by distinguished men have been collected in Janet's *La Philosophie de la Révolution Française*. In the early years of the nineteenth century French thought was divided into the schools of the counter-revolution and the supporters of ' the principles of 1789.' The most powerful opponent of the Revolution who used the French language was Joseph de Maistre. The Savoyard nobleman, who summoned the survivors from the revolutionary flood to rally round the principle of authority embodied in the Pope, may be approached in John Morley's essay in his *Miscellanies* and in Cogordan's volume in the *Grands Écrivains français*. The moderate Liberals, who admired the principle of ' the separation of powers ' enshrined in the British Constitution, were known as Doctrinaires. Both schools of thought are included in the first volume of Faguet's incomparable *Politiques et moralistes du dix-neuvième siècle*, which dissects the ideas of de Maistre and de Bonald, Madame de Staël and Benjamin Constant, Royer-Collard and

Guizot. The most comprehensive and illuminating survey of French political thought since the Revolution is to be found in the fine work of Henri Michel, *L'Idée de l'État : essai sur l'histoire des théories sociales et politiques en France depuis la Révolution.*

The extension of the principle of equality of rights, which was the gospel of the Revolution and the main-spring of its energies, proceeded in ever-widening circles throughout the nineteenth century, like a huge stone thrown into a stagnant pond. The novel conception of common citizenship rendered it impossible to maintain the disabilities of the Jews or to tolerate slavery ; nor was it logical any longer to evade the demand for equal rights and equal opportunities for the sexes. Above all the principle of equality gave an incalculable impetus to socialism. The nationalisation of the land makes frequent appearance in the pamphlets of the revolutionary era ; and with the conspiracy of Babeuf in 1797 socialism ceased to be merely a speculative doctrine and became a political programme. The wholesale transfer of land, and the circumstances under which it took place, under-mined the idea of the sacredness of property ; and when the promised equality of political rights failed to secure the welfare and happiness of the masses, the elastic principle of equality was stretched to the economic sphere. The Tiers État having extracted from the Revolution most of the benefits that it could provide, it is in the socialist movement that the operation of its governing principle is most clearly traceable at the present time.

If equality of rights and opportunity was the central tenet of the revolutionary faith, the sovereignty of the people was its necessary corollary. When the doctrine of hereditary privilege was abandoned, the death-knell of autocracy, enlightened or unenlightened, was sounded, and power could only reside in the mass or the majority of citizens. The third watchword of the Revolution, nationality, was foreign to the cosmopolitan teaching on which its leaders were nourished, nor did it make its

appearance till Europe began to threaten interference ;
but it arose naturally enough from the conception of
popular sovereignty. Before 1792 men had thought
of States as territorial units subject to a certain authority rather than as communities bound together by ties
of blood, religion, language, common traditions and
aspirations. The French Revolution astonished mankind by the spectacle of a nation thinking and acting
independently of its Government. The conception
of nationality was ignored at Vienna ; but the idea had
taken root, and the arrangements of the Congress in
which the principle was violated were those which were
most speedily upset.

The doctrine of nationality was no more invented by
the Revolution than the doctrines of equality and popular
sovereignty ; but their adoption by France opened a
new chapter in the life of humanity, and their proclamation by the revolutionary trumpet carried the gospel of
democracy to the uttermost parts of the earth.   ' France
did more than conquer Europe,' writes Sorel in an eloquent passage ; ' she converted her. Victorious even
in their defeat, the French won over to their ideas the
very nations which revolted from their domination. The
princes most eagerly bent on penning in the Revolution
saw it, on returning from their crusade, sprouting in the
soil of their own estates which had been fertilised by the
blood of French soldiers. The French Revolution only
ceased to be a source of strife between France and Europe
to inaugurate a political and social revolution which in
less than half a century had changed the face of the
European world.'

THE POLITICAL BACKGROUND OF GOETHE'S LIFE.[1]

THOUGH it is generally agreed that Goethe's was an essentially unpolitical nature, his lot was cast in such an eventful time and he touched life at so many points that his relation to politics deserves more attention than it has received. Despite the overwhelming number of monographs on the greatest figure in German literature, there is still need for a detailed record of his contacts with public life and a comprehensive study of his opinions on government and society. Of the larger biographies, that of Hume Brown alone is the work of a trained historian ; but the distinguished Edinburgh Professor spoke with greater authority on Scottish than on German history. Sir John Seeley, the learned author of the *Life and Times of Stein*, and a close student of Goethe, might have given us the book that we need ; but he unfortunately contented himself with a birdseye survey of the man and the writer in his little volume *Goethe after Sixty Years*. In the present address I can do no more than suggest the interest and importance of a comparatively neglected department of Goethe studies.

I

The notion of Gervinus that Goethe deliberately averted his gaze from the pageantry of events and buried himself in art, literature and science, is without

[1] Read before the Society at a meeting at King's College, University of London, on February 3, 1926.

foundation. No citizen of Frankfurt could fail to be vividly aware of the existence and significance of the system under which Central Europe had lived for a thousand years. The Holy Roman Empire, in regard to which Voltaire caustically inquired in what sense it was either holy, or Roman, or an Empire, was a mere ghost of its former self ; and the revellers in Auerbach's Keller shouted in disrespectful mirth :

> Das Heilige Römische Reich,
> Wie hält es doch zusammen ?

Yet its gigantic frame still sprawled across Germany, and its wheels, rusty though they were, continued to revolve. The Emperor, though nominally elective, had for centuries reigned at Vienna ; the Diet with its three Colleges of Electors, Princes and Free Cities, sat at Regensburg ; the Supreme Court was located at Wetzlar. Behind the decorative façade of the central machinery were the Circles or larger administrative units, the ecclesiastical and secular principalities, the Free Cities, and finally the Imperial Knights, whose duodecimo possessions were sprinkled by hundreds over the map. It was, indeed, the consecration of anarchy and particularism. ' In my childhood,' wrote Wieland, ' I was told a great deal about duties ; but there was so little about the duty of a German patriot that I cannot remember hearing the word German used with honour. There are Saxon, Bavarian, Frankfurt patriots ; but German patriots, who love the Empire as their fatherland, where are they ? ' Well might Friedrich Karl Moser cry in the bitterness of his heart that the Germans were a great but despised people. Yet while publicists and pamphleteers lamented in chorus the creeping paralysis of an institution which had once filled Europe with its prowess and fame, none of them could suggest an effective remedy. The Empire had virtually ceased to exist, but it seemed unable to die.

The mortal sickness of the Holy Roman Empire never clouded the spirits of the youthful Goethe, who, like his fellow-citizens, saw rather the glamour than the rottenness of a picturesque survival. ' If we can find a place where we can rest with our belongings,' he wrote in 1773, ' a field to support us, a house to shelter us, have we not a fatherland ? And do not thousands in every state possess it ? Wherefore then the vain striving for a feeling which we cannot and indeed do not desire to entertain, which is the result of special circumstances in certain peoples at certain times ? ' The mighty past appeared to revive for a moment in the coronation pageantry at Frankfurt, where the Arch-Chancellor, the Elector of Mainz, crowned the Emperor. The new ruler received the homage of the Estates on bended knee, and the herald brandished his sword towards the four quarters of heaven in token that all Christendom was subject to his master's sway. It was a great event in the life of the Imperial city, fully described in *Dichtung und Wahrheit*, when on April 3, 1764, the high-souled Joseph II was acclaimed in the Römersaal ; and when in 1792 his nephew Francis was the central figure, the spectators were blissfully unaware that the last successor of Charlemagne had been crowned.

Goethe's brief residence at Wetzlar in 1772 was calculated rather to diminish than to increase the respect for the Empire which he had imbibed in his native city. The Court of Imperial Appeal, like the Court of Chancery in the time of Lord Eldon, had earned an unenviable reputation for procrastination, and its name was tarnished by suspicions of venality. Moreover, its prestige was impaired by the fact that most of the important cases were reserved by the Emperor for the Aulic Council at Vienna. If a few petty tyrants were thwarted or punished by its decrees it was too weak to strike at powerful offenders. Young jurists spent a month or two in the sleepy little town to learn the routine of Imperial law ; but Goethe's heart was never in his profession, and Wetzlar alike to Goethe and to the world stands for Werther and Lotte, not for the musty memories of the Reichskammergericht.

Goethe was wholly free from the contempt for the Empire which was felt by so many of his contemporaries ; but he combined benevolent neutrality towards the system under which he lived with an ardent admiration for Frederick the Great. In a well-known passage in the autobiography he records how his victories awoke Germany from her slumbers, supplied the poets with an inspiration which they had hitherto lacked, and aroused respect for German prowess throughout the West and South scarcely less than in the Protestant north. It was, however, a personal as well as a transitory sentiment for a daemonic personality. ' He was Prussian,' he writes, ' or, to be more accurate, Fritzian (fritzisch) ; for what was Prussia to us ? It was the personality of the great king which appealed to every one.' It was to the Seven Years' War that the poet also owed his first experience of a French occupation, in which a French officer was quartered in his father's house.

An essential part of the Imperial system was the little principality whose fortunes depended on the virtues or vices, the smiles or the frowns of its autocrat. While Goethe was growing to manhood, Germany could boast of some of the best and some of the worst rulers of the age. On the one hand, men like Charles William Ferdinand, Duke of Brunswick, and Karl Friedrich, Duke of Baden, were fathers of their people ; on the other, the Landgrave of Hesse-Cassel sold his subjects to George III as mercenaries for the American War, and the Duke of Württemberg's tyranny aroused the attention of Europe. The abominations of selfish autocracy are enshrined for ever in the fiery pages of *Emilia Galotti* and *Kabale und Liebe*.

Goethe's autobiography records his debt to the writings of Karl Friedrich Moser, who denounced the soulless autocrat and preached the gospel of service ; but of the darker features of princely rule the poet had no personal experience. While Schiller chafed under the yoke of an extravagant despot, Goethe was privileged

from the age of twenty-six to co-operate with one of the
most enlightened rulers of his time. The young Karl
August inherited a principality with only 100,000 inhabitants and an infertile soil ; but after sowing their wild
oats the prince and the poet resolved to make the Duchy
of Weimar a model principality. At this task Goethe
laboured with unflagging zeal for a decade and his
master for half a century. On the birth of an heir in
1783, the Duke gave expression to his gratitude. ' Here
is a hook on which I can hang my pictures,' he wrote to
Merck. ' With the help of Goethe and good fortune I
will paint them in such a way that posterity will perhaps
say *Anch' egli fu pittore.*' The poet's admiration for the
ruler is enshrined in the beautiful lines in the *Venetian
Epigrams*, written after he had laid down the more
exacting burdens of public life :

> Klein ist unter Germaniens Fürsten freilich der meine ;
> Kurz und schmal ist sein Land, mässig nur was er vermag.
> Aber so wende nach innen, so wende nach aussen die Kräfte
> Jeder ; da wär's ein Fest Deutscher mit Deutschen zu sein.

His gratitude to the man was no less sincere than his
respect for the prince :

> Denn mir hat er gegeben, was Grosse selten gewähren,
> Neigung, Musse, Vertraun, Felder und Garten und Haus.
> Niemals frug ein Kaiser nach mir, es hat sich kein König
> Um mich bekümmert, und Er war mir August und Mäcen.

Elected Councillor of Legation in 1776, Privy
Councillor in 1779, President of the Council in 1782,
Goethe threw himself heart and soul into the tasks of
government.[1] To Herder he was ' the Weimar-fac-
totum,' to Knebel ' the backbone of affairs.' He promoted the development of agriculture, industry and
mines, the reform of education and finance, the ameliora-
tion of the lot of the poor. He was in fact a capable,
energetic and conscientious official. Though he returned
to literature after ten years of ministerial activity, his
experiences of public life left deep traces on his life and

[1] See the essay ' Goethe als Staatsmann ' in Schöll, *Goethe.*

thought.   All that he had done and all that he had wished to do had been or could be accomplished by the will of a benevolent autocrat.   The elements of any political structure in Weimar other than paternal government were absent.   The people had a right, not indeed to govern themselves, but to be well governed.   He stood mid-way between the legitimists, to whom princely power was sacrosanct, and the democrats, to whom the voice of the people was the voice of God.   He was a conservative reformer, convinced that reforms must come from above, that changes must be gradual, and that order was heaven's first law.

Goethe's love of order and economy, combined with his humane feelings, aroused in him a life-long detestation of war.   The extravagance of Karl August was a sore trial to his minister, and he was haunted by the fear that the blood and treasure of the little duchy might be poured out in quarrels not its own.   As a boy he had been dazzled by the flashing sword of Frederick the Great, but as a man he had no desire to see Weimar tied to his chariot-wheels.   Karl August, like other rulers of little states who are born for action, fretted at his impotence, and sought an outlet for his energies by revolving round a larger sun.   The later years of Frederick were troubled by the restless ambitions of Joseph II, and in 1778, when yet another struggle between Prussia and Austria seemed inevitable, Goethe accompanied his master to Berlin to make arrangements.   The storm blew over, but in 1785 the Fürstenbund, the last achievement of the great King, was formed to hold Joseph in check.   The demonstration sufficed, and Bavaria was saved ; but in 1790 Frederick William II, alarmed by Austrian operations against Turkey, led Prussian troops into Silesia.   Karl August hurried to the front and ordered Goethe to join him at Breslau ; but for a third time a conflict was avoided.   Though the worst had not occurred, Goethe throughout disapproved the policy of adventure which appealed so strongly to his master.   The duty of rulers was to provide good govern-

ment for their subjects, to ignore the siren calls of
ambition, and to conduct their business on the principle
of limited liability.

II

The impressions and convictions formed during his
years of active service at Weimar provided the compass
by which Goethe steered his course through the tempests
of the revolutionary era.[1]   Being well aware that mis-
government brought its nemesis, he was not one of those
whom the French Revolution caught unprepared. ' As
early as 1785,' he wrote long after in the *Annals*, ' the
history of the Diamond Necklace had made an indelible
impression on me.   Out of the bottomless abyss of the
immorality in city, court and state there emerged, spectre-
like, the most horrible apparitions.   These so affected my
behaviour that the friends with whom I was living when
the news arrived have confessed to me that I appeared
like one demented.' The figure of Cagliostro haunted
him, and on his visit to Palermo in 1787 he sought out
the family of the impostor.

' Hardly had I settled afresh into the life of Weimar,'
we read in the *Annals*, ' than the French Revolution
attracted the attention of the world, and I followed the
development of the drama with close attention.'   We
cannot expect to find in Goethe the enthusiasm which
the birth pangs of a new world inspired in elderly men
like Kant and Klopstock, Wieland and Herder, and in
younger men like Forster and Johannes Müller.   He was
the subject, the friend and the counsellor of a model
prince.   His administrative experience had convinced
him of the practicability and the value of reforms carried
out from above.   His sojourn in Italy had strengthened
his preference for classical harmony and measure.   The
phase of *Sturm und Drang* was over, and he believed that
the ship of State should be steered by the brain, not by
the emotions.   His contempt for the political capacity

[1] See Gooch, *Germany and the French Revolution*, ch. 7.

of the masses was revealed in *Egmont*. Though recognising the justice of the punishment that fell on the monarchy and the privileged classes in France, he never for a moment expected any benefit to arise from the violent methods of the reformers ; and the Declaration of the Rights of Man, which was music to the ears of some of his Weimar friends, was to him as meaningless as to Bentham and Burke.

The first literary expression of Goethe's views on the French Revolution is to be found in the *Venetian Epigrams*, written during his second visit to Italy in the spring of 1790 :

> Alle Freiheitsapostel, sie waren mir immer zuwider,
> Willkür suchte doch nur jeder am Ende für sich.
> Willst Du viele befreien, so wag es vielen zu dienen.
> Wie gefährlich das sei, willst Du es wissen ?   Versuchs !

> Könige wollen das Gute, die Demagogen desgleichen,
> Sagt man ; doch irren sie sich : Menschen, ach, sind sie wie
> wir.

> Nie gelingt es der Menge, für sich zu wollen, wir wissens.
> Doch wer verstehet für uns alle zu wollen, er zeigs.

> Frankreichs traurig Geschick, die Grossen mögens bedenken ;
> Aber bedenken fürwahr sollen es Kleine noch mehr.
> Grossen gingen zu Grunde, doch wer beschütze die Menge
> Gegen die Menge ?   Da war Menge der Menge Tyrann.

These are the strong, simple outlines of his unchanging political faith.   Since the masses cannot save themselves, it is the duty and the privilege of their rulers to save them.   To princes and people alike the Revolution brought a solemn warning.   For the prince to do too little and for the people to attempt too much was to invite disaster.

Goethe made several attempts to embody the Revolution in dramatic form, but without complete satisfaction to his readers or himself.   *Der Grosscophta* is a satirical study of a corrupt and credulous society. Cagliostro, the hero, is an impostor in the grand style,

and the history of the Diamond Necklace lays bare one
of the festering sores of the *Ancien Régime*. Though not
a directly political play, its analysis of social and moral
decay embodies the conviction that monarchical France
was sick and in need of a physician. Goethe thought
better of the work than did his friends. ' It was a good
subject,' he remarked to Eckermann, ' for it was not
merely of moral but of historical significance. The
Queen, through being implicated in the unlucky story
of the Necklace, was no longer respected. Hate injures
no one ; it is contempt that drags men down.' Whatever we may think of the literary merits of this sinister
drama, no reader can regard its author as an apologist of
the *Ancien Régime*.

In the spring of 1792 the Girondins compelled
Louis XVI to declare war against feudal Europe, and the
poet accompanied his master to the front. ' Goethe
with the army ! ' wrote Heyne ; ' what profanation ! '
The invitation was unexpected and not wholly welcome,
for he was deep in the study of optics. Yet he promised
himself an interesting experience, and it was expected
that the Coalition army would reach Paris without delay.
' After home and bed and kitchen and cellar,' he wrote
to Jacobi from Frankfurt, ' life in a tent will indeed be
a change, all the more since the death of both aristocratic
and democratic sinners leaves me cold.' At Mainz he
made his first acquaintance with the Émigrés, and passing
through Trier and Luxemburg he reached the Duke of
Brunswick's camp at Longwy on August 27.

With the aid of his letters and diary we can follow
his movements almost day by day ; and in the *Campaign
in France*, worked up in 1820 from his own materials and
from the Memoirs of Dumouriez and other protagonists,
he has told the story of one of the most memorable
episodes in his life. The surrender of Longwy, the first
French town, seemed to confirm the assurance of the
Émigrés that the invaders would be welcomed with open
arms ; and on the capitulation of Verdun after a brief
bombardment he wrote to Christiane that he would

soon be with her again and would bring her something from Paris.   A week later he wrote in a more chastened mood.   ' It is very interesting to be here.   To see the ways of war under so great a general, and to learn to know the French nation, affords even an idle spectator plenty of entertainment.   What is to happen next ? We are all wondering.   The business is lengthening out. It is a stupendous enterprise, even with all our resources.' The September massacres, the answer of Danton to the Brunswick Manifesto, seemed to him likely to facilitate the invasion ; but the blood-bath in the prisons proved the beginning not of anarchy but of organised resistance. A week later the battle of Valmy, in which Goethe received his baptism of fire, turned the tide.   In the most celebrated passage of the book he described the Allied camp on the evening after the brief conflict. ' People avoided each other's glances.   We could not even light a fire.   After a time some one asked me what I thought, as I had often amused the circle with oracular utterances.   On this occasion I remarked, '' Here and to-day commences a new epoch of world-history, and you can boast that you were present at its birth ! '' ' It was a bold prophecy ; but a century dominated by the forces of nationality and democracy was to prove its truth.

The retreat began under conditions which prompted the witticism that Jupiter Pluvius had turned Jacobin. ' I hasten back to my flesh-pots,' he wrote to Herder, ' there to awake from a bad dream.'   Though he kept his spirits and his health, his letters and diary are filled with lamentations.   ' In six weeks we have borne and seen more misery and danger than in the rest of our lives.   No pen and no tongue can describe the plight of the army.   This campaign will cut a sorry figure in history.'   Yet despite its failure and its horrors, he was glad to have taken part.   ' In these four weeks,' he wrote to Knebel a few days after Valmy, ' I have learned much. I am happy to have seen everything with my own eyes, and I can say of this historic epoch, '' Quorum pars minima fui.'' '

Ranke has complained that the *Campaign in France* makes no real contribution to history, since the author was never in the confidence of Brunswick, the King of Prussia, or the other leaders of the ill-starred enterprise. Other historians have expressed a higher view of its value, and the reader can see for himself with what power and skill the atmosphere is reproduced. It is, however, less as a footnote to history than as a revelation of mind and character that the book retains its place. To his courage and serenity Goethe added a clearness of vision to which few if any of his companions could lay claim. There is not a word of hatred or recrimination in the *Campaign* or in the letters on which it is based. Aristocrats and democrats, he feels, have sinned alike, and the French people is the victim of its rulers, old and new. He was temperamentally unfitted to scale the heights and plumb the depths of the Revolution ; yet he never shared the delusion that it was merely the outpouring of human wickedness or that it could be suppressed by the sword alone. His heart is filled with compassion for the victims of war,—for the civilian sufferers no less than for the combatants. His pages breathe a genuine humanity, and the sufferings of the humble never fail to strike a responsive chord in his heart. He returned home with a shuddering horror of war, more convinced than ever that revolutions were not worth their price, and that the highest duty of rulers was to render them unnecessary.

The repulse of the invaders was followed by the execution of Louis XVI. ' Who was there who had not from childhood shuddered at the execution of Charles I,' wrote Goethe, ' and comforted himself with the hope that such scenes would never recur ? Imagine the feelings of those who had marched forth to rescue the King and now were impotent to intervene in the trial or to prevent the execution of the sentence ! The world appeared to me bloodier and more bloodthirsty than before ; and if the death of a King in battle counts like a thousand, it is of far greater significance in a constitutional struggle.' The unfinished fragment of a philosophic tale, written at this moment, *The Sons of Megaprazon*, which only saw the light a century later, describes the terrific experiences of the volcanic island of Monarchomany (France), and the devastating effects of the eruptions on the dwellers in neighbouring lands. It is a sombre little study of confusion and delusion ; but the author's emphasis on the fact that an ancient law forbade the tillers of the soil ever to satisfy their hunger reveals his unchanged conviction that the revolution was not without a cause.

After recovering from the distracting experiences of the campaign, a sudden inspiration in the spring of 1793 seized the poet, who threw off the sparkling little one-act play *Der Bürger-General* in three days. The French were now on the Rhine, and incendiarism, it was feared, might set the whole countryside ablaze. George and Rose, a newly-married couple, are happy and contented in their little holding, the landlord of which is a kindly nobleman. Old Martin, however, Rose's father, has caught the Jacobin fever, and is egged on by Schnaps, the villain of the piece, who proceeds to illustrate French principles by removing some eatables from the cupboard. He is arrested, and the judge proceeds to unravel the threads of what he believes to be a formidable conspiracy. At this moment the landlord appears, and proclaims the familiar Weimar gospel of the duties of man. ' My children,' he says to Rose and George, ' love each other and look after the land and your household.' Old Martin is advised to let foreign countries settle their own affairs. ' Let every one begin with himself, and he will find plenty to do. Let him honourably seek the advantage of himself and those dependent on him, and he will thus contribute to the general welfare.' The judge breaks in with a plea for punishment, only to receive an admonition in his turn. ' Not too fast ! Vindictive penalties only breed trouble. In a land where the prince is accessible to all, where all classes live in harmony, where no one is hindered in his activity, where useful knowledge is universal, there will be no parties. The drama of the world will attract attention, but seditious opinions will find no entry. Let us be thankful to have the blue sky over our heads when too many fields are ravaged by hailstones. It means something that we can laugh at the cockade and the cap and the uniform which have brought so much evil on the world.' Beneath the sunlit ripples of this merry little satire—the most successful of his efforts to portray the Revolution on the stage—lies the major part of the poet's political creed.

Shortly after completing *Der Bürger-General*, Goethe once more emerged from his sheltered home at the bidding of the Duke to witness the wild surge of war. Custine had seized Mainz when Brunswick was thrown out of France, and had held it throughout the winter ; but his forces were small and at length the French garrison found itself besieged. The poet's appetite for campaigning had been fully satisfied in 1792, but the expulsion of the invader appealed to his sympathies much more than the Brunswick Manifesto. Once again we can follow his adventures and emotions both in his letters and in the finished narrative *Die Belagerung von Mainz*, which he compiled in later years. The horrors of war, though on a smaller scale than in the previous year, awoke the old compassion for the combatants on both sides, and for the civilians whose sufferings were often scarcely less poignant. ' My friends can be thankful,' he wrote, ' not to witness the misery in unhappy Mainz.' He displayed the same bravery as before. ' Every moment one was filled with anxiety for the Duke and one's dearest friends, and one forgot to think of one's own safety. As if enchanted by the confusion, one rushed to the danger-points and let the cannon-balls fly over one's head and burst by one's side.' Once again there is no bitterness against the French, whom he watched march out of the city singing the *Marsellaise*. ' It was a poignant spectacle as the cavalry rode past. Individually they looked like Don Quixote, but in the mass extremely impressive.' His rebukes are reserved for the Clubists, or German Jacobins, who co-operated with the invaders ; yet he witnessed with shame and indignation the sack of their houses and the pillaging of shops. Though he told Jacobi that the closing days of the strife and the capitulation were among the most interesting of his life, his second and last campaign intensified the loathing of war which was one of the master-passions of his life.

On his return home Goethe sketched a new play on the Revolution, with the revealing title *Die Aufgeregten*. The subject was once again the effect of propaganda on the ignorant masses ; but while *Der Bürger-General* skated lightly over thin ice, its successor dealt more comprehensively with the causes and the results of agitation. The unfinished play embodies the most complete dramatic statement of his political creed. The scene is laid in a village, the inhabitants of which have been grievously wronged by a deceased landlord and a fraudulent steward. The grandfather of the youthful Count had remitted some feudal burdens ; but the charter of emancipation had disappeared, the son of the benefactor had exacted the old dues, and his widow, fearing to compromise the rights of her son, made no change, though her kindly heart yearned for restitution. At this point the French Revolution brings to a head the discontent of the villagers, who plot to obtain restoration of their rights. The second act opens with the return of the Countess from Paris, where her experiences have made her more, not less, inclined to concessions. Thus at the very moment that the villagers are preparing to secure their rights by force, the Countess is about to do justice by her own free will. From this point we only possess the outlines of the play, with a few scenes worked out in detail. The revolt begins, but tragedy is averted by the masculine daughter, who at the point of her gun compels the villain who possesses the secret to produce the lost charter from its hiding-place. Thus the play ends harmoniously. The rustics are depicted as usual with good hearts and no brains ;

but the Countess embodies the spirit of liberal conservatism which severed Goethe as much from the
Émigré as from the Jacobin. ' With the words I have
put into her mouth,' observed Goethe to Eckermann,
' I have expressed how the nobility ought to think. She
has convinced herself that the people may be ruled but
not oppressed, and that the revolutionary outbreaks of
the lower classes are the consequence of the injustice
of the upper classes.' The moral of the play is that
abuses should be corrected without waiting for the
explosion.

Of a second unfinished revolutionary drama *Das
Mädchen von Oberkirch*, a tragedy in five acts, only two
scenes were composed, and we have no clue as to the
probable development of a story which opens with the
Jacobin dictatorship in Strassburg. Goethe was indeed
in no mood for sustained literary composition. ' To
have been an eye-witness of revolutions threatening the
peace of the world,' he writes in the *Annals* for 1794,
' and to have seen with one's own eyes the greatest
misfortunes that can befall citizens, peasants and soldiers,
clouded my mind with sadness. Robespierre's deeds had
terrified the world, and all sense of happiness had been
so utterly extinguished that no one presumed to rejoice
over his destruction, least of all while the horrors of war
were in full blast. French revolutionary songs floated
about in secret. News of fugitives flowed in from all
quarters. There was not a family, not a circle of friends,
which had not suffered. Several times I offered my
mother a quiet residence with me, but she had no fear
at Frankfurt, finding comforting passages in the Psalms
and Prophets.'

His disgust with the times led Goethe to refashion
the old beast-epic *Reinecke Fuchs*, whose fierce onslaught
on the follies and baseness of mankind were in tune with
his own sombre feelings. ' As I had hitherto occupied
myself *ad nauseam* with the revolts of the mob, it was a
real pleasure to hold up the mirror to Courts and rulers.'
The epic tells its tale and points its moral without

ambiguity ; but Goethe could not resist the temptation of interpolating a few lines of his own.

> Doch das Schlimmste find ich den Dünkel des irrigen Wahnes,
> Der die Menschen ergreift : es könne jeder im Taumel
> Seines heftigen Wollens die Welt beherrschen und richten.
> Hielte doch jeder sein Weib und seine Kinder in Ordnung,
> Wüsste sein trotzig Gesinde zu bändigen, könnte sich stille,
> Wenn die Thoren verschwenden, in mässigen Leben erfreuen.
> Aber wie sollte die Welt sich verbessern ?   Es lässt sich ein jeder
> Alles zu und will mit Gewalt die anderen bezwingen.
> Und so sinken wir tiefer und immer tiefer ins Arge.

The Revolution obsessed Goethe to such an extent that he seemed unable to write without direct or indirect reference to its problems.   In the winter of 1794 he amused himself with a new Decameron, the French armies playing the disruptive part which in the distant days of Boccaccio had been taken by the plague.   The stories in the *Unterhaltungen* are flimsy enough, but some of the contrasted types are of interest, and their heated discussions obviously reflect the distressing scenes which the author knew only too well.   The siege of Mainz provokes a passionate altercation on the Clubists and other German champions of France.   ' They will fall into the hands of the Allies,' cries one, ' and I hope to see them all hanged.'   ' And I hope,' snaps another, ' that the guillotine will reap a rich harvest in Germany and that no guilty head will be spared.'

At a time when Goethe complained that some of his old friends were behaving in a way that bordered on insanity, the new friendship with Schiller proved particularly welcome.   Schiller had outgrown the romantic radicalism of his youth, had tired of politics, and had embraced the classical tradition ; and though one of the friends had known autocracy at its best and the other at its worst, they were now in close agreement on political theory and practice.   The first-fruits of their co-operation was the *Xenien*, which the authors compared to foxes sent into the land of the Philistines with burning tails to destroy the harvest of the inhabitants.   It was their wish that the winged words of the German Dunciad should be regarded as their joint work ; but we catch the authentic accents of Goethe in the couplets which reiterate the familiar message of Weimar :

Majestät der Menschennatur ! Dich soll ich beim Haufen
   Suchen ? Bei wenigen nur hast Du von jeher gewohnt.
Willst Du frei sein, mein Sohn, so lerne was rechtes, und halte
   Dich genügsam, und sieh niemals nach oben herauf.
Wisst ihr auch wie der kleine was ist ? er mache das Kleine
   Recht. Der Grosse begehrt just so das Grosse zu thun.
Freiheit ist ein herrlicher Schmuck, der schönste von allen,
   Und doch steht er, wir sehn's, wahrlich nicht jeglichem an.
Das Verfassung sich überall bilde, wie sehr ist's zu wünschen,
   Aber ihr Schwätzer verhelft uns zu Verfassungen nicht.
Zur Nation euch zu bilden, ihr hoffet es, Deutsche, vergebens.
   Bildet, ihr könnt es, dafür freier zu Menschen euch aus.
Was das Luthertum war ist jetzt das Franztum in diesen
   Letzten Tagen, es drängt ruhige Bildung zurück.

Yet Goethe is as ready as ever to dissociate himself from the sterility of legitimism :

Wer ist wirklich ein Fürst ? Ich hab es immer gesehen,
   Der nur ist wirklicher Fürst, der es vermochte zu sein.
Was ist das würdigste Glied der Regierung ? Ein würdiger
      Bürger,
   Und im despotischen Land ist er der Pfeiler des Staats.

The progress of French arms and the extension of the war to Italy filled Goethe with apprehension and sorrow. ' Into what misery has that beautiful land fallen ! ' he wrote to a friend in 1796. He was anxious about his mother, and thankful that Weimar at least was at a distance from the storm. Prussia and the North had withdrawn from the fray in 1795 ; and though Frederick William II was denounced for leaving his allies in the lurch, no one more whole-heartedly approved the Treaty of Basel than Goethe. ' We have all cause to be thankful,' he wrote to Karl August ; ' for there is no question that the French could and would ravage us as they ravaged the districts of the Rhine and the Main, or even worse.'

' For me it was a new spring,' wrote Goethe in

thankfully recording his friendship with Schiller, 'in which everything secreted in my nature burst into joyous life.' Having recovered his poetic inspiration he turned from the controversial fireworks of the *Xenien* to the miniature epic of *Hermann und Dorothea*. Though it is a great deal more than a political poem, it would never have been written without the stimulus of the French Revolution. 'I have tried to smelt the life of a German village in the epic furnace,' he explained to a friend, 'and to reflect the great movements and changes of the world arena in a modest mirror.' The poem is saturated with politics, and familiar axioms are proclaimed anew. The bonds of the world are unloosed ; who will rejoin them ? States fall to pieces when the restraints of law are removed. To build and maintain one happy home serves mankind better than all the talk about the rights of man. Goethe's own experiences of war gave poignancy to his picture of the sufferings of the refugees flying before the armies of Republican France, and it is against the dark background of war and confusion that the angels of Love and Hope stand out in sharp relief.

Hermann und Dorothea is a sermon on war ; but once more it is the monster itself that is denounced rather than the warriors. And once again Goethe recognises the gold as well as the dross in the revolutionary ore.

> Denn wer leugnet es wohl dass hoch sich das Herz ihm erhoben,
> Ihm die freiere Brust mit reineren Pulsen geschlagen,
> Als sich der erste Glanz der neuen Sonne heranhob,
> Als man hörte vom Rechte der Menschen, das allen gemein sei,
> Von der begeisternden Freiheit und von der löblichen Gleichheit ?
> Damals hoffte jeder sich selbst zu leben ; es schien sich
> Aufzulösen das Band das viele Länder umstrickte,
> Das der Müssigang und der Eigennutz in der Hand hielt.
> Schauten nicht die Götter in jenen drängenden Tagen
> Nach der Hauptstadt der Welt, die es schon so lange gewesen
> Und jetzt mehr als je den herrlichen Namen verdiente ?
> Waren nicht jene Männer die ersten Verkünder der Botschaft
> Namen den höchsten gleich, die unter die Sterne gesetzt sind ?
> Wuchs nicht jeglichem Menschen der Mut und der Geist und die
> Sprache ?

In the summer of 1797 Goethe paid one of his rare visits to Frankfurt. ' It is very interesting to be here just now,' he wrote to a friend ; ' intercourse with people who have known almost all the important actors in this war-drama is most instructive. One sees the French Revolution and its effects much more directly, because it has had such great consequences for the city and because here one is in such manifold relations with that nation. What a curious people they are ! The Frenchman is never still for a moment ; he walks, chats, jumps, whistles, sings, and makes such a noise that one expects to see a larger number of them than there is. If one does not understand them, they grow irritable ; but if one can talk with them they are at once *bons enfants*. In the armies of this kind one sees a peculiar energy and power at work. Such a nation must be terrible in more than one sense.' He had no desire to see Germany under the yoke of the Republic ; but no word of hatred for France and the French ever escapes this cool observer who stands above the battle.

Ten years after the meeting of the States-General at Versailles, Goethe made a final attempt to embody the stupendous cataclysm in dramatic form. The plan of *Die natürliche Töchter* was suggested by the Memoirs of Stephanie Louise de Bourbon-Conti, published in 1798. ' Into this work, as into a vessel, I desired to pour reflections of many years on the French Revolution.' The story was to be unfolded in three full-length dramas, the first of which appeared in 1803. Eugenie, the Natural Daughter, ranks high among Goethe's heroines. She is born for great deeds and great sacrifices in the crisis which is drawing near in the French monarchy. We are acutely conscious of the approach of tragic issues, of the throbbing unrest, of the ferment of revolutionary ideas. The finely moulded drama deserved and received the approval of the poet's friends ; but the coldness of the public discouraged the author, and the later parts of the trilogy remained unwritten.

Of all Goethe's attempts to embody the French

Revolution in literary form, *Hermann und Dorothea* alone can be pronounced a complete success ; and that glittering jewel is the least directly concerned with politics.   That so many were unfinished testifies not only to his dissatisfaction with his efforts but to the irresistible fascination of the theme.   His nature yearned for harmony in life as in art, and was thrown out of gear by the storm and the earthquake.   Moreover, his incapacity to love or to hate the doctrines for which men fought and died cut him off from the deepest springs of inspiration.   The Revolution, in his mature judgment, was a lesson alike to rulers and ruled.   ' I could be no friend to the Revolution,' he remarked to Eckermann in 1824, ' but I was as little a friend to arbitrary rule. Indeed, I was perfectly convinced that a great revolution is never the fault of the people.   Revolutions are utterly impossible so long as Governments are just and vigilant. If there exists an actual necessity for a great reform, God is with it and it prospers.'   Eckermann describes his master as a mild aristocrat, but Goethe preferred another title.   ' Dumont is a moderate Liberal, as all rational people are and ought to be, and as I am myself.'   Whatever political label we may ultimately affix to his name, he cannot at any rate be placed in the camp either of indifference or reaction.

III

The stupendous figure of Napoleon claims as large a space in the life and thought of Goethe as the French Revolution ; but his opinions of the Emperor are to be found rather in his conversations and correspondence than in his literary works.[1]   Like everyone else he had followed with breathless interest the lightning ascent of the young General during the Italian and Egyptian campaigns ; he welcomed Brumaire as the end of the Revolution and the inauguration of an era of efficiency and order ; and he accepted the proclamation of the

---

[1] See A. Fischer, *Goethe und Napoleon.*

Empire as the obvious reward of incomparable services. It was not, however, till 1806 that the greatest of historic men won an abiding place in the foreground of Goethe's consciousness and claimed an allegiance which never waned or wavered till death.

Prussia had retired from the conflict with France in 1795 and re-entered it in 1806, and in both cases Weimar followed her lead. To join Russia and Austria in 1805 might have been wise, but to plunge after Austerlitz was madness. In July 1806 the Rheinbund was formed by sixteen Princes under the presidency of Napoleon, and in August the Emperor Francis proclaimed the dissolution of the Holy Roman Empire. The announcement, declared Goethe, disturbed him less than a quarrel between his servant and his coachman on the box seat ; nor did he in any way regret the appearance of the Rheinbund. He had had enough of war and dissensions, and was ready to accept any system, national or anti-national, which seemed likely to promise a quiet life. He had always disapproved his master's close association with Prussia, and the quartering of the Duke's Prussian cavalry in Weimar had provoked complaints of the officers' arrogance. The army of Frederick the Great had not yet encountered Napoleon, and Goethe never shared the delusion that it would prove invincible. There was no talk this time of his joining Karl August in the field ; but since the Duchy lay right athwart the track of the French advance, he could not escape the gathering flood of war by staying at home. Alone of the Ducal family the valiant Duchess Luise remained in the capital, where she and the poet anxiously awaited the march of events.

October 14, 1806, was the most terrible day of Goethe's life. The thunder of the cannon at Jena reverberated through the little town, and bullets whistled over the gabled roofs. The appearance of Prussian soldiers in headlong flight soon told the citizens who had won, and the pursuing soldiers proceeded to exact the usual price of defeat. Some Alsatian Hussars, who entered Goethe's house, behaved tolerably well, and an officer soon arrived to report that Augereau would establish his headquarters there. The Marshal only arrived next day, and during the night two soldiers broke in, forced their way to the poet's bedroom and threatened his life. The bravery of Christiane at this moment was rewarded three days later by marriage. On the following morning Ney appeared and left a guard, and Augereau spent two days under Goethe's roof. The soldiers drank twelve casks of wine, and the owner estimated his losses at 2,000 Thalers.

Goethe cared as much for the Duchy of Weimar as he cared little for Germany ; and the political framework of Weimar was saved by the Duchess, whose courage and personality made a deep impression on Napoleon. Karl August was to leave the Prussian army, pay an indemnity, and enter the Rheinbund ; and the presence of French troops guaranteed the fulfilment of the terms. The settlement was better than Goethe had dared to hope ; and when peace was restored by the Treaty of Tilsit, it seemed as if Germany might for a time live quietly under the aegis of the Emperor whom he resolutely declined to regard as an enemy or a barbarian. He had never loved Prussia, and he shed no tears over her overthrow. Moreover, the fascination of a daemonic figure, ' beyond good and evil,' impersonal as fire or water and irresistible as fate, laid its spell on him and blinded him to everything but the splendour of creative genius.

At the Erfurt Congress in 1808 Napoleon was the central figure of a dazzling throng, which included not only the Tsar but more than forty kings, princes and dukes. He had brought Talma and his troupe from Paris, and it was his wish to appear as the ruler of the most civilised no less than of the most powerful country in the world. Karl August summoned the most distinguished of his subjects to the rendezvous, and on October 2 the two greatest men in the world met face to face. When the poet entered the room, Napoleon—

as a rule the least impressionable of men—exclaimed :
' Vous êtes un homme ! ' The conversation turned on
drama and on *Werther*, which the Emperor took with
him on his campaigns and knew almost by heart, and
ended with questions on his personal affairs and his
relations to the Ducal family. Goethe was treated
throughout as an equal, and on his leaving the room the
Emperor ejaculated : ' Voilà un homme ! ' It was the
most memorable day in his life, and every detail of the
audience combined to heighten its effect. The value of
the Emperor's admiration for *Werther* was enhanced by
his criticisms, which struck the author as both penetrating and just. ' I gladly confess,' he wrote to Cotta,
' that nothing higher or more gratifying could occur in
my life than thus to stand before the Emperor. Of the
great ones of the earth I can truly say that no one had
received me in such a manner—I mean on terms of such
confidential equality.'

Four days later Napoleon visited Weimar, and again
conversed with Goethe at the ball which followed the
performance of Voltaire's *La Mort de César*. The poet
was exhorted to write a tragedy on the same theme which
would prove that the murder of Caesar was a blunder.
Tacitus was condemned for his partisanship and Shake-
speare for mixing comedy with tragedy. Goethe was
invited to Paris, where he was assured that he would
widen his outlook and find rich material for his craft.
The Emperor also conferred the Cross of the newly-
founded Legion of Honour on Goethe and the aged
Wieland. The Man of Destiny was in a gracious mood,
for fortune had smiled on him. Having decided to
spare the dynasty, he proceeded to win its good-will by
exempting the Duchy from providing troops for Spain,
and by idemnifying the town of Jena for the damage
wrought by the battle.

The Emperor's pressing invitation—' je l'exige de
vous '—to settle in Paris occupied Goethe's thoughts
for a time, and led to inquiries as to the practical questions involved in such a step. His worship of Napoleon

strengthened his life-long desire to see ' das ungeheure Paris,' and the provincialism of Weimar lay heavy on him. The project was dropped, though not from any doubt as to the permanence of his favour. Indeed Goethe's fidelity to his hero survived all the vicissitudes of fortune, and he defiantly continued to wear the Legion of Honour after the French yoke had been broken. He never pretended to approve all the Emperor's actions and he sympathised with his brother Louis, King of Holland, whom he met at Karlsbad and whose ' goodness ' he warmly admired ; yet he never lost the conviction that Napoleon was such a unique, daemonic, almost supernatural genius that he could not be weighed in the scales of ordinary humanity.

Though he constantly talked and wrote of Napoleon and enjoyed the society of the French Minister, Baron de St. Aignan, it was not till 1812 that he rendered poetical homage to the lord of the world. The presence of Marie Louise in Karlsbad during her annual sojourn inspired the poem : *An Ihro der Kaiserin von Frankreich Majestät*. The structure was suggested by the firmament, where Jupiter and Venus were close together in May. The Emperor is Jupiter, the Empress Venus, and the French Revolution night. Jupiter-Napoleon terminates the confusion, banishes the darkness and rules by power and wisdom :

> Worüber trüb Jahrhunderte gesonnen,
> Er übersieht's in hellstem Geisteslicht ;
> Das Kleinliche ist alles weggeronnen,
> Nur Meer und Erde haben hier Gewicht.
> Ist jenem erst das Ufer abgewonnen,
> Dass sich daran die stolze Woge bricht,
> So tritt durch weisen Schluss, durch Machtgefechte
> Das feste Land in alle seine Rechte.

The dynasty, he adds, is established by the birth of an heir, and the poem ends with the hope that the Emperor, ' der alles wollen kann,' may will peace.

The French yoke in the Duchy was light, and in Goethe's view it was neither necessary nor possible to overthrow it ; but the *débâcle* in Russia gave North-German patriots their chance. The poet, however, stubbornly declined to believe that the end was near, and cynically observed that the burning of Moscow was nothing to him. As the Emperor passed through Weimar on his way home, he inquired about Goethe, and sent a direct greeting from Erfurt. The French garrison surrendered to a body of Russians and Prussians a few days after he had left his home, taking some valuables with him and burying others. On his way to Teplitz, where he hoped to escape from the blinding storm of war, he broke the journey at Dresden, where he witnessed the entry of Frederick William III and the Tsar. There Arndt found him ' much depressed, with neither joy nor hope in the changed condition of affairs.' When the elder Körner and his greater son gave vent to their enthusiasm, he uttered his second famous prophecy : ' The man is too great for you ; you may shake your chains, but you will not break them.'

On his return home, three months later, Dresden was French again, and Napoleon's birthday was cele-brated by illuminations and processions. No wonder that at this moment he bet a gold ducat that the French would not be driven beyond the Rhine. The bet was lost, for in October the slaughter of Leipzig made Germany free. French troops had marched through Weimar to the battlefield, and after the titanic conflict the little capital once again witnessed a flight from the striken field. In 1806 the Germans were pursued by the victorious French ; in 1813 the French were chased by the triumphant Allies. Once again the town was filled with wounded men, and once again officers were billeted in Goethe's house ; but his inconveniences were minimised by the friendly intervention of Metternich. ' It is uplifting,' he wrote, ' to obtain an insight into the views of such men as he who directs the stupendous whole, by the smallest fraction of which the rest of us feel oppressed and indeed overwhelmed.'

Goethe watched the march of events with heavy

heart.   If the French triumphed their revenge would be
terrible ; if they were beaten, arrogant Prussia and
savage Russia would be supreme.   He, at any rate,
would not lift a finger to aid the national cause.   When
Karl August, emerging from his neutrality, appealed for
volunteers, August Goethe desired to serve ; but the
father interposed on the ground that his son was acting
as his secretary and could not be spared.   During these
weeks of national exaltation he found himself a lonely
man wherever he went, and when Fouqué recited some
patriotic verses at the house of Johanna Schopenhauer
he refrained from joining in the applause.   Yet when
the Allies had entered Paris in the spring of 1814 and
Napoleon was caged in Elba, Iffland invited him to
contribute to the festivities which were to welcome the
allied sovereigns to Berlin.   He replied that he was busy
with another theatrical piece, and that a month was too
short ; but a day or two later he wrote that an idea had
occurred to him, and he thanked the Director of the
Berlin Theatre for enabling him to tell the German
people how he had sympathised with its joys and sorrows.
His heart, however, was not in his work, and *Des
Epimenides Erwachen*, like Gerhart Hauptmann's *Festspiel*
in 1913, was deemed unworthy both of the occasion and
the author.   Of the tumultuous emotions of the War
of Liberation there was not a trace, and indeed no one
could tell who Epimenides was intended to be.   The
concluding chorus, however, was clear enough, and
embodied the poet's longing that now at last his countrymen would find peace :

> So rissen wir uns rings herum
> Von fremden Banden los.
> Nun sind wir Deutsche wiederum,
> Nun sind wir wieder gross.

Six years later Goethe paid his last homage to the hero
by translating Manzoni's fine ode *Il Cinque Maggio*.
    When the long peace of the Restoration had de-
scended on tired Europe, Goethe's thoughts constantly

turned to Napoleon. On one occasion Eckermann observed that the poet had been reproached for not taking up arms at that great time. ' How could I take up arms without hatred ? ' rejoined the old man. ' And how could I hate without youth ? I have never shammed. I have never given utterance to what I have not experienced. I have only composed love-songs when I have loved. How could I write songs of hate without hatred ? And between ourselves I did not hate the French, though I thanked God when we were free of them. How could I, to whom culture and barbarism are alone of importance, hate a nation which is among the most cultivated on earth, and to which I owe so great a part of my own possessions ? There is a stage where national hatred vanishes altogether, and where one stands to a certain extent above the nations, and feels the weal or woe of a neighbouring people as if it were one's own.' It is the voice of the last and greatest of the cosmopolitans whose spiritual home was in the eighteenth century. In his own way and in his own mind Goethe, too, was a patriot ; but patriotism was to him the life-long endeavour to enrich German culture and to set it in the forefront of the march of civilisation.

IV

The last chapter in the story of Goethe's political contacts is a time of relative tranquillity. Europe desired and required to recover breath after the exhausting struggle ; revolutionary doctrines were discredited, and a period of quiet growth, such as the poet loved, seemed at hand. Moreover, Weimar had emerged from the fiery ordeal not only unscathed but enlarged. The Duchy had doubled its territory, Karl August had become a Grand Duke, and his prestige stood higher than ever. Goethe might well have looked forward to a tranquil eventide, untroubled by wars, invasions and revolts.

On the disappearance of the Holy Roman Empire

and the collapse of the short-lived Rheinbund, a new political framework was provided by the Deutscher Bund, a loose federation of forty states with its Diet in permanent session at Frankfurt. The Bund was a decided improvement on the decrepit Holy Roman Empire ; but it lacked power and prestige, and the control of affairs remained in the hands of its component units. Generous hopes had been aroused and encouraged during the exaltations and agonies of the War of Liberation ; but when victory was achieved the two strongest members, the King of Prussia and the Emperor of Austria, determined to continue the system of autocracy in which they had been bred, and Goethe was the last man to blame them for their resolve.

The ' ideas of 1789 ' had been temporarily discredited by the Terror and the revolutionary wars ; but the doctrine of political self-determination had been scotched, not killed, and the celebrated article XIII of the Constitution of the Bund provided that every member of the confederation should introduce a constitution with assemblies of Estates. The South German rulers proceeded to grant constitutions, Karl August himself courageously leading the way in 1816 by reviving and expanding the provisions of the Constitution which he had granted in 1809. The Privy Council was succeeded by a Ministry of which Goethe became the head. Yet the rise in his worldly fortunes, combined with an increase in his salary, brought him no joy ; for in his heart he disapproved his master's concessions, which included election by ballot of representatives to all Estates, and liberty of the Press. His apprehensions of the latter were quickly confirmed by the journals which sprang up like mushrooms throughout the Duchy, and to which both the teachers and students of Jena made outspoken contributions. It was his wish to suppress the more radical organs, but the Grand Duke loyally upheld the privileges which he had granted. It was a painful duty for the Prime Minister to stand at the right hand of his master in 1816 when the dignitaries paid homage for the Constitution. Still more distressing was the discovery that as President of the Commission for Art and Science he was obliged to report to the Landtag. He flatly declined to make a statement on his expenditure, and it required the tactful intervention of the Grand Duchess to induce the Landtag in this instance to waive its rights.

The Wartburg festival intensified Goethe's conviction that his master had embarked on the wrong track. Young Germany had combined in the Burschenschaften to work for unity and self-government, and on October 18, 1817, the German Burschen met at the Wartburg at the invitation of the Jena branch to commemorate the tercentenary of the Reformation and the fourth anniversary of the battle of Leipzig. The festival was organised with the approval of the Government, and the speeches were harmless enough, but the proceedings ended with a bonfire of reactionary writings, among them those of Kotzebue. Two years later, when the dramatist, who had become an agent of Russia, was murdered at Mannheim by the student Sand, Metternich exploited the panic to issue the Karlsbad Decrees, which muzzled not only the Press but the Universities. The arch-reactionary, who throttled the political life of Germany for a generation, held Karl August in large measure responsible for the dangerous spirit of the German youth ; and Goethe, who visited him at Karlsbad, shared his opinion. For the remaining thirteen years of his life the poet lived in a country which possessed scarcely more freedom than it had enjoyed in his youth.

Goethe grew up in the eighteenth century, when the ruling conceptions of the élite were benevolent autocracy and cultured individualism ; and he remained to the end a child of his age. He was a stranger in the new century, whose ideals of democracy and nationality were to change the face of the world. Democracy meant to him the enthronement of inexperienced mediocrity, for he lacked the belief in the instinctive wisdom of the people which is the kernel of the democratic faith. Nationality recalled to him visions of the French on the Rhine and the Wars of Liberation, with their tumultuous emotions which he never shared. Throughout life he looked down on the struggling masses as from the housetops, wishing them well, but utterly unconvinced of their capacity to work out their own salvation. The world swings rapidly forward, and few of us can keep pace with all its moods and tenses. Goethe's services to his countrymen and to mankind were manifold enough to dispense with the title of political prophet and pioneer.

GERMANY'S DEBT TO THE FRENCH REVOLUTION.[1]

DURING the years preceding the French Revolution Germany presented a pathetic spectacle of political decrepitude. The Holy Roman Empire was afflicted with creeping paralysis, and Justus Möser truthfully remarked that no Curtius would leap into the abyss for the preservation of the Imperial system. Germany, cried Friedrich Karl Moser in the bitterness of his heart, is a great but despised people. Every nation, he added, had a governing principle. In England it was liberty, in Holland trade, in France the honour of the King, while in Germany it was obedience. Pamphleteers lamented the anæmia of the Fatherland, but not one of them could suggest a remedy. The political framework of central Europe was the consecration of anarchy, and the country was racked by an incurable particularism. Few competent observers believed that it could be reformed, and an increasing number turned their eyes to Prussia as to a possible saviour. The Fürstenbund, or League of Princes, formed by Frederick the Great to resist Hapsburg ambitions, was welcomed in certain quarters as the dawn of a better age. Johannes Müller hailed it as a bulwark against the world-domination of the Emperor, a defence of the rights of every member of the Empire, and a beneficent revolution from above ; and when it fell to pieces on the death of its founder he uttered a cry of despair. ' Without law or justice,

[1] For a full discussion of the subject here briefly surveyed, see Gooch, *Germany and the French Revolution*.

without security against capricious burdens, uncertain
of maintaining our children, our liberties, our rights or
our lives for a single day, the helpless prey of superior
power, without national feeling—that is our *status quo.*
I cannot understand how we Germans have lost the
courage and intelligence to advance from hoary pedan-
tries to an effective Imperial constitution, to a common
patriotism, so that we could at length say, We are a nation.'
' It is a rickety house,' echoed Thugut from Vienna ;
' one must either leave it alone or pull it down and build
another.'   It was, indeed, past mending, and only waited
for an order of demolition.

No less urgent was the need of reform in the majority
of the units which composed the Empire.   While Germany could boast of a certain number of rulers of conscience and capacity, such as Karl August of Weimar
and Karl Friedrich of Baden, the Duke of Brunswick
and the Duke of Gotha, nowhere in Europe was absolutism more repulsive than in the little Courts where
Frederick's doctrine of service had never penetrated,
where mistresses ruled supreme, where venality placed
the unfittest in office, and where reckless ostentation
stood out in glaring contrast to the poverty of the people.
' The peasant,' wrote a satirist grimly, ' is like a sack
of meal.   When emptied there is still some dust in it ;
it only needs to be beaten.'   For the most part the
victims suffered in silence ; but discontent found powerful interpreters in Moser and Schlözer, Schubart and
Weckerlin, while the revolt of the American Colonies
and the establishment of a democratic republic free from
courts and armies, feudalism and poverty, was at once
a warning to rulers that there was a limit to tyranny
and an inspiration to downtrodden peoples all over
the world.   At the same time the intellectual revival
which had given birth to the *Aufklärung* or Enlightenment began to produce its effect on the political plane.
During the generation of peace which followed the
Seven Years' War Germany learned to read, to think
and to ask questions.   The critical spirit, once aroused,

spread rapidly, finding nourishment in the rank evils which overspread the land. In an age of obscurantism and repression every leader of thought was on the side of the Opposition. ' In my youth,' wrote Goethe in 1790, ' it hardly occurred to anybody to envy the privileged class or to grudge them their privileges ; but knights, robbers, an honest Tiers État and an infamous nobility—such are the ingredients of our novels and plays during the last ten years.' The poet was thinking above all of Schiller, whose passionate denunciations of tyranny moved his audiences to frenzied enthusiasm.

Thus the lethargy which had weighed on Germany in the first half of the eighteenth century was passing rapidly away. The personality and victories of Frederick the Great, the object-lesson of the American War, the leaven of Voltaire, Rousseau and Montesquieu, the challenge of the *Aufklärung*, the radicalism of the dramatists, the barbed arrows of the journalists,—these crowding and converging influences and experiences set the mind of the nation in a ferment. To borrow the words of Kant in 1784, it was not an enlightened age but an age in process of enlightenment. Change was in the air, and the fragility of traditional institutions and ideas was widely recognised. In Germany as in France prophetic voices gave warning of the wrath to come, and skilled observers felt the earth trembling beneath their feet. On the eve of the Revolution the mass of the population was poor, ignorant, ill governed, discontented and helpless ; and when the Rights of Man were proclaimed from the banks of the Seine the German people, fast bound in the fetters of feudalism and autocracy, was ready to welcome the virile message as a gospel of deliverance.

The opening scenes of the French Revolution were watched with delight by most of the leaders of German opinion. The Declaration of the Rights of Man put into words the muffled aspirations of the masses all over Europe, and gave to the humble and disinherited a new sense of human dignity. When France in trumpet tones decreed the downfall of feudalism, proclaimed the

equality of burdens, and declared every man possessed
of certain inalienable rights, generous hearts in Germany, no less than in England, were thrilled by the
warmth and glory of the sunrise.   Johannes Müller, the
historian of Switzerland's struggles for freedom, pronounced the destruction of the Bastille the happiest
event since the birth of Christ.   Many a Sultan in the
Empire, he hoped, would tremble and many an oligarchy
would learn that there were limits to human endurance.
Klopstock, the Nestor of German literature, regretted
that he had not a hundred voices to celebrate the birth
of liberty.   It is glorious, cried Georg Forster, to see
what philosophy has ripened in the brain and realised
in the State.   The philosophic Herder proclaimed the
Revolution the most important movement in the life
of mankind since the Reformation, and welcomed it as
a no less decisive step towards human freedom.   'The
spirit of the time is strong within me,' exclaimed Gentz,
the most brilliant of Prussian publicists.   'I am young,
and the universal striving for freedom arouses my
warmest sympathy.   I should regard the shipwreck of
this movement as one of the greatest disasters that ever
befell mankind.   It would be felt that men were happy
only as slaves, and every tyrant, great and small, would
revenge himself for the fright the French nation had
given him.'   'You cannot be more convinced than I,'
wrote Wieland in an Open Letter to the French reformers,
'that your nation was wrong to bear such misgovern-
ment so long ;   that every people has an indefeasible
right to as much liberty as can co-exist with order ;   that
the person and property of every citizen must be secured
against the caprices of power, and that each must be
taxed in proportion to his wealth.'

In the crowded salons of Henriette Herz and Rahel
Levin the intellectual *élite* of the Prussian capital applauded the moving drama on the Seine.   Cosmopolitan
Hamburg and tolerant Brunswick welcomed the dawning
age of reason with enthusiasm ;   and in distant Königsberg the greatest of German thinkers made no secret

of his joy. Opinion was more critical in Hanover, where Brandes and Rehberg asserted the superior virtues of the British Constitution and exalted Burke above Rousseau ; while, in Weimar, Goethe and Schiller, though in no way blind to the sins of the *Ancien Régime*, lamented that the work of reform had fallen into the hands of the multitude and that the frail bark of culture was in danger of shipwreck in the revolutionary rapids. A more balanced view was advanced by Humboldt, who, while foretelling a short life for the new Constitution, maintained that the benefits of the great upheaval would be felt beyond the frontiers of France rather than in the land of its birth. Many of the most vociferous of its admirers, led by Klopstock and Gentz, changed their note when the reform movement degenerated into murder and anarchy ; but others, like Kant and Herder, refused to allow even the Terror to blind them to the enduring value of its work for humanity.

The favourable impression made by ' French ideas ' at the outset was enhanced by the appearance of the first batches of refugees on the Rhine. ' One must distinguish between the voluntary and compulsory emigrations,' wrote Madame de Stael. ' After the fall of the monarchy we all emigrated.' This distinction between ' the emigration of pride ' and ' the emigration of necessity ' was fully appreciated in the frontier lands in which the newcomers sought temporary shelter from the storm. Though they were kindly welcomed by the ecclesiastical Electors and provided with every luxury, the citizens of Coblenz and Mainz watched their arrogance, their extravagance and their immoralities with indignation, Each haughty aristocrat seemed a fresh argument for the necessity and the utility of the Revolution ; and even those who cared nothing for the Rights of Man sympathised with a nation which had been subject to such unworthy masters. A brief experience of their character and methods aroused no less anger and contempt in the breasts of the Emperor Leopold and Kaunitz than among the easy-going bourgeois of the

Rhineland.   The detestation they provoked was intensified by the cruel and disparaging tone in which many of
their leaders referred to the sovereigns whom they had
deserted.   ' Till his death,' writes Ernest Daudet, the
historian of the *Émigration*, with just severity, ' Louis
XVI had no worse enemies than the Émigrés, who were
the principal authors of his troubles.   The Princes were
disobedient to their brother and disloyal to their country.'
The result of their intransigence was clearly foretold by
Mirabeau.   ' By threatening us with the return of
despotism,' he cried bitterly in 1790, ' they will drag us
willy-nilly to a republic.'

     In his dispassionate work on the causes of the war
of 1792, Ranke argued that a conflict between the new
France and the old Europe was virtually inevitable ; to
which Sybel replied that its outbreak was solely due to
the chauvinism of Brissot and his fellow Girondins, who
believed that war would strengthen the position of their
party.   If the former explanation was too vague, the
latter was too narrow.   The antagonism between the
doctrinaire radicalism of the French reformers and
the unimaginative traditionalism of the Great Powers
rendered a conflict probable enough ; but hostilities need
not have broken out but for the two concrete problems
of the abolition of feudal rights in Alsace and the gathering of armed Émigrés in the cities of the Rhineland.
In the first case the German princes had a legitimate
grievance, in the second the French Government ; and
there were plenty of men in Paris, Berlin and Vienna
who were eager to fan the smouldering embers into a
flame.   The first shot was fired by France ; and after a
decade of desperate struggle, the victorious Republic
pushed its frontier to the Rhine and established itself as
the most formidable military Power in Europe.   ' I
observe that minds are fermenting in that Germany
of yours,' wrote Mirabeau to Mauvillon at the end of
1789.   ' If the spark falls on combustible material, it
will be a fire of charcoal not straw.   Though perhaps
more advanced in education, you are not so mature as

we, because your emotions are rooted in the head ; and since your brains are petrified with slavery, the explosion will come with you much later than with us.' The great tribune's prophecy proved correct ; for the main effects of the Revolution were manifested in Germany some years after the acute crisis in France was past.

The combined influence of the ideas of 1789 and of the Great War which followed their proclamation produced concrete results in Germany of incalculable importance—one of a negative, others of a positive character. The first was destruction of the political framework of the country. The patent weakness of the Empire in the war, the desertion of Prussia and the North at the height of the struggle, and the collapse of the ecclesiastical Electorates, left no attentive observer in doubt that the old firm was in liquidation. No ambitious and aggressive State could have wished for a neighbour less fitted by its traditions and institutions to parry the thrust of its conquering sword. Well might Napoleon write to the Directory from Rastadt, ' If the Germanic Body did not exist, we should have to create it expressly for our own convenience.'

When the left bank of the Rhine was annexed to the French Republic, Görres wrote his celebrated obituary. ' On December 30, 1797, at three in the afternoon, the Holy Roman Empire, supported by the Sacraments, passed away peacefully at Regensburg at the age of 955, in consequence of senile debility and an apoplectic stroke. The deceased was born at Verdun in the year 842, and educated at the court of Charles the Simple and his successors. The young prince was taught piety by the Popes, who canonised him in his lifetime. But his tendency to a sedentary life, combined with zeal for religion, undermined his health. His head became visibly weaker, till at last he went mad in the Crusades. Frequent bleedings and careful diet restored him ; but, reduced to a shadow, the invalid tottered through the centuries till violent hemorrhage occurred in the Thirty Years' War. Hardly had he recovered when the French

arrived and a stroke put an end to his sufferings.   He
kept himself unstained by the *Aufklärung*, and bequeathed
the left bank of the Rhine to the French Republic.'
Görres was right.   The Empire was not buried till
1806 ; but it was slain by the Revolution.   It perished
unwept, unhonoured and unsung ; and its ghost had to
be laid before Germany could be reborn.

Secularisation was in the air before 1789 ; and,
when the Republican armies reached the Rhine, the
princes whose interests were affected sought compensation for their losses on the right bank.   When rude
hands were laid on the ark of the covenant they quickly
found imitators.   By the Recess of 1803 the ecclesiastical
Electorates and principalities were swept away ;   the
Free Cities, with the exception of Hamburg, Bremen,
Lubeck, Frankfurt, Nürnberg and Augsburg, disappeared ;   and the old organisation of the Circles was
broken in pieces.   In the College of Princes the Protestants obtained a majority ;   and power passed from
south to north, from the Austrian to the Prussian camp.
The Hapsburg ascendancy was overthrown by the eviction of the ecclesiastics and by the aggrandisement of
Bavaria, Baden, Württemberg and Hesse.   ' Few among
the great transformations of modern history,' declares
Treitschke with truth, ' seem so detestable, so base and
so mean as this Princes' Revolution.   Not a glimmer of
a bold idea, not a spark of noble passion illuminated
the colossal breach of public law.   And yet the overthrow was a great necessity.   All that was buried was
already dead.   The ancient forms of the State vanished
in an instant, as if they had been swallowed up in the
earth.'

The Princes' Revolution left the historic structure
little more than a ruin, and it was clear that its respite
would be brief.   A year later, when the First Consul
crowned himself in Notre Dame, the Hapsburg monarch
assumed the title of Emperor of Austria.   In 1805 the
cannon of Austerlitz battered down what remained of the
crumbling walls and towers of the Holy Roman Empire.

In the following summer the curtain was rung down on a thousand years of German history. The Holy Roman Empire, with the Emperor, the Electors, the Diet, the Court of Appeal, the Ecclesiastical Princes, the Imperial Knights and Free Cities, collapsed like a house of cards at the touch of Napoleon's spear. When the German Bund emerged from the Congress of Vienna, there were only forty-one States in place of the motley multitude which had composed the Empire. The outward transformation of Germany was as wholesome and almost as rapid as that of France ; and it was accomplished without the savagery and sufferings which disgraced the noble experiment of 1789. On the other hand, the simplification of political geography brought gain rather to the princes than to the nation ; for Germany as a whole secured neither unity, liberty nor strength.

The second momentous result of the Revolution was the renaissance of Prussia ; but it was not till the *débâcle* of 1806 that her slow-witted ruler began to realise that he must take a lesson from his terrible neighbour. ' The Prussian Monarchy,' declared Mirabeau, ' is so constituted that it could not cope with any calamity ' ; and the calamity had now arrived. The work of Stein and Hardenberg was rendered possible as well as urgent by Napoleon's thunderbolts ; but the ideas to which they gave practical shape were in large measure those of 1789. The counsellors of Frederick William II and his successor were men like Mencken, Lombard and Beyme, who academically desired the application of French principles in diluted form ; and young Custine pronounced Struensee, the Minister of Finance, as much a partisan of the French Revolution as a Prussian Minister could be. But they were not statesmen of the first rank, and they lacked the resolution to carry out the changes which they knew to be necessary. The hour of reform only arrived when the logic of the stricken field had revealed the need of building from the depths, and when men of ability and determination received the more or less reluctant assent of the monarch to carry out some of the most essential tasks.

Republican and Imperial France had shown how to develop and apply the latent strength and capacity of a nation ; and the grandeur of her achievement impressed even those who suffered from her ringing blows. The regenerators of Prussia, whether Prussians or not, shared the conviction that the supreme need of the time was to revive the courage and mobilise the resources of the nation by inviting it to share in the burdens, the privileges and the responsibilities of government. ' The military as well as the political chiefs,' writes the French historian Cavaignac with patriotic pride, ' were penetrated by the example of the Revolution, imbued with its spirit, convinced that Prussia and Germany could only find salvation by following the paths it had opened.' This was recognised as frankly by Stein and Niebuhr, by Scharnhorst and Gneisenau, who hated it, as by the eclectic Hardenberg and by Schön, the radical *doctrinaire*.

The Revolution had been saddled and bridled before Stein was called, in middle life, to play a commanding part on the Prussian stage ; but its influence on his reforming ideas and achievements is indubitable. After his appointment as Minister, shortly before the battle of Jena, he drew up a memorandum comparing the State of his adoption to a machine which only functions properly when controlled by a superman, and demanding a limited monarchy. The memorandum was seen by the Queen, but was considered too outspoken for the eyes of the King. Of greater importance was the ' Nassau Programme,' written in Stein's ancestral home on the eve of his appointment as First Minister. ' If the nation is to be uplifted,' he declared, ' the submerged part must be given liberty, independence, property and the protection of the laws.' He agrees with the French reformers with regard to the emancipation of the peasants, the liberation of industry, the equalisation of taxes and the abolition of patrimonial jurisdiction. ' Here is no catalogue of the Rights of Man,' comments his admiring biographer

Lehmann ; ' but the emphatic demand for the right of a nation to administer itself rules out the patriarchal system of old Prussia and implicitly contains the whole charter of citizenship.' Stein's historic Ministry was cut short before he had time to carry out more than a fraction of the Nassau Programme ; but the emancipation of the peasants and the grant of municipal self-government stand out as everlasting monuments of his brief rule. Emancipation owed as much to Schön, who had drunk deeply at French springs, as self-government to Frey, who had diligently studied the French decree of 1789 on municipalities.

' What was it,' asks Lehmann, ' that attracted these thoroughly German minds in Königsberg to the revolutionary legislation of France, which they only approved with large reservations ? The answer is that they desired to attain for their country the position of power which those laws had secured for France.' Reform in the direction of equality was in the air ; and Stein and his colleagues were merely the agents of a change rendered inevitable by the ferment of the Revolution. As the abstract ideas of 1789 appealed to the writers and thinkers of Germany in the decade of revolution, their concrete results converted conservative German statesmen in search of a policy in the opening years of the nineteenth century. The sensational returns secured by France by every approximation towards equality and by every release of individual aptitudes were writ large on the map of Europe ; and every statesmanlike brain in Prussia grasped the fact that, if their nation was to live and grow, it must learn wisdom from its conquerors.

The new spirit of reforming zeal was passionately denounced by Marwitz, the spokesman of the impenitent Junkers who looked back to the autocracy and feudalism of the Frederician system as to the golden age. ' Stein,' he complains, ' brought the Revolution into our country. He collected a gang of ideologues, drones and chatterers about him, and began revolutionising the Fatherland, inaugurating the war of the landless against property, of industry against agriculture, of crass materialism against the divine order. He inaugurated the so-called regeneration of the Prussian State with laws based on the principles of Rousseau and Montesquieu. The ideologues, from the Garonne to the Niemen, hailed the Emancipation Edict with a hymn of praise.'

The impeachment has been adopted and confirmed with patriotic pride by a long series of French historians. ' It needed half a century to establish throughout Germany the social principles born of the French Revolution,' writes Doniol in his work on the Revolution and Feudalism. ' Finally they took possession even of the most recalcitrant of the States. There was no longer room in people's minds for other laws than those fitted to endow both the people and the land with the independence which the French Revolution had made the indispensable condition of social vitality. Prussia led the way. Stein's Edict of 1807 was the Prussian Fourth of August.' ' France did more than conquer Europe,' echoes Sorel ; ' she converted her. The French won over to their ideas the very nations which revolted against their domination. The princes most eagerly bent on penning-in the Revolution saw it, on returning from their crusade, sprouting in the soil of their own estates which had been fertilised by the blood of French soldiers.' Cavaignac's massive volumes, *La Formation de la Prusse Contemporaine*, are one long plea for the recognition of French influences on the transformation and modernisation of the Hohenzollern State. Stein's debt to France has been contested in Ernst von Meier's elaborate treatise on Prussia and the French Revolution ; but Lehmann, whose biography called forth the protest of the Hanoverian jurist, never suggested that France was more than one source of his hero's inspiration or that he made uncritical use of foreign models. ' He never surrendered himself, says Lehmann, to the ideas of 1789. His desire was to modify them and to combine them with the inherited conditions of Prussian and Protestant ideals.'

The political derivation of Hardenberg gives rise to

no such controversy. 'While Stein swam against the stream of the time,' writes Meier, ' Hardenberg allowed himself to be borne along with it. He was an adherent of the French Revolution, and he desired to imitate it.' An enemy alike of autocracy and democracy, he greeted the Revolution and many of its early measures as making for the limited monarchy of his dreams. France travelled too far and too fast for a liberal conservative who abhorred violence ; but he never for a moment doubted that a new era had dawned, and that the task of statesmanship was to apply the lessons of the cataclysm. In a memorial written in 1807 at the King's request, he declared that the dominant principle of government should be the application of the ideas of the French Revolution to Prussia ; for such was their power that any State which rejected them would either collapse or be forced to accept them. There must be a revolution in the good sense, he argued—a revolution from above, in which the wisdom of the Government would foster the ennobling of humanity. The form most suited to the spirit of the age would be a combination of democratic principles with monarchical rule. A government must work in harmony with the scheme of Providence, and should not shrink from the principal demand of the age, namely the utmost possible liberty and equality. He prescribed the same medicine for the State when he assumed power in 1810. 'Your Majesty, we must do from above what the French have done from below.'

He was as good as his word. He completed the creation of a free peasantry begun by Stein, and carried forward the reform of the central and local administration ; and it was not his fault that Prussia had to wait for a constitution till 1848. Like Stein, he was denounced by Marwitz and the Junkers as a leveller ; and from their narrow standpoint they were right, for he had grasped the force latent in the conception of social equality. Throughout Europe a truceless conflict was in progress between the *Ancien Régime* and the ideas of 1789 ; and when a statesman decided to break with feudalism, he was compelled to study and to some extent to adopt French methods. ' Hardenberg's work,' testifies Cavaignac, ' is the most indubitable testimony to the action of the French Revolution on European society.' A mind so receptive to new influences and yet so firmly anchored in historic realities was of infinite value in the critical period following the battle of Jena ; and Ranke, who edited his papers, justly declared that no statesman had engraved his name more deeply on the brazen tablets of Prussian history.

The lessons of the French Revolution were taken to heart by the reforming soldiers of Prussia no less than by the reforming civilians. The powerful intellect of Scharnhorst focussed on national strength, and he complained that the Declaration of the Rights of Man dealt only with the rights of individuals, not with those of the State ; but he recognised that the upper classes were as a rule too selfish and too stupid to make concessions, and he declared that things could not go on as they were. In a pregnant dissertation on the French War, written in 1797, he argued that the evil fortune of the Allies was due not to accidents or details but to much deeper causes. The first of these was ignorance of the strength of the foe, due to the false reports of the Émigrés, who led the Powers to believe that the Revolution was the work of a small minority. The second reason was the lack of stomach for the fight. ' When the French Revolution began, a large number of the noblest minds were fired by the ideal of a more perfect and more beneficent government, especially among young men of lively imagination with a generous feeling for right and for the sufferings of the less fortunate class. France employed all her material and moral resources, while the Allies only utilised a portion of their strength and were sadly lacking in *moral*.' The main reasons for the loss of the first round of the match between revolutionary France and feudal Europe were thus to be sought on the moral and political rather than on the material plane. Every citizen of the Republic had been prepared for any sacrifice

to defend his territory and his independence ; and necessity generated a marvellous energy alike in the Government, the army and the nation. If the Powers were to
triumph, they would have to penetrate the secret of
national determination which had carried France through
unprecedented trials and dangers.

Though Gneisenau, like Scharnhorst, cared more for
order than liberty and more for obedience than self-
realisation, he drew the same lesson as his political and
military colleagues from the crowning event of his time.
' One cause above all has raised France to this pinnacle
of greatness,' he wrote after Jena in memorable words.
' The Revolution awakened all her powers and gave to
every individual a suitable field for his activity. What
infinite aptitudes slumber in the bosom of a nation !
In the breast of thousands resides real genius. Why do
not the Courts take steps to open up a career to it wherever
it is found, to encourage talents and virtues whatever the
rank ? Why did they not seize this opportunity to
multiply their powers a thousandfold, and to open to the
simple bourgeois the Arc de Triomphe through which
only the noble can now pass ? The new era requires
more than old names, titles and parchments. The
Revolution has set the whole strength of a nation in
motion, and by the equalisation of the different classes
and the equal taxation of property converted the living
strength of men and the dead strength of resources into
a productive capital, and thereby upset the old relations
of States and the old equilibrium. If other States desire
to restore this equilibrium, they must employ the same
instruments. They must appropriate the results of the
Revolution, and then they will reap the double advantage
of being able to mobilise their whole national strength
against another Power, and of escaping the danger of
an upheaval which threatens them so long as they refuse
to obviate a violent change by a voluntary transformation.'
Here are the same ideas and almost the same phrases
as those we have met on the lips of Stein and Hardenberg.
Their programme was never carried out in its entirety ;

but the partial application of ' French ideas ' produced
the desired result in the Wars of Liberation, and enabled
Prussia to cast off the yoke of the tyrant with the resolute
passion of a united people.

While Prussia suffered more poignantly at the hands
of France than any other German State and looked back
with loathing on the mighty Emperor, the west and
south of Germany received a far more direct and permanent impress from the ideas and institutions imported
by the Revolution.   The three ecclesiastical Electorates,
which ought to have been the bulwark of the Empire,
collapsed at the first assault ; and what was known as
the Pfaffengasse or Parsons' Lane was ruled by France
for twenty years.   The Republic of Mainz, established
by Custine in the autumn of 1792, only lived till the
recapture of the city in the following summer ; but the
experiment created extraordinary interest, and the fate
of Georg Forster and Adam Lux, its deputies to Paris,
had thrown round it something of the halo of romance.
When the French armies again reached the Rhine in
1794, the Left Bank entered on a period of rapid change.
The invaders were never popular, for instead of liberty
and fraternity they brought crushing burdens and military rule, administrative corruption and anti-clerical
intolerance.   Their watchword ' War on the palaces,
peace to the cottages ' was a parrot's cry, and was dropped
when it had done its work.   The only disinterested
friend of German liberty among the soldiers and statesmen of the era of the Directory was Hoche, whose premature death left the Rhineland a prey to the vultures.
In burning words Görres denounced ' the heartless
and mindless men who are sent to govern us, adventurers
who are the scum of France.   Many of us believed that
the French had been transformed by the Revolution into
angels ; but the arrogance of the conquerors waxed day
by day, and there was no end to their extortions and
exactions.   Everything combined to create a universal
detestation of the French.   The cause was soon identified

with its representatives, and hatred was felt not only for
republicans but for republicanism and liberty. In my
belief the century for the introduction of democracy has
not yet dawned and will not dawn in a hurry. We say
with Vergniaud, We have deceived ourselves not in
liberty but in the hour. We believed we were in Rome,
but we found ourselves in Paris.' A mission to the
capital shortly before Brumaire convinced the high-
souled idealist that the agents of the Republic were no
worse than those who had sent them. He bitterly compared the Revolution to a balloon which had soared
majestically into the air and then exploded and sunk to
the earth in flames.

The anger, if not the disappointment, of Görres
was shared by his fellow-victims on the Left Bank.
Conscription was the first and the most detested of
the penalties of conquest. The importation of English
goods was prohibited, and the loss of the German market
was but partially balanced by the commercial current
directed towards France. The army of occupation lived
on the country, and the burden of taxes and requisitions
was increased by the dishonesty of unpaid and rapacious
officials. The shock to religious sentiment was particularly resented. The clergy lost their endowments
without receiving an indemnity from the State. Pil-
grimages and processions were forbidden, while the
republican Calendar, with its three Decades a month,
virtually suppressed Sunday. Under the fanatical Commissioner Lakanal the yoke became almost intolerable.
Churches were closed, houses were searched, and
incautious critics found themselves in prison.

Though the decade of republican rule inflicted
grievous hardships on the Rhineland, there were nevertheless substantial entries on the credit side of the balance-
sheet. On the outbreak of war the Left Bank had been
ruled by nine Archbishops and Bishops, two religious
Orders, seventy-six Princes and Counts, four Free
Cities and a host of Imperial Knights. Every one of
these rulers and systems of government had been swept

away by the broom of the war-god ; and the nobility, with few exceptions, had fled across the Rhine. Feudal dues and tithes, privileges and exemption from taxation were abolished. The sequestration of the lands of the dispossessed pointed to their sale in the near future. Liberty of industry was secured by the suppression of the gilds with their harassing rules and limitations, while French weights and measures and the decimal system gave a further impetus to trade. An efficient police guaranteed tolerable public security ; a uniform legal procedure took the place of the innumerable tribunals of spiritual and temporal lords ; and the mild criminal code of 1795 was applied. The gates of the ghetto at Bonn were thrown open, and the Protestants of Aachen and Cologne built their first churches.

A brighter day dawned in 1802 after the definite cession of the Left Bank by the Treaty of Lunéville. The office of Commissioner was abolished, and the country was henceforward governed as an integral part of France. The local assemblies and municipal councils were mere shadows, and there was as little liberty in the Rhineland as in the rest of Napoleon's dominions ; but the reconciliation with the Church was welcomed by pious inhabitants, and material progress was quickly registered. The property of the secular and ecclesiastical princes, the Émigrés, the Corporations and the Communes was now open to purchase by the peasants and burghers, who, in working for their own profit, rendered the soil more productive. The last traces of serfdom disappeared ; education was extended and systematised ; and the navigation of the Rhine was improved. The Code substituted uniform procedure and modern ideas for a chaos of outworn practices. Roads were constructed, fruit-trees planted, agriculture and stock-breeding encouraged. Under model prefects such as Jean Bon Saint-André and Lezay-Marnésia, the Left Bank experienced a period of tranquil advance after a decade of war, billetings, exploitations and assignats.

' In the relatively short period of twenty years,' writes

Sagnac, the latest French historian of the Rhineland, in a passage of eloquent pride, ' the French accomplished an immense work of which the Germans would never have dared to dream. The country was divided up into ninety-seven little States, jealous of one another and incapable of self-defence. It had remained feudal, and, being occupied by the petty interests of caste, was incapable of any comprehensive activity. It was called, not immediately but little by little and at the request of a large part of the inhabitants, to enter into a modern and centralised State, rich and powerful, and vitalised by economic liberty. To these weak and disunited peoples France gave what they needed most—protection and security. Having gone to war to liberate the peoples, not to enslave them, she brought all the free institutions which she had won in ten years of terrible strife. She abolished feudalism, liberated the soil, and transformed the peasant serfs into free proprietors. She sold to the burghers and the peasants the possessions of the late rulers and the lands of the Church and even a portion of the communal property, in order to multiply small freeholders and insure them a competence. She established civil liberty and equality. In these Germanic lands, so unfamiliar with equality of rights and with liberty, so respectful of ecclesiastical and noble castes, it was a veritable revolution. No more distinction between citizens ; no more religious intolerance ! Protestants and Jews found themselves on the same footing as the Catholics, who for centuries had governed the country in their own interest. The unity of laws was established. The Civil Code facilitated transactions from end to end of the Rhineland, and gave to the Rhinelanders the profound sentiment of the unity of their country and of their intimate union with France, who brought law and liberty in the folds of the tricolour.'

History thus seen through the invaders' spectacles overlooks not only the burdens imposed by an Emperor perpetually at war but the healthy dislike of civilised Europeans for alien rule. The dominant feeling of the

Rhineland was in favour of a return in due course to German rule, combined with the retention of the reforms introduced by the conquerors. No one ever dreamed of the restoration of the sway of the crozier and of the feudal order which had been swept into the dustbin by the revolutionary blast ; but absolutism had been unknown in the ecclesiastical Electorates, and the *Ancien Régime* had left no such bitter memories of oppression and humiliation as in France. Moreover, attachment to the Church had continued unbroken, and had been strengthened by the attacks upon its practices and beliefs. In a word, the Rhineland as a whole was neither Jacobin nor reactionary, neither nationalist nor anti-national ; and for this reason, though not immune from the fell visitation of war, it was spared the horrors of revolution and counter-revolution. When peace returned to the world in 1815, the Left Bank reverted to German allegiance without regret and without enthusiasm. The reforms which had been introduced into the mushroom principalities of Westphalia, Berg and Frankfurt were for the most part swept away on the fall of their creator ; but in the Rhineland, divided though it was between Prussia, Hesse-Darmstadt and Bavaria, twenty years of French occupation and assimilation left abiding traces. Friendly memories of the tricolour and legends of the Petit Caporal lingered on till they were swallowed up in the pride and glory of the German Empire ; and the Civil Code remained as a link with the past till it was superseded by the Imperial Code in the closing year of the nineteenth century.

While the western fringe of the Empire was linked to France before the Revolution by many ties, and almost completely detached from the intellectual currents beyond the Rhine, Bavaria had deliberately cut herself off from contact with the world outside her frontiers. The country defined by Frederick the Great as an earthly Paradise inhabited by animals had sunk into a material and spiritual decadence without parallel among the larger States of central Europe. When the French

Revolution burst upon the world the realm of the Wittelsbachs was rotten to the core. The Illuminati had been suppressed ; reaction and superstition reigned supreme ; and the later years of Karl Theodor, surrounded by his bastards, are among the darkest in Bavarian history. The Government's method of confronting the perils of the time was to tighten the censorship, to forbid the circulation of French newspapers, to bring education under stricter control, and to compel candidates for office to swear that they belonged to no secret association. The spiritless and ignorant people had sunk so low that for a few years longer these miserable expedients availed to stave off the inevitable change ; but, on the death of its degenerate ruler in 1799 and the accession of his cousin Max Joseph of Zweibrücken, ' French ideas ' flowed into the country like a torrent and carried away the ancient landmarks of Church and State.

Max Joseph, the last Elector and the first King of Bavaria, had been a colonel in the French army and lived with his regiment in Strassburg till the outbreak of the Revolution, when he migrated to Mannheim. To his easy-going nature rancorous hate was impossible, and he never lost his old affection for France. ' I was born there,' he remarked to the French *chargé d'affaires* on his accession, ' and I beg you to regard me as a Frenchman. Please inform the Directory that it has no truer friend than myself.' The British Minister in Munich promptly reported the atmospheric change at Court, and drew an unflattering portrait of the new ruler. ' The character of the present Elector is such, I fear, as offers little prospect of happiness to his subjects, the more so as he is surrounded by persons supposed to be devoted to the French Government, particularly a certain M. de Montgelas, who governs him. Fomenters of revolution remain unmolested here at a moment when many respectable but unfortunate Emigrés are persecuted and ill-treated. I have seen with pain the hordes of Jacobins with which this place swarms, and have in secret condemned the system by which they are tolerated.'

These conversations naturally reached the ears of the Elector, who showed himself decidedly chilling in the only audience that he granted, and revenged himself by asking for another Minister.

Montgelas, the chief of the ' Jacobins,' possessed the drive and ability which his weak and benevolent master lacked. The creator of modern Bavaria was the grandson of a Savoy official, whose son emigrated to Bavaria and married a German wife. The future statesman entered the service of the State at the age of twenty, but like many other clever young men he listened to the siren voices of Illuminati. On the dissolution of the Order he lost the favour of the Elector, and resolved to seek his fortunes at Zweibrücken, where he won the friendship and confidence of Max Joseph, the brother of the reigning Duke. When the Bavarian throne fell to his master, he returned to Munich and became the real ruler of the country for eighteen years.

The Dictator looked like a French noble and wrote and spoke French in preference to German. His aim was to accomplish peacefully for Bavaria what France had achieved at the cost of anarchy and bloodshed. He approached his task with the critical detachment of a foreigner, and made no secret of his contempt for ' cette nation bornée.' He determined to remove all institutions which were likely to thwart his will, beginning with the Estates and the Communes. Serfdom was abolished, the monasteries were thinned, and the material regeneration of the country taken energetically in hand. Protestants received equal rights from a prince who had married a Protestant and a Minister who felt equal contempt for every variety of religious belief. His most successful reforms were in the sphere of education. To root out Jesuit influence, the University of Ingoldstadt was abolished and a new seat of learning established at Landshut. The Academy of Sciences was revived, and scholars were imported from the Protestant north. Elementary education was freed from clerical control and rendered compulsory. In a few crowded years the accumulated rubbish of centuries was swept away, and Bavaria was transformed from the most backward into one of the most advanced of German States. 'We are in the middle of a complete but bloodless revolution,' cried Anselm Feuerbach, the author of the new criminal code. The Minister was as little of a democrat as Frederick the Great ; but his lucid and logical mind was offended by the fantastic absurdities of the traditional system, and like Hardenberg he had learned from France that revolutions could only be avoided by drastic reform.

The work of destruction and reconstruction accomplished by Stein and Hardenberg in Prussia and by Montgelas in Bavaria was carried out with even more uncompromising determination by the last Duke and the first King of Württemberg. When Frederick succeeded to the throne in 1797 he found the duchy small and poor and the power of the ruler circumscribed, at any rate in theory, by constitutional rights granted as far back as the Reformation. The liquidation of the Empire and the distribution of the smaller units among the larger States gave the ambitious autocrat the opportunity which he sought. With the new Catholic territories falling to his share he could do as he pleased ; but he refused to rule over a country in a portion of which his will was fettered by traditional rights and claims. He therefore made a clean sweep of ' the good old law,' and introduced a uniform system of administration throughout his dominions. ' The *coup d'état*,' comments Treitschke, ' was the outcome not simply of a tyrant's overweening love of power but also of an undeniable political necessity. Over the united old and new Württemberg all the terrors of despotism now raged ; but the autocracy endowed the country with indispensable institutions of the modern State. The edict of religions, King Frederick's best work, overthrew the dominion of the Lutheran Church and gave equal rights to both creeds. By the secularisation of Church property and the abolition of the treasury of the Estates, unity of national economy was established and the duty of paying regular taxes was carried into effect. The defenceless country once more acquired a little army fit for war. With revolutionary impetuosity the enemy of the Revolution established modern legal equality in his own State.' The debauched and extravagant monarch was heartily detested by his subjects, but the firm outlines of his work remained. Without the example of France to warn, to inspire and to guide, neither Montgelas nor Frederick could have overthrown the entrenched forces of tradition nor carried out the revolution from above of which South Germany stood in such desperate need.

In the third leading State of southern Germany the transition from the old world to the new was more gradual and far less violent ; for Karl Friedrich, the father of modern Baden, had not waited for the storm to break before setting his house in order. As a life-long friend of France and a correspondent of Voltaire and the elder Mirabeau, the Duke regarded her efforts for liberty with considerable sympathy ; and neither the atrocities of Paris nor the horrors of invasion shook his belief in the wisdom and necessity of unhasting and unresting change. When he died in 1811, after a reign of seventy years, he had increased his territory tenfold and left behind him one of the freest, best educated and most prosperous States in Germany.

The fall of Napoleon restored their independence to the Rheinbund princes, but the foreign leaven remained. The French Revolution left an abiding mark on the rulers and peoples, the institutions and ideas of the south as well as the west of Germany ; and men of a later generation looked back on it with gratitude as the inauguration of a better age. ' My birth and childhood,' wrote Welcker, the leader of Baden liberalism in the middle decades of the nineteenth century, ' synchronised with the Revolution, before which nobody thought of a Constitution.' While Prussia remained in tutelage till 1848, the South German States were furnished with Parliaments within a few years of the conclusion of peace. For a generation after Waterloo the Liberals of the south

and west looked to Paris for their inspiration as the
Liberals of the north looked to England, and spoke
more of the French occupation than of the Wars of
Liberation. In the celebrated controversy between
Thibaut and Savigny on the project of a Code for
Germany, the Baden jurist appealed to reason and the
Berlin Professor to tradition. The two most popular
historical works of the Restoration era were the world-
histories of Schlosser and Rotteck, which stretched
priests and kings on the rack and shed tears over the
sufferings of the oppressed masses. The central doctrine
of the French Revolution—that the destinies of a country
should be controlled by the people as a whole and in
the interest of the majority—found far fuller acceptance
in the south than in Prussia, and has coloured its political
thought and practice ever since.

The wish was expressed by Georg Forster, the most
eminent of the German victims of the Revolution, that
his country should warm itself at the flame that had
been kindled in France, without being burned. The
aspiration was destined in large measure to be fulfilled.
While in England the reform movement was thrown
back forty years by the earthquake and tempest, in
Germany it was strengthened and accelerated. If Saxony
and Mecklenburg remained unaffected by the Revolution,
and the old governments of Hanover, Brunswick and
Hesse-Cassel on their return restored most of the old
abuses, Prussia, the Rhineland and the south learned in
a generation of conflict and suffering at least some of
the secrets of enduring advance. Even Treitschke is
compelled to admit that the constitutional ideas of the
Revolution everywhere struck root in German soil ; and
without the Revolution the famous Article 13 of the
Act creating the German Federation would never have
seen the light. The political unification of the nation
was deferred for a couple of generations ; but the signal
for its deliverance from the thraldom of medieval institutions and antiquated ideas was sounded by the tocsin
which rang out in 1789.

GERMAN THEORIES OF THE STATE

GERMANY has produced no political thinker so widely influential as Machiavelli and Hamilton, Hobbes and Locke, Montesquieu and Rousseau, Burke and Bentham ; but Kant and Hegel are stars of the first magnitude, and several of her lesser luminaries shine with considerable lustre. Moreover, her teachers, great and small alike, mirror the changes through which the German mind has passed during the century and a half in which it has seriously reflected on the fundamental problems of political science.[1]

The land which Bismarck hammered into a united empire was in the eighteenth century nothing but a geographical expression. The creeping paralysis of the Holy Roman Empire found its natural counterpart in cosmopolitanism. In literature and society French influence was supreme, and men of culture felt themselves in literal truth to be citizens of the world. Patriotic feeling was regarded as a mutilation of the mind, a culpable limitation of intellectual interest and sympathy. 'I have no conception of the love of country,' wrote Lessing, 'and it seems to me at best a heroic failing which I am well content to be without.' 'There are Saxon, Bavarian, Frankfurt patriots,' wrote Wieland ;

---

[1] There is no satisfactory survey of the evolution of German political ideas. The student may consult Bluntschli, *Geschichte des allgemeinen Staatsrechts* ; Meinecke, *Weltbürgertum und Nationalstaat* ; Meinecke, *Die Idee der Staatsräson* ; Merriam, *History of the Theory of Sovereignty since Rousseau* ; Ruggiero, *History of European Liberalism* ; Veit Valentin, *Geschichte des Völkerbundgedankens in Deutschland*. The useful series entitled *Der Deutsche Staatsgedanke* contains some of the classics of German political literature.

' but German patriots, where are they ? ' ' Ubi bene ibi patria,' wrote Goethe in 1773 with eloquent brevity ; and the youthful Schiller defined himself in 1784 as a citizen of the world who served no prince.

Before the French Revolution no German of the front rank devoted himself to the science of politics which has claimed many of the ablest minds in France, England and Italy for a couple of centuries. For generations the stage had been occupied by the Cameralists, a school of writers who accepted the Absolute State as an axiom and discussed how best to satisfy the fiscal needs of the ruler.[1] Cameralism, which was the science of administration rather than the science of politics, was restated and brought up to date by Justi, whose writings reflect and idealise the theory and practice of benevolent autocracy in the age of Frederick the Great. The common weal is presented as the goal of the State and the happiness of the governed receives lip-homage ; but Justi assumes that it is secured by absolute government. As the contemporary of Montesquieu and Rousseau, he is aware of the growth of moral demands which form a standard for rulers ; but he never suggests that the people may enforce it. The revolt of the American colonies caused a stirring of the stagnant waters ; but even the boldest journalists like Schlözer and Schubart contented themselves with attacking the grosser abuses of feudalism and autocracy. Moser's famous treatise *Der Herr und der Diener (Master and Servant)*, published in 1759, the most ambitious political dissertation of the age, sharply castigates the evils of personal government—the wild extravagance, the sordid favouritism, the unblushing ignorance, the naked selfishness of the German princelets who made the lives of their subjects a perpetual misery. But he never looks beyond the reform of the system. His ideal is a conscientious paternal ruler, assisted by honest ministers like himself.

The French Revolution destroyed the Holy Roman

[1] See Albion Small, *The Cameralists*.

Empire, but it taught Germany to think. Every German writer of distinction, except Goethe, began to discuss the nature and duties of the State. Though the sweeping reforms of Stein, Hardenberg, Montgelas, and other statesmen only came some years later, the ground had been prepared not only by the example of France, but by eager and fruitful discussion at home. Rapid as was the march of events, the current of thought kept pace with them. The transition from the eighteenth century to the nineteenth, from the old Germany to the new, is reflected in the writings of Humboldt, Kant and Fichte.

Wilhelm von Humboldt's treatise on *The Limits of State Action* was finished in 1792 and portions appeared in the reviews ; but no publisher was willing to risk a conflict with the censorship, and the book was published sixty years later by the author's brother.[1] It is the German equivalent of Mill *On Liberty*, and Mill has expressed his indebtedness to his famous predecessor. The German nobleman writing under Frederick William II of Prussia, and the philosophic Radical living in Mid-Victorian England, reached the same conclusions ; and though the English manifesto enjoys the greater celebrity, Humboldt's volume remains one of the classics of political literature. There are two questions, he begins, involved in the attempt to frame a constitution. The first is, Who shall govern ? The second relates to the sphere to which the Government shall extend its operations. The former problem was being discussed on all sides, while the latter, which was far more important, was utterly neglected. Constitutions are only machinery for ministering to the needs and developing the capacities of the individual. While France was demanding freedom for a nation, Humboldt pleads for freedom for himself. The most important of all political questions, he argues, are those which affect the private life of the citizen. As civilisation advances there is less need of government, and the question of its

[1] See Gooch, *Germany and the French Revolution*, ch. 4.

form becomes of secondary importance. His demand is not for a better government, but for less government. It is a modest request to address to a ruler, and can be granted without waiting for a revolution. ' If to behold a people breaking their fetters asunder is a beautiful and ennobling spectacle, how much better is it to witness a prince himself unloosing the bonds of thraldom and granting freedom to his subjects ! '

The true end of man, proceeds Humboldt, is the harmonious development of his powers, and reason demands a condition of things in which every man enjoys the most abundant opportunities of self-realisation. The unceasing effort of the State to promote the welfare of its citizens is harmful, for it creates uniformity, suppresses spontaneity, discourages energy, and thereby hinders the natural growth of the individual. What a man does under instruction or guidance fails to enter into his being and remains alien to his true nature. Legislation necessarily bears a general character, and therefore fails to meet the need of particular cases. Moreover, the greater the activity of the State the greater the army of functionaries. In a sentence which has a twentieth-century ring he complains that every decade the number of officials increases and the liberty of the subject proportionately declines. The sole duty of the State is to watch over the security of the nation. ' The State should not proceed a step further than is necessary for the protection of its citizens against foreign enemies. It should abstain from all solicitude for their positive welfare.' Voluntary association is better than any arrangements that the Government can ever make. Civilisation has reached a point beyond which it cannot aspire to still loftier heights save through the development of individuals ; and therefore all institutions which in any way obstruct this development are now far more hurtful than in earlier and less advanced ages.

After this introductory bombardment of government and legislation the author carries on the siege in a series of chapters devoted to the ordinary activities of the State.

National education turns out all its scholars on the same pattern. A State Church, by encouraging certain opinions, gives a bias to the citizen and discourages freedom of thought. National supervision of morals might produce a peaceable and prosperous community, but its members would be like a flock of sheep, not free and independent men. No serious consequences need be apprehended from the abuse of liberty. ' The State is merely a means to which man, the true end, must never be satisfied.' Its duty is to provide security, which the citizen cannot provide for himself.

This earnest and eloquent work, like most other pleas for individualism, assumes that human nature is on the whole good, just as champions of autocracy assume that it is on the whole bad. ' Man,' he declares cheerfully, ' is naturally more disposed to beneficent than to selfish actions.' But an even bolder assumption underlies his structure of argument and paradox. Humboldt universalises himself. He believes that the world is full of men like himself, who possess sufficient virtue and wisdom to make their life a thing of beauty without the guidance of authority. Many years later, when he became Minister of Education in Prussia, he realised that the alternative to bad government was not philosophic anarchy but good government, and that wise action by the State may be one of the most powerful factors in the development of a rich and harmonious personality. Despite his exaggerated individualism, which sometimes anticipates the paradoxes of Nietzsche, the youthful Humboldt remains an impressive figure ; and his teaching that a State must be judged, not by its power and riches, but by the spiritual quality of its citizens, shines out like a ray of light in the evil days of Frederick William II. The treatise was carefully studied by his friend Schiller, and the doctrine that the perfecting of the individual is a more urgent and fruitful task than the search for new institutions reappears in the *Letters on the Aesthetic Education of Man*.

By his individualism and his cosmopolitanism Kant,

no less than Humboldt, belongs to the eighteenth century ; but the greatest of philosophers was also one of the boldest and most suggestive of political thinkers.[1] His interest in affairs was aroused by the American War of Independence, which won his whole-hearted sympathy. Though nearly seventy at the outbreak of the French Revolution, he welcomed it with enthusiasm, and for the rest of his life his talk was mainly of politics. One of his colleagues records the fearlessness with which he championed the principles of the Revolution at a time when everybody who had a word to say for it was entered on the black books of the authorities as a Jacobin. His pen was as bold as his tongue. In his study of *Religion*, published in 1793, he counters the argument that the French are not ripe for liberty with the axiom that men only become ripe for liberty when they are set free. ' We must be free in order to use our powers wisely in freedom. The first attempts will naturally be imperfect ; but experience will show the way, for God has created mankind for freedom.' In his *Philosophy of Law*, published four years later, he declares that liberty, equality and personal independence are the alienable attributes of the citizen, and that the highest criterion of legislation is that it represents the will of the people. Throughout life he taught that man is a rational and moral being, and that politics must be based on reason and morality.

In the most arresting of Kant's political works, *Perpetual Peace*, we catch the highest notes ever struck by a German publicist. If law, based on reason and morality, was the foundation of the life of the State, it should equally regulate the relations of States to one another. Humanity needed a constitution not less than France or Prussia ; for so long as each State recognised no authority above itself and no duty except to itself, wars would continue. He does not waste time in proving the evil of war. Writing in 1795 he takes it for granted, and plunges at once into a discussion how

[1] See Gooch, *Germany and the French Revolution*, ch. ii.

it may be avoided. He first enumerates what he describes as the preliminary articles of peace : (1) No treaty shall be valid if it contains a secret reservation of materials for a future war. (2) No State shall be acquired through inheritance, exchange, or purchase ; for it is not a property, but a society of human beings. (3) Standing armies shall one day be abolished, for they are always threatening other States with war. Rivalry in armaments begins, and armed peace becomes so oppressive that war may seem a preferable alternative. (4) No national debt shall be incurred except for purely internal affairs. (5) No State shall forcibly interfere with the constitution and administration of another.

These injunctions and exhortations are, of course, merely counsels of perfection so long as the destinies of nations are in the hands of irresponsible autocrats. The second part of the little treatise, therefore, proceeds to establish the fundamental conditions, or, as Kant phrases it, definite articles of permanent peace. The first is that all States must become republican, a term in which he includes every kind of genuinely constitutional government. ' The only constitution which is rooted in the idea of the original contract, on which the lawful legislation of every nation must be based, is the republican.' It recognises the dependence of the State on law and on the equality of its members. It is also the only constitution which ensures peace ; for if the consent of the community is needed for war, it will think twice before undertaking such a bad business. On the other hand, where the subject is not a citizen with a vote, plunging into war is the easiest thing in the world, for the ruler loses nothing by it, and continues to enjoy his sport and the delights of the table. Indeed, it requires no greater effort on his part than to issue orders for a hunting expedition. When selfish and capricious autocracies are replaced by representative institutions, a new system of relations between States will become possible. The second article therefore demands a federation of free States. By war and victory, remarks Kant, the

question of right can never be decided.   Anticipating
our League of Nations, he declares that if some powerful
and enlightened people should form a republic, that is,
should become master of its own fate, it would serve as
a nucleus for other States, and the federation would
gradually increase in size and authority.   The only
absolute security for perpetual peace would be a world-
republic, which he laments that the nations will not
accept.   ' Hence, if all is not to be lost, we must obtain
the negative substitute for it, a federation averting war.'
But even then there will be constant danger.   The third
article claims what Kant describes as universal hospitality
for individuals in whatever State they may find themselves.   The idea of cosmopolitan right, or, as we may
say, of world-citizenship, is the complement of the
unwritten code of law for the public rights of mankind.

In one of the brief supplements to the treatise the
philosopher offers some reasons for his great hope.
Nature, he boldly announces, points us towards peace,
for she makes harmony spring from discord, even
against the will of man.   She fills the earth with con-
tiguous peoples, who gradually learn their interdependence.   The commercial spirit cannot co-exist with war,
and sooner or later it takes possession of every nation.
But his faith in man is even greater than his faith in
nature or commerce.   In noble words, which crystallise
his political as well as his moral philosophy, he declares
that ' man cannot get away from the idea of right.'
Germans who desire to become good Europeans need
only resort to the oracle of Königsberg.

While Humboldt and Kant express the loftiest ideals
of the eighteenth century, Fichte represents the transition to the dominant principle of German thought in
the nineteenth century.[1]   Attracted to politics by the
French Revolution he made his début as a publicist in
1793 with an anonymous pamphlet entitled *A demand
for freedom of thought presented to the Princes of Europe*

[1] See Léon's great work, *Fichte et son Temps*, of which two volumes have
been published.

who have hitherto suppressed it. In scathing terms he attacks the rulers of his country. ' One of the sources of our misery,' he cries, ' is our exaggerated estimate of these folk. Their minds are warped by false teaching and superstition. I reckon as virtues all the vices they do not possess, and I thank them for all the evil acts they do not commit. Let us rid ourselves of the notion that it is for the princes to secure our happiness. We shall now dare to ask those who claim to rule us, By what right ? If they reply, By inheritance, we rejoin that man cannot be inherited like flocks and herds. He is governed by conscience alone. If he admits any other rule, he sinks to the level of the animals. The prince obtains the whole of his power from his contract with society. It is indecent for thinking men to crawl at the foot of the throne and beg leave to be the doormat of kings. The strength of our rulers lies in the ignorance of their subjects.' This passionate attack on despotism and obscurantism combines Humboldt's cult of the individual with the full-blooded doctrine of the sovereignty of the people newly imported from France.

A longer and less rhetorical treatise appeared in the same year entitled *A Contribution to the formation of a correct judgment on the French Revolution.* That great event, declares Fichte, is of importance for the whole of mankind. Now is the time to make the people acquainted with freedom, which he who seeks will surely find. ' Things have become the subject of conversation of which no one had dreamed. Talk of the rights of man, of liberty and equality, of the limits of the royal power, has taken the place of fashions and adventures. We are beginning to learn.' While deprecating violent change, he stoutly upholds the rights of revolution. As man is or ought to be subject to the moral law alone, every citizen may terminate his share in the contract at his own discretion. As the contract was freely made, so it may be freely changed. Neither power nor privileges can be handed down. Man is born with certain inalienable rights, and he is under no obligation to a government or a social system which fails to respect them. If the individual is thus master of himself, how much more is it the right and duty of a whole people to remove all obstacles to the pursuit of a free and elevated existence.

With such unbridled individualism at work the life of the State is like the flame of a candle ; and Fichte, whose mind never stood still, quickly realised that his position was untenable. In his treatise, *The Foundations of Natural Law*, published in 1796, he begins to construct breakwaters against the tide of popular passion. Though clinging to the sovereignty of the people and the social contract, he creates a small body of Ephors with the power to veto the decisions of the government and check the tendency to revolution, which, though justifiable, often produces greater evils than it cures. He was not long in perceiving that his Ephors were men of straw ; but the proposal shows that he is feeling his way towards the necessity of stable government. In his curious economic work, *The Isolated Commercial State*, published in 1800, we note a further departure from his original standpoint in his demand that the State concern itself with wages, prices and other factors of material well-being.

Fichte's evolution was still incomplete, for in his lectures on *The Characteristics of the Present Age*, delivered in the year before Jena, he asks ' Which is the fatherland of the truly cultured European ? ' It is Europe, he replies, and more particularly that State which at any given time has reached the highest point of culture. Animated by this cosmopolitan sentiment, we need not worry about the fortunes of particular States. But this was the last utterance of the spirit of the eighteenth century. Nationalism is the child of the French Revolution, and Prussia learned at Jena what France had learned at Versailles. Our philosopher now becomes the most fervent and eloquent champion of the national State, and the *Addresses to the German Nation*, delivered within earshot of the French garrison in Berlin and at peril of his life, proclaim the birth of the political gospel of which his

countrymen were one day to become devotees. He no
longer paints his princes black and their subjects white.
All, he cries, are responsible for the great collapse, and
all must co-operate in the work of reconstruction. The
nation had become self-conscious, and nationality involves
the recognition of the necessity, the utility, and the
majesty of the State.

While Kant and Humboldt failed to grasp the full
significance of the nation and the State, and Fichte only
realised it when Prussia lay prostrate before the invader,
Hegel made it the starting-point of his philosophy.[1]
He pronounces nationality to be the foundation of all
higher life. He was also the first German thinker to
concern himself long and deeply with the nature of the
State, and no subsequent writer of the first rank, except
Nietzsche, has belittled it. As a student at Tübingen he
had coquetted with the French Revolution, but the
sufferings of his country during the great war taught him
to seek remedies for her weakness. In his remarkable
book *The German Constitution*, written about 1802 but
not published till long after his death, he bitterly bewails
the helplessness of his countrymen. He surveys the
Holy Roman Empire in its different organs and branches,
and concludes that Germany can no longer be called a
State ; for only that country deserves the name which
can provide for the defence of its possessions. He
speaks enviously of other nations which have created a
State, and thereby entered upon a period of power,
wealth and prosperity. Order is the first need of society.
Europe, he declares, had become less sensitive to the
cry of freedom since the horrors of the French Revolution. ' In this bloody drama there has melted the cloud
of liberty in embracing which the peoples have fallen into
an abyss of misery. A settled government is necessary
for freedom.' He adds that the people must co-operate
in the making of the laws, and that representation is
essential to liberty. He concludes with proposals for

[1] The fullest account of the evolution of Hegel's political views is in
Rosenzweig's admirable volumes, *Hegel und der Staat*.

the reform of the constitution as the sole means of avoiding partition. Had this honest and practical treatise been published when it was written, it would have prevented the growth of the legend that he was so immersed in philosophy that he was indifferent to the fate of his country.

Hegel had reached the height of his influence and had been called to Berlin when he published his *Philosophy of Right* in 1820. Since the War of Liberation had rendered the German people fully self-conscious, the demand for some measure of political liberty had become general, and the South German States were granted constitutions by their princes. In Prussia, on the other hand, reactionary influences combined with the King's timidity to retain autocracy unimpaired. The students' demonstrations on the Wartburg and the murder of Kotzebue had been followed by the Carlsbad decrees, which muzzled the Universities and the press. At this moment, when Metternich was in command, the most influential philosopher in Germany issued what was in some quarters regarded as a manifesto of the reaction. A famous witticism affirmed that he had mistaken the kingdom of Prussia for the kingdom of heaven. The accusation was groundless, for he demanded representative institutions a generation before they were granted. He had stoutly championed the reforming king of his native Württemburg in his struggle with the feudal interests, and part of an article on the English Reform Bill, written just before his death, was suppressed by the Prussian censor. Hegel was a moderate conservative, not a reactionary.

The State, we read in the *Philosophy of Right*, is the realised ethical idea. A people must embody its sense of right in a constitution, which, however, is not a mere manufactured article, but the work of centuries. The best form is hereditary monarchy, which guarantees the unity and continuity of the State, and is raised above faction by ruling through ministers. Montesquieu's ideal of the separation of powers is rejected on the ground that it tends to endanger the strength of the State.   A Legislature is essential, but ultimate decisions must not be made by the people, which does not know what it wants.   ' To know what we want, and still more to know what reason wants, and what is good for the State, is the fruit of deep knowledge and insight, and is therefore not the property of the people.'   The right of criticism is the most valuable that the community possesses. ' Public opinion deserves both to be esteemed and de- spised—despised in its concrete expression, esteemed in its essential basis.'   Hegel's notion of government is that it is a very difficult task, requiring highly-skilled operators for its success.   The sovereignty of numbers and the abstract Rights of Man are emphatically re- pudiated.   He lacked that confidence in the average citizen which inspired the French Revolution, and which lies at the base of the democratic faith.   In his political, not less than in his philosophical system, the individual sometimes tends to be engulfed in the larger whole.

In his doctrine of the relation of States to one another Hegel represents a sharp and deplorable reaction from Kant.   While the elder philosopher proclaimed the overlordship of humanity, the younger denied the exist- ence of moral relations between States.   The State is its own master, and is subject only to the world-process. Thus international law is no real contract, and no State is legally or morally bound by it.   Differences between States can only be settled by war, which is neither good nor evil, but natural.   Indeed, it has its uses as a national scavenger and in emphasising the unimportance of material things.   In deciding on war the State must consult nothing but its own interest.   Yet Hegel's teaching is widely different from the militarism of a later age, which glorifies aggression and thinks exclusively in terms of force.   A State, he declared, is bound together, not by force, but by a deep-rooted instinct of order.   It is a spiritual structure, the highest embodiment of reason, the guardian of liberty.   Such a teacher, whatever his faults, is on the side of the angels.

Hegel's doctrine of the State was too rationalistic for romantic mystics of the type of Adam Müller, and too rigid for the large and growing body of men who bitterly regretted that the constitution promised to Prussia during the War of Liberation had never been granted. South German Liberals looked for inspiration to France, while North Germans cast wistful glances across the North Sea.[1] The expulsion of the Bourbons from France in 1830 and the passage of the English Reform Bill in 1832 increased the ferment. It was at this time that Dahlmann, from his chair at Göttingen, like Guizot in Paris, loudly proclaimed the virtues of constitutional government as practised in England.[2] His treatise on political science, published in 1835, for some years the Bible of North German Liberalism, applied the historical method of Eichhorn and Savigny, judging ideas and institutions, not in abstraction, but in their evolution and operation. The book is a spirited plea for representative government, and its illustrations are drawn almost exclusively from English history. Though not a man of profound scholarship, Dahlmann's nobility of character made him one of the most impressive figures of modern Germany. His ardent nationalism and his deep conviction of the rightness of the popular thirst for liberty influenced generations of University students ; and his manly protest against the revocation of the Hanoverian constitution in 1837, promptly followed by his expulsion from Göttingen, increased his authority with the bourgeoisie, which he described as the kernel of the population and the centre of gravity of the State. He lived to play a leading part in the Frankfurt Parliament of 1848, and to witness the collapse of the promising movement for a Germany at once united and constitutional. He left no successor, and the liberal nationalism which was the dream and inspiration of his life withered away.

[1] See T. Wilhelm, *Die Englische Verfassung und der Vormärzliche Deutsche Liberalismus.*

[2] See Springer, *F. C. Dahlmann*, and Treitschke's fine tribute in his *Historische und Politische Aufsätze*, Vol. I.

During the years between the Frankfurt Parliament and the dictatorship of Bismarck, the atmosphere of Prussia was once more oppressive with reaction. When Frederick William IV presented his people with the constitution under which Prussia lived till the revolution of 1918, he took care that it should leave the authority of the crown intact. Moreover, he grudged even this attenuated concession, and left secret instructions to his successor to revoke it. The dominant creed of clerical Conservatism found its strongest exponent in Stahl,[1] whom Lord Acton described as the ablest Jew since the destruction of Jerusalem. Born of a Lutheran family in Bavaria, Stahl had won fame by his work *The Philosophy of Law*, in which he vindicated what he described as the Christian State against Liberalism in all its manifestations. He demands the return of the human mind from the arrogance of reason to the shelter of revelation. As the goal of the State is the realisation on earth of the moral kingdom, it must be built, not on the law of nature, the source of all revolution, but on Christian principles. His system centres in the royal prerogative, which he declares the sole effective rival to the doctrine of the sovereignty of the people. The rule of man over man needs a religious consecration to make it palatable. In words at which Frederick the Great would have scoffed but which his pious successor accepted as a gospel, he declares that a divine radiance rests upon the wearer of the crown. On the political battlefield he sees only two combatants—the Christian State *versus* the Revolution, Authority *versus* Majorities, the ordering of God *versus* the will of man. He rejected the notion of Karl Ludwig von Haller, an echo from the far-off days of our English Filmer, that power was the private property of the prince, and he accepted the principle of representation where the predominance of the conservative elements was amply secured ; but in spite of these

[1] The full treatment of Stahl which has long been needed is supplied by Masur, *F. J. Stahl*. The first volume, published in 1930, covers the years 1802–40.

concessions he stands out as the chief creator, or at any rate the chief formulator, in modern Prussia of the doctrine of divine right.

This able and scholarly champion of Christian Byzantinism was summoned by the King to Berlin University, where he preached his gospel with tongue and pen.   When the constitution of 1850 was granted, Stahl became leader of the Conservative majority in the Upper House of the Landtag, and throughout the fifties, now Metternich was gone, he was the most impressive figure of European Conservatism.   In his scheme the King occupies the place which in Hegel's system is reserved for the Government.   He is the champion of the ruling classes—the princes, the nobles, the clergy, the army.   On the other hand, the bourgeoisie, the peasants, the workers are frowned on as the natural prey of democracy, socialism, and the revolution.   Stahl, not Hegel or Radowitz, was the father of the Conservative party which dominated the Prussian Parliament till 1918, and his views of the royal office found a zealous disciple in the Emperor William II.

While the rival squadrons of Dahlmann and Stahl were quarrelling over the power of Kings and Parliaments, Bismarck was maturing the policy which was to turn the current of thought from constitutional to national and international issues.   As Fichte had reflected the change from the individualistic humanitarianism of the eighteenth century to the idealistic nationalism of the Wars of Liberation, so Treitschke spans the transition from the aspirations of 1848 to the era of blood and iron. His magnetic personality, his passionate conviction, and his incomparable eloquence, of which I was one of the last hearers, made him an educative force of the first magnitude.   Though in history he founded no school, his flamboyant patriotism exerted enormous influence in Prussia for half a century.

In 1860, at the age of twenty-five, Treitschke struck the dominant note of his political teaching in his little book *The Science of Society*, which he bluntly asserted to have no existence.[1] The only science was that of the State, which was society organised as a unit. The State was as necessary as language, and no contract was needed to create or maintain it. Two years later, in an article on Liberty, suggested by Mill's essay, he unfolds his ideal of a State both strong and constitutional. The State has the right to dominate the individual, because the individual cannot live a worthy life without its protection and guidance. Far from being a mechanical structure for strictly limited purposes, it is the supreme moralising agency of the world. It is bound, however, by no moral code, for the only law of its existence is to exist and develop. Self-preservation, which is merely an instinct with the individual, is the supreme duty of the State. But though the State is force, it is much more than force. ' We want free men in a free State,' he cries. He speaks of the rights of conscience and liberty of thought with scarcely less fervour than Mill. Moreover, the liberty of the individual can only flourish under the protection of political liberty. All that was new and fruitful in the nineteenth century was the work of Liberalism. Applying his doctrine to the problem of German politics, he contends that Prussia can only become a rallying point for all Germans as a genuinely constitutional State. This gospel, which bore the stamp of his beloved teacher Dahlmann, he continued to preach till the guns of Sadowa blew what was left of German Liberalism into thin air.

On the eve of the war with Austria Bismarck pressed Treitschke to accompany the army and write manifestos, promising him a Chair at Berlin as the reward. The historian refused on the ground that he could not become a Prussian official till the constitution was once again respected. But the Seven Weeks' War dissolved his scruples, and he became one of Bismarck's stoutest supporters in domestic no less than in foreign affairs. This Saxon of Slavonic descent was more Prussian than the

[1] See Gooch, *History and Historians in the Nineteenth Century*, ch. 8.

Prussians. He learned to admire the Junkers, flung himself into the Anti-Semitic crusade, and declared that Socialism should be met with force, not argument. He became the intellectual leader of the reaction, and after helping to create united Germany he devoted his matchless energies to teaching its citizens the detestable philosophy of chauvinistic absolutism.

Treitschke's famous work on the history of Germany in the nineteenth century grew under his hands to such an extent that he was unable to realise his life-long dream of a systematic treatise on political science ; but the lectures which he delivered for a generation to crowded audiences in Heidelberg and Berlin were published after his death, and the two large volumes set forth his opinions with a clearness that leaves nothing to be desired.[1] His message is the moral and spiritual grandeur of large and powerful States. The State stands high above the individuals who compose it, and it exists in order to realise ideals far above individual happiness. This it can only do if it is strong. It is no part of its duty to inquire whether its actions are approved or disapproved by its subjects. It is the guardian of the national tradition and a trustee for the interests of unborn generations. Hereditary monarchy buttressed by a vigorous aristocracy is most conducive to national strength, and the executive must be independent of the ebb and flow of opinion. In like manner the State owes no allegiance to any external authority. International law is a mere phrase, and no tribunal can arbitrate between sovereign States. Treaties are a voluntary self-limitation, and no State can hamper its freedom of action by obligations to another. It must ever be ready for war, which, when undertaken for honour or for some supreme national interest, is wholesome and elevating. For war is not a necessary evil but an instrument of statesmanship and a school of patriotism. Only in war for the Fatherland does a nation become truly and spiritually united. It is

---

[1] An English translation entitled *Politics* appeared in 1916, with an Introduction by Lord Balfour.

indeed the only medicine for a sick people.   It is idealism
that demands war and materialism which rejects it.
Dreams of perpetual peace are the mark of a stagnant
and decadent generation, for conflict is the law of life.
' The hope of banishing war is not only meaningless but
immoral ; for its disappearance would turn the earth
into a great temple of selfishness.'   We catch the echo
of Moltke's classical aphorism : ' Perpetual peace is a
dream, and not even a beautiful dream.'

Der Staat ist Macht—the State is Power.   All its
institutions and practices must be directed towards this
goal.   The youth of the country must be trained to arms,
and courage must be fostered by duelling.   Germany
has been welded into a mighty State, respected and self-
respecting, by the blows of Thor's hammer.   The battle
is to the strong and the race to the swift.   Such is the
gospel of Treitschke, the Bismarck of the Chair, in its
ultimate form.   Its fruits may be seen in the pages of
Bernhardi, who adopts all that is most repulsive in his
teaching, and mixes it with the cold realism of
Clausewitz and crude generalisations from Darwinian
biology.

A notable utterance on the nature and duties of the
State is to be found in Delbrück's *Regierung und Volkswille*
(*Government and the Popular Will*)—a course of lectures
delivered in Berlin University a few months before the
war.   The successor to the Chair of Treitschke was
known to scholars by his life of Gneisenau and his *History of the Art of War* ; but he was familiar to a wider
circle as editor of the *Preussische Jahrbücher*, and, like
Treitschke, he possessed parliamentary experience.   The
object of the book is to show that democratic government
is a fraud, and that Germany possesses the best government in the world.   Defining the ideal of democracy as
the realisation of the will of the people, he points out
that even with a liberal franchise the actual voters are but
a small proportion of any community, and that many
men qualified to vote make no use of their privilege.
Thus the whole body of representatives is elected by

a mere fraction of the people ; and the majority, often only a little more numerous than the minority, represents a still smaller proportion of the nation. Moreover, an election is not a *bona fide* expression of opinion, but a campaign in which victory often falls to the party with the longest purse and fewest scruples. Thus the discovery of the popular will by the machinery of votes, which is the chosen method of democracy, is impossible, and self-government is a sham. Even were it otherwise, what reason is there to believe that the majority is right ? Again, a popularly-elected Legislature in possession of supreme power falls a ready victim to corruption, though he admits that the record of England is much better than that of France and America.

This resounding attack seems to point to autocracy as the ideal, but Delbrück rejects it as decisively as democracy. The weakness of the system of Frederick the Great, he declares, was revealed at Jena. Some connection between the Government and the people is essential, and it was their co-operation which rescued Prussia in 1813. Two generations later Bismarck created not only the German Empire, but a constitution which was worthy of it. The Reichstag enjoys far less power than other Parliaments, but it has as much as any Parliament ought to possess. What would happen to the German Empire if it were ruled by changing majorities, a Socialist Government following a Catholic, and each party proscribing its enemies ? Indignantly repudiating the elder Liebknecht's description of the Reichstag as a mere fig-leaf to cover the nakedness of absolutism, he pronounces it a mighty organ of criticism and control. Its members, he contends, influence and modify legislation far more than is the case at Westminster. His only criticism is that it does not attract the best talent in the country, since its members never rise to a position of authority. The capital fault of democratic States is that power is in the hands of a single body. The shining merit of the German constitution is that it is a dualism, Princes and Reichstag playing parts of equal importance, and between them representing the interests as well as the will of the nation.

This reading of the German Constitution is so different from the view generally entertained that Delbrück attempts to establish his position by attributing to the Reichstag the fall, not only of Bülow, but of Bismarck himself, maintaining that the Emperor only dared to dismiss his Minister because he knew that the majority was hostile to him. Yet he is too honest to conceal the fact that the supreme power is in the hands of a single man. Discussing the much-debated problem as to where sovereignty is to be found, he concludes that it rests with the man or the body of men whom the army obeys. Tried by this test sovereignty in England and France rests with the majority of the Lower House, in Germany with the Emperor. In a passage of extraordinary interest he declares that Prussian officers have always served the King rather than the State. ' He is their comrade, and they cleave to him as their war lord, and that is the foundation of our national life. The essence of our monarchy lies in its relation to the army.' Even were there no other arguments against Parliamentary government, this would be decisive. ' Everybody who knows our officers is well aware that they would never tolerate the rule of a War Minister drawn from the Reichstag.' This attitude he fully approves, for he is convinced that democracy means not only corruption, but weakness. The Governments of France, England and the United States do not possess the strength, patience, or continuity to deal successfully with foreign policy or a great war. Thus the German Constitution, adapted to the requirements both of peace and war, needs no change, for it represents by far the highest form of political organisation existing in the world. Defeat in the World War failed to modify these convictions, and in a new edition, published in 1920, Delbrück argued once more that dualism alone was suited to German conditions. He added that the terrible struggle confirmed his view of the superiority of the German Constitution, since no other country could have held out so long against a world of enemies.[1]

The finality of the Bismarckian Constitution was reiterated by a far more influential voice than that of Delbrück. ' The German Empire,' wrote Prince Bülow in his *Imperial Germany*, published in 1913, ' situated in the middle of Europe and insufficiently protected by nature on its frontiers, is, and must remain, a military State ; and strong military States have always required monarchical guidance. The Crown is the corner-stone of Prussia and the keystone of the Empire. The dividing line between the rights of the Crown and of Parliament is immutably fixed.' While fully recognising, like Delbrück, that a modern monarchy requires the co-operation of the people, he pronounces against all alterations in the sphere of constitutional law. He laments the relative apathy of the people and the lack of the sentiment of responsibility shown by the members of the Reichstag ; but he proposes to deal with these evils, not by enlarging popular rights, but through the spread of political education, a task to be carried out by the cultured classes. Political talent, he declares, is not among the many great qualities of the German nation, and, in particular, the parties which would benefit by the extension of Parliamentary power are lacking in political judgment and training. Neither the Prince nor the Professor had mastered Mill's axiom that while the schoolmaster does all his pupils' sums they will never learn to do them for themselves.

Though democratic ideas were scouted by the governing classes, traces of the ideas of 1848 were still to be found among the bourgeoisie, and the demand for a more elastic theory of the State was strengthened by the growth of the Socialist movement. In his lectures on German parties, delivered in 1910,[2] Friedrich Naumann, the most eloquent spokesman of the Freisinnige, or

[1] An American translation of the second edition, entitled *Government and the Will of the People*, appeared in 1923.
[2] *Die Politischen Parteien.*

Radical Party, in the Reichstag, sharply challenged Prince Bülow's estimate of the political capacity of the German nation. ' The word self-government signified in the mouth of the old Liberalism, not merely a scheme of franchise, but the will of every individual in his parish, in his province, and in his nation to have his share in political activity. Thus arose in Germany the great idea of a political people in which each member possesses an importance of his own. We parties of the Left must hold fast to our conviction that the idea of nationality will only reach its full height if it is saturated with the conception of free, self-governing citizenship.' There is an immense capacity for development latent in the German people, he declares, which only awaits the over-throw of the parties of the Right. ' We wish,' he concludes, ' to enter into ennobling competition with the Englishman and the American as to which of our nations shall make the greatest contribution to the future civilisation of the world.'

I have now briefly traced what may be called the curve of German political thought from the eighteenth century to the eve of the World War. The individualistic cosmo-politanism of the eighteenth century was only possible in the dying days of the Holy Roman Empire. The French Revolution taught Germany to think and to hope, and the tyranny of Napoleon created the national idea. The value of the State, discovered by Fichte, was con-firmed by Hegel, and has ever since remained the common property of all schools of thought. The middle decades of the century witnessed an attempt to combine liberty with authority ; but the dazzling victories of Prussia ushered in a period of soulless realism in which the claims of the individual were overlooked and the partnership of nations was repudiated. The idolatry of the State reached its logical issue in the elevation of force to the sovereign principle in national life and in inter-national relations. The pendulum could swing no further in the direction that it had followed for half a century. The titanic struggle and the revolution of 1918

set it swinging back towards the more generous inspira-
tions of Germany's greatest and wisest teachers.

The collapse of the Hohenzollern Empire and the
institutions by which it was supported encouraged the
reappearance of ideas and ideals which had been submerged by the Bismarckian tide. German democracy,
which was born in the trenches, found expression in the
Weimar Constitution. In an article in the *Berliner
Tageblatt*, five days after the Revolution and the flight of
the Kaiser, Professor Hugo Preuss, a leading authority
on constitutional law and the history of institutions, and
a Liberal of the school of Bamberger, Rickert and
Theodor Barth, had voiced the demand for self-government.[1] Not classes and groups, he cried, not parties
and estates in hostile isolation, but the whole German
people embodied in a fully representative National
Assembly could erect the new democratic state. Moreover it must act quickly, for the alternative was Bolshevism. Democracy, he added, was only fit to rule
when it was national in sentiment, that is when it was
penetrated by the consciousness of its identity with the
State and of its full responsibility. But a truly democratic policy could only be national, since the conception
of democracy was inseparable from that of national solidarity. Preuss was appointed Home Secretary in the
first Republican Ministry, and proceeded to embody his
convictions in the first draft of the Weimar Constitution.

'The German Constitution is a Republic,' runs the
first of the 181 articles ; 'supreme power emanates from
the people.'[2] If the first part creates a *Volksstaat*, the
second ordains a *Rechtsstaat*. The sovereignty of the
People is supplemented and consecrated by the Rights
of Man. In the clauses devoted to the *Grundrechte* are
mirrored the changes of thought and feeling which
produced or sprang from the Revolution. In these

---

[1] Preuss, *Staat, Recht und Freiheit*, 365–8. The writings on the Weimar
Constitution are collected in Part IV of this large volume.

[2] See H. Oppenheimer, *The Constitution of the German Republic*, and Gooch,
Germany, ch. 9.

philosophic axioms and categorical imperatives we are back to the generous inspiration of 1848. A Liberal breeze is blowing again. The reign of the great Leviathan is ended. The spiritual worth of the individual is proclaimed, with all his obligations and his rights. The formulation of Fundamental Rights occupied the members of the Frankfurt Parliament, and their work was used as a model by their successors. While a minority of the legislators, like Bismarck in his day, considered them superfluous, the majority welcomed them as a confession of faith, a declaration of solidarity with the humane ideas of the modern world. If Hugo Preuss, the Professor of Constitutional Law, is the chief architect of the Weimar Constitution in its structural aspect, the insertion of the *Grundrechte* is mainly due to Friedrich Naumann, the eloquent idealist who began his career as a pastor, and who urged that they should be presented as aphorisms so that they might become ' the political Bible of the people.' In times of revolution, he argues, it is good to proclaim general truths. Thus the wheel has come full circle. The story of German theories of the State, which begins with the Liberalism of Humboldt, Kant and Fichte, ends with the Liberalism of Preuss, Naumann and their colleagues who drafted the first operative Constitution which the German nation has been privileged to construct for itself.

THE STUDY OF BISMARCK

THE student of recent European history will exclaim of Bismarck, as Victor Hugo exclaimed of Napoleon, *Toujours lui, lui partout*.[1] Next to the great Emperor he fills by far the largest space on the nineteenth century stage, and the two figures stand together and alone in the first class of men of action of the modern world. Richelieu, Cromwell and Frederick the Great are not very far behind, and Cavour, had he lived, might have pushed closer to the front rank than any of them. For there is no more consummate achievement of brain and will than the making of a nation. Bismarck, like Napoleon, was a ruthless destroyer ; but, unlike the Emperor, he was even greater as an architect. Though Germany has changed her institutions, shed territory at home and abroad, and lost her allies, she remains a Great Power and a united people. The Iron Chancellor seems to assume almost superhuman proportions in contrast with his bungling successors. The World War has focussed attention on the principal author of the international system which perished in its flames, and German historians in particular, by scores and by hundreds, are busily working the rich Bismarckian seam. Most of them find in him an oracle the neglect of whose principles led to the catastrophe, while a few may be found to challenge the philosophy of force of which he was the supreme embodiment. But hero-worshippers

[1] The latest surveys of the literature are by Maximilian von Hagen, *Das Bismarckbild in der Literatur der Gegenwart* (1929), and Lawrence D. Steefel, ' Bismarck,' in the *Journal of Modern History*, March, 1930 (Chicago).

and critics are at one in their recognition of his towering stature and in the zeal with which they explore every aspect of an incomparable personality.

I

Students of the master-builder may take their choice whether they approach him through his own writings, speeches and table-talk, or whether they shall form a preliminary impression of his work from selected biographers and historians. The latter method is usually preferred and is probably the best. Ranke's work on the leader of the Catholic forces in the Thirty Years' War bore the significant title, *Geschichte Wallensteins*, for the personal life of the man was merged in the history of his time. If we decide to begin with one or more biographies, the English reader who commands no tongue but his own is better off than the citizen of any other foreign country. The first serious survey of Bismarck's career was attempted in 1885 in the volumes of Charles Lowe, *Times* Correspondent in Berlin, revised in 1892, which are still worth reading as the work of a contemporary and in some cases an eye-witness. A shorter but far more scholarly performance was published soon after the Chancellor's death in the *Heroes of the Nations* series by J. W. Headlam, afterwards Sir James Headlam-Morley. While Lowe was merely a competent journalist, Headlam wrote as a trained scholar who had mastered the whole mass of printed material then available, and could set his subject in the framework of German history. On the other hand the proportions of his book are radically faulty ; for the stream shrinks to a trickle after the foundation of the Empire, and the reader never learns to know Bismarck as a legislator and a man of peace. The most interesting of Headlam's verdicts approves the annexation of Alsace and condemns the annexation of Lorraine. The third English biography, by Sir Charles Grant Robertson, published in 1919, devotes adequate attention to the later decades of dictatorship which interested our fathers so much less than the earlier years. Though the work appeared before the opening of the German archives, it remains the best guide for English readers, as Paul Matter's three-volume biography (in its second edition) is the chosen method of approach for the French.

The first serious attempt in Germany to record the achievements of his career in detail was made in the six volumes *Fürst Bismarck und seine Zeit*, published in 1894–5 by Hans Blum, Member of Parliament and journalist ; but the narrative of this devoted and uncritical admirer is now out of date. Among single-volume presentations by German historians the first and still the most important is Lenz's *Geschichte Bismarcks*, which appeared in its original form in the *Allgemeine Deutsche Biographie*. It is a careful chronicle of events by a scholar of the first rank who lived through the whole Bismarckian era, and was scarcely less interested in its military than in its political triumphs. Its fault is that the twenty years of peace are merely a sketch. Smaller in size but superior in proportion and style is *Otto von Bismarck : Ein Lebensbild*, by Erich Marcks, like Lenz a Professor at Berlin and a no less ardent admirer. Written for the Centenary in six weeks during the first winter of the war, he presents to his countrymen a hero ' the contemplation of whom is strength and comfort and courage and hope and faith.' Despite the overwhelming emotions of the struggle the author kept his head and provided the best popular introduction to the study of Bismarck ever written. The most original feature of the book is the discussion of the *Kulturkampf*, which is exhibited as a virtually inevitable clash between national and super-national concepts. Still smaller in scale, but hardly less authoritative, is A. O. Meyer's richly illustrated *Bismarck* in the well-known series *Velhagen und Klasings Volksbücher*.

The centenary, synchronising with the first intoxications of the World War, inspired not only a large crop of popular biographies but two co-operative enterprises of enduring value. The more substantial of the two, *Erinnerungen an Bismarck*, edited by Brauer, Marcks and K. A. v. Müller, contains contributions from friends and associates, among them Schweninger, the faithful doctor, who always found him simple and natural, and Dryander, the Court theologian, who describes him as a pious evangelical. The second collection, *Das Bismarckjahr*, edited by Lenz and Marcks, and covering a wider field less thoroughly, contains brief articles, in addition to those by the editors, by Brandenburg, Hintze, Meinecke, Oncken, Rachfahl, and a dozen other specialists on various aspects of his mind and policy.

When the student has familiarised himself with the personality of the principal actor in one or more of the best biographies, he should seek a closer acquaintance with the stage of events. English readers are fortunate in possessing two authoritative guides to the history of modern Germany in Sir Adolphus Ward and W. H. Dawson, who combine serenity and erudition with life-long knowledge of the country and its people. Though written when he was approaching his eightieth year, the survey of German history during the nineteenth century by the *doyen* of English historians betrayed no sign of failing powers. The first volume, covering the years from 1815 to 1852, provides the best account of the revolution of 1848–9 that we possess in English. The second, bringing the story to 1871, narrates the process of unification with sovereign impartiality. To a mind wearied and confused by the partisanship of Sybel and Friedjung, Ollivier and La Gorce, it was an emancipation to follow the unravelling of Prussian, Austrian and French diplomacy by a scholar who knew all there was to be known of the rival cases and who stood securely above the battle. In his youth he had spent several years in Germany ; and it adds to the personal interest as well as to the value of the book that his account of the later developments of the Schleswig-Holstein question utilised the papers of his father, William Ward, who was accredited to the Hanse cities during the critical decade

1860–70. The third volume, which carries the story to the fall of Bismarck and briefly sketches the reign of William II down to 1907, is smaller in bulk and of inferior importance.

If the Master of Peterhouse knew more of the history of Germany from 1815 to 1871 than any man born beyond her frontiers, Mr. Dawson possesses a many-sided acquaintance with the Germany created by Bismarck which no living Englishman can approach. Though written during the war, like the volumes of Ward, his work is no less honourably free from the passions and even the unconscious bias which render many of the historical writings of that distracted period little better than old newspapers. It is a striking testimony to the fair-mindedness and scientific method of British scholarship at its best that these two works, written in complete independence of each other, should reach approximately the same conclusions on the policies and personages of modern German history. Yet though their attitude of discriminating sympathy is almost identical, the differences in treatment are so great as to render them complementary to one another. Ward, the professional historian, wrote for students of history, while Mr. Dawson, the publicist, catered for the needs of the general reader. Though his book bears the title *The German Empire 1867–1914 and the Unity Movement*, by far the larger part of the two volumes is devoted to Bismarck, whom the author visited at Friedrichsruh while pursuing his studies in Berlin.

However suggestive foreign interpretations may be, the history of a country can never be fully understood without the aid of its own sons, who alone can tell us how they think and feel. By far the most illuminating introduction to an intensive study of the problems which Bismarck had to solve is Treitschke's *History of Germany in the Nineteenth Century*, which comes down to 1847. Despite its immense length and its violent prejudices, no other book conveys such a vivid impression of a great but disunited nation awaiting the touch of the

magician's wand.   The best substitute or supplement is
to be found in Brandenburg's *Die Reichsgründung*, the
first volume of which sketches the evolution of ideas
and institutions down to the call of Bismarck in 1862.
Readers of Treitschke's incomparable masterpiece, while
missing its splendour and glow, will be grateful to the
Leipzig Professor for the sobriety of his judgment.
The era of propaganda has given place to the era of
science.

II

After thus obtaining a nodding acquaintance with
the man, the problem, and the achievement, we must
make closer acquaintance with Bismarck in his writings
and correspondence, his conversations and his speeches.
When the most powerful man in the world suddenly
found himself at seventy-five in the ranks of the un-
employed, he set himself, like fallen demigods before
and after, to fight his battles over again.   Accepting an
offer from Cotta to publish his Memoirs, he secured an
ideal assistant in his old associate of the Foreign Office
and secret agent, Lothar Bucher, who knew more of his
master's secrets than anyone else and who, unlike the crafty
Holstein, remained loyal when the shades began to fall.
Encouraged by his old collaborator, who resided for
long periods at Friedrichsruh and Varzin and pored
over the materials, the Prince dictated fragmentary
reminiscences and reflections, sometimes spontaneously
and sometimes in answer to questions, which Bucher
sorted out into chapters.   The work grew under his
hands, and when ' Büchlein,' as the faithful old scribe
was called by Princess Bismarck, passed away in 1892
the foundations had been well and truly laid.   In the
following year the first version was set up in type and
served as a basis for the extension and revision which
continued till the end.   The circumstances of its composition are reflected in the character of the work.   It
bears little resemblance in form to the apologias of

Clarendon, Guizot and Bülow, who told their story with consummate art and in orderly sequence from beginning to end. Yet despite its mistakes and misstatements it is incomparably the greatest of its class, not only on account of the almost superhuman dimensions of its author, but owing to its wealth of reflection on the dynamics of politics and diplomacy.

The first two volumes which were published directly after his death and end with the reign of the Emperor Frederick, are of infinitely greater interest than the scolding supplement which could not be published till the Hohenzollern Empire was a memory. The narrative of his fall, which forms its exclusive theme, is written with a pen of gall and damages its author more than the young ruler whom he hated and despised. Though his picture of William I, painted with affectionate gratitude, is essentially true to life, his comments on some of his rivals and enemies are vitiated by the gnawing bitterness of Prometheus chained to his rock. But the faults of temperament which diminish the importance of the work as a contribution to history, and compel us to check every one of his statements, enhance its value as a revelation of personality. In the *Reflections and Recollections* we find the whole authentic man. The student should read and re-read the most impressive of political apologias at intervals as his knowledge of the period grows, keeping at his elbow Marcks' critical commentary *Fürst Bismarcks Gedanken und Erinnerungen*.[1]

Our next step in cultivating personal acquaintance is to read some of the principal speeches in the fourteen sumptuous volumes edited by Horst Kohl, or in the new edition in volumes X–XIII of the *Gesammelte Werke*. Bismarck was never an orator and occasionally hesitated for the right word ; but though he had far less difficulty in finding ready expression for his thoughts than Cromwell, his utterances sometimes recall the great Protector

[1] Horst Kohl's well-known *Wegweiser durch Bismarcks Gedanken und Erinnerungen* was avowedly written for the general reader, and is of no value to the student.

in their rugged strength. Of the declarations on domestic policy none exceed in interest those of his first storm-tossed years as Prussian Premier, collected in the second volume, when he bluntly declared that Germany would be unified not by speeches and resolutions but by blood and iron. In the field of foreign affairs the two great surveys of the European situation delivered in 1887 and 1888, and printed in the twelfth volume, stand out as imperishable statements of the maxims by which he steered his perilous course. Though far less witty and urbane than those of Bülow, Bismarck's speeches impress us by their sincerity and the range of their vision.

While the apologia and the speeches were addressed to the world, the despatches were written for the eye of his official superiors, and, when he had succeeded to the command of the ship, for the subordinate officers. Nothing is more instructive in the literature of diplomacy than to follow his reports from Frankfurt in the fifties. Appointed to the most difficult post in the Prussian service without any technical training, he quickly transformed the situation. Instead of being the mouthpiece of his Government, he worked out a policy of his own, explained it to his superiors in Berlin, and shaped his conduct by its principles. While Prussia was still ruled by Frederick William IV, who accepted the primacy of Austria as he accepted the Christian creeds, Bismarck was forming the resolution that Prussia should take the lead. That the situation in central Europe was about to enter a new phase was sensed by Austria's harassed representatives at the Diet of the Bund before it was proclaimed to the world at the cannon's mouth. The Frankfurt despatches were published in the early eighties by Poschinger in four volumes under the title of *Preussen im Bundestag*, with the omission of certain passages deemed offensive to the susceptibilities of Austria, now no longer a rival but a trusted ally. Twenty years after Bismarck's death his despatches from St. Petersburg and Paris during 1859–1862 were published by Raschdau, the last survivor of the Bismarckian Foreign Office. Though they do not compare in bulk or importance with the dramatic story of the prolonged duel at Frankfurt, they are of interest for their glimpses of Gortschakoff and Napoleon III on the eve of his promotion to the highest office in the State.

The despatches from Frankfurt were republished forty years later—without the omissions which political considerations had imposed—when both Hapsburgs and Hohenzollerns had passed away, as a portion of the ambitious enterprise launched by a defeated nation in homage to its greatest son. The first and most important section of *Bismarck : die gesammelten Werke* contains the Political Writings. The first three stately quartos cover the period down to his appointment as Premier and Minister of Foreign Affairs in 1862, and reproduce from the original texts the larger part of the volumes edited by Poschinger and Raschdau. Neither of these two collections, however, can be set aside, since the new edition for reasons of space makes no pretence to completeness. On the other hand it contains some new letters and reports, and includes the private correspondence with Schleinitz.

The second section of the *Politische Schriften*, edited with valuable prefaces by the indefatigable Thimme, embraces the years of the Prussian Premiership, and is of far greater importance to the student of today, since more than three-quarters of the documents are new. The three volumes on 1862–6 throw welcome light on the internal history of the era of unification, which had previously been envisaged too exclusively as a problem of diplomacy and war. But the main interest in this opulent budget of fresh material lies in the modification of our traditional reading of Bismarck's attitude to Austria. The notion of an implacable Prussian sharpening his knife for Austria's throat over a long period of years fades away, and we discover a pillar of Conservatism accepting Austro-Prussian collaboration as a bulwark against the democratic flood. The annexation of the

Elbe Duchies turns out to have been no part of his original plan ; and even after the campaign of 1864 a conflict with Austria was rather a possibility than a postulate. Austrian approval was to be sought for a North German Confederation under Prussia and a South German Confederation under Austria, or, if she refused, under Bavaria. Only when the plan miscarried did he press on to a *Kleindeutsch* and warlike solution, and Thimme believes that the strife of 1866 was due to the intransigence of Vienna rather than to the policy of Berlin, where compromise was favoured till the eleventh hour. The latest double volume, which brings us to the opening of 1869, reveals Bismarck in a gentler mood towards France than was hitherto supposed.

With the return of peace in 1871 we embark on the vast collection of documents from the archives of the Foreign Office, entitled *Die Grosse Politik der Europäischen Kabinette*, which illustrates the development of German policy with growing fullness till the outbreak of the World War. Though no more than six of the fifty-four volumes are devoted to the reign of Bismarck, they suffice to reveal the main lines of his statecraft when the principal task was to safeguard his conquests by the isolation of France. Every step by which he built up his gigantic system of insurance of the *status quo* deserves careful study ; but no portion of the story is more dramatic than his creation of the alliance with Austria in 1879 and his conversion of the Russophil Emperor. If it is a fact, as Bismarck asserted, that true history cannot be written from official documents, it is equally certain that it cannot be recaptured without their aid.

Bismarck's private letters, if less historically significant than his official papers, are essential to our understanding of his temperament and outlook. By far the most important item is the correspondence with William I, which was published immediately after his death by his express desire, as he considered that it would best reveal the nature of a unique relationship. Beginning in 1852 and ending in the winter of 1887, these letters reveal the two men at their best, the monarch abounding in affectionate gratitude for incomparable services, the Chancellor fully conscious of the value of unfaltering support. A second volume contains correspondence with his colleagues and other public men selected by Bismarck himself. The two volumes, which appeared in an English translation in 1903,[1] were designed by Bismarck to authenticate and supplement his autobiography, and they should therefore be taken as an elaborate appendix to his apologia.

Next in importance to the correspondence with his old master are the letters to his wife, published at the wish of Herbert Bismarck in 1900.[2] Beginning with the request to Herr von Puttkamer for the hand of his daughter in 1846, and ending in 1892, the letters reveal the softer side of ' Ottochen.' Husband and wife were seldom parted for long after 1866 ; but for the first two decades of his public life, which began in the year of his marriage, the stream is steady and copious. The letters written during the French campaign, which were not at first to be found, were published later in a little volume of a hundred pages, and subsequently added to the larger work. Johanna gave him the loving care that he needed, and her moderate intellectual equipment saved her from the temptation to have a will of her own. The letters to his sister Malwine von Arnim and her husband, covering an even longer period, were edited by Horst Kohl in 1915, and the shorter series to his son Bill was published by his daughter-in-law in 1922. The letters of the fifties to General Leopold von Gerlach were published in 1896 with the writer's consent by the indefatigable Horst Kohl, who also published the much smaller budget of letters to Kleist-Retzow, leader of the Conservatives in the Prussian Upper House. The correspondence with the Foreign Minister Schleinitz, covering the years 1858 to 1861, appeared in 1905. Other letters and memoranda are to be found in the successive volumes of the *Bismarck-Jahrbuch*, edited by

---

[1] *The Correspondence of William I and Bismarck, with other Letters.*
[2] English translation, *The Love Letters of Prince Bismarck*, 2 vols.

Horst Kohl, and the *Bismarck-Portefeuille*, edited by Poschinger. The private letters are to form a section of the *Gesammelte Werke*. A handy selection from the writings and speeches is available in *Otto von Bismarck : Deutscher Staat*, edited with a thoughtful introduction by Rothfels, in the series entitled *Der Deutsche Staatsgedanke* ; and Gunther Franz's admirable little monograph *Bismarcks Nationalgefühl* traces the development of his ideas on the making of Germany.

The greatness of Bismarck was so unmistakable from the moment of his appointment as Premier in 1862 that notes of his conversation were made and kept by large numbers of friends and colleagues, agents and visitors. The *Gespräche* are collected and arranged in chronological order by Willy Andreas in volumes VII–IX of the *Gesammelte Werke*, which take their place with the table-talk of Luther and Goethe among the treasured possessions of the German people. The most celebrated of reporters was Busch, whose *Bismarck und seine Leute während des Krieges mit Frankreich*, published in 1878, made him a creature of flesh and blood to his countrymen. The voluminous diary, continued up to the fall of the Dictator in 1890, was published in 1898 directly after his death, the English edition, entitled *Secret Passages from the Life of Bismarck*, containing a few passages omitted in the German original. Busch possessed no Boswellian magic ; but his employment in the management of the press gave him a close-range insight into some of the Chancellor's methods, and his unquestioning discipleship counteracted any temptation to conceal details of an awkward character. The garrulous journalist must of course be checked by other witnesses ; but his three volumes will always attract readers as a living picture of the superman at work with his chosen *entourage*. Less entertaining and less important is Poschinger's *Fürst Bismarck und die Parlamentarier : Die Tischgespräche des Reichskanzlers*, which contains copious records of the varied conversation at the *Bierabende* and *Frühschoppen* to which Members of Parliament were invited. The three large volumes have been skilfully abridged by Charles Lowe in an English version entitled *Bismarck's Table-Talk*.

Next to Busch no diarist has gathered such a harvest of ripe grain as Lucius von Ballhausen, a leading Conservative member of the Reichstag and Minister of Agriculture from 1879 to 1890, whose *Bismarck Erinnerungen*, published in 1921, cover the last two decades of the dictatorship. While Busch was a tool, ready at any moment to fetch and carry for his master, Ballhausen was a colleague of independent position and lofty character, a valued friend, not an obsequious satellite. His accounts of the Ministerial Councils afford precious glimpses into the working of the machine, and the record of the final crisis is impressive in its unadorned simplicity. The much slighter testimony of another Ministerial colleague, the *Erlebnisse und Gespräche mit Bismarck* of Adolf von Scholz, Minister of Finance, illustrates the domestic policy of the later years of the Prince, whom he continued to revere in the days of eclipse, and whom he depicts in an attractive light. Bismarck is seen from another angle in the two little volumes *Erinnerungen an Bismarck* by Mittnacht, the Prime Minister of Württemberg, who shared the responsibilities of Versailles and paid the Chancellor frequent visits in Berlin, in his country homes, and at Kissingen and Gastein. In his *Persönliche Erinnerungen an Bismarck* Hans Blum, the admiring biographer, describes his contacts with his hero from the first meeting in 1867 till the end. Christoph von Tiedemann's *Sechs Jahre Chef der Reichskanzlei*, which forms the second volume of his Memoirs, covers the years 1875-81. Though he spent weeks at a time in Varzin and kept a diary, the book, which is almost entirely concerned with domestic politics, is rather dull reading.

The Memoirs of the agents and diplomatists through whom Bismarck carried on his complicated game provide a rich feast. Keudell's *Fürst und Fürstin Bismarck*, the work of an intimate friend as well as a trusted associate,

covers the early years 1846–72, before his appointment as Minister to Constantinople. Of far greater
political importance, though lacking personal intimacy,
are the two volumes of the *Denkwürdigkeiten* of General
von Schweinitz, who represented his country in Vienna
and St. Petersburg during the whole of the Bismarckian
era, and whose carefully written diaries are an authority
of primary rank. The diaries of Prince Hohenlohe,
the greatest political figure on the German stage after
Bismarck himself, supply a mass of information on his
mind and moods. Hohenlohe was a *Grand Seigneur* to
his finger-tips, and the two men were never intimate ;
but they respected each other, and for decades worked
together in the cause of German unity. Of equal fame
are the first two volumes of the *Denkwürdigkeiten* of
Count Waldersee. Moltke's right-hand man and successor as Chief of the Staff was at least as much a
politician as a soldier, and in his later years was credited
with the ambition to succeed Bismarck as Chancellor.
The two men had no love for each other, but they never
quarrelled openly, and their paths constantly crossed till
the end. The *Aufzeichnungen und Erinnerungen* of
Radowitz, son of the friend and Minister of Frederick
William IV, are useful for the whole period of the dictatorship, especially for the seventies, when he worked
in the Foreign Office, during the Berlin Congress, of
which he was one of the Secretaries, and for the hectic
days of his fall. The fourth volume of Bülow's Memoirs
offers glimpses of Bismarck over a period of forty years.
But none of these witnesses has drawn such a vivid
picture of the ageing statesman in his family circle, in
sunshine and in storm, as Prince Eulenburg in his
fascinating recollections *Aus 50 Jahren.*

We derive little of our knowledge of Bismarck's
personality from his foreign visitors ; but two Anglo-
Saxon witnesses at least have a claim to be heard. In
the *Correspondence* of Motley, his friend of Göttingen
days, we catch some fleeting but delightfully intimate
and attractive glimpses of the actor off the stage. The

host, wrote the famous American historian and diplomat, was so simple and friendly that it was difficult for the guest to remember that he was staying with the greatest German since Luther. Equally appreciative are Sidney Whitman's *Personal Reminiscences of Prince Bismarck*, which record a series of visits after the catastrophe of 1890, and present a picture of greater gentleness and refinement of feeling than we find in the portrait of any other artist. Before we return from the man to the statesman we should not fail to consult the excellent study by Otto Baumgarten, *Bismarcks Religion*, which traces the intellectual and spiritual evolution of a Prussian Protestant, to whom church-going and dogma made no appeal, but who believed in Providence and felt himself responsible for his actions to a higher Power. ' He experienced God as a reality before which he seemed to himself small.'

III

For intensive study of the master-builder we must grapple with the more important of the monographs which exist in overwhelming numbers and in many languages. Twenty years ago Erich Marcks set out to produce a biography which, if not official in the sense of the stately records of our British statesmen, enjoyed at any rate the approval of the family. His unrivalled knowledge of the period, his psychological insight and his literary skill rendered Marcks the ideal biographer ; but the *magnum opus* began and ended with the first volume, which only brings the story down to 1848 and therefore falls into the category of monographs. No portion of his career has been so adequately portrayed as in this masterly reconstruction of his youth and early manhood. It is deeply to be regretted that the biographer withdrew after the first round ; and where Marcks felt unequal to the struggle, no lesser champion is likely to try his hand.

The four stormy years from the election to the

United Landtag in 1847 to the appointment as Prussia's representative at Frankfurt are the least known and the least documented of his public career. At this stage he was Prussian, not German, a royalist of the extreme right who poured scorn on the ideals of constitutional liberty. Thus he was completely out of touch with the Frankfurt Parliament, which strove earnestly and nobly for a free and united Germany. In attempting to reconstruct the stage on which he made his *début*, and to understand the ideas which inspired the various groups in the middle of the century, we should seek assistance from Meinecke's classical treatise *Weltbürgertum und Nationalstaat* and Veit Valentin's monumental *Geschichte der deutschen Revolution 1848–9*, of which the first volume has recently appeared.

On the seminal Frankfurt period we are fortunate to possess one of the best monographs in German historical literature. The Prussian envoy's reports, already mentioned, only gave one side of the grim struggle between the two leading members of the Bund, and no satisfactory reconstruction was possible till the Austrian version was also in our hands. It is the merit of Arnold Oskar Meyer, in his *Bismarcks Kampf mit Oesterreich am Bundestag zu Frankfurt 1851 bis 1859*, to have provided the first full account from the Prussian and Austrian archives of his hero's apprenticeship in the diplomatic art, combining an ardent admiration of the Prussian champion with vivid sketches of Thun, Prokesch and Rechberg, the Austrian representatives. The story has subsequently been outlined from another angle by the Hungarian historian Wertheimer in the first chapter of his work *Bismarck im politischen Kampf*, based on the reports of the Austrian representatives, which he had studied before Meyer.

While Bismarck at Frankfurt was planning his campaign to deliver the Bund from the Austrian yoke, Frederick William IV surrounded himself with members of the so-called Christo-Germanic school, inspired by Stahl and led by the Gerlach brothers. Bismarck agreed with the ruler and his friends in detesting Liberalism ; but the ruthless realist was just as hostile to the flabby romanticism of his master, whom he despised both for his subservience to Austria and for his weakness of will. The two men met from time to time, and the King was aware of the volcanic fires that burned in his envoy. But the note written against his name—' only to be employed in a crisis '—was a sentence of exclusion from high office during the reign of a gifted dreamer who had had enough of crises in the year of revolution to last him the rest of his life. Bismarck's personal relations with the ruling clique are mirrored in his correspondence with Leopold von Gerlach, and are carefully analysed by Augst in *Bismarck und Leopold von Gerlach*, which presents the younger man as the friend but never as the disciple of the old General.

Our acquaintance with the three years in Russia, hitherto known from the official despatches and the private letters to Schleinitz, received a welcome enrichment with the publication in 1921 of Kurt von Schlözer's *Petersburger Briefe 1857–1862*. ' My new chief,' wrote the exasperated First Secretary of the Prussian Legation after a brief acquaintance, ' is a man without consideration, a man of might who aspires to *coups de théâtre*, who desires to shine, who knows everything without having seen it, and is omniscient though there is much that he does not know. He has been used in Frankfurt to young *Attachés* who trembled at his approach.' A year later Schlözer reported that they were getting on splendidly, though he added : ' A devil of a fellow ! Where is he making for ? ' The greatness of the man conquered him, and he remained a friend up to and after 1890, if indeed the Titan can be said to have had any friends in the ordinary sense of the term.

The first full and authoritative record of the diplomacy of the eight years which followed Bismarck's summons was attempted by Sybel, who, after sharply attacking the Premier's unconstitutional proceedings in Parliament, was converted by the victory of Sadowa into one of his trustiest henchmen.   The suggestion that the famous historian should devote his closing years to describing the founding of the German Empire came from Bismarck himself, who promised him the use of the archives.   The first five volumes, published in 1889, brought the story to the end of 1866 ; but the young Emperor considered that his adored grandfather had not received his due, and excluded him from the archives of the Foreign Office after the quarrel with his patron in the following year.   Thus the last two volumes, which reach the outbreak of war with France, lack the documentary value of their predecessors, though the fallen statesman gave what help he could.   Whatever else we read on the most eventful years of his life, Sybel's narrative, though nearly half a century old, must be read too.   When asked his opinion of the book by Justizrat Philipp, Bismarck replied that Sybel had written with discretion, but that, despite the necessary omissions, the work was thoroughly reliable in all essentials.   Thus in reading Sybel we must remember that we are listening to the story in the shape that the chief actor desired it to be told.   Rössler wittily remarked that the title *The Founding of the German Empire by William I* contained a misprint, and that it should have been ' despite ' instead of ' by.' [1]   This, however, is not the criticism that we should make today.   The real weakness of Sybel is in his Prussian partiality and his failure to paint the hero with his warts.   A critic complained with humorous exaggeration that he had transformed the tiger into a tame cat.   The German Empire was not founded by a Sunday school teacher, and the Bismarck of the sixties was more like Vulcan in his forge.

The dynastic vanity of William II, which had been wounded by Sybel, was soothed by Ottokar Lorenz in his famous counterblast, *Kaiser Wilhelm I und die Gründung des Reiches 1866–1871*, published in 1902. Utilising materials supplied by Ernst, Duke of Coburg, the rulers of Baden and Weimar, and various South

[1] *Trotz* for *durch*.

German statesmen, he presented a picture strikingly different from that with which the world had grown familiar, and hailed the old Emperor as the real founder of the German Empire. But the pendulum now swung too far in the other direction, and Lorenz was sharply challenged by his brother specialists. He vigorously defended himself in a little book entitled *Bismarcks Verkleinerer* ; but his work, despite its power and erudition, has failed in its purpose of upsetting established judgments. The personal and political relations between the old Emperor and his Minister are most fairly depicted in Marcks' classical biography *Kaiser Wilhelm I.* For later and more judicial versions than that of either Sybel or Lorenz we may turn to the second volume of Brandenburg's *Die Reichsgründung* (with its pendant *Untersuchungen und Aktenstücke zur Geschichte der Reichsgründung*, which deals with Prussia in 1848–9 and Franco-German relations 1863–6) and to the eighth, ninth and tenth volumes of Alfred Stern's cool and authoritative *Geschichte Europas 1815–1871*, written in the temperate zone of neutral Switzerland. For the rival French view of the sixties we look to the *Histoire du Second Empire* of La Gorce and to Ollivier's voluminous apologia ; for the Austrian version to Friedjung's famous book *Der Kampf um die Vorherrschaft in Deutschland*, which Srbik is about to supplement.

The most important addition since Sybel to our knowledge of the diplomatic game in Western Europe in the sixties is contained in Oncken's three volumes of documents *Die Rheinpolitik Kaiser Napoleon III von 1863 bis 1870*, which reveal the innermost thoughts of the Imperial adventurer in his declining years. The astonishing story of ambition and intrigue unfolded in the reports of Metternich, the Austrian Ambassador at Paris, is summarised in the Introduction, which has appeared separately in English as *Napoleon and the Rhine*. It is a fascinating if not precisely elevating occupation to watch the two chess-players at their game, Napoleon aiming at the control of the Rhineland,

Bismarck at the unification of Germany, the one plunging wildly, the other skilfully exploiting his mistakes. *Grossherzog Friedrich I von Baden und die deutsche Politik von 1845 bis 1871*, edited by the same distinguished scholar, covers part of the same ground. The correspondence, memoranda, and diaries of the son-in-law of the Emperor William are of equal value for the relations between North and South Germany and for the conflicts from which the Empire emerged. A luminous Introduction furnishes the key to the two weighty volumes, and enables us to visualise the wisest of Bismarck's collaborators. The vast official publication *Les Origines diplomatiques de la Guerre de 1870–1* begins its long journey in 1862. The first volume appeared in 1909, and the ground has now been covered as far as 1867. The work, in which we may follow Bismarck's conversations with the French Ambassadors at Berlin, has been completed in manuscript, and only the printing of the later portion remains.

Since the whole of Europe was involved in the birth-pangs of the German Empire, it is not surprising that erudite monographs on the sixties follow each other in rapid succession. The intricate story of the promise in Article V of the Treaty of Prague of a plebiscite in North Schleswig, and of its cancellation in 1878, has been told in *Bismarck und die Nordschleswigsche Frage 1864–1879*, published in 1925 by order of the German Foreign Office. In his Introduction to the extensive collection of documents Platzhoff challenges the traditional belief that Bismarck never intended to fulfil the pledge, and points out that he was ready to surrender the frontier districts on condition that the transferred German minority should be protected and the honour of Germany maintained. That all attempts at a peaceful understanding failed, concludes the editor, was due not to Bismarck but to the obstinacy of the Danes, who demanded a plebiscite in the whole of Schleswig.

Zechlin's *Bismarck und die Grundlegung der deutschen Grossmacht* grew out of a plan to describe the making of the Constitution ; but the interaction of foreign and domestic politics proved to be so close that the work developed into a panoramic survey of Bismarck's policy in the sixties. So comprehensive indeed has the scheme become, and so great the mass of fresh material, that this volume of 600 pages, after an introductory survey of the European situation and of Bismarck's political ideas, only covers ' the new era ' during 1862 and 1863. The end of the same decade has been illuminated, with the aid of fresh material from the Prussian Foreign Office, by Horst Michael's *Bismarck, England und Europa, 1866-1870*. Special emphasis is laid on the importance of the problems of the Near East, and we are warned not to dwell too exclusively in the west in reconstituting the foundation of the German Empire. The essential condition of a victorious struggle with France, which Bismarck anticipated rather than desired, was the neutralisation of Austria ; and in these pages it is the angry Beust, who was summoned from Dresden to the Ballplatz after the *débâcle* of 1866, who claims our attention rather than the more histrionic figure of Napoleon III.

The latest important contribution to our understanding of the diplomacy of the sixties is provided from a foreign angle in Wertheimer's *Bismarck im politischen Kampf*, based on research in the archives of Vienna and Berlin. The official biographer of Andrassy is a patriotic Hungarian ; but he assures his readers that he writes with the love of a life-long friend of Germany and that his book, the fruit of many years of labour, is a sign of his special reverence for the greatest statesman of German blood. After a careful introductory survey of Bismarck's apprenticeship at Frankfurt, St. Petersburg and Paris, he deals at length with the background of the war of 1866, Bismarck's relations to Hungary, the visit of the monarchs to the Paris exhibition of 1867, and the relations of Bismarck with Prince Jerome Napoleon. The longest chapter describes the domestic and other obstacles which had to be overcome before the King of Prussia could assume the Imperial title. A

final chapter on Bismarck's relations to Taaffe takes us
to the period of peace. A curious addition to our
knowledge of the struggle with Austria has been made
in Hermann Wendel's *Bismarck und Serbien im Jahre
1866*, which reveals the plan of stirring up Serbia as
well as Hungary against the Hapsburg foe.

The internal history of the founding of the Empire
has received far less attention than the diplomatic side,
and we must collect our information from many sources.
Bismarck's work was facilitated—it may almost be said
rendered possible—by the *Nationalverein* founded in
1859 by Rudolf von Bennigsen. The Hanoverian
statesman, who owed his influence at least as much to
his high character as to his ability, has found a sympathetic biographer in Oncken, whose enormous volumes,
stuffed with political correspondence, are indispensable
for the domestic history of the whole Bismarckian era.
A full-length portrait of his eloquent collaborator Miquel,
who found his way from Marx to Bismarck, is being
painted by Wilhelm Mommsen, whose first volume
reaches 1866. The Dictator's relations with Lassalle
received fresh illumination when in 1927 a forgotten
chest in the Foreign Office collapsed from old age and
disclosed the lost correspondence, which Gustav Mayer
has published with an admirable Introduction as *Bismarck und Lassalle : Ihr Briefwechsel und ihre Gespräche*.
For his conflict with the Liberals we have the recent
collection of letters published with the title *Deutscher
Liberalismus im Zeitalter Bismarcks: eine Politische Brief-
sammlung*, edited by Geritzcke and Heyderhoff, of which
the first volume reaches to 1875. His dealings with
the Conservatives are sketched in the first lecture in
Siegfried von Kardorff's *Bismarck*, which utilises material
supplied by his distinguished father ; described in detail
in Gerhard Ritter's *Die Preussischen Konservativen und
Bismarcks Deutsche Politik, 1858–1871* ; and receive
occasional illustration from the *Denkwürdigkeiten* of
Roon.

When the Deutscher Bund perished on the battle-

field of Sadowa Bismarck set to work to construct a
constitution for the newly founded North German Confederation, which, in the fullness of time, could be enlarged
to embrace the South German states.   The classical
presentation of the new constitutional structure is in
Laband's *Deutsches Staatsrecht* ; but those who shirk
the German Anson will find an excellent substitute in
B. E. Howard's *The German Empire*. That united
Germany might have come earlier into the world if the
attitude of Hesse-Darmstadt had been more forthcoming is the argument of Schüssler's learned monograph
Bismarcks Kampf um Süddeutschland 1867. The constitutional relations of the Empire to its largest unit
are traced in Hans Goldschmidt's *Das Reich und Preussen
im Kampf um die Führung : von Bismarck bis* 1918.

On the immediate causes of the last of Bismarck's
three wars we possess *The Origin of the War of 1870* by
the Harvard historian, R. H. Lord, who prefaces a translation of the most important Prussian documents with a
critical discussion of his policy.   There is a vivid account
of the historic scene at Ems in the life of Abeken, the
Secretary of King William, translated under the title
Bismarck's Pen.   No German historian has devoted so
much attention to the last days of peace as Fester, who
has collected the relevant material in *Briefe, Aktenstücke
und Regesten zur Geschichte der Hohenzollernschen Thron-
kandidatur in Spanien*.   The *War Diary* of the Crown
Prince Frederick, 1870–1871, from which Geffcken had
published some sensational extracts in 1888, appeared in
1926, and the Diary of the Grand Duke Frederick of
Baden concludes the second volume of his papers to
which attention was called above.   The important *rôle*
of the Bavarian Government and dynasty in the creation of the Empire is authoritatively described from a
Bavarian standpoint in Döberl's *Bayern und die Bis-
marckische Reichsgründung*, which pays fitting tribute to
the statesmanship of Bray.   Johannes Haller's suggestive little book *Bismarcks Friedenschlüsse*, one of the
best Bismarckian monographs, compares and discusses

the contrasted settlements of 1864, 1866 and 1871. Nikolsburg, he contends, was a perfect peace, while Frankfurt was in some degree vitiated by the failure to take Belfort.

IV

With the return from Versailles we enter on the second and less eventful chapter of the twenty-eight years of personal rule. Till then Bismarck had lived the feverish life of a gambler playing for high and ever higher stakes. He had won every round in the game owing to an unparalleled combination of skill and luck ; but the ground was never firm beneath his feet till German unity under Prussian leadership had been attained. A French triumph in 1870, like an Austrian victory in Bohemia in 1866, would have flung him headlong from his lofty pedestal of power and prestige. The great adventure was now at an end. No one was tempted to attack the strongest state on the Continent, which had struck down its two rivals within a space of five years. Henceforth his position was unassailable. He had enemies by the score, but no rivals ; for the laurels were thick on his brow, and he enjoyed the unchanging confidence of the modest old ruler whom he had raised to the pinnacle of earthly fame.

The sources for a study of Bismarck's diplomacy in the nineteen years following his crowning victory accumulate from year to year. The first six volumes of the *Grosse Politik* provide the groundwork for an interpretation ; but the inexhaustible treasures of the Wilhelmstrasse have as yet only been tapped. Meanwhile there is much to learn from the *Documents Diplomatiques Français*, which, like the *Grosse Politik*, begin in 1871. The two volumes of the first series already published help to fill in the outline drawn in the poignant Memoirs of the sorely-tried French Ambassador Gontaut-Biron and in the slighter volumes, *La Mission du Comte de St. Vallier*, constructed by Ernest Daudet from the papers of his happier successor. From the Austrian side we derive precious assistance from the third volume of Wertheimer's biography of Andrassy, and from Pribram's revelations of the *Secret Treaties of Austria-Hungary*, which are prefaced by an illuminating sketch of the formation and evolution of the Triple Alliance. From the British side some useful material has recently become available in the official biographies of Disraeli and Salisbury, the second and third series of Queen Victoria's correspondence, and the quivering *Letters of the Empress Frederick*, edited by Sir Frederick Ponsonby.

No detailed study of Bismarck's later diplomacy has been attempted on the scale of Sybel. A meritorious sketch by Hans Plehn, *Bismarcks Auswärtige Politik nach der Reichsgründung*, written from printed sources alone, has been superseded since the publication of the *Grosse Politik*, and Rachfahl's enormous volume, *Deutschland und die Weltpolitik*, consisting of his University lectures, lacks notes and references. We owe the best birdseye view of the period to Japikse, whose work has appeared in German as *Europa und Bismarcks Friedenspolitik*. Standing outside the traditions and rivalries of the Great Powers, the verdict of the distinguished Dutch historian is of peculiar weight when he asserts that from the defeat of France till the day of his dismissal the governing principle of Bismarck's foreign policy was the maintenance of peace. The same conviction inspires A. O. Meyer's brochure *Bismarcks Friedenspolitik*, which contains a little fresh material supplied by the family.

This reading of twenty years of Bismarckian diplomacy, though now generally accepted by historians, has been challenged within and beyond the frontiers of the Fatherland. The severest of competent critics is the American scholar Joseph Vincent Fuller, who launched a preliminary attack in an essay on the war scare of 1875 published in the *American Historical Review*, January, 1919. Rejecting the Prince's contention in his apologia that he was the innocent victim of designing soldiers, Fuller argues that the crisis was in effect the

Chancellor's own work. Herzfeld responded to the challenge in his brochure *Die deutsch-französische Kriegsgefahr von 1875*, which surveyed all the evidence then available. The most damaging factor in the indictment is the report by Gontaut-Biron of an after-dinner conversation with Radowitz, a high official of the Foreign Office, in which the latter was stated to have spoken openly of a preventive war. The publication in the *Grosse Politik* of Radowitz' very different account of the conversation sets the problem in a new light, though it is highly improbable that the Ambassador invented the incident which caused him so much alarm. Wahl has analysed the place of the *Kulturkampf* as a factor in Bismarck's *crise de nerfs* in his little book *Vom Bismarck der 70er Jahre* ; and Holborn has cleared up the mystery of Radowitz' visit to St. Petersburg in his documented monograph *Bismarcks Europäische Politik zu Beginn der 70er Jahre und die Mission Radowitz*, in which the vain old Gortchakoff is the villain of the piece. The latest and best discussion of a complicated problem is in the articles of Miss Taffs in the *Slavonic Review* (December, 1930, and March, 1931), which utilise the new French official documents, the correspondence of the British Ambassador, Lord Odo Russell, and fresh material from the archives of Berlin. She reaches the conclusion that Bismarck was neither as white as he painted himself nor as black as the Quai d'Orsay believed. It is as clear that he rattled the sword as it is that he had no desire to draw it from its scabbard. Moreover, the instantaneous rally of Russia and Great Britain to the side of France showed him, as it showed the world, that he had made a mistake, and taught him to be more cautious in the remaining years.

A more sustained attack by Fuller on Bismarck's reputation as a man of peace after 1871 was delivered in his learned volume *Bismarck's Diplomacy at its Zenith*, a study of the European crisis inaugurated by the revolutionary unification of Bulgaria in 1885. Unlike most historians, who see in Bismarck the giant whose mighty arm kept Austria and Russia from flying at one another's throats, he depicts the Chancellor as an angry bungler, whose duplicity and brutality left Germany at the conclusion of the crisis between two potential foes about to join hands across her frontiers. No student can neglect the book, but few of its readers are likely to be convinced by its argument.

Hardly less severe is the criticism of the handling of the same dangerous incident in *Bismarcks Friedenspolitik und das Problem des deutschen Machtverfalls* by Ulrich Noack, though the indictment is of a strangely different character. While the American scholar accuses the Dictator of playing with fire, the young German historian paradoxically condemns him for his short-sighted pacifism. Bismarck, he declares, lost an opportunity which could never recur of ending by a fourth victorious war the growing Slav danger. He should have joined with Austria against Russia, and after the victory have satisfied the autonomous aspirations of the various Slav races, from the Baltic to the Aegean, within the orbit of Austro-German hegemony. The task of remodelling Eastern Europe shirked by the Man of Destiny in the eighties, according to his principle of avoiding preventive wars, was taken up and solved thirty years later by the victorious allies at the expense of the Central Empires. Very different in tone and conclusions is Otto Becker's masterly treatment of the same group of problems in *Bismarcks Bündnispolitik*, the first volume of a work which passes beyond the later phases of the master's diplomacy to the tragic blunders of his successors, and vindicates the secret treaty of reinsurance concluded with Russia in 1887 as serving the interests of each of the three Empires.

Smaller in scale and far less controversial than the writings of Fuller and Noack is the little book by Rothfels, *Bismarcks Englische Bündnispolitik*, which discusses our relations to the New Empire down to the offer of an alliance in 1889. While Germany remained a Continental power there was no conceivable reason for British antagonism ; but the Dictator's decision in 1884 to follow the fashion by carving some slices off the African joint led to temporary friction. A comprehensive survey of the creation of a colonial Empire is given in Maximilian Hagen's extensive monograph *Bismarcks Kolonialpolitik*, which it is interesting for English readers to compare with the account in Lord Fitzmaurice's biography of Granville. How Bismarck mended the wire to St. Petersburg in 1881 after the dangerous tension of 1879 we learn from the *Memoirs* of Saburow, the Russian Ambassador at Berlin, edited with an Introduction by J. Y. Simpson. The European chessboard during Bismarck's final years in the Wilhelmstrasse and on the morrow of his fall is skilfully reconstituted in the opening chapters of W. Langer's remarkable book *The Franco-Russian Alliance 1890–1894*.

In his domestic policy after the foundation of the Empire Bismarck was as fallible as lesser mortals. At a time when it was desirable to rally all the forces of national life round the new Imperial structure, he engaged in a struggle with the Roman Church which stirred millions of loyal subjects to passionate anger and from which he emerged, not indeed completely defeated, but badly bruised, and saddled with a powerful permanent *Centrumspartei* under the leadership of the formidable Windthorst. His struggle with the Catholics, the one spectacular failure of his life, is described from the Government side in Erich Förster's fully documented life of Falk, the Minister whom he used as his tool in the days of his wrath and who, when he came to recognise the futility of the struggle, was unhesitatingly thrown aside. The story is excellently told from the Catholic side in Kissling's three-volume *Geschichte des Kulturkampfes im Deutschen Reiche*, the first volume of which traces Prussian policy towards Catholics down to 1870. The settlement with the Papacy is vividly described in the *Letzte Römische Briefe 1882–1894* of Kurd von Schlözer, Prussian Minister to the Vatican. Suggestive sketches of the long quarrel are to be found in Adalbert Wahl's booklet *Vom Bismarck der 70er Jahre*, which explains the Chancellor's action by considerations of foreign policy, and in the closing lecture in Siegfried von Kardorff's *Bismarck*, which describes the mission of peace of Prince Hatzfeldt Trachenberg in 1886 from material furnished by the envoy.

The battle with the Socialists was equally unsuccessful, though in this case Bismarck is not open to the charge of provoking an unnecessary conflict. Socialism was a world-wide problem, the child of modern industrialism, and he can hardly be blamed for not knowing how to deal with such a novel phenomenon. But his repressive legislation was a failure, and the working-class movement developed in bitter hostility to the State. The Socialist version of the long duel may be read in the fourth volume of Mehring's standard *Geschichte der deutschen Sozialdemokratie* and in Bebel's artless autobiography,—the latter available in an English translation. The Government's constructive policy of state-aided insurance and pensions, which followed the passing of the anti-socialist law of 1878, is sympathetically outlined in W. H. Dawson's *Bismarck and State Socialism*. His unceasing struggle with the Liberals is reflected in the second volume of the work *Deutscher Liberalismus* which has been mentioned above. His relations with the Conservatives are summarised in the opening lecture of Siegfried von Kardorff's *Bismarck*.

The sharpest condemnation of the whole spirit of Bismarck's domestic policy has been passed by Ziekursch in the first two volumes of his spirited and controversial *Politische Geschichte des neuen deutschen Kaiserreiches*. The Dictator, he complains, gave the dynasty such an excess of power that a Frederick the Great on the throne or a Bismarck on the steps of the throne was required to avert disaster. The edifice that he erected was top-heavy, for it rested on a quasi-autocratic Government which was bound to become increasingly out of touch with the spirit of the age. The unpardonable error of the Chancellor, he argues, was the omission to train the nation for self-determination. It is true that the hard-working *bourgeoisie* had no burning desire for a larger share of power ; but a statesman of deeper faith and longer vision would have realised that an orderly, educated and prosperous community could not be kept in leading-strings for ever. The lack of contact between the Government and the people, as he points out, was to be manifested during the war and to be one of the contributory causes of the revolution of 1918.

A very different reading of Bismarck's statesmanship is presented in Wahl's *Deutsche Geschichte 1871–1914*, the first two volumes of which bring us to 1890. Though Wahl writes with authority on foreign policy, he devotes most of his space to internal affairs,—the institutions and parties of the Empire, the fortunes of its component units, the social and economic legislation of the first Chancellor, his conflict with the Socialists and Catholics, the triumphs of science and scholarship, the achievements of literature and art. While Ziekursch lectures Bismarck on his blindness to the merits of Democracy, Wahl applauds him as the author of a constitution which retained the organic elements in the State and was capable of resisting the assaults of radicalism and socialism, No recent work on Bismarck has emphasised so strongly his services to Conservatism in the broadest sense of the term. Ardent, however, as is Wahl's admiration for his hero, he is in no way blind to the spots on the sun. The *Kulturkampf*, which he treats in great detail, was admittedly a failure, and his fall was in part the result of faults of temperament and domestic policy.

The accession of William II in 1888 was the beginning of the end, though the crisis of March, 1890, took two years to develop. There is already a substantial literature on the fall of the Dictator, and as despatches of the diplomatic representatives of other States come to light it will grow. The two parties to the quarrel have presented their case to the world, the old gladiator in the third volume of his apologia, the monarch through the medium of Nowak's *Kaiser and Chancellor*, published in 1930 as the first volume of a survey of his reign utilising written and oral material from Doorn. The historian has made out a better case for the fallen ruler than he made for himself in his self-righteous Memoirs. The Prince is depicted as drunk with power and past his prime. An appendix reprints the letter to Francis Joseph dictated by William II on April 3, 1890, describing the events of the critical days in vivid detail, which was first published in an Austrian review in 1919. The valuable memoranda of Bötticher, the Minister of the Interior, and Rottenburg, the Secretary of the Chancellor's office, were published in Epstein's *Bismarcks Entlassung*, which establishes Bötticher's loyalty both to the Kaiser and the Chancellor. The first critical summary of the abundant evidence was provided in Schüssler's *Bismarcks Sturz*, for which the Austrian and Bavarian archives were explored; and Wilhelm Mommsen's *Bismarcks Sturz und die Parteien* analyses the Parliamentary and Press reactions of the catastrophe. The work of Gradenwitz, *Bismarcks letzter Kampf 1888–1898*, which despite its title is almost wholly concerned with his resignation, utilises the reports of Baden's Minister at Berlin. In the first volume of *Bismarcks Entlassung* Gagliardi, the Swiss historian, who sides with the Emperor rather than with the Chancellor, reviews the internal aspects of the crisis, adding new light from Swiss and Austrian archives and from reports of the envoys of the minor German states at Berlin. When the sequel on the international aspects of the crisis is in our hands, we shall possess as satisfying a picture of a historic event as we could wish.

The impression left on the mind after studying the evidence now available is that the breach was psychologically inevitable, resulting as it did from a clash not only of temperaments but of generations. The dropping of the pilot was clearly a danger to the navigation of the ship; on the other hand the young Emperor was right in rejecting the Chancellor's advice to adopt violent courses against the strikers and Parliamentary opponents. The little known story of his unconstitutional projects, which was hinted in Delbrück's little book *Bismarcks*

Erbe, published in 1915, has been recently repeated in the pages of Nowak, and has been worked out in detail by Zechlin in *Die Staatsstreichpläne Bismarcks und Wilhelms II*. It is piquant to learn that the dangerous idea of attacking the Reichstag, which was rejected by the young ruler in 1890, was seriously considered by him four years later.

The last eight years of the old campaigner must be reconstructed from the abundant material collected in Penzler's seven volumes, *Bismarck nach der Entlassung* ; in the two volumes entitled *Fürst Bismarck 1890–1898*, edited by Hofmann, editor of the *Hamburger Fremdenblatt*, which contains the articles inspired by the mighty *frondeur* ; in the third volume of the *Gespräche* in the *Gesammelte Werke* ; and in Julius von Eckardt's *Aus den Tagen von Bismarcks Kampf gegen Caprivi*. The conflict of Potsdam and Friedrichsruh reached its climax when the fallen statesman, on his visit to Vienna for the wedding of his eldest son, was publicly boycotted by order of the German Government. His retaliation in a memorable series of speeches at Jena and elsewhere as he returned home through Germany is described in Gradenwitz' little monograph *Akten über Bismarcks Grossdeutsche Rundfahrt vom Jahre 1892*.

Among the many pilgrims to Friedrichsruh in the years of eclipse none possessed a quicker mind or a sharper pen than Maximilian Harden, who defended the Bismarckian tradition against the new regime in *Die Zukunft*, and whose memories were embodied in the essay on Bismarck published in the first volume of his *Köpfe*. The sympathetic study of Johanna Bismarck in the same volume brings the unselfish companion of his stormy life vividly before our eyes. The most recent addition to our knowledge of the closing years is contained in the little volume *Bismarck-Gespräche*, published in 1927, recording conversations from 1878 to 1896 with Justizrat Philipp, his legal adviser. The most interesting part of a rather uninspiring narrative concerns the circumstances of his fall and his attitude to William II, on whom he

THE STUDY OF BISMARCK 265

repeatedly enlarged with his usual unmeasured bitterness. The publication of selections from Herbert Bismarck's papers, to which we may look forward in the next few years, will be a precious addition to our knowledge of his father, to whom in filial devotion he sacrificed first his domestic happiness and finally his political career.

V

The unwearying researches of the last decade have brought our knowledge to a stage which allows us to pronounce judgment on a unique career with considerable confidence. In his challenging little brochure *Bismarcks Schatten*, published in 1921, Hermann Kantorowicz argued that Germany's path of deliverance led over the ruins of his cult, and foretold that in another generation he would be recognised as the great seducer who had led Germany astray. While others were shouting Back to Bismarck ! he cried Away from Bismarck ! A no less fundamental repudiation came in the same year from F. W. Förster, Germany's leading pacifist, whose brochure *Bismarcks Werk im Lichte der föderalistischen Kritik* revived the arguments of the half-forgotten *Grossdeutsch* publicist Constantin Frantz, and condemned the *Kleindeutsch* or Prussian solution of the problem of German unity. Such criticisms, however, have found little acceptance at home or abroad. For most people are convinced that the omelette could not have been made without breaking eggs, and that Bismarck and Cavour had as much right to unite their nations as had Lincoln to keep a nation united. Neither country could call its soul its own till Austria was excluded, and as she declined to go she had to be expelled by force of arms. Such elemental occurrences as the fashioning of Germany and Italy are indeed beyond good and evil. The conditions which enabled England and France to become strong homogeneous nations by leisurely process were lacking in Cental Europe. If the work were to be done at all it had to be achieved in a few brief years of passionate endeavour in the middle of a Continent filled with jealous competitors. Moreover the nineteenth century witnessed the coming of age of nationalism. A generation which blundered into the world war, and is only now beginning to recognise the theoretical and practical imperfections of the concept of self-sufficing sovereignty, has little right to throw stones at the supreme interpreter of the spirit of his age.

To admit that the forcible unification of Germany was within the rules of the game as played by statesmen and peoples in the nineteenth century in no way pledges us to approve every step of the path which led to the goal or to admire the use that was made of a spectacular victory. The annexation of a portion of Lorraine, however natural a penalty for aggression and defeat, was an error of the first magnitude ; for though Alsace might conceivably have been disarmed by tact and kindness, Lorraine was French in blood, speech and sentiment. Metz could only be held by the bayonet, and in the endeavour to hold it Europe was transformed into an armed camp. Moreover though it was easy enough to keep France in quarantine while she was weak, it was impossible to perpetuate her isolation when she recovered her breath. The momentous choice of Austria in preference to Russia in 1879 was inevitable under the circumstances ; but henceforth a Franco-Russian *rapprochement* was in the logic of events. Though no irrevocable step was taken while Bismarck was at the helm, the process had begun in 1875 and was in full swing before his fall. ' We Germans fear God and nothing else in the world,' declared the Dictator in the ringing utterance of 1888. It was not strictly true ; for he himself confessed that he was haunted by the spectre of coalitions. For such a re-grouping of the Powers he paved the way by the annexation of Lorraine, which rendered a high-spirited nation an irreconcilable foe, biding her hour till the international situation brought the ball to her feet. Force alone could not guarantee a settlement that was passionately resented by millions of civilised human beings, any more than it could break the force of Catholic claims or Socialist ideals.

The weakness of the ' realists '—and Bismarck was the greatest of the tribe—is that they define reality too narrowly and tend to think more of immediate than of ultimate returns. Vast and splendid as was his intellect, the vision of a new international order resting on a partnership of contented self-governing national units was beyond his ken. The main task of the twentieth century as it emerges from the shattering ordeal of the war is the organisation of a shrinking world. To 'the shaping of the human spirit for that supreme adventure Bismarck contributed nothing either by example or precept. He was content to work for his country alone and was satisfied with its rapturous applause.

GERMAN HISTORICAL STUDIES SINCE THE WAR

THOUGH the material and psychological conditions of Germany since the World War have been exceptionally unfavourable to historical research and production, a great deal of valuable work has been accomplished during the last decade. The *Notgemeinschaft der deutschen Wissenschaft*, founded in 1920 and generously supported by the Government of the Reich, has enabled many a learned society to survive, many a veteran scholar to continue the task to which he had set his hand in happier days, and many a promising student to win his spurs. Taking quality and quantity together, Germany retains her place, which she won a century ago with Ranke and Böckh, at the top of the list in the field of historical studies. No other country can show such a record as is revealed in the *Jahresberichte für deutsche Geschichte*, edited by Brackmann and Hartung, with the aid of dozens of expert collaborators. A few of the veterans have described their activities in the volumes *Die Geschichtswissenschaft der Gegenwart in Selbstdarstellungen.*

A brief revew of a vast territory must necessarily devote most attention to the achievements of the older generation, and much of the best work has been produced by septuagenarians. Some admirers of Eduard Meyer may be tempted to regret that the time devoted in the evening of his life to his *Ursprung und Anfänge des Christentums*, despite the high merits of portions of the treatise, was not spent on the revision of the first volume of the great *Geschichte des Altertums*, which the progress of research in Egypt and Mesopotamia since 1913 rendered urgent.   The task, he declared, was too formidable to be undertaken by a man of his age, who desired to spend his remaining years in revising the later portions of his panoramic survey ; but as a partial substitute he published a small monograph, *Die ältere Chronologie Aegyptens und Assyriens*.   The second volume, however, covering the period from 1500 B.C. to the beginnings of historical Greece and portraying the New Kingdom in Egypt at its height, appeared in a revised form in 1928. The promised revision of its successors was frustrated by his death in 1930.   For a picture of Mesopotamian civilisation in the light of the latest discoveries we may turn to the writings of Meissner, whose illustrated volumes *Babylonien und Assyrien* embody in popular form the labours of a lifetime.   Students of Kittel's *Geschichte des Volkes Israel* may now read the first two volumes of his masterpiece in a fresh revision, and the recently published first half of the third volume describes the Exile and return.   A shorter but no less authoritative survey is supplied in Sellin's *Geschichte des Israelitisch-Jüdischen Volkes*, the first volume of which brings the story down to the Exile.

In the department of Greek history the outstanding event is the completion of the second edition of Beloch's *Griechische Geschichte*, which grew from four volumes to eight, of which the last half has appeared since the war. After a prolonged and unwelcome interruption caused by the entry of Italy into the conflict, he returned to his home in the Eternal City.   It was his boyish ambition to supersede Curtius, and the dream was fulfilled in the most arresting history of Greece since Grote.   It was the dearest wish of the veteran scholar, whose interest increased rather than flagged with the Hellenistic era, that he might live long enough to carry his narrative through the little known period from the third century to Sulla ; but it was not to be.   Work of the finest quality has been accomplished in a neighbouring portion of the vineyard by Wilcken, whose attention was directed

to the papyri by Mommsen over forty years ago.   His
latest achievement, the sumptuous *Urkunden der Ptolo-
mäerzeit*, furnished with an imposing Introduction and
commentary, throws fresh light on the religion of Ptole-
maic Egypt.   Among the contributions of a younger
generation none holds a higher place than Kahrstedt's
Griechisches Staatsrecht, of which the first volume deals
with the institutions of Sparta.   The second will be
devoted to Athens, and the third to the minor city states.
The delightful *Recollections* of Wilamowitz, published in
1928, the author's eightieth year, are at once the record
of a life devoted to the interpretation of classical Greece
and a contribution to the history of German scholarship.

In the world of Roman studies no book of such
outstanding importance has appeared as the *Storia dei
Romani* of Gaetano de Sanctis or Camille Jullian's
Histoire de la Gaule.   Beloch's *Römische Geschichte bis
zum Beginn der Punischen Kriege* is lively and suggestive,
but too controversial to be of much use for the un-
instructed reader.   Largely owing to the wealth of new
material garnered in the *Corpus Inscriptionum*, one of
Mommsen's favourites among his numerous progeny,
the attention of scholars has turned to the Empire rather
than the Republic.   Otto Seeck lived long enough to
complete his *Geschichte des Untergangs der antiken Welt*
by a sixth volume which brings his story to the fall of the
Western Empire.   Seeck marched on a broad front,
and we hear as much of Augustine, the heresies, and the
Theodosian Code as of the invasions of Huns and
Vandals ; but the book is slightly marred by his hostility
to the Church and to some of its greatest figures.   The
most important work on the Empire published since the
war is Dessau's *Geschichte der römischen Kaiserzeit*.   Our
fathers hoped that Mommsen would one day supplement
the immortal achievement of his early manhood by a
history of the Empire, but they had to content themselves
with the *Staatsrecht* and the *Roman Provinces*.   Domas-
zewski's well-known volumes, *Geschichte der Römischen
Kaiser*, a series of personal studies from Augustus to

Diocletian, written rather for the general public than for specialists, in no way filled the void ; and the path was clear for Dessau, another pupil of Mommsen, who has grown grey in the study of the *Corpus*. The whole of his first volume is claimed by the mighty figure of Augustus, and the first half of the second reaches Vitellius. The second half of the second volume surveys the conditions and administration of the different parts of the Empire during the first century. His goal is Constantine. Despite its sound scholarship the book lacks inspiration, and it is too early to judge whether it will meet one of the most urgent needs in historical literature.

Only second in importance to the work of Dessau is the *Geschichte des spätrömischen Reiches*, by Ernst Stein, a scholar of a younger generation. The first volume, published in 1928, covers the two centuries from Diocletian to the fall of the Western Empire ; and it will be interesting to compare his picture of the age of Justinian, when the next volume is ready, with that of Bury. While the administrative system, political events, and the personalities of the Emperors are clearly described, he is less successful in dealing with religion, art and social life. The distinguished Austrian scholar, Ludo Hartmann, added a fourth volume to his *Geschichte Italiens im Mittelalter*, but his *magnum opus* was interrupted by death when it had reached the tenth century. In Byzantine history no large work of outstanding importance has appeared. The second volume of Karl Holl's *Gesammelte Aufsätze zur Kirchengeschichte* is of the first quality ; and Heisenberg, the editor of the *Byzantinische Zeitschrift* and author of innumerable monographs, received a well-deserved compliment on his sixtieth birthday in the shape of a *Festschrift* which filled the whole of the thirtieth volume of the great journal which he directs.

The chief work of the last years of Harnack's laborious life was his treatise on Marcion, a theme on which he had won a prize half a century earlier as a student at Dorpat. Hauck's monumental *Kirchengeschichte Deutsch-*

lands, which he had hoped to bring down to the Peace of
Augsburg in 1555, had only reached the fourteenth
century at his death in 1918 ; but the second half of
the fifth volume, covering the period till the eve of the
Council of Basel, was sufficiently advanced for post-
humous publication.   Of equal importance is Hans
von Schubert's *Geschichte der Christlichen Kirche im Früh-
mittelalter*.   The imposing *Handbuch* of eight hundred
large and closely printed pages begins with Clovis and
ends with the fall of the Carolingians.   The whole of
Europe is included, and no aspect of religious life,
thought and institutions is ignored.   In the first volume
of his *Geschichte des Papsttums von den Anfängen bis zur
Höhe der Weltherrschaft*, published in 1930, which bears
the title *Römische Kirche und Imperium Romanum*, Erich
Caspar has inaugurated a work which amply fulfils the
promise of his earlier monographs.   He explains in his
Preface that a history of the Papacy must be more than
a history of the Popes : it must be first of all the history
of an idea,—the origin and development of the conception of the primacy of Rome.   The imposing volume
ends with Leo I in the middle of the fifth century, when
the fall of the Western Empire leaves the stage free for
the Papacy.   The author has received well-deserved
congratulations on the successful completion of the most
difficult portion of his arduous task—the most outstanding contribution to Church history of the last
decade.   From the Catholic camp we welcome Dempf's
massive treatise *Sacrum Imperium*, of which the sub-
title is *Geschichte und Staatsphilosophie des Mittelalters und
der politischen Renaissance*.   Writing entirely from the
sources, the author traces the development of political
ideas and ideals from the New Testament, the early
Church and Augustine to Hildebrand and Aquinas,
Dubois and Marsilio, Dante and Wiclif, concluding with
the age of the Councils.

In the secular field the outstanding achievement in
medieval studies is Dopsch's *Wirtschaftliche und Soziale
Grundlagen der europäischen Kulturentwicklung*, from

Caesar to Charlemagne. The Viennese Professor, who made his name before the war by his volumes on the social history of the Carolingian era, pushed his researches back to Caesar and Tacitus, and constructed an immense panorama of the factors of medieval civilisation—political institutions, land systems, the classes, the Church, the towns, industry and trade. For such a survey of a vast field every student must feel grateful ; but the author's interpretations have aroused widespread criticism and, indeed, hostility. Reacting against the nationalism of a good deal of nineteenth century scholarship, Dopsch proclaims in ringing tones the abiding influence of Imperial Rome. The battle between the Roman and the Teuton still rages in the lecture rooms, and Dopsch stands forth as the doughtiest Romanist since Fustel de Coulanges. We are presented with a continuity of cultural development, the Germans taking over the Roman heritage without much wanton destruction or uncompensated waste. He is not without disciples who help him to fight his battles. But he tends to under-estimate the worth of the ' barbarian ' contributions to medieval civilisation and to exaggerate the vitality of Roman institutions and traditions, and Vinogradoff used to complain that he was stronger in economics than in law. His later and more popular *Naturalwirtschaft und Geldwirtschaft in der Weltgeschichte* covers a far wider field, both in time and space, for he begins with primitive society and takes Asia in his stride. Less individual but no less useful is Kötzschke's *Allgemeine Wirtschaft-geschichte des Mittelalters*, which, as the author explains, attempts to describe conditions, not to elaborate a theory. The picture is brightly painted, and we are advised to regard the Christo-German Middle Ages as a time of power and creativeness, full of promise for the new world. In the field of law Freiherr von Schwerin has edited and largely rewritten the second volume of Brunner's classical *Deutsche Rechtsgeschichte*, which the master's death in 1915 prevented him from revising.

In the latter half of the Middle Ages two works begun

long before the war call for notice.   Cartellieri has completed in a fourth volume his full-length portrait of
Philipp August II König von Frankreich; and Davidssohn
has added a fourth volume, so large that it has appeared
in three successive portions, to his *Geschichte von Florenz*,
—that incomparable picture of the medieval life of the
fair city which he has made his home.   Gebhardt's well-
known co-operative *Handbuch der Deutschen Geschichte*
increases in value with every successive edition.   The
spirited study of the Emperor Frederick II, *stupor mundi*,
by Ernst Kantorowicz, was acclaimed by the public but
frowned on by some of his fellow specialists.   In the
province of Islamic history the *Islamstudien* of Carl
Becker, for some years Minister of Education, claim
the attention of the historical student no less than of the
Orientalist, for they present an admirable picture of
Mohammedan civilisation in popular form.

On reaching the sixteenth century the first event to
be recorded is the new edition of Ranke's *Deutsche
Geschichte im Zeitalter der Reformation*.   The star of the
greatest of modern historians shines as brightly as ever
in the heavens, and the centenary of his earliest book
witnessed the first instalment of a critical edition of his
works.   If the *History of the Popes* remains the favourite
of the wider world, the *Reformation* is the special pride
of German Protestants.   The Introduction and Notes by
Professor Joachimsen are worthy of a historical classic,
and new material from Ranke's papers illustrates not only
the composition of the book but the development of his
studies and ideas from early manhood onwards.   The
Preussische Geschichte is the next item on the list.

On Kawerau's death in 1918 the presidency of the
Luther Commission (which is responsible for the mag-
nificent Weimar edition of *Luthers Werke*), and, perhaps
we may add, the primacy among Reformation specialists,
passed to Karl Holl.   No recent work on the German
Reformation equals in importance the first volume of
his *Gesammelte Aufsätze zur Kirchengeschichte*, which
bears the simple title *Luther*, and contains addresses and

dissertations dating from before, during and after the war.   While Holl's penetrating studies appeal primarily to specialists, Gerhard Ritter, one of the most distinguished of the younger historians, presented the fruits of critical scholarship in popular form in a striking little volume on Luther, which devotes special attention to the derivation and development of his theology.   Among Kalkoff's learned monographs his two volumes *Hutten und die Reformation* and *Huttens Vagantenzeit und Untergang* stand first.   Those of us who read David Friedrich Strauss in their youth will be surprised to find how much less romantic and enlightened his hero appears today ; but there is general agreement that the pendulum has now swung too far the other way, and that Holborn's briefer biography hits the happy mean.   An admirable survey of the century from the political rather than the religious point of view entitled *Deutsche Reformation und Gegenreformation*, forming the second volume of a *Deutsche Geschichte* edited by Erich Marcks and intended for the general reader, has been furnished by Karl Brandi, the distinguished Göttingen Professor.   The work appeared in two parts, and the second half is particularly welcome to those who lack time or courage to master Moriz Ritter's monumental treatise on the Counter-Reformation.

No recent work by a Protestant scholar on the ecclesiastical history of the sixteenth century compares in range and importance with Pastor's *Geschichte der Päpste seit dem Ausgang des Mittelalters*.   A striking passage in his autobiography describes how his friend and teacher Janssen gave him a copy of Ranke's *History of the Popes* at Frankfurt in 1873, and how the ambition to rewrite the story from the Vatican archives took root in his mind.   He began work in Rome in 1878 at the age of twenty-four, and carried it on with unflagging energy till his death half a century later.   The first volume of the vast enterprise, which has been translated into English and other languages, appeared in 1886, and the thirteenth, published in 1928, brought the narrative

down to 1644. Never for a moment does Pastor allow
the reader to forget that he is a Catholic, and many of
his judgments only carry conviction to members of his
own communion. But he is not afraid to criticise and
condemn, and the value of his work is incomparably
greater than that of the *magnum opus* of Janssen on the
Reformation and its consequences. He has reared his
towering structure, not on the archives of the Vatican
alone, but also on those of several of the great Roman
families and on the treasures of the provinces. No book
of our time in any field has made a larger or more enduring contribution to historical knowledge.

No German historian of our generation possesses
such a philosophical mind as Meinecke, the editor of the
Historische Zeitschrift, whose masterpiece, *Weltbürgertum
und Nationalstaat*, published in 1908, recently appeared
in a seventh edition. Only second in importance is his
more recent volume *Die Idee der Staatsräson in der
neueren Geschichte*, an analysis of Macchiavelli's political
teaching and a survey of its influence through the
centuries. Students of Lord Acton's famous Introduction to Burd's edition of *The Prince* will find in
Meinecke a penetrating discussion of selected publicists of different countries who occupied themselves
with the relations of ethics and politics. Among them is
Frederick the Great, the only ruler in the portrait gallery,
who denounced the tempter in his *Anti-Machiavel* before
his accession, only to emerge as a disciple when he found
himself on the throne. No such illuminating contribution to the history of modern political ideas has been
made in Germany since Gierke's *Althusius* appeared half
a century ago. Another Berlin veteran, Hans Delbrück,
who lived just long enough to celebrate his eightieth
birthday in 1928, lost nothing of his industrious zeal
in the years after the war. The fourth volume of his
*Geschichte der Kriegskunst im Rahmen der politischen
Geschichte*, bringing the narrative from the Renaissance to
Napoleon, completed the chief historical venture of his
life. Himself a soldier in early life and the biographer

of Gneisenau, his authority in this field is recognised by military students. The evolution of armies, the development of munitions, the literary pundits from Macchiavelli to Clausewitz, the commanders from Gustavus Adolphus to the Wars of Liberation, and the historic battles are his themes. The book, however, as the author explains, was written, not for soldiers, but for lovers of history and as a contribution to the story of mankind. The completion of the *Gesçhichte der Kriegskunst* was followed by five volumes of *Weltgeschichte*, based on his lectures at Berlin. The fifth, covering the period from 1852 to 1888, is enriched by Delbrück's personal acquaintance with the Reichstag and the Imperial Court.

Of the four centuries which compose modern history the seventeenth and eighteenth have recently received far less attention than the sixteenth and nineteenth, and nothing comparable in importance to Koser's *Friedrich der Grosse* can be recorded. Oswald Redlich, the *doyen* of Austrian medievalists, was persuaded to continue the *Geschichte Oesterreichs* which Alfons Huber had brought down to the Treaty of Westphalia, and has published a comprehensive survey of the long reign of the Emperor Leopold I, the contemporary of the Great Elector and Louis XIV. Englishmen watch with special interest the progress of Michael's *Englische Geschichte im achtzehnten Jahrhundert*, the first instalment of which appeared as long ago as 1896. A second volume, published shortly after the war, only covered the years 1717–1720 ; but we may expect before long further light on the reign of Walpole, which the veteran Freiburg Professor is the first modern historian to explore in elaborate detail.

In Germany and Austria more than anywhere else the World War has for obvious reasons focussed attention on nineteenth-century history. By far the most important recent work on the first half of the century is Heinrich Ritter von Srbik's *Metternich : Der Staatsmann und der Mensch*. A full-length portrait based on the archives was urgently required, and the two bulky volumes are more likely to be supplemented than

superseded. The new material alone would render the
book indispensable ; but its outstanding feature is the
exhaustive analysis of the statesman's ' system.' The
Viennese Professor, himself a nobleman, a Catholic, and
a moderate Conservative, naturally presents a more
sympathetic picture than we find in the Liberal writers
of England and France or in the malicious pages of
Treitschke. Metternich was much more than a timid
reactionary, and his ideas on revolution and Austria's
European mission are well worth study ; but Srbik
never suggests that he was creative, or denies that he
was blind to the significance of the constructive principles
proclaimed by the French Revolution. A good deal of
the same ground is covered from a very different point
of view in the work of his Viennese colleague Viktor Bibl,
Der Zerfall Oesterreichs, the first volume of which
attempts a panoramic survey of the reign of the Emperor Francis II, and sharply arraigns the short-sighted
statesmanship of Metternich. The second volume,
bringing the story down to the collapse of 1918, becomes sketchy and hurried in the later decades. Kähler's
powerful study, *Wilhelm von Humboldt und der Staat*,
is perhaps a little less than fair to the most distinguished
mind in the service of Prussia between Stein and Bismarck. Gerhard Ritter's study of Stein, to which we
are eagerly looking forward, and of which we have had
a foretaste in articles in the *Historische Zeitschrift*, will
show that the last word on a great subject was not said
by Max Lehmann.

Despite its immense importance and its human
interest, the revolution of 1848 has been strangely
neglected. It was a tragedy that Treitschke only lived
long enough to carry his masterpiece down to 1847,
and that the eagerly awaited sixth volume remained
unwritten. Meinecke's study of the philosophic but
ineffectual adviser of Frederick William IV in *Radowitz
und die deutsche Revolution* was a weighty contribution
from the Prussian side ; but no serious attempt to fill
the void was made till in 1930 Veit Valentin published

the first volume of his *Geschichte der deutschen Revolution,* *1848-9,* the fruits of twenty years of toil and the fulfilment of an ambition formed in youth. His fitness for the exacting task had been proved by a series of monographs, and his researches in the archives of Frankfurt, Berlin, Vienna, and the smaller capitals have furnished him with a wealth of material such as no scholar has ever possessed. His book, he explains, is written for the public as well as for experts. After five massive chapters on Austria, Prussia, Bavaria, the smaller States, and Germany as a whole, in which every aspect of political, social and intellectual life is surveyed, the narrative begins with the March revolution, and the first volume of the most important work on modern German history published since the war ends with the meeting of the Frankfurt Parliament.

The object of this article is to survey historical writings, not collections of documents ; but an exception must be made when we reach the Bismarckian era. Never has the Iron Chancellor been so intensively studied both by friend and foe, at home and abroad, as since the collapse of the Empire which he built. *Die Grosse Politik der Europäischen Kabinette, 1879–1914,* edited by Thimme, the Berlin archivist, and Mendelssohn Bartholdy, the Hamburg Professor, fills fifty-four volumes, of which only the first six relate to the years before his fall ; but the references to his policy and ideas are innumerable, and his mighty spirit broods over the whole era. Only second in importance as a contribution to our knowledge of Bismarck is the series of stately quartos entitled *Die Gesammelten Werke,* begun in 1921, as we are told in the Preface, as a monument erected by Germany in her deepest distress. By far the most valuable section, the *Politische Schriften,* includes most of the famous despatches from Frankfurt, published by Poschinger in the early eighties under the Chancellor's directions, and those from St. Petersburg and Paris published by Raschdau long after his death. The second and more important series, beginning with his appointment to the highest office in the State in 1862, is largely fresh material and presents his relations to Austria down to the war of 1866 in a new and unexpected light. Three volumes contain the *Gespräche*, collected from Busch, Poschinger and numberless other reporters, and arranged in chronological sequence. The *Reden* fill four volumes, and the *Privatbriefe* are promised. The editors, Petersdorff, Thimme, Andreas and Schüssler, have performed their task with modesty and skill, and the enterprise inaugurates a new chapter in the history of Bismarckian studies.

Since Erich Marcks discontinued his large-scale record of Bismarck after producing an admirable volume on his youth, no one is likely to attempt a full description of a life which belongs to history rather than to biography. Suggestive summaries appear from time to time, but for real illumination the student must turn to the monographs. Of these the most important since the war is Arnold Oskar Meyer's *Bismarcks Kampf mit Oesterreich am Bundestag zu Frankfurt, 1851–1859*. The Frankfurt Embassy, hitherto known only from the Prussian reports, may here be studied in the light of the despatches in the Vienna archives from Prokesch and the other Austrian representatives with whom Bismarck engaged in unrelenting strife. Meyer is a whole-hearted admirer and commands a spirited style rare among German historians. We feel the greatness of his hero on every page, but we can also understand the growing exasperation of his adversaries.

If Arnold Meyer aids us to understand the Bismarck of the fifties, many scholars have provided new clues to the following decade. The three large volumes entitled *Die Rheinpolitik Kaiser Napoleons III von 1863 bis 1870*, edited by Hermann Oncken, reveal the most secret thoughts of the Imperial dreamer at Paris, and throw a flood of light on the diplomacy of central Europe. It is an astonishing story of ambition and intrigue that is revealed in the reports of Metternich, the Austrian Ambassador, and is summarised in the lengthy Introduction, which has appeared separately in English as *Napoleon III and the Rhine*. An admirably dispassionate narrative of the making of the Empire has been supplied by the eighth, ninth and tenth volumes of Alfred Stern's *Geschichte Europas 1815-1871*, a work based on decades of research in the archives of many states.

No recent study of Bismarck's achievement has caused more stir than Ziekursch's *Politische Geschichte des deutschen Kaiserreichs*, though it is an argument rather than a contribution to knowledge. While most Germans, exasperated by humiliation and defeat, glorify him at the expense of his clumsy successors, Ziekursch declines to prostrate himself before the national idol. He gave the Hohenzollerns such enormous power, complains the historian in his first volume, entitled *Die Reichsgründung*, that a Frederick the Great on the throne or a Bismarck beside it was required for its wise use. The edifice that he erected was top-heavy, and the democratic *Zeitgeist*, which he scorned, has proved victorious. The second volume, *Das Zeitalter Bismarcks*, brings the story to the fall of the Chancellor, over which Ziekursch sheds no tears ; but the Emperor's action, he argues, was only justifiable if intended as a prelude to the scrapping of absolutism. That the maintenance of national unity demanded a completely new system forms the argument of his third volume, which carries the narrative till the fall of the Empire. In foreign affairs the Emperor and his advisers stumbled from one blunder to another. At home the Prussian Conservatives prevented the transformation needed to identify the masses with the State in preparation for the hour of danger. It was in vain that the fallen Bismarck, speaking in the market-place of Jena in 1892, demanded a more virile Parliament ; for the instrument which he had himself broken could not be so easily or so quickly repaired. Thus when the testing time came in 1914 Germany lacked the institutions and the solidarity needed to confront the fiery ordeal. Ziekursch is stronger in domestic than in foreign affairs, and he tends to be too cocksure ;

but such a ringing challenge to the political system of the Empire from an academic historian is a new and interesting experience.

Adalbert Wahl takes up the cudgels for Bismarck in his elaborate and scholarly work, *Deutsche Geschichte 1871–1914*, the first two volumes of which come down to 1890. While Ziekursch writes as a fervent democrat the Tübingen Professor, in an argumentative Introduction, wages war on the shibboleth of progress. In many European States, he declares, there has been a decline since the French Revolution, and it has not yet reached its end. Outward and material progress, it is true, has been made, but at the cost of inward and spiritual decline. The peoples have been robbed of a precious inheritance ; for the notion of utility has been enthroned in place of the idea of right, and what constitutes utility is difficult for short-sighted man to determine in advance. One of the most significant results of the French Revolution is the domination of wealth, with its resultant deterioration of the moral fibre of a nation. The State has been rationalised and mechanised, and organic elements such as the Estates have yielded to a levelling Parliamentary democracy. It was Bismarck's incomparable achievement not only to found the German Empire but to provide it with an ideal Constitution, capable of defending the State and the community against predatory Socialism and doctrinaire cosmopolitanism. Whether or no we share Wahl's reading of nineteenth-century history, we can all profit by the first panoramic presentation of Germany during the first two decades of the Empire,—the foreign and domestic policy of the Reich, the fortunes of its component States, its institutions, its economic development and its cultural life.

Of the numberless histories, monographs and biographies relating to the reign of William II only a few call for mention in a brief review. In his classical volumes *Die Reichsgründung*, published during the war, Erich Brandenburg displayed commendable freedom from the passions and prejudices of Treitschke and Sybel, and his later work *Von Bismarck zum Weltkrieg* maintains the lofty standard of its predecessor.   The English translation of the second edition is a well-deserved tribute to a book written straight from the archives of the Wilhelmstrasse, and remarkable for its balanced judgment. Of almost equal importance in the field of diplomatic history is Otto Becker's *Bismarck und die Einkreisung Deutschlands*, which, despite its title, belongs mainly to the reign of William II.   For, after a slender introductory volume on Bismarck's system of alliances, he passes to a detailed investigation of the Franco-Russian alliance, and will reach the Triple Entente in due course. The work contains new material from the Austrian archives and other sources, which he employs to drive home his charges against Bismarck's blundering successors.   Johannes Haller's full-length biography of Eulenburg is not only a life-like portrait of a fascinating personality but a revealing study of the character and methods of William II.   And finally Nowak, the author of several widely-read works on the World War, has begun a comprehensive review of the reign of the last of the Hohenzollerns with the aid of material supplied by the fallen ruler himself.   The first volume, *Kaiser and Chancellor*, covering the two opening years of his reign, retells the dramatic story of the quarrel with Bismarck, who appears in these pages not only as drunk with power but as in some respects already past his work. Prince Bülow's scintillating but ill-natured *Memoirs* must be described rather as materials for history than history itself.

No single volume published in German since the war has added so much to our knowledge of recent history as Pribram's *Die Geheimverträge Oesterreich-Ungarns, 1879–1914*, the English edition of which, published under the auspices of the late Professor Coolidge of Harvard, is known to every Anglo-Saxon student of war origins.   The value of the work of the *doyen* of Austrian historians is enhanced by a luminous record of the negotiations preceding the conclusion of the Triple

Alliance in 1882 and its successive renewals and modifications, based on the Vienna archives. An earlier period of Francis Joseph's long reign is illuminated in Redlich's monumental work *Das Oesterreichische Reichs- und Staatsproblem*. A brilliant summary of the creation of the machinery of the Austrian State by Maria Theresa and Joseph II precedes the commencement of the detailed narrative in 1848. Neither Friedjung nor any other earlier historian had access to the records of the Ministerial Councils and conferences by which the internal development of the Hapsburg Empire after the Metternich era was shaped. The first of the two enormous volumes brings the story to 1861, while the second is confined to the six difficult years ending with the *Ausgleich* of 1867. If the mass of constitutional detail is intended for the specialist, the summaries of problems and situations are well within the grasp of the general reader ; and the portraits of Bach, Schmerling, Beust, Deak, and other protagonists are vividly conceived. Those of us who have learned to think of Francis Joseph as a rusty old machine rather than a human being will discover in these chapters an energetic and impetuous young ruler, who took his full share in the discussions no less than in the decisions of a period crowded with formidable events. In his masterly biography, *Emperor Francis Joseph of Austria*, Redlich presents the results not merely of his studies in the archives but of his personal knowledge of many of the Emperor's later Ministers and associates ; for, as a member of the Reichsrat before the war and a Minister during the dying agonies of the dynasty, he has seen a good deal of Austrian history in the making. Friedjung's *Das Zeitalter des Imperialismus*, which was interrupted by the author's death when the third volume was nearly completed, is chiefly of value for its treatment of Balkan questions, above all the Bosnian crisis, in regard to which his acquaintance with Aehrenthal brought him a good deal of inside knowledge.

In economic history three works may be mentioned, though in the narrower sense of the term none of the

authors is commonly reckoned a historian.   For half a
century Brentano has been the chief of the Liberal, Free
Trade, South German economists, and has maintained
a running fight with Schmoller, Wagner, and other
Conservative champions of the North.   But his knowledge of economic history is in no way inferior to that
of the members of the so-called Historical School, and
generations of students in Munich and elsewhere have
enjoyed his lectures on England, a country which he
knows almost as well as his own.   These courses have
been worked up by the ever-youthful octogenarian into
a comprehensive survey entitled *Eine Geschichte der
wirtschaftlichen Entwicklung Englands*, the fourth and last
volume of which is devoted to the British Empire.
Though the latest monographs are not always utilised,
the freshness and lucidity arouse gratitude in those who
began their studies of economic history with his little
book on *Guilds and Trade Unions* published as long ago
as 1870.   Smaller in bulk but richer in ideas are the
lectures, recently translated under the title *General
Economic History*, of the lamented Max Weber, socio-
logist, economist, historian, publicist, the most fertile
and encyclopaedic mind of his time in the academic
world of Germany with the single exception of Tröltsch.
The volume was compiled from the notes of the Professor and some of his hearers, and appeared without
revision after his death in 1920.   Far more important
than either is Sombart's masterpiece *Der moderne Kapital-
ismus*, begun many years before the war and recently
completed by the volumes on the eighteenth, nineteenth
and twentieth centuries which are described as the era
of *Hochkapitalismus*.   The sub-title of the work is
*Historisch-systematische Darstellung des gesamten Euro-
päischen Wirtschaftslebens von seinen Anfängen*.   Sombart
complains that he has not succeeded in obtaining recognition as a historian, and it is true enough that he has
been sharply attacked by such formidable gladiators as
Below and Brentano.   But no student of his six weighty
volumes is likely to challenge the assertion that they are

crowded with historical material of the greatest interest, and that his analysis of the material and psychological factors in the evolution of capitalism through the centuries ranks among the most stimulating works of the present century.

Seldom does the modern historian care or dare to move far from his fortified base, to expose himself to the rebukes of his fellow experts, and to challenge the centuries in their flight. It was, however, a wise resolve when Johannes Haller, yielding to many requests from his pupils, published his favourite course under the title *The Epochs of German History*. Equally at home in medieval and modern times, a master of lucid narrative and suggestive generalisation, the Tübingen Professor has written a book which deserves its popularity and its English translation. Defeat, he argues, necessitates self-knowledge, and his analytical commentary on German history exposes with unsparing hand the errors of the past. The princes who ruined the medieval empire ; the Protestant rulers whose quarrels limited the triumph of the Reformation ; the Hapsburgs, ' who have brought nothing but misfortune for the German people up to our own days ' ; Frederick William III, who withheld a Constitution, and Frederick William IV, who refused an Imperial crown ; the *doctrinaires* of the Frankfurt Parliament, who built castles in the air—it is a story of lost opportunities only partially redeemed by the genius of Bismarck, whose precious gift his countrymen have not known how to retain. Haller laments the political flabbiness in which, he declares, his countrymen surpass all other nations. Such a verdict reveals the bitterness of the hour ; but his manly and clear-sighted patriotism should serve as a tonic to a sorely tried nation once more struggling to its feet.

To omit all reference to Spengler's *Untergang des Abendlandes* on the ground that it is not a purely historical work would be pedantry ; for its sub-title is *Outlines of a Morphology of History*, and its arguments have claimed the attention of professional historians. The Agadir crisis of 1911, he tells us, turned his thoughts to the issues of the day, and his first instinct was to write on some political phenomena of the age and the conclusions to which they pointed. ' I then discovered not only that I must go much further back in order to understand the present, but that a political problem cannot be understood on the purely political plane, and indeed that no fragment of history could be understood till we penetrate the secret of world-history, which no one has ever achieved.   Then all the connections began to become clear, and I envisaged the approaching war as the type of an historical occurrence which has its predetermined place within a great historical framework. At last I saw the solution plainly before me in immense outlines and in all its logical necessity.   My book contains the irrefutable formulation of an idea which cannot be contested.   Its narrower theme is an analysis of the decline of the culture of the West, but the goal is nothing less than the problem of civilisation.'   The title of his treatise was chosen in 1912, the first draft was finished before the outbreak of war, and the first volume was published in 1918.   Thus the book, far from being the offspring of defeat and despair as the world concluded from its title and the date of its appearance, was planned at the meridian of the Empire and completed when Germany still counted on victory.

' In this book,' the author explains, ' the attempt is made for the first time to determine history in advance, to follow up the fate of the civilisation of Western Europe in the stages through which it has still to pass.' The principle of history is declared to be multiple periodicity, a succession not of stages, as previous thinkers had believed, but of completed cycles.   The unity of mankind is a biological fact and nothing more. Civilisation passes through the stages from childhood to old age not once alone but again and again.   One civilisation after another moves onward to its appointed end.   Western civilisation is the latest but not the last of the recurring cycles which advance and recede like the tide on a shelving beach.   The traditional classification—ancient, medieval and modern—is a barren chronological sequence, not a sociological interpretation ; and Spengler substitutes four cycles of civilisation, the Indian, the Antique, the Arabian and the Western, the latter beginning about A.D. 900.   Each is subdivided into Spring, Summer, Autumn, Winter, and each is studied in the various manifestations of its historic life. Thus successive civilisations work to a time-table, and the civilisation of the West, now entering the winter months and replacing spiritual activities by practical aims, has only about a couple of centuries to run.   A second stout volume, published in 1922, with the subtitle *World-historic Perspectives*, analysed the life of early man, the State, and other problems of historical sociology. Casting his gaze first backward, then forward, Spengler discovers no enduring progress, no guiding spirit, no ultimate goal.   Such questions, however, are the concern of the philosopher rather than of the historian, whose task is to reconstruct the life of humanity, not to speculate on the nature and purpose of the universe.

THE CAMBRIDGE CHAIR OF MODERN HISTORY

A CENTURY before the foundation of the Regius Professorship of Modern History, a gallant attempt to provide historical instruction in the University of Cambridge was made by Fulke Greville, first Lord Brooke, the friend of Philip Sidney and Spenser, of Bacon and Giordano Bruno, the counsellor of James I, the patron of Camden and Speed.[1]   The regulations which he drew up in 1627 for 'A Publique Lecture of Historie' prescribed the conditions of appointment and the duties of the lecturer in great detail.   No clergyman nor married man was to be eligible, nor anyone whose occupation would distract him from his studies.   A mastery of Latin, Greek, geography and chronology was essential.   ' Such as have travelled beyond the seas and so have added to their learning knowledge of modern tongues and experience in foreign parts, and likewise such as have been brought up and exercised in public affairs shall be accounted most eligible.'   The lecturer should be at liberty to choose any province of secular or ecclesiastical history.   Lectures were to be delivered twice a week, and on a third day he was to discuss difficult points with his class.   The appointment was for five years, the salary to be £100 a year.   Lord Brooke's design that the presentation should remain for ever in his family was altered after his death, and the patronage was vested in the University.

[1] See Mullinger, *History of the University of Cambridge*, III. 81–90, and 674–7, and Cooper, *Annals of Cambridge*, II. 201–2, and V. 370–1.

In his anxiety to obtain the best available scholarship, the founder wisely inserted a clause authorising the appointment of distinguished foreigners. Finding no suitable candidate in England he invited Gerard Vossius to fill the new Chair ; but the great scholar was unwilling to leave Leyden. A less distinguished son of the same University, Isaac Dorislaus, who had for some time resided in England and was married to an English wife, was approached, and accepted the offer. Dorislaus began his lectures at the end of 1627, but the course was destined to be brief. Selecting the *Annals* of Tacitus as his text-book, his reflections on Kingship, moderate as they were, scandalised the Anglican divines who dominated the University. The Vice-Chancellor forbade the continuance of his course, and the prohibition was confirmed, at the instigation of Laud, by royal injunction. Many years later the unfortunate scholar was assassinated by royalist refugees, while representing the Commonwealth at The Hague, in revenge for his share in the trial of Charles I. After this ill-starred commencement the story of the Chair is involved in obscurity, and the office was probably a sinecure. The names of two subsequent Readers have been disinterred ; but there is no evidence that they delivered lectures, and the endowment appears to have lapsed.

In 1724, a century after Lord Brooke's noble scheme had been wrecked by royalist intolerance, King George I founded twin Chairs of Modern History and Languages at the two great English Universities. In his masterly biography of Edmund Gibson Dr. Norman Sykes [1] has shown how the project was initiated and carried through by the learned Bishop of London, himself an Oxford man, and has thrown a flood of light on the purposes and the nature of the enterprise. The ambitious prelate never realised his dream of the Primacy, but he was for many

---

[1] *Edmund Gibson*, 94–107. Cp. Firth, ' Modern History at Oxford, 1724–1841,' in *English Historical Review*, 1917 ; Firth, *Modern Languages at Oxford, 1724–1929*, ch. 1 ; Oscar Browning, *Cambridge Review*, November 25 and December 9, 1897 ; and J. W. Clark, *Endowments of the University of Cambridge*, 183–92.

years the ecclesiastical adviser of the Whigs, and his practical mind realised the importance of converting the Universities to the Hanoverian regime. He reminded Townshend that it was the intention of the Universities to train persons for the service of God in the State as well as the Church, and that a supply of men with a knowledge of foreign languages was necessary for the effective functioning of our diplomacy. The lack of such linguists, he pointed out, led to the employment of foreigners by British Embassies and the engagement of foreign tutors by the nobility and gentry to accompany their sons on their travels. Moreover the honour of the Universities demanded that they should be the seat of universal learning. His plan was to appoint two Professors proficient in modern languages to be ' the chief directors ' of the study of modern languages and history, who would instruct, both in speaking and writing, twenty Bachelors of Arts nominated by the Crown ; and each Professor was to have qualified assistants in his task.

The scheme worked out by Gibson and Townshend was announced by the King in a letter of May 16, 1724, countersigned by Townshend, to the Vice-Chancellors of the two Universities. ' We, being greatly desirous to favour and encourage our two Universities, and to enable them more effectually to answer the trend of their institution by sending forth constant supplies of learned and able men to serve the public both in Church and State, and having observed that no encouragement or provision has hitherto been made for the study of Modern History and Modern Languages, and having seriously weighed the prejudice from this respect, persons of foreign nations being often employed in the education and tuition of youth both at home and in their travels, and great numbers of the young nobility and gentry being either sent abroad directly from school and taken away from the Universities before their studies are completed, and opportunities frequently lost to the Crown of employing and encouraging members of Universities by conferring on them such employment, both at home and abroad, as require a competent skill in writing and speaking the modern languages. In order therefore to remedy these inconveniences, we have determined to appoint two persons of sober conversation and prudent conduct, skilled in Modern History and in the knowledge of Modern Languages, to be Professors of Modern History, who shall be obliged to read lectures in the Public Schools. They shall have a stipend of £400 per annum, and out of the said stipends shall be obliged to maintain with sufficient salary two persons at least well qualified to instruct in history and speaking the said languages, which said teachers shall be under the direction of the Professors and shall be obliged to instruct *gratis* in the Modern Languages twenty scholars of each University, to be nominated by us, and each scholar so nominated shall be obliged to learn two at least of the said languages. Professors and teachers shall be obliged once every year to transmit an attested account of the progress made by each scholar to our principal Secretary of State to be laid before us, that we may encourage the diligence of such amongst them as shall have qualified themselves for our service by giving them suitable employments, either at home or abroad, as occasions shall offer.'

The response of Cambridge was as grateful as that of Jacobite Oxford was grudging. The Royal Letter, wrote the Vice-Chancellor on May 10, after the holding of a Congregation, had been read in the Senate, ' intimating your Majesty's gracious and princely intentions of establishing a new Professorship, with an appointment so ample as well nigh to equal the stipends of all our other Professors put together. We are firmly persuaded that when your Majesty's noble design shall have taken effect, there shall be a sufficient number of academical persons well versed in the knowledge of foreign courts and well instructed in their respective languages ; when a familiarity with the living tongues shall be superadded to that of the dead ones, when the solid learning of antiquity shall be adorned and set off with a skilful habit of conversing in the languages that now flourish, and will be accompanied with English probity, our nobility and gentry will be under no temptation of sending for persons from foreign countries to be entrusted with the education of their children ; that the appearance of an English gentleman in the courts of Europe, with a governor of his own nation, will not be so rare as hitherto, and that your Universities, thus refined and made more completely serviceable to the education of youth, will be able to furnish you with a constant supply of persons every way qualified for the management of such weighty affairs and negotiations as Your Majesty's occasions may require.'

In September the Royal Letters Patent were despatched to both Universities, setting forth among other regulations that the Professors were to be appointed for one year only, with a right to apply for renewal,—a precaution suggested by the frowns of Oxford and the desire of the Government to retain control of a foundation which was political rather than academic in character. The first of a long line of Professors was Samuel Harris, a Fellow of Peterhouse, Doctor of Divinity and Fellow of the Royal Society. He delivered his inaugural lecture in 1725, and the *Oratio Inauguralis* was published at Cambridge in the same year.[1] In ponderous Latin he laments the moral dangers incurred by young men who have to repair abroad to learn languages, and congratulates his hearers that the necessity is at an end. Turning to the other aspect of the foundation he credits the King with the hope that the knowledge of the achievements of their ancestors in peace and war would fire the imagination and mould the character of the students, some of whom might perhaps rise to the highest posts in the State. The discourse, which in its emphasis on the practical aim of historical studies is a curious anticipation of Seeley, closes with a fulsome panegyric on the royal founder. He never lectured again, and no other lecture was delivered from the Chair for nearly half a century.

[1] A copy is in the British Museum.

Though the Professor took his duties lightly, a French and an Italian instructor were appointed, and twenty scholars were duly chosen. In 1726 Harris reported their progress. In one or two instances he wrote ' perfect ' against the names, and he dutifully added that the effects of the new foundation were already visible in the University in the increase of loyalty and useful learning. A second report, drawn up in April, 1727, announced that two Trinity men had become secretaries to the British envoys at Turin and Ratisbon, and that one or two were learning German and Spanish. During the same month some more scholars were selected. When the enterprise had been auspiciously launched the indefatigable Bishop of London left its supervision to the Secretary of State ; but the Government soon lost interest, and the ensuing vacancies were left unfilled. In 1728 George II confirmed his father's foundations and ordered that the Professors should retain their chairs ; but with the disappearance of their scholars the posts became sinecures.

' The late Royal Institution for the study of History,' wrote Warburton hopefully in 1727, ' must produce the master-builders to give us that promising body of English history so long wanted and till now despaired of.' It was, however, a false dawn. No builders, still less master-builders, came forward in the Cambridge of the eighteenth century to erect the temple of historical learning.

Harris died in 1733, and two years later *A Commentary on the fifty-third chapter of Isaiah* was published in London,[1] dedicated by his widow to Queen Caroline. A preface of fifty pages reveals the author's knowledge of classical literature, his interest in Hebrew philology and the ancient world, and his impeccable orthodoxy. These qualities, however estimable in themselves, do not explain his appointment to a Chair of Modern History, and the clue is doubtless to be found in his

[1] A finely bound quarto, bearing the arms of George III, is in the British Museum.

strident loyalty to the Hanoverian dynasty. ' I am very sure that under the most auspicious and happy reign of his present Majesty King George, the glorious guardian of our religious as well as civil liberties, force will never be made use of to compel men in matters of religion, except it be such a force as arises from his own illustrious example.'

After the death of Harris the Chair remained vacant for over a year. On the appointment of his successor, Shallett Turner, a Cosin Scholar, later Fellow and Junior Dean of Peterhouse and a student of law, the Government woke up for a moment and asked for information. The new Professor replied that it was over seven years since the last list of King's scholars was made, and that all the places were consequently vacant. He added that the documents and nomination forms would doubtless be found in the office of the Secretary of State. No further steps were taken, and the long tenure of the second Professor, who never delivered a lecture, is a blank. At the end of the summer term of 1737 Gray wrote ironically to Horace Walpole : ' Not to tire you with my travels, you must know that Mr. Turner is come down. His list is vastly near being full notwithstanding which, and the cares and duties of his office, he says he thinks to go to Paris every year.' [1] An anonymous pamphlet, *Free Thoughts upon University Education*, published in 1751,[2] asserted that if the Professor of History would reside at Cambridge with his proper assistants, a numerous audience would regularly attend his lectures or classes ; but this confident prediction was never put to the test.

As the Professor advanced in years the question of his successor began to be eagerly discussed, and among the aspirants to the coveted sinecure was the greatest poet of his age, a Peterhouse man who had recently

[1] *The Correspondence of Gray, Walpole, West and Ashton* (1734–71), ed. Paget Toynbee, 1915, I. 151–2.
[2] Cp. T. A. Walker, *Peterhouse*, ch. 7. A copy is in the Library of Trinity College. See Wordsworth, *Scholae Academicae*, 150.

296 STUDIES IN MODERN HISTORY

migrated to Pembroke, though a Fellow of neither.
'Old Turner is very declining,' wrote Gray to a friend
in 1759, 'and I was sounded by Dr —— about my
designs (so I understood it). I assured him that I
should not *ask* for it, not choosing to be refused. He
told me two people had applied already. N.B.—All
this is secret.' [1] 'Old Turner' lingered on for three
years more and when the end came Gray attempted to
mobilise his friends.

To JOHN CHUTE [*undated*].

MY DEAR SIR :

I was yesterday told that Turner (the Professor of
Modern History here) was dead in London. If it be true, I conclude it is now too late to begin asking for it. But we had (if
you remember) some conversation on that head at Twickenham,[2]
and as you have probably found some opportunity to mention it
to Mr. W. since, I would gladly know his thoughts about it.
What he can do he only can tell us : What he will do, if he can,
is with me no question. If he could find a proper channel,
I certainly might ask it with as much or more propriety than any
one in this place. If anything were done it should be as private
as possible, for if the people who have any sway here could prevent
it, I think they would most zealously.

The result of the application was announced to
Warton in the course of a long letter dated December 4,
1762, describing a country tour.[3] '. . . When I
arrived here (London) I found Professor Turner had
been dead above a fortnight, and being cockered and
spirited up by some friends (though it was rather of the
latest) I got my name suggested to Ld. B. You may
easily imagine who undertook it, and indeed he did it
with zeal. I received my answer very soon, which was
what you may easily imagine, but joined with great
professions of his desire to serve me on any future
occasion.'

The glittering prize fell to Laurence Brockett, a

[1] *Gray's Letters*, ed. Tovey, II. 262.
[2] Horace Walpole's house, Strawberry Hill.
[3] *Gray's Letters*, ed. Tovey, II. 268.

Fellow of Trinity, who shares with Shallett Turner the claim to be the least distinguished holder of his chair, but possessed the qualification of having been tutor to the son-in-law of Lord Bute, in whose hands the appointment lay.   We catch a glimpse of him in 1757, when Gray wrote to ask him, ' when he has occasion to go into Trinity Library,' to be good enough to inquire for some old English books.[1]   The new Professor was more interested in University politics than in academic studies, and his shadowy figure assumes flesh and blood for the first and last time in the fierce contest for the post of High Steward left vacant by the death of Lord Hardwicke in 1763.   After months of conflict [2] the second Lord Hardwicke succeeded his father, and the assault on the authority of the Duke of Newcastle, the Chancellor of the University, was repulsed ; for the defeated candidate was the unsavoury Lord Sandwich, the boon-companion of Wilkes.   Despite his unenviable notoriety Sandwich was supported by the Court and Ministry, and among his champions in the University none was more active than Brockett, who was reported to Newcastle as ' most violent in his counsels.' [3]   When the Master of Trinity died early in 1768, Brockett was mentioned as a competitor for the post.[4]   Six months later, returning from a visit to Lord Sandwich at Hinchinbroke, he fell off his horse—' drunk I believe ' commented Gray—and died three days later.

Gray's hour had come at last.   Disheartened by his previous rebuff he refused to renew his application; but his friend Stonhewer, Fellow of Peterhouse, and Secretary to the Prime Minister, was ready for action.[5]   The appointment took place without delay, and the joyful news was communicated to Mary Antrobus on July 29.

[1] *Gray's Letters*, ed. Tovey, II. 1.
[2] The full story is told in Winstanley, *The University of Cambridge in the Eighteenth Century*.
[3] Winstanley, 117.
[4] *Gray's Letters*, ed. Tovey, February 3, 1768, III. 180.
[5] In 1769 Gray described him as his best friend, and he left him £500 in his will.

DEAR MARY,

I thank you for all your intelligence (and the first news I had of poor Brockett's death was from you) and to reward you in part for it I now shall tell you that this day, hot as it is, I kissed the King's hand ; that my warrant was signed by him last night, that on Wednesday I received a very honourable letter from the D. of Grafton, acquainting me that His Majesty had ordered him to offer me this Professorship, and much more which does me too much credit by half for me to mention it. The Duke adds that from private as well as public considerations he takes the warmest part in approving this measure of the King's. These are his own words. You see there are princes (or Ministers) left in the world that know how to do things handsomely ; for I profess I never asked for it, nor have I seen his Grace before or after the event.[1]

The new Professor expressed his gratitude to his benefactor in a graceful letter of which the draft is dated Cambridge, July, 1768.[2]

MY LORD,

Your Grace has dealt nobly with me ; and the same delicacy of mind that induced you to confer this favour on me, unsolicited and unexpected, may perhaps make you averse to receive my sincerest thanks and grateful acknowledgements. Yet your Grace must excuse me, they will have their way. They are indeed but words ; yet I know and feel they come from my heart, and therefore are not wholly unworthy of your Grace's acceptance. I even flatter myself (such is my pride) that you have some little satisfaction in your own work. If I did not deceive myself in this, it would complete the happiness of, my Lord, your Grace's most obliged and devoted servant.

A letter of August 3 to the Rev. Norton Nicholls added one or two details.[3] '. . . You are to say that I owe my nomination to the whole Cabinet Council, and my success to the King's particular knowledge of me. This last he told me himself, though the day was so hot and the ceremony so embarrassing to me that I hardly know what he said.' The Professor's satisfaction continued

---

[1] *Gray's Letters*, ed. Tovey, III. 199–200. A shorter account was sent to Warton on August 1, III. 202–3.
[2] *Ib*. III. 198.   [3] *Ib*. III. 205.

to bubble over in letters to his friends. ' It is the best thing the Crown has to bestow (on a layman) here,' he wrote to James Beattie on October 31, 1768 ; [1] ' the salary is £400 per annum, but what enhances the value of it to me is that it was bestowed without being asked. . . . Instances of a benefit so nobly conferred, I believe, are rare ; and therefore I tell you of it as a thing that does honour not only to me but to the Minister.'   The debt was partially repaid by the Ode for Music written on the Duke's installation as Chancellor a few months later. None of his friends was more delighted or surprised than Horace Walpole. ' Yes, it is my Gray, Gray the poet,' he wrote on August 9, ' who is made Professor of Modern History, and I believe it is worth five hundred a year. I knew nothing of it till I saw it in the papers, but believe it was Stonhewer that obtained it for him.' [2]

' It is only to tell you,' wrote the new Professor to Mason on August 1, 1768,[3] ' that I profess Modern History and Languages in a little shop of mine at Cambridge, if you will recommend me any customers.'   That this was no mere meaningless phrase is suggested by an undated document in Gray's handwriting published in 1926.[4] The scheme may have been drawn up when he was hoping to succeed Turner in 1762 ; but it more probably dates from the fulfilment of his hopes in 1768, when, as Mason tells us,[5] he laid before the Duke of Grafton three different schemes of choosing his pupils, one of which found so much favour that it was sent to Oxford for the benefit of the new Regius Professor in the sister University.

1. That the Professor shall apply to the several Heads of Colleges : and desire them to recommend one or more young Gentlemen, who shall be instructed without expense in some of

[1] *Gray's Letters*, ed. Tovey, III.
[2] To Hon. H. S. Conway, *Letters of Horace Walpole*, ed. Toynbee, VII. 211–2 ; cp. the letter of September 20 to Warton, VII. 227–8.
[3] *Gray's Letters*, ed. Tovey, III. 203–4.
[4] In a letter of Dr. Paget Toynbee in the *Times Literary Supplement*, March 4, 1926.
[5] *Memoirs of the Life and Writings of Thomas Gray*, first edition (1775), 397.

the modern languages, and attend such lectures as he shall give. The number (if each smaller College send one, and the larger two) will amount in the University of Cambridge to nineteen.

2. That the Profr. shall nominate and pay two Praeceptors, qualified to instruct these Scholars in the French and Italian tongues.

3. That He shall reside the half of every Term at least in the University (wch. half-terms at Cambridge make about a hundred and ten days, almost one-third of the year) and shall read publickly once at least in every Term a lecture on modern History to his Scholars, and to any others, that shall be present.

4. That He shall besides at short and regular intervals give private lectures to his Scholars on the same subject, prescribe a method of study, direct them in their choice of Authors, and from time to time enquire into the progress they have made in the Italian and French tongues.

5. That if he neglect these duties, he shall be subject to the same pecuniary mulcts, that other Professors are according to statute.

We learn from Mason [1] that immediately after his appointment Gray sketched out an Inaugural lecture in Latin. ' He also wrote the exordium of this thesis, not indeed in a manner correct enough to be here given but so spirited in point of sentiment as leaves it much to be lamented that he did not proceed to its completion.' He engaged and paid teachers of French and Italian, and he fretted that no ' customers ' came to his shop. ' Notwithstanding his ill-health,' writes Mason, ' he constantly intended to read lectures, and I remember the last time he visited me at Acton in the summer of the year 1770 he expressed much chagrin on this subject and even declared it to be his steadfast resolution to resign his Professorship if he found himself unable to do real service in it. What I said to dissuade him from this had so little weight with him that I am almost persuaded he would very soon have put this intention into execution. But death prevented the trial.' The prickings of conscience continued

[1] *Memoirs*, 395–9.

till the end.   On May 24, 1771, he wrote to Warton of his cough and of his idea of a visit to the Continent in the summer.   ' My own employment so sticks in my stomach and troubles my conscience, and yet travel I must or cease to exist.'   Two months later Gray was dead. ' I know that till he did accept the Professorship from the Duke of Grafton,' wrote Horace Walpole to Mason,[1] ' it was my constant belief that he would scorn any place.' A tribute from the same life-long friend [2] fittingly commemorates the only Immortal among the occupants of the Cambridge Chair.   ' The loss of him was a great blow to me and ought to be so to the world, as Mr. Mason tells me he has left behind him nothing finished, which might have compensated his death to them, tho' not to his friends.   He was a genius of the first rank, and will always be allowed so by men of taste.   You sir will be honoured by them for having done justice to his merit ; and as he was so averse to receiving favours, it will be a great proof that he did justice to yours in consenting to be obliged to you.'

To Gray's successor John Symonds, Fellow of Peterhouse and a man of wide reading and liberal views, belongs the merit of being the first occupant of the Chair to discharge his duties.   The most interesting of his writings, *Remarks upon an Essay intituled the History of the colonisation of free states of antiquity applied to the present contest between Great Britain and her American colonies*, published in 1778, attacked the argument that, as the free states of antiquity taxed their colonies, Great Britain had a right to tax hers.   A survey of ancient colonisation, based on classical sources and modern French and English commentators, leads to the conclusion that the human race has advanced and that the American colonies are in the right.   ' We live not under the Commonwealth of a Carthage, an Athens or a Rome ; but (thanks be to the virtue of our ancestors !) we live under a monarchy

[1] March 2, 1773. *Letters*, VIII. 247.
[2] Published by Paget Toynbee in the *Times*. The letter is dated September 16, 1771, and was probably addressed to Stonhewer.

where the meanest subject may assert his rights, consistently with the duty which he owes his sovereign ; and yet nothing is wanting to a necessary authority any more than a rational liberty. This is a short answer to a thousand precedents of antiquity ; but every good Englishman will think it a satisfactory one.' His later volumes on the revision of the New Testament contain one or two passages of personal interest. The *Observations upon the expediency of revising the present English version of the four Gospels and the Acts*, published at Cambridge in 1789, is dedicated to the Duke of Grafton, Chancellor of the University, who was not quite so bad as Junius urged his readers to believe. 'By your recommendation, unsolicited and even unasked, I have for many years had the honour of enjoying a distinguished appointment in this University, and you have ever since ranked me in the number of your particular friends.' He adds that the Duke in repeated conversations has shown his interest in a subject so near to the author's heart. 'The more frequently I reflect upon the important truths of Christianity, the more ardently I wish to see our version revised by proper authority.'

The *Observations on the Epistles*, which followed in 1794, contains a preface replying to an attack on the earlier work. Among the charges was that of speaking well of Priestley, whose political and theological views were not in favour with rigid traditionalists ; but Symonds has no apology to offer. 'Ever since his *Lectures upon History* were published I have constantly recommended them to the students in our University as the best book in its kind which has fallen within my observation.' An allusion to 'my excellent friend Bishop Watson' confirms the impression that the Professor was a man of the left centre ; and it is a feather in his cap that Arthur Young [1] refers to 'the admirable essays of my valuable friend Professor Symonds upon Italian agriculture,' which appeared in the *Annals of Agriculture*.

When Symonds succeeded Gray in 1771 he lost no

[1] *Travels in France*, ed. C. Maxwell, i.

time in getting to work, and the set of rules which he proposed was accepted in 1773.[1] The fees of the noble-men, Fellow-Commoners and their attendant private tutors were to be devoted to remunerating the teachers of languages and the purchase of books and maps. He collected and bequeathed nearly a thousand volumes for the use of his pupils, each bearing the title *Scholae Historicae Cantabridgiensis Liber*, thus founding the Historical Library to which his successor was to make large additions.[2] Some printed notices survive of the commencement of his courses, which included hints on text-books and the study of history. In his survey of European civilisation since the Roman Empire we are not surprised to learn that he reprobated ' intolerance in religion and civil government.'

Symonds was succeeded in 1807 by William Smyth, the fifth Peterhouse occupant of the Chair, and the first of the Professors to make a serious study of history. An Irishman, educated at Eton and King's, and later a Fellow of Peterhouse,[3] he became tutor to Sheridan's son and, as a *persona grata* in Whig circles, he obtained the post through the influence of the youthful Lord Henry Petty, Chancellor of the Exchequer during the brief Grenville Ministry which followed the death of Pitt, and Member for the University. In her obituary of the third Marquis of Lansdowne, written nearly half a century later,[4] Harriet Martineau speaks with some severity of the appointment. Cambridge, she declares tartly, would have no more of the young Liberal ; but he indulged himself in a last act of patronage in securing the appointment of Smyth, whom his friends called the ' amiable and accomplished.' ' It was, like most of

---

[1] C. Wordsworth, *Scholae Academicae*, 1877, 147–51.

[2] See J. W. Clark, *Endowments of the University of Cambridge*, 184–5. A MSS. volume of his lectures, 640 pages, quarto boards, undated, bearing the names at the end Panting, Coll. John Cant. 1790, recently appeared in a catalogue priced 21*s*.

[3] Two windows in Peterhouse Chapel perpetuate his memory. Walker's *Peterhouse*, 31, note.

[4] *Biographical Sketches*, ed. 1885, 94–5.

Lord Lansdowne's appointments, an act of kindness to the individual, but scarcely so to the public. There is no saying what benefit might have accrued to British statesmanship if a man of more vigour, philosophy and comprehensiveness of mind had been appointed to so important a chair.'

Harriet Martineau had a sharp tongue, and her censure seems a little excessive.   It is true that in 1810 Gillray depicted Smyth lecturing to a few slumbering students.[1]   Modern history was then regarded as a subject of little importance, and it is improbable that British statesmanship would have profited by a different appointment.   No one at any rate could deny that Smyth was a man of active mind.   In his leisure hours he composed lyrics, which passed through five editions and earned the praise of the *Edinburgh Review*, and a work on the Evidences of Christianity.   His first historical publication, *A List of Books recommended and referred to in the Lectures on Modern History by Professor Smyth*, appeared in 1817.   The brochure of 21 pages suggested, even for the shortest course of reading, selected chapters of Gibbon, Hume, Robertson, Coxe, Voltaire, with parts of Clarendon, Burnet and other memoirs.   But the pupil was encouraged to throw his net wide.   ' Adam Smith should also be studied, and the late work of Mr. Malthus, with the best works in morals and metaphysics.' The bibliographical guide reveals a wide knowledge of the English and French works then available, and in reprinting it in 1819 with his Lectures he called attention to Hallam and Lingard, Mignet and Thiers, Sismondi and other bright lights in the new firmament.

If Symonds was the first Professor to lecture, Smyth was the first to publish his lectures, and the volumes which appeared in 1840 enable us to test his quality. The first two, entitled *Lectures on Modern History*, were dedicated to his benefactor Lord Lansdowne.   ' It has always been a source of pride to me to have owed my Professorship to your Lordship's favourable opinion.'

---

[1] *Caricatures of James Gillray*, ed. by T. Wright, 360.

The survey of the centuries from the fall of Rome to the Reformation is very brief, and the continual comments on modern historians impede the flow of his tale. The course ends with a full treatment of the American War of Independence which reveals the orthodox Whig. ' I know not how any friend to his species, much less any Englishman,' he concludes, ' can cease to wish with the most earnest anxiety for the success of the great experiment. What efforts can be made for the government of mankind, so reasonable as these—a limited monarchy and a limited republic ? Give civil and religious liberty and you give everything ; deny them and you deny everything.' Three volumes of *Lectures on the French Revolution*, the first delivered in 1826-7, carry the story to the fall of Robespierre, examine the state of opinion in England, and sketch the teaching of Burke, Godwin and other gladiators. The work concludes with half a dozen supplementary discourses of later date. During the crisis of the Reform Bill he declared that he never intended in his lectures to mix himself up in the politics of the day, but he added that the lesson he had always endeavoured to enforce was the duty of moderation. In a lecture of 1832 he warned his hearers against Robert Owen and other revolutionists. He never wearied of drawing lessons from the French Revolution, which revealed ' what man becomes when he attempts to be wiser than the God that made him.' Smyth's utterances, without being in any way distinguished, mark a considerable advance on anything that had been heard in the realm of history in either University. They found an honoured place in many an early Victorian home, and received the honour of a reprint in Bohn's Library.

On the death of Smyth in 1849 the Prince Consort as Chancellor of the University was anxious to secure a scholar of real eminence, and the most famous historian of the age was invited to fill the vacancy. ' To the Palace,' wrote Macaulay in his diary on July 1, 1849.[1]

[1] Trevelyan, *Life and Letters of Macaulay*, II. 261.

'The Prince, to my extreme astonishment, offered me the Professorship, and very earnestly, and with many flattering expressions, pressed me to accept it. I gratefully and respectfully declined. It would be strange if, having sacrificed for liberty a seat in the Cabinet and £2500 a year, I should now sacrifice liberty for a chair at Cambridge and £400 a year. Besides I never could do two things at once. If I lectured well my History must be given up ; and to give up my History would be to give up much more than the emoluments of the Professorship.' It was a wise decision, though it is tempting to reflect on the crowds who would have flocked to hear the most eloquent voice of his time.

A fortnight after Macaulay's refusal Lord John Russell recommended Sir James Stephen. 'It seems to me,' wrote the scholarly Prime Minister to the Prince Consort on July 20, 'that experience in the practical business of life is a good foundation for an historian. Xenophon, Tacitus, Davila, Guicciardini were all men engaged in political or military affairs.' [1] At the Prince's request Stephen explained his view of the duties of the office in a Memorandum which found entire satisfaction, and a personal interview was followed by the appointment. 'Sir James Stephen has after all become Professor of History in Cambridge,' wrote the Prince to the faithful Stockmar. 'We have had him here, and I was able to have much conversation with him. Never have I seen an Englishman with a mind more open and free from prejudice. I understand now why he was unpopular ; for he hits hard at the weak points of his countrymen.'

The father of the new Professor had been a prominent member of Wilberforce's evangelical circle, and had taken an active part in the struggle against the slave-trade. His mother was a daughter of John Venn, a leading member of the Clapham Sect.[2] Sir James himself, after studying at Cambridge, spent his early years at the Bar ; but in 1834 he became Under-Secretary in

[1] *Life of the Prince Consort*, II. 203.
[2] See Leslie Stephen, *Life of Sir J. F. Stephen*, ch. 1.

the Colonial Office.[1] During the next decade his strong hand and powerful brain were felt in every detail of legislation and administration, above all in the abolition of slavery and the grant of responsible government to Canada ; and Sir Henry Taylor, his colleague in the Colonial Office, declared that he literally ruled the Colonial Empire. The commanding personality of the greatest civil servant of his time is suggested, perhaps a little unkindly, in the titles King Stephen, Mr. Over-Secretary Stephen, Mr. Mother-Country Stephen (the latter attributed to Charles Buller) by which he was familiarly known. Though his work was continuous and exacting he stole time from sleep and relaxation to write articles for the *Edinburgh Review* which, when collected and revised in 1849 under the title of *Essays in Ecclesiastical Biography*, enjoyed a popularity second to those of Macaulay alone. The vigour of his style, his wide knowledge and broad sympathy with leading figures of different Churches—Hildebrand and St. Francis, Luther and Loyola, the French Benedictines and the Port-Royalists—won innumerable friends, and the book may still be read with pleasure and profit.[2]

The new Professor was hardly in the saddle before he was exposed to a virulent attack for the views on eternal punishment which he had expressed in an Epilogue to the *Essays*. The danger of daring to say what most educated men had already begun to think was to be proved four years later when the saintly Maurice lost his chair in London ; but Maurice was a Professor of Theology, and his case was complicated by extraneous factors.[3] An anonymous pamphlet[4] entitled *The Government Scheme of Education in the University of Cambridge*

---

[1] See *The First Sir James Stephen.* Letters with biographical notes by his daughter C. E. Stephen. Printed for private circulation, 1906. Cp. the brief biography by his son James to the fourth edition of the *Essays in Ecclesiastical Biography.*

[2] A reprint in the Silver Library in 1907 has secured new readers in the post-Victorian world.

[3] See Hearnshaw, *History of King's College, London,* 206–16.

[4] A copy is in the British Museum.

argued that religious errors in the Professor would vitiate his teaching of Modern History. ' It is the clear duty of the members of the Senate,' declared the author, ' to prove to the country at large that they are watching with godly jealousy over the faith and morals of the youth committed to their charge.' The attempt to secure an inquiry by the Senate was frustrated by a modest and wholly admirable letter to the Vice-Chancellor.[1] Stephen protested his orthodoxy, recalled the fact that he had subscribed to the Thirty-nine Articles only a few weeks before, and resented the insinuation that he would use the Chair to attack the doctrines of the Church which he loved. He was indeed a deeply though unobtrusively religious man, and he made his public reply to his critics in the Inaugural *On certain so-called Philosophies of History*, rejecting the fatalist and positivist attitudes and acclaiming the theory of Providence.[2]

Stephen had long been a celebrity, and his first impressions were favourable. ' Conyers Middleton was certainly mistaken,' he wrote to Henry Taylor, ' in thinking that there has been an end of all miracles since the time of the Apostles. My own lectures prove it. Gownsmen and gownswomen, filling room or college hall, the female students of history occupying the gallery, while I at the other end address my audience in a sonorous voice and with an assurance which the most intrepid of your Downing Street bores might envy.' Two years later he expressed his pleasure in resuming his gown at Cambridge and writing lectures on history, believing that ' though there were many men much more conversant with the events of former times, there was no candidate for the office who could in any degree claim equality with myself in that kind of historical knowledge which is derived from a long and intimate connexion with the actual government of mankind.'

---

[1] This letter is printed and the Cambridge years are described in *The First Sir James Stephen*, chs. 5–8.

[2] *Selected Epigraphs*, by L. S. Wood (Historical Association Leaflet No. 80), analyses the Inaugural Lectures of the Regius Professors at Oxford and Cambridge since 1841.

Stephen chose for his first courses the history of France, after consulting John Austin, who advised him to explain the institutions of the old French monarchy, and Macaulay, who emphasised the claims of the wars of religion.[1] He had retired from the Colonial Office owing to ill health in 1847, and he never regained his strength, though his intellectual energy was unabated. After delivering his first series in 1850 he fell dangerously ill, and completed the second series in Paris during the winter of 1851. The two solid volumes covering the internal history of France from Roman Gaul to the eve of the Revolution received a warm welcome, and a third edition, with large additions, appeared in 1857. ' I claim no place among historians,' he write in a modest preface ; ' I have written only as a commentator.' No apology was needed, for the lectures reveal the same sterling qualities as the *Essays*. His survey is singularly lucid, comprehensive and well arranged. Among its most valuable features are the addresses on the rise of the municipalities and the results of the Crusades, the administration of justice and the collection of revenue, and the full narrative of the meetings of the States-General. The three lectures on the Power of the Pen contain attractive portraits of thinkers and scholars, saints and sinners, from Abelard and Bernard to Rabelais and Descartes. Leslie Stephen was justified in pronouncing his father's lectures to reflect his experience of administrative work and to reveal an unusual appreciation of the constitutional side of French history. In his study of the *Ancien Régime* he anticipated some of the results of Tocqueville, who expressed cordial appreciation of his work. His hope of following it up with a survey of French foreign policy was never fulfilled.

The interest in the new Professor soon flagged, and he reported that his audiences had dwindled. In 1855 he became Professor of Modern History and Political Economy at the East India College at Haileybury,

---

[1] See the dedicatory letter to Whewell in Vol. I. of the first edition of the *Lectures on the History of France*, 1851.

holding the two Chairs at the same time, and writing out
lectures on the history of India which were never published.
He found the new audience more satisfactory than the
old. ' The difference is that here the boys listen with
anxiety to get up the subject for their exams. At Cambridge they listen or not as it happens to interest them.'
Stephen was gowing old and weary, and in 1858 decided
that he would resign in the following year. He died in
1859 at the age of 70. His successor paid public tribute
to his ' large-hearted humanity,' and his decade of office
notably enhanced the prestige of the Chair.

The vacant post was offered by Palmerston to Charles
Kingsley. ' He accepted it,' records his wife, ' but with
extreme diffidence.' [1] His hesitation was intelligible.
He was a popular preacher and lecturer, a moralist, a
poet, a novelist, a pamphleteer, a country parson and
Chaplain to the Queen. Though he was the author of
Hypatia and *Westward Ho!* he had never made any
systematic study of history. ' It is with a feeling of awe,
almost of fear,' he declared in his Inaugural,[2] ' that I find
myself in this place upon this errand.' He cut the knot
by delivering a sermon. To understand history we
must understand men. Biography and autobiography
were essential. Human welfare was founded not on
mind but on morals. ' As the fruit of righteousness is
wealth and peace, strength and honour, the fruit of un-
righteousness is poverty and anarchy, weakness and shame.
For not upon mind, gentlemen, not upon mind, but upon
morals is human welfare founded. So far from morals
depending upon thought, thought, I believe, depends
upon morals.' Thus prosperity was the correlative of
morality. In a word history was the record of God's
education of man. It was the same message which
Thomas Arnold had brought to his Oxford hearers in
1841.

The seed sown in the Inaugural ripened in his first

---

[1] *Charles Kingsley: Letters and Memories of his Life.* Edited by his wife,
Vol. II. ch. 20.

[2] Printed separately and reprinted in *The Roman and the Teuton.*

and most celebrated course, *The Roman and the Teuton*. The rejuvenation of Europe by the unspoiled races from the north was a theme after Kingsley's own heart. From the paralysis of the ancient world we pass to the swarming barbarians, who are speedily civilised by the joint influence of Christianity and Rome. Huns, Goths and Lombards sweep across the stage. The closing lecture bears the characteristic title, ' The Strategy of Providence.' The conquest of Rome by the Teutons, he declares, was directed by God. ' Was this vast campaign fought without a General ? No ! the hosts of our forefathers were the hosts of God.' There are passages of genuine eloquence and skilful dramatisation ; but there is little learning, and the reflections are commonplace. His brother-in-law and admiring friend, Max Müller, admits that he would have done better to write a historical novel or drama on Theodoric.[1] ' History,' he adds, ' was but his text ; his chief aim was that of a teacher and preacher.' The Professor's peculiar gifts were well understood by his audience. ' He preached,' writes a pupil, ' without seeming to do so. Men all over the world have thanked God for the lessons of manliness, charity and godliness they learned in his lecture-room.' The lecturer would have valued such a testimonial far more than any tribute to his scholarship.

Kingsley's second course, on the History of America, suggested by the outbreak of the Civil War, ended with the words, ' If I have convinced you that well-doing and ill-doing are rewarded and punished in this world as well as in the world to come, I shall have done you more good than if I had crammed your mind with many dates and facts.' It was utterances of this sort which moved Lord Morley to declare that Kingsley had less of the historic sense than any other Professor who ever sat in a Chair of History. Though he attracted one of the largest audiences in Cambridge and held it enthralled, his lectures did not lead to serious study. His quick sympathy, fervent emotions and robust personality made him the

[1] *Chips from a German Workshop*, Vol. II.

idol of young men, and he was chosen by the Prince Consort to teach history privately to the Prince of Wales during his residence in Cambridge ; but he knew that he was unfitted for an academic career. *The Roman and the Teuton* was sharply criticised, and his later courses were never published. He was not much in residence, and was happiest in his Rectory at Eversley. A newspaper attack in 1868 turned his thoughts to resignation, and in 1869 he withdrew from the post which he ought never to have accepted. ' My brains as well as my purse,' he explained, ' rendered the step necessary.'

Gladstone's choice fell on Seeley, who had won fame as the author of *Ecce Homo*, and had been for some years Professor of Latin at University College, London.[1] In his Inaugural he recalled Stephen's lectures, which he had attended as an undergraduate. ' The recollection is discouraging. I do not hope to give better lectures than Sir James Stephen. It was—and I think the Professor felt it—a painful waste of power. There was teaching of the highest kind, and no demand for it. The causes which were at work to depress the study of modern history have not quite ceased to operate, though they may operate less powerfully, and it is in no sanguine spirit that I commence my labours.' His theme was the Teaching of Politics. Why should history be studied ? he asked. Because it is the school of statesmanship, came the reply. ' Our University is and must be a great seminary of politicians. Without at least a little knowledge of history no man can take a rational interest in politics, and no man can form a rational judgment about them without a good deal.' That this truth was so little recognised was due to the common error that history dealt with the remote past. It was to modern history that he invited the attention of the young men ' from whom the legislators and statesmen of the next age must be taken.' ' As the indispensable thing for a lawyer is a knowledge of law and for a clergyman of

[1] See Gooch, *History and Historians in the Nineteenth Century*, ch. 19.

divinity, so the indispensable thing for a politician is a knowledge of political economy and history.'

The new Professor found time to write several books of outstanding significance. The earliest and the largest, *The Life and Times of Stein*, the first important historical work written by a holder of the Cambridge Chair, approached the history of Napoleon from a new angle. It contained no revelations, for he consulted no manuscripts; but he mastered the whole mass of printed authorities. Though hero-worship was no temptation to his austere temperament and biographical detail had no attraction for him, he does not conceal his admiration for the strong, silent man whom he ranks with Turgot among the leading political architects. If the work has a fault it is its portrait of the Emperor. His *Short History of Napoleon*, written some years later, once more revealed his inability to measure the greatness of a genius whose policy he abhorred.

If the *Life of Stein* met with less than its legitimate success, his next work brought generous compensation. *The Expansion of England* occupies a place in our political history as well as in the annals of scholarship ; for it appeared at a moment when the nation was becoming genuinely interested in the colonies and the Empire. The two courses of lectures dealt with the conquest of Canada and India, explaining with crystal clearness the relation between the foundation of the British Empire and the conflict with France. His thesis was less original than he believed, but he was the first to work it out. He knew how to produce effects by focussing a brilliant light on the principal factors, and exhibiting the connection between a number of apparently isolated phenomena. He loved large surveys, international problems, comprehensive generalisations. The book was read throughout the British Empire, and quickened the sense of the magnitude as well as the responsibility of our heritage. He rejects the notion that its vastness proves either our invincible heroism or our genius for government, and his pages stimulate reflection rather than exaltation. If the book was as much a political dissertation as a scientific inquiry, it was enriched by ample knowledge and carried out in an objective spirit.

The last ten years of Seeley's life were devoted to the composition of a work on British foreign policy. Like Ranke, to whom he owed most, he regarded history as concerned mainly with the fortunes of states. Intending at first to begin with 1688, he pushed his starting-point ever further back. He finally commenced his survey with Elizabeth, and was overtaken by death when he had reached William III. *The Growth of British Policy*, though but a fragment in two volumes, contains some of his most effective work. His power of marshalling facts was unrivalled, and no one but Ranke has been more successful in making the reader feel the diplomatic unity of Europe. He believed that the destiny of a State depended less on its institutions than on its place in the world. If he occasionally traced results too exclusively to diplomatic factors and was blind to the full importance of internal development, his mastery of foreign relations often placed domestic occurrences in a new light.

Seeley's long tenure of the Cambridge Chair will ever remain memorable. He was the first scholar of the front rank to hold the post, and the first to realise the immense significance of German scholarship. He had very definite ideas of his own, and he worked hard for their realisation. He had a horror of lazy thinking and careless scholarship, and scorned the literary purveyors of the picturesque. No one has more ardently proclaimed the capacity of history to guide the footsteps of the statesman and the citizen. When the Historical Tripos was established in 1875 [1] he claimed a leading place in it for political science. Politics, he declared, were vulgar when they were not liberalised by history, and history faded into mere literature when it lost sight of its relation to practical politics. The unwearying attempt to build up a science of politics was pursued in the Conversation Classes held at his own house to which

---

[1] The Law and History Tripos had begun in 1870.

many Cambridge men, myself among them, look back with gratitude. Despite the obvious limitations of his method, Seeley's twenty-five years at Cambridge raised the whole level of historical study and production in the University.

Lord Acton's appointment by Lord Rosebery in 1895 aroused unusual interest.[1] Though his name was unknown in the market place, he had been a conspicuous figure for nearly forty years in the republic of learning. He had taken a leading part in opposing the Ultramontane movement which culminated in the Vatican decrees, he was familiar with the statesmen no less than the scholars of the Continent, and he was the most erudite Englishman of his time. Half a German by birth and training, he brought an international atmosphere into the University. Though he had never written a book, his articles and reviews in the Catholic journals which he had edited, in the *Quarterly Review* and the *Nineteenth Century*, and more recently in the *English Historical Review*, were appreciated throughout Europe. A Catholic Professor of History was a novelty ; but the choice was justified not only as a fitting tribute to a scholar of world-wide reputation but from the narrower standpoint of the Cambridge historical school. Though not the greatest historian, he was the most commanding personality who has held the Chair of Modern History. The University has never possessed a teacher more capable of inspiring his students to research and reflection or one more ready to enter into their interests. For himself it was an Indian summer after a life of controversy and disappointment. ' Cambridge is really a haven of delight,' he wrote to Gladstone at the opening of 1896, ' and I am grateful to them all round for the way they tolerate and even accept me.' [2]

The Inaugural lecture on the Teaching of History sounded a note which had never been heard at either University. In his opening paragraphs he struck off

[1] See Gooch, *History and Historians in the Nineteenth Century*, ch. 20.
[2] Lord Acton's *Correspondence*, I. 157.

the fetters in which Seeley had bound himself and attempted to bind his pupils. ' Politics and history,' he declared in those deep, strong tones which his hearers will never forget, ' are interwoven but not commensurate. Ours is the domain that reaches further than affairs of State. It is our function to keep in view and to command the movement of ideas, which are not the effect but the cause of public events.' The first of human concerns was religion, the second liberty ; and their fortunes were intertwined. Passing from the scope of the science to the spirit which should govern its study he emphasised the sanctity of the moral code. ' I exhort you never to debase the moral currency, but to try others by the final maxim that governs your own lives, and to suffer no man and no cause to escape the undying penalty which history has power to inflict on wrong. If in our uncertainty we must often err, it may be sometimes better to risk excess in rigour than in indulgence.' The fear that he would shield his own Church disappeared when it was realised that the severest sentences were passed where religion should have taught men better. In judging men and things, he declared, ethics go before dogma, politics and nationality. He practised what he preached, and he never wrote a word as Regius Professor which revealed him as member of a particular Church.

The message that history embraced the whole life of man and the whole process of civilisation came like a breath of spring after the rather wintry rule of Seeley ; but his almost passionate exhortation to moral severity provoked lively opposition. In his Presidential address to the American Historical Association on Ethical Values in History, Henry Charles Lea, the historian of the Inquisition, joined direct issue. The new gospel, he declared, presupposed a fixed and unalterable standard of morality, together with the comfortable assurance that we have attained to that absolute knowledge of right and wrong which enables us to pass final judgment on the men of the past. Every age has similarly flattered itself, and presumably every succeeding one will continue to cherish the same illusion. We must judge men, declared the Nestor of American historians, by their time. To transport ethical ideas into bygone centuries was to introduce subjectivity into what should be purely objective. Philip II, for example, conscientiously believed that in his mortal struggle with heretics he was rendering the highest service to God and man. To censure him was unjust, for the real culprit was the age. Even Acton's most devoted disciples must admit the substantial justice of this measured criticism.

The Professor delivered two courses of lectures, which were published after his death without the author's revision. 'My tendency to read everything I can get that relates to my subject,' he wrote to Gladstone, ' proves a drawback and a vice when I have to lecture, and I am always a little late and hurried.' [1] The course on Modern History covered the centuries from the Renaissance to the French Revolution. Designed as it was for students reading for an examination, it naturally contains a great deal of familiar information ; but we catch his personality in the judgments and reflections with which it abounds. Though necessarily dealing with events rather than with ideas, his dominant theme is the advance of man towards ordered freedom. In a striking phrase he pronounces the emancipation of conscience from authority the main content of modern history. He is at his best in the sixteenth century, and the lecture on Luther is a triumph of impartial interpretation. It is piquant to hear a Catholic assurance that the Reformer was ' a profound conservative and a reluctant innovator,' though he adds on a later page that ' with all the intensity of his passion for authority, he did more than any single man to make modern history the development of revolution.' He understands as fully as any Protestant historian why the Reformation occurred, and he admits the debt of his Church to her enemies. ' Rome, with a contested

[1] Lord Acton's *Correspondence*, I. 157.

authority and a contracted sphere, developed greater
energy, resource and power than when it exercised
undivided sway over Christendom in the West.' Next
in interest to the judgment on Luther is that suggested
by the fate of Strafford, Laud and Charles I. ' It is
certain that they were put to death illegally and therefore unjustly. But we have no thread through the
enormous intricacy and complexity of modern politics
except the idea of progress towards more perfect
and assured freedom and the divine right of free
men. Judged by that test the three culprits must be
condemned.'

More significant and personal is the course on the
French Revolution, which Acton once described to me
as the greatest subject in history. The volume is
equally distinguished by its erudition and its sanity, its
eloquence and its strength. ' The Revolution,' he
declared, ' will never be intelligently known till we
recognise that it is not utterly singular and exceptional,
that other scenes have been as horrible and many men
as bad.' In contrast to Taine's highly coloured picture
of the actors he declares them to have been for the most
part average men, with a large number above the
common standard, while Mirabeau and Sieyès possessed
some claim to genius. Of the Declaration of the Rights
of Man he speaks with enthusiasm. ' It is the triumphant proclamation of the doctrine that human obligations
are not all assignable to contract or to interest or to force.
This single page of print outweighs libraries, and is
stronger than all the armies of Napoleon.' Yet it had
one great fault. It sacrificed liberty to equality, and the
absolutism of the King was succeeded by the absolutism
of the Assembly. Like Aulard he attributes the main
responsibility for the degradation of the reform movement to the Court. The well-meaning King was surrounded by evil counsellors, and the worst of them was
the Queen ; yet the Revolution, despite its horrors, was
a great effort at emancipation. ' The best things that
are loved and sought by men are religion and liberty,

not pleasure or prosperity, not knowledge or power. Yet the paths of both are stained with infinite blood.'

A few months after his appointment Acton received an invitation from the University Press to edit a comprehensive history of the modern world.[1]   ' We shall avoid the needless utterance of opinion or service of a cause.   Ultimate history we cannot have in this generation, but we can dispose of conventional history.'   He looked forward with special pleasure to the later volumes, which could be enriched with secrets not learned from books.   He drew up a list of specialists and secured the acceptance of the greater number ; but in 1901 he was struck down by illness, and died in 1902, a few months before the appearance of the first volume.   The introductory chapter in which he intended to assess the legacy of the Middle Ages, and the survey of the later Gladstonian era which he thirsted to undertake, were never written.   The work was carried out with admirable loyalty to his plan, and will always be connected with his name.

On the death of Acton the Chair was offered by Balfour to his old friend and political opponent John Morley, who wisely declined.   Acton's successor, Bury, his rival in learning, had already won European reputation by his histories of Greece, Rome, and the early Byzantine Empire and by his incomparable edition of Gibbon ; and he may fairly be described as the greatest historian who has ever held the Cambridge Chair.   His Inaugural Lecture, entitled ' The Science of History,' revealed an attitude in sharp contrast to those of his three predecessors.[2]   To Kingsley history was theology, to Seeley politics, to Acton morals ; to the new Professor it was science.   History, he declared, was a science, no less and no more.   This famous aphorism, which lends

---

[1] See *The Cambridge Modern History, An Account of its Origin, Authorship and Production,* 1907.

[2] Bury's writings on the nature of history are collected in his *Selected Essays,* edited by Professor Temperley.   Cp. the Memoir by Norman Baynes, and R. H. Murray's Introduction to the *Lectures on the History of the Papacy in the Nineteenth Century.*

itself to misunderstanding if quoted *in vacuo*, is fully explained in the course of the lecture. 'The transformation which historical studies are undergoing is a great event in the history of the world. A revolution is slowly and silently progressing. Erudition has been supplemented by scientific method. History has been enthroned among the sciences.' We owed the beneficent transformation to Germany, where it was inaugurated by Wolf, Niebuhr and Ranke. Nationalism had encouraged research, but the twentieth-century historian must emancipate himself from its yoke. The doctrine of human development, enunciated by Leibnitz, was necessary for the understanding of history ; but the historian *qua* historian had no business with philosophical or teleological interpretations. 'Though she may supply material for literary art and philosophical speculation, she is herself a science, no less and no more.'

Old as is the human race, Bury reminds us, we are still at the beginning of the story, and our experience is much too short for confident generalisations. 'We must see our petty periods *sub specie perennitatis*,' and approach their study without presuppositions. Ranke's gospel—*Ich will bloss sagen wie es eigentlich gewesen ist*—was still the watchword. For the first time in a pronouncement from the Cambridge Chair we sense the full impact of scientific discovery on the thought and perspective of the historian. Freeman had usefully proclaimed the unity of history, but he had lived in a very limited world. History, as rightly envisaged by Bury, embraced human life in all its length and all its breadth. Its theme was 'the material and spiritual development of man.' If the lecture seems on cursory reading to lack colour and warmth, it was from no tepid devotion of the new Professor to his calling. 'In prosecuting historical research,' he concludes, 'we are not indulging in a luxury but doing a thoroughly practical work and performing a duty to posterity.' In a sentence which revealed an aspect of his mind of which more was to be known later, he added that history would become

' a more and more powerful force for stripping the bandages of error from the eyes of men, for shaping public opinion, and advancing the cause of intellectual and political liberty.'

The ideas scattered by the Inaugural in rich profusion were developed in Bury's later utterances. ' The place of Modern History in the perspective of knowledge,' an address delivered at St. Louis in 1904, renewed the solemn warning against taking short views. Philosophies of history, such as that of Hegel, are splendid failures, for they are all imposed from without. In whatever period he lives the historian is under the spell of the present, and in our day it is tempting to believe that Christianity, Democracy and other familiar landmarks are the last word. ' Historical relativity triumphs over the Procrustean principle. Our syntheses and interpretations can only have a relative value.' This absence of finality in no way diminishes the interest and importance of particular eras, and the scholar who gave most of his life to antiquity and the early Middle Ages stresses the special importance of modern history. For full knowledge—including knowledge of the mind and feeling of the time—is necessary for full understanding ; and it is less difficult to know and therefore to understand the modern world than more distant and different epochs.

Five years later, in 1909, Bury contributed a paper on ' Darwinism and History ' to a centenary volume entitled *Darwinism and Modern Science*, which reiterates the leading ideas of the Inaugural. ' The growth of historical study in the nineteenth century has been determined and characterised by the same general principle which has underlain the simultaneous developments of the study of nature, namely the genetic idea. The conception of history as a continuous, genetic, causal process has revolutionised historical research and made it scientific. History is the reconstruction of the genetic process.' The meaning of genetic history was not fully realised till the first quarter of the nineteenth century, and its implications had not yet become axioms. 'History cannot become a science until it is conceived as lying entirely within a sphere in which the law of cause and effect has unreserved and unrestricted dominion.' Darwinism emphasised continuity, and 'the perspective of history is merged in the larger perspective of development.'

Though the human process is depicted as part of the genetic process, Bury points out that general laws were insufficient to explain historical development ; for the part played by coincidence and individuals rendered it impossible to deduce the past or predict the future. This, however, was also the case in organic development. The element of contingency is analysed in the essay ' Cleopatra's Nose,' published in 1916. Among his illustrations of apparently fortuitous synchronism of men and events are such outstanding occurrences as the invasion of Silesia by Frederick the Great, the loss of the American colonies by George III, and the conversion of Constantine to Christianity. With the advance of democracy and science, he concludes, contingencies will become less important in human evolution. The idea of contingency haunted him and prompted his oft-quoted confession: ' In days when I am a determinist I look on history in one way, and on days when I am an indeterminist in quite another.' It is significant that in dealing with the fall of the Roman Empire in the later edition of his greatest work he pronounces general causes alone insufficient to explain the catastrophe.

The substantial volume, *The Idea of Progress*, published in 1920, boldly grapples with the doctrine which Bury describes as the animating and controlling idea of western civilisation. Its practical utility is frankly recognised, for it carries with it the elevating conception of duty to posterity. But this consideration is irrelevant to the question of its truth. ' The progress of humanity belongs to the same order of ideas as Providence or personal immortality. It is true or it is false, and like them it cannot be proved either true or false. Belief in it is an act of faith.' The idea involved a belief not only in advance during the past but in an indefinite advance in the future. The classical world and the Middle Ages knew nothing of it, and its principal sponsors were sons of France. Evolution was a purely neutral conception, compatible either with optimism or pessimism ; and he labels believers in progress the optimists. He ends on a note which reveals the very depths of his thought. The idea of progress, he reminds us, had to overcome the illusion of finality, and in so doing it had rendered a most valuable service. But there was no finality in the notion itself. 'A day will come, in the revolution of centuries, when a new idea will usurp its place. And it too will have its successors.' This ever-present sense of the duration of the drama and the vastness of the stage partly accounts for the fact that he was less interested in individuals than in institutions, movements and ideas.

No survey of Bury's activities at Cambridge, however brief, could omit a reference to the *History of Freedom of Thought*, contributed in 1913 to the Home University Library, in which, to use a popular expression, he let himself go. We might be listening to Buckle or other mid-Victorian rationalists as we read his narrative of the struggles of the European mind to break the cramping fetters of dogma, superstition and ecclesiastical authority. For the first and last time the grave Professor left his desk for the market-place, and laid about him with a big stick. To a mind filled with the doctrine of relativity such notions as a chosen people, a final revelation and an infallible church were anathema. We find the same mixture of exasperation and contempt in his lectures on the Papacy in the nineteenth century, which, despite their interest, betray a curious lack of understanding of the varieties of religious experience.

The appointment of George Macaulay Trevelyan to succeed Bury in 1927 restored to Cambridge the best-known English historian of our time. His early works on the fourteenth and seventeenth century had won him readers outside professional circles, but it was from the Venetian colouring of the Garibaldian trilogy that we learned that the spirit of his great-uncle was reincarnate. His conception of the functions of the historian was stated in the brilliant and challenging manifesto entitled *Clio, a Muse*, published in 1913. Two generations earlier, he declared, history was a part of our national literature, but its popular influence had diminished as the expert displaced the amateur. If there was a gain in the deeper academic life of the nation, there was also a loss in its wider cultural life. The modern German idea of history as a science is unfavourably contrasted with the older English ideal of conveying the results of learning to a wide public in attractive form. Carlyle combined warm human sympathy with the highest imaginative powers, and his interpretations of the French Revolution and Cromwell were still alive. Historical sources could never tell us all that we wanted to know, and imagination was essential to discover the causes of human action. ' To recover some of our ancestors' real thoughts and feelings is the hardest, subtlest and most educative function that the historian can perform.' The historian has three tasks,—the scientific, the imaginative and the literary. To Seeley, who attacked narrative and told his students, ' Ask yourself questions, set yourself problems,' he rejoins that the principal craft of the historian is the art of narrative. ' History is a tale,' not a science. The historian should write for the nation, not merely for his fellow-students ; for ' the ultimate value of history is not scientific but educational.'

The Professor's Inaugural Lecture, entitled ' The Present Position of History,' renewed the plea for ' the true English tradition,' but in a less provocative tone.[1] His *History of England* had displayed a serene impartiality which has made it the chosen companion of every school of thought, and his official declaration of 1927 breathes the rich maturity of middle age. Though he

[1] The 1930 edition of *Clio, a Muse*, contains the Inaugural as well as the essay of 1913.

now speaks with more respect for research, he once again pays homage to the time-honoured ideal of a liberal education, and argues that literature and learning should still go hand in hand.   While Bury wrote primarily for scholars and envisaged history first and foremost as intellectual enlightenment, his successor is penetrated by a sense of its value for the enrichment of character and life.   ' The truth about the past, if taught or read with broad human sympathy, can give a noble education to the mind of the student, not only in politics but in all kinds of civic and social relationship, and even in the domain of personal, religious and ethical ideals.' The appeal of history, he concludes, is in the last analysis poetic, for the historian is consumed with the longing ' to know what really happened in that land of mystery which we call the past.'   Some of us possess this urge to peer into the magic mirror in a greater degree than others ; but it exists in us all.   History is too precious, too wonderful, too inspiring to be the monopoly of the experts ; for the past ' gathers round it all the inscrutable mystery of life and death and time.'   ' Let the science and research of the historian find the fact, and let his imagination and art make clear its significance.'   That Professor Trevelyan can realise his own lofty ideal, that he inherits the mantle of Macaulay without his partisanship, he has shown once again in his panoramic vision of the crowded age of Anne.

The story of the Chair of Modern History at Cambridge is a record of steady growth, a mirror of the changing habits and ideas of two centuries, a chapter in the development of national education.   But it is also a reminder that, though historians are honourably associated in the common pursuit of truth, each one of them differs from his comrades in training and inheritance, in mind and temperament, and in consequence regards the human pageant from a different angle.   For in the temple of Clio there are many mansions.

THE STUDY OF FOREIGN AFFAIRS

THE Social and Political Education League was founded by Sir John Seeley, whose unceasing endeavour was to relate learning to life.[1]   Why should history be studied ? asked the Regius Professor of Modern History in his Inaugural Lecture on succeeding Kingsley in the Cambridge Chair in 1869.   Because it is the school of statesmanship, came the unhesitating reply.   ' Our University is, and must be, a great seminary of politicians. Without at least a little knowledge of history no man can take a rational interest in politics, and no man can form a rational judgment about them without a good deal.'   That this obvious truth was so little recognised was due, he argued, to the common error that history dealt with the remote past.   It was to modern times that he invited the attention of the young men from whom, as he declared, the legislators and statesmen of the next age must be taken.   His special interest was in the relation of States to one another, and he reproved our insular historians for believing that their main task was to trace the development of our institutions. English eyes, he complained, were always bent upon Parliament.   ' The expansion of England is the great fact of modern English history,' he cried in the most famous of his works, which summoned his hearers and readers to turn from the domestic wrangles of the eighteenth century to the titanic spectacle of France and England wrestling for the domination of India and the New World.   Seeley's later years were devoted to a

[1] Presidential Address to the Social and Political Education League, 1921.

history of British foreign policy, but he died when he had traced the story from Elizabeth to William III. Though his two volumes are only a fragment, few historical works leave such an impression of lucidity and grasp. He believed that the destiny of a State depended less on its institutions than on its place in the world, and no one except Ranke, his illustrious model, was more successful in making the reader envisage the diplomatic unity of Europe. My old teacher's conception of history as mainly concerned with the relations of States was impossibly narrow ; but no British scholar has done so much to arouse interest in the study of foreign affairs.

If our historians have not always realised the importance of our foreign relations, a similar charge may with even greater justice be brought against our legislators. Since the first Reform Bill the British Empire has been ruled by the House of Commons ; but in no Parliament since 1832 can we discover more than a handful of men who devoted themselves before their election, or proceeded to devote themselves after their election, to what is perhaps the most important branch of public affairs. It is not enough for members to wake up when a crisis is at hand ; and Flournoy's *Parliament and War* reminds us how little the House had to say in the initiation of our conflicts from the Crimean War to the conflagration of 1914. The long peace following the downfall of Napoleon allowed men to forget the whole in the part, and neither Gladstone nor Disraeli displayed an interest in international relations till they reached middle age. Even during the second half of the nineteenth century, when war again became a fashionable pastime, there were few who apprenticed themselves to this exacting study. Among the little band were Grant Duff, whose annual addresses to his constituents in the Elgin Burghs in the sixties and seventies were devoted to a survey of the wider world, and Dilke, who, while still a young man, won for himself by travel and observation a recognised position among European publicists. That the House of Lords always

possesses a few specialists is no substitute for lack of
knowledge in the Chamber which is supposed to control
the executive Government. Cabinet Ministers themselves are almost always far too occupied with their own
departments to digest the information regularly supplied
to them by the Foreign Office. 'Where is Annapolis?'
asked the Duke of Newcastle in a famous aside ; and
in our own day Mr. Lloyd George confessed that he
had never heard of Teschen.

If our rulers set such an example, it is no wonder
that most of our fellow-citizens should regard foreign
affairs with massive unconcern. We devote as much
attention to politics as the inhabitants of any other
country, but our interest in our external relations and
obligations has always been spasmodic. Long periods
of lethargic repose are followed by orgies of excitement
aroused by war or the menace of war, and the coloured
information about actual or potential enemies supplied
at such times produces the same effect on our heads as
alcohol on an empty stomach. Every journalist, every
Member of Parliament, and every Minister who has
tried the experiment is aware how difficult it is in time
of peace to arouse and sustain intelligent curiosity about
international problems. Yet the effort must be cease-
lessly renewed ; for if we do not educate ourselves and
our masters when the sky is clear, we shall find it is too
late when the lightning begins to play and the thunder
rolls. No one ever laboured more diligently to dispel
the complacent indifference of his fellow-countrymen
than David Urquhart, who instituted Foreign Affairs
Committees in many of our large cities at the time of the
Crimean War ; but before the death of their founder in
1877 they had one and all ceased to exist.

Whatever excuses could be made in an earlier generation, no one would now dare to deny the interdependence
of nations or the domination of domestic problems by
external factors. Talleyrand wrote home from the
Congress of Vienna that he was trying to be a good
European as well as a good Frenchman ; but today

each one of us must aim at being not only a good Englishman and a good European, but a good citizen of the world. With the standardisation of culture, the triumphs of applied science, the growth of commercial enterprise, and the extension of political groupings, the world has become like a pond into which a stone thrown from any of its banks produces ripples, or even waves, over the entire surface. Thanks to the telegraph, remarked Lord Dufferin, our globe has become a mere bundle of nerves. The aphorism of Terence, *Homo sum ; nihil humani alienum puto*, is now not merely a philosophical commonplace but a political axiom. Civilisation is like a train, the travellers in which know little and care less about their fellow-passengers in other compartments, though the safety of them all depends on the skill and trustworthiness of the engine-driver and the signalman. Since the revolver shots rang out at Serajevo on June 28, 1914, we can no longer argue that any part of the earth is too remote or any State too insignificant to concern our interests and to claim our attention.

If the interdependence of nations, with all its fateful possibilities, is thus admitted, we may proceed to inquire what ought to be done. The first requisite is of course the provision of facilities for teaching and study. When France lay bleeding and humiliated in 1871, some far-sighted patriots, led by Taine and Émile Boutmy, founded the École Libre des Sciences Politiques to train the diplomatists, the administrators, and the Civil Service of the Third Republic. As an old pupil of the school, I can testify to the practical character of its curriculum and the authority of its teachers, which included such celebrities as Albert Sorel and Alfred Rambaud. Our own School of Economics and Political Science, established a generation later, now possesses a Chair of International Politics, following the precedent of Aberystwith. Oxford stands third in the list, and other Universities impatiently await the appearance of a fairy godmother. The Royal Institute of International Affairs, one of the few entirely beneficent results of the Peace Congress of 1919, has become a fruitful centre of expert discussion, while its *Journal* and Professor Toynbee's *Annual Survey* should be our inseparable companions. The Institute of Historical Research, which we owe mainly to the zeal of Professor Pollard, includes in its programme advanced instruction in modern diplomatic history. It is increasingly recognised that the teaching of modern history in every centre of higher education should bring the record up to or within sight of the day and hour in which we live and move and have our being. If it be objected that the nearness of events and the passions of party disqualify contemporary history for a place in the academic curriculum, we reply that the origins of the World War are not more controversial than the Reformation and the French Revolution, and that in England as elsewhere there are scholars who can steer with a steady hand through the stormiest waters. The United States can boast of the Council of Foreign Relations, with its *Annual Survey of American Foreign Relations* and its authoritative quarterly *Foreign Affairs*, to which statesmen and scholars of the Old World freely contribute. In Germany we may note the Institut für Auswärtige Politik at Hamburg which, under the direction of Professor Mendelssohn Bartholdy, encourages research and issues a valuable monthly *Europäische Gespräche*, and the Hochschule für Politik in Berlin founded by Professor Jäckh. All these ventures belong to the post-war world.

The overwhelming experiences of the war, added to the discovery of secret commitments both in the years preceding the outbreak of hostilities and during their course, have created a demand not only for the study but for the control of foreign policy. The topic has been discussed with inside knowledge in Lord Ponsonby's *Democracy and Diplomacy* and in Sir George Young's little volume *Diplomacy*, while an interesting chapter on ' Democracy and Foreign Policy ' in Lord Bryce's last work, *International Relations*, is devoted to the theme. ' The voices which demand the abolition of secret diplomacy

and the control by the people of all foreign relations,'
declares the latter, ' appeal to an incontestable principle,
because a nation has every right to deliver its opinion on
the issues of peace and war. If Ministries were to
become more and more anxious to keep as close a touch
with the feelings of the nation in foreign as they seek to
do in domestic affairs, the risk that any nation will be
irrevocably entangled in a pernicious course would
diminish. And if there be less desire to get the better
of other nations in acquiring territory or concessions
abroad, if a less grasping and selfish spirit should rule
foreign policy, fewer occasions will arise in which secret
agreements will be required. The thing now most
needed by the people and its representatives is more
knowledge of the outside world, with a more sympathetic
comprehension of the minds of other peoples. History
shows that the people determine the general aims of
foreign policy at least as wisely as monarchs or oligarchs,
or the small groups to whom, in democratic countries,
the conduct of foreign relations has been left, and that
they have evinced more respect for moral principles.'

The problem of popular control only concerns us in
its relation to the study of foreign affairs ; but, if we
accept Lord Bryce's reading of history, any increase in
the number of people endowed with the knowledge and
concerned with the discussion of international problems
would be welcome. A Foreign Affairs Committee,
drawn from both Houses of Parliament, is overdue ;
and there is no reason to suppose that it would hamper
the Executive any more than it has impeded it in France.
The old demand that no treaty or commitment should
be regarded as binding till it has been communicated to
and approved by Parliament has now been met. In a
country with compulsory education and adult franchise
there should be no *arcana imperii*. When the life and
fortunes of every citizen are involved in the successful
conduct of our relations to other States, it is our right to
know what is being done in our name and to be informed of
the responsibilities which we are called upon to shoulder.

The Treaty of Locarno is a solid political fact because the obligations which it imposes on us are understood and accepted.   The Treaty of 1883, on the other hand, binding Roumania to the Central Powers, proved a scrap of paper in 1914 because its very existence was unknown to the people.   The Great War was caused by the bungling of a handful of highly placed individuals in different countries ; and as we gaze at the result of their follies, can any one desire that foreign affairs should be the preserve of a little group of supermen ?   The revelation by the Bolshevists of the secret treaties concluded between the members of the Entente during the world war came as an unpleasant shock, and the publication of *The Secret Treaties of Austria-Hungary* by Professor Pribram in 1920 revealed the old Europe tied up in a network of unknown or imperfectly known obligations. The details of diplomacy will always have to be worked out by experts ; but the wise statesman will desire the informed co-operation of Parliament and the sustained interest of an intelligent electorate.

How shall the citizen prepare himself for this special branch of his responsibilities ? In answering the question I have in mind not the average voter, who has neither opportunity nor inclination for serious study, but the man who is prepared to devote time to the task.   To understand the world of States in which we are living, we must begin by knowing something at any rate of the recent history of the Powers—of Great Britain since Chatham, of France since the Revolution, of Germany since Frederick the Great, of Russia since Peter the Great, of Austria since Maria Theresa, of Italy since Cavour, of the United States since the Civil War, of Japan since the voyage of Commodore Perry ; and in each case our first object should be to discover the governing tendency of their policy.   In our own case it has been the utilisation of our island position for commercial and territorial expansion overseas, and the maintenance of the Balance of Power as a means to that end.   France has striven for her ' natural frontiers,' as she calls them—the

Pyrenees, the Alps, and the Rhine. Ice-bound Russia has sought for access to warm water ports. Italy has struggled to bring all her children within her fold. The Hapsburgs have endeavoured to prevent Russia from dominating the Near East. Prussia and, later, Germany resolved to compensate for their lack of natural frontiers by rigorous discipline and formidable armaments. The policy of the United States is enshrined in the Monroe Doctrine with its twofold precept—no fresh European interference on the American Continent, and no American interference in the Old World. Japan seeks opportunities for her overflowing millions to colonise and exploit the territories of Eastern Asia. For such a general acquaintance with the main tendencies and events the budding student may turn to the *Cambridge Modern History* and to an up-to-date handbook such as Grant and Temperley, *Europe in the Nineteenth Century*.

His next task should be to follow the evolution of British statesmanship, beginning with the *Cambridge History of the British Empire* and the *Cambridge History of British Foreign Policy*, and advancing to the monographs in which, as a nation, we are unusually rich. Professor Basil Williams will introduce him to Chatham and Professor Holland Rose to Pitt. The work of Castlereagh in rebuilding Europe should be studied in Professor Webster's volumes and Professor Alison Phillips' lectures on the Holy Alliance. For Canning we turn to Professor Temperley, for Palmerston to Evelyn Ashley, for Russell to Spencer Walpole, for Aberdeen to Lady Frances Balfour. The later history of Whig and Liberal diplomacy is to be found in the lives of Clarendon and Granville, Gladstone, Rosebery and Dilke, and the autobiography of Lord Grey, while the Conservative record may be traced in Lord Malmesbury's *Memoirs*, the later volumes of Mr. Buckle's life of Disraeli, Lady Gwendoline Cecil's biography of her father, and Lord Newton's portrait of Lansdowne. If we add Lord Morley on Cobden, Professor Trevelyan on Bright, and *The Letters of Queen Victoria*, we shall have a fair acquaintance with British policy in the nineteenth century. Some suggestive comments and arguments are to be found in Sir James Headlam-Morley's *Studies in Diplomacy*, Mr. Algernon Cecil's *British Foreign Secretaries*, and Mr. A. L. Kennedy's *Old Diplomacy and New*.

Having surveyed British statesmanship at work in Downing Street, let us transport ourselves beyond the frontier to watch its formation and execution through the eyes of some of our representatives. An ambassador was defined by Sir Henry Wotton as a man sent to lie abroad for the good of his country ; and whether he lies or tells the truth, a diplomat of clear-cut views and resolute will has often been a maker of history. Lord Aberdeen, the most pacific of men, would hardly have drifted into the Crimean War without the vigorous initiative of Stratford Canning, whose biography recalls the opportunities for independent action before the telegraph transformed our Ministers into the mouthpiece of official instructions. But though there is now no longer need for a diplomat to take momentous decisions on his own responsibility, the advice of the man on the spot may be of decisive effect in the Cabinet deliberations at home. If Stratford Canning ranks as the most spectacular personality among our modern Ambassadors, Lord Lyons may be taken as the type of the wise counsellor, little known to the public, but prized at his true worth by his official chiefs. No ambassadorial biography of recent years surpasses in interest and importance Lord Newton's volumes on the man who represented Great Britain at Washington during the Civil War and at Paris before and after the collapse of the Second Empire. The work of his two most eminent successors in the task of bringing and keeping together the British and American nations may be studied in Professor Mowat's life of Lord Pauncefote and Mr. Herbert Fisher's life of Lord Bryce. In another field Mr. Harold Nicolson's biography of his father, Lord Carnock, should not be overlooked. Among autobiographies those of Sir George Buchanan and Sir Rennell Rodd stand high, while the

Letters of Sir Cecil Spring Rice and the Diaries of Lord d'Abernon are a sheer delight.

The technique of diplomacy has been authoritatively explained to the layman in Sir Ernest Satow's classical volumes, *Guide to Diplomatic Practice* ; Jules Cambon's *Le Diplomate* ; Sir George Young's *Diplomacy : Old and New* ; Baron Szilassy's *Traité Pratique de Diplomatie Moderne* ; and Sir Rennell Rodd's brochure in Benn's Sixpenny Library. In an admirable chapter on the duties and qualifications of an ambassador, the latter advises him to try to see things with the eyes of the people among whom he is living, so as to be able to make their point of view perfectly understood. ' He will be serving his own country best by endeavouring to obtain a fair hearing for them and due consideration for their legitimate interests. With this in view, he must be always accessible and in touch with men of every class and calling. . . . As it is his business to maintain harmonious relations and a good understanding with the Government or Court to which he is accredited, he must have the courage to tell his own people if the moment for carrying out an instruction or making a certain communication appears to him to be inopportune, or if the form in which he has been directed to make it is liable to be taken amiss.'

To master a diplomatic incident or unravel a tangled controversy we must penetrate behind histories, biographies and memoirs, and set sail on the ocean of official publications. No connected narrative of our foreign policy, however, can be built up from such sources ; for many cardinal occurrences and transformations leave scarcely a trace in the catalogue of Blue-books or in the annual volumes of *State Papers, British and Foreign,* inaugurated in 1812. For instance, if we confine ourselves to the twentieth century, we were at the time presented with the articles of the Japanese alliance, the treaty with France in 1904, and the treaty with Russia in 1907 without the correspondence and memoranda which preceded the conclusion of those epoch-making agreements ;

and the Algeciras Conference, the Bosnian crisis and the Agadir crisis were far too inflammable topics even for the most emasculated of official publications.   For all such matters the world had to wait till the great struggle had come and gone and the secrets of our policy could be revealed in the *British Documents on the Origins of the War, 1898–1914*, edited by Gooch and Temperley.   On the other hand, we were nearly smothered by the pile of Blue-books relating to our policy in Persia, Macedonia and the Congo.   Few lines of research are more fascinating than to follow the development of a complicated situation, the relations of Downing Street and its agents, the play of personality, the gradual formation and formulation of a policy.   For instance, to read Lord Curzon's Viceregal despatches on the Russian menace in Persia and the contumacy of the Dalai Lama of Tibet is to be introduced not to a spectral official, but to a very human individual, arguing hotly for a programme of his own.

The study of official documents must be supplemented by the Parliamentary debates.   The single day annually allotted to the Foreign Office vote in the House of Commons usually produces little beyond piecemeal criticism, and on other occasions it is the topic of the moment that is discussed.   It is disquieting to remember that during the critical decade before the outbreak of war our relations to the Powers and our obligations to one of the two groups into which Europe was divided were never brought under review nor surveyed as an organic whole.   The nearest approach to a discussion of fundamentals was on the occasions when some commanding topic focussed public opinion, such as the debate on the Anglo-French Treaty of 1904, or that of November 27, 1911, when Sir Edward Grey unfolded the moving story of the Agadir crisis.   Perhaps the most adequate discussion of a great issue in recent years was the two days' debate in the House of Lords at the opening of the session of 1908 on the Anglo-Russian Convention of 1907, in which the attack was brilliantly opened by Lord Curzon, and the Ministerial spokesmen were reinforced by the weighty approval of the veteran Lord Sanderson. Yet there has been nothing in our lifetime to compare with the Don Pacifico debate of 1850, when Palmerston defended his policy from the dusk of one summer day to the dawn of the next, when Gladstone made his first considered declaration on the principles of foreign policy, and when the voice of Peel was heard for the last time.

So far we have confined our attention to British sources ; but we shall never master the secrets of foreign affairs if we keep our watches set by the meridian of Greenwich. We may gather from our own observers and recorders what foreign statesmen have done ; but why they have done it we can best learn from themselves. The historian, with his cooler head and his wider knowledge, is able to understand men who could never understand one another ; and the student of foreign affairs, if he is not to waste his time, must keep several pairs of spectacles on his table. The conduct of a nation is often unintelligible to us because we lack the key, and the attribution of discreditable motives to our rivals and antagonists is as common between peoples as between individuals, and even more childish. We smile, for instance, when we read in Reventlow that we denounced the scandals in the Belgian Congo because we desired to add it to our possessions, or that the sympathy of ' the Vampire of the Continent' with the victims of Abdul Hamid veiled our greedy resolve to partition the Turkish Empire. In like manner the well-informed German smiles when he reads in certain French and English books that German intervention in Morocco in 1905 and 1911 was utterly unprovoked. The Austrian in turn marvels at our ignorance of the Russo-Serb intrigues against the integrity of the Hapsburg dominions, in which he finds the root cause of the war of 1914. Before the reconciliation of 1904 the Frenchman was amused or angered, according to his temperament, at the British claim to special rights in the valley of the Nile. Our first discovery when we seriously study foreign affairs is that they present problems of infinite complexity, in which there are often not merely the proverbial two sides, but three or four or five, each with a good deal to say for itself ; and we must understand them all. We may learn something of the difficult art of comprehension from such a work as Professor Fay's treatise, *The Origins of the World War*.

In the last decade an immense impetus has been given to the study of diplomacy and diplomatists by the decision of the Governments of all the Great Powers of Europe to publish selections from their archives on a generous scale. The Germans (who set the example) and the French begin in 1871, the British in 1898, the Austrians in 1908, the Italians with the unification of Italy, the Russians with the close of the Crimean War. Only the latter include the World War in their programme. The new material is almost overpowering in bulk ; but the mariner who sets sail on this mighty ocean is rewarded not only by precious discoveries in detail but by an ever clearer vision of the rivalries and apprehensions, the traditions and ambitions out of which the conflict arose. If it is true, as Bismarck declared, that diplomatic history cannot be written from official documents, it is equally true that it cannot be reconstructed without their aid. The statesmen who sign despatches and deliver speeches become creatures of flesh and blood, and we learn something of the share of the permanent Civil Servant such as Holstein and Eyre Crowe in the making of policy. We also discover that an Ambassador may still play a part of immense historic importance. During his fifteen years at Constantinople, for instance, Marschall von Bieberstein reduced the influence of Russia, Great Britain and France to a shadow, and convinced not only Abdul Hamid but the Young Turks that Germany was their friend. During his twenty-three years in London Paul Cambon was one of the main architects of the *Entente cordiale*. ' He won the friendship of the sovereigns,' writes his brother in affectionate admiration,[1] ' the confidence of the Government, the respect of the British

[1] Jules Cambon, *Le Diplomate*, 60.

nation. His loyalty dispersed all the misunderstandings which existed between our country and England.' Of scarcely less significance was the work of Barrère, who did more than any other man to disintegrate the Triple Alliance and to bring Italy into line with the Triple Entente.

If the Englishman has instinctively based his policy for centuries on the command of the narrow seas, the Frenchman has fixed his gaze on the open frontier in the east. It was the supreme merit of Sorel's masterpiece to relate the policy of the Revolution and Napoleon to that of the *Ancien Régime* by establishing the continuity of the principle of *les frontières naturelles*. While the professional student of history will plunge into the great *Recueil des Instructions données aux Ambassadeurs et Ministres de la France depuis les Traités de Westphalie jusqu'à la Révolution*, a series to which no other country can offer a parallel, most people will content themselves with the four volumes of Émile Bourgeois' *Manuel Historique de Politique Étrangère* and René Pinon's sumptuous quarto *Histoire Diplomatique, 1515–1928*, which forms the ninth volume of the *Histoire de la Nation Française* edited by Hanotaux. No corresponding work exists in Germany. Droysen's colossal presentation of Prussian policy only reaches Frederick the Great and is vitiated by his thesis of Prussia's prophetic mission. Treitschke and Sybel together cover the ground up till 1870, but are too general and detailed to be read in their entirety except by specialists. The best historical introduction to a study of Imperial Germany is provided in Emil Brandenburg's admirable volumes *Die Reichsgründung*, and its translated sequel *From Bismarck to the World War*. For recent Austrian policy Professor Pribram's authoritative little sketch, *Austrian Foreign Policy, 1908–1918*, and Professor Joseph Redlich's masterly study of Francis Joseph are ready to hand. Though Russia is justly proud of Martens' *Recueil des Traités et Conventions conclus par la Russie avec les Puissances Étrangères* (Austria, Germany, England, France), no history of Russian policy exists in any language ; and since there are no biographies of Nesselrode, Gortschakoff or Giers to take its place, we have to fall back on monographs such as Goriainoff's *Le Bosphore et les Dardanelles*. No authoritative survey of Italian policy since Cavour exists in the peninsula, but Professor Salvemini is at work on the history of the Triple Alliance. For the policy of the United States, which has touched the Old World at so many points, we turn for guidance to the ten co-operative volumes on the Secretaries of State edited by Professor Bemis, supplementing them by the official biographies of Roosevelt, John Hay and Henry White, the Letters of Walter Page, and the *Private Papers* of Colonel House.

After thus acquainting ourselves with the various standpoints as reflected in the summaries of national historians, we must listen to the testimony of the statesmen who have borne the burden and heat of the day. Political apologias are not history, but they contain material and clues to character which the historian cannot neglect. Ollivier will tell us his version of the outbreak of the Franco-German War, Freycinet of the first two decades of the Republic, Poincaré of the last years of peace and the first years of war, Clemenceau and Tardieu of the argumentative conflicts that went to the making of the Treaty of Versailles. William II and his first, fourth, fifth, sixth and eighth Chancellors have defended their stewardship of Imperial Germany. None of the Foreign Ministers of Austria since Beust has left memoirs ; but Berchthold may be expected to enter the witness-box before long. Witte, Izvolsky and Sazonoff have told the tragic tale of Russia in war and peace under the last of the Romanoffs. The *Memoirs* of Giolitti reveal with unblushing realism how the Tripoli War was engineered, and Salandra's vivid volumes enable us to trace every step of the path which led Italy through neutrality to intervention in 1915. Why Bulgaria joined the Central Powers is authoritatively expounded by the Prime Minister Radoslavoff, whose testimony can be read in a German translation entitled *Die Weltkrise*. Differing fundamentally in the policies which they describe and defend, these witnesses are alike in contemplating their labours with satisfaction, and in the conviction—which victory confirms and defeat is unable to shake—that in the larger issues at any rate they could have chosen no other path.   One and all they declare that they acted in accordance with the tradition and the wishes of their respective countries, and in the anarchical world before the League of Nations was born none of the actors had much right to frown on the morality of his fellows.

If we desire to enter the innermost shrine of diplomacy, to watch a master-builder fashioning an Empire and bending events to his will, we should study the achievements of Bismarck with care.   His *Reflections and Reminiscences*, dictated after his fall, are not only the most interesting of political autobiographies but also an imperishable treatise on the theory and practice of diplomacy.   Though the record is naturally an apologia, and, like other apologias, incomplete and often misleading, we learn from its pages the technique by which the Iron Chancellor solved the problem of the unification of Germany which had baffled his predecessors.   The greatest triumphs are never achieved without luck ; and Bismarck was favoured by a whole series of fortunate incidents and accidents—the discredit of German academic Liberalism since 1848–9, the stanchness of King William of Prussia, the skilled collaboration of Moltke and Roon, the attempt of the King of Denmark to trample on the autonomy of Schleswig and Holstein, the selection of Benedek to command at Sadowa, the eviction of Queen Isabella from Madrid and the search for a foreign ruler, and finally the crazy resolve of Louis Napoleon, after the Hohenzollern candidature had been withdrawn, to telegraph a humiliating demand to the King of Prussia without consulting his own Prime Minister.   These openings and opportunities were gifts of the gods ; but what other statesman of the nineteenth century except Cavour would have known how to use them to the full ?

Since Francis Joseph would never voluntarily abdicate his position in the Bund, war with Austria was inevitable ; and since Napoleon III would scarcely stand idly by while Prussia grew into the strongest Power on the Continent, a conflict with France was also highly probable. It was therefore essential that the two struggles should not synchronise, and equally necessary that no other Power should intervene while they were in progress. Great as was his confidence in himself and in the Prussian Army, Bismarck believed that one enemy was enough at a time. For this reason he determined to win and to retain the goodwill of Russia. Prussia was not to join in the Crimean War, and was to aid in the suppression of the Polish rebellion of 1863. Italy, again, who was as anxious to drive Austria out of Venetia as was Bismarck to expel her from the Bund, was a predestined ally. Thus, when the decisive moment arrived in 1866, Russia remained neutral, and Italian troops engaged the Austrian Army south of the Alps. And when the sword of Moltke had struck down the Austrian Army at Sadowa, Bismarck promptly terminated hostilities without annexing an acre of Hapsburg territory, partly to give Napoleon III no time to intervene in the struggle, and partly because he was already looking ahead to an alliance of Berlin with Vienna. It was the greatest single achievement of his life when, after three days of wrestling with the King and his Generals, he forced them by threats of resignation to sacrifice the march on the capital to his own long-range view of present perils and dawning possibilities.

The diplomatic preparation for the struggle with France was as consummate as that for the reckoning with Austria ; and when Napoleon III declared war, the conditional promises of support from Austria and Italy on which he had relied melted into thin air. For if Francis Joseph and Beust had endeavoured to reverse the verdict of 1866 they would have had Russia on their backs ; and few Italians except Victor Emmanuel himself desired to assist the ruler who had taken Savoy and Nice and buttressed the Temporal Power of the Pope. The manipulation of the Ems telegram was a smart conjuring trick ; but it was a smaller offence than Louis Napoleon's old plan to annex Belgium, which Bismarck sent to the *Times* at the outbreak of the war, and which destroyed any lingering sympathy for the Imperial gambler. Yet if the Chancellor's far-sighted moderation in 1866 was the greatest moment in his career, his failure to override the soldiers in 1871 is a blot on his statesmanship. Germany, like other victors, insisted on the extension of her territory, and the voice of the people united with the demand of the Generals for the return of the Rhine provinces. Alsace was German in blood and language, though not in sentiment, and nobody except a few Socialists opposed its annexation ; but Bismarck himself had qualms about Lorraine, remarking that he did not want so many Frenchmen in his house, and that Metz might be dismantled and a milliard added to the indemnity. His doubts were shared by the Grand Duke of Baden, the son-in-law of King William ; but Moltke refused to guarantee the security of the frontier while Lorraine remained a sally-port in French hands. Perhaps it would have been beyond the Chancellor's strength to carry his point ; but at any rate he yielded without a struggle. Alsace might have been assimilated, but Lorraine was as indigestible as Posen. From that disastrous error in judgment dates the division of Europe into two armed camps, the victors seeking allies to guarantee their new possessions, the vanquished craving associates to reverse the verdict of Sedan.

When he had unified Germany in three wars, Bismarck devoted the rest of his life to the maintenance of the *status quo* ; and since France was too weak to disturb it by her unaided efforts, his task was to keep her in quarantine. The *entente* with Russia continued, despite the jealousy of Gortschakoff and the restlessness

of Alexander II ; and when Bismarck was forced by
Russian menaces to take sides with Austria in 1879, he
repaired the damage by the Three Emperors League in
1881, which he renewed with both partners in 1884 and
with Russia alone in 1887.   The Eastern Question, he
declared, was not worth the bones of a Pomeranian
grenadier ; and he made no secret of his view that if
Russia wanted Constantinople, she could have it.   Equal
pains were taken to avoid crossing the path of Great
Britain.   ' In Bulgaria,' he used to say, ' I am Russian,
in Egypt I am English.'   If Great Britain's command
of the sea remained unchallenged and her instinct for
Colonial expansion was not thwarted, there was nothing
to interfere with the friendship of the two Powers.
Italy was driven into the arms of the Austro-German
alliance by France's seizure of Tunis ; the Hohenzollern
King of Roumania bound his country to the Central
Powers by a secret pact ; and Serbia under King Milan
entrusted her foreign policy to the control of the Ballplatz.   Thus Bismarck bestrode Europe like a colossus,
maintaining his conquests and keeping the peace till
his fall.   Next to Napoleon his is the most wonderful
career in modern times, and for the student of the art of
diplomacy it is of much greater importance ; for the
Emperor's statesmanship was ruined by his inability to
limit his vaulting aims.   English readers ignorant of the
German tongue are well supplied with materials for the
study of Bismarck ; for, in addition to the scholarly
biographies of Sir James Headlam-Morley and Sir
Charles Grant Robertson, we possess excellent narratives
of the founding of the German Empire by Sir Adolphus
Ward and Mr. William Harbutt Dawson.

If Bismarck's *Reflections* picture the greatest of
modern statesmen at work, Prince Bülow's scintillating
but ill-natured *Memoirs*, like his *Imperial Germany*,
reveal the mistakes and miscalculations into which a
powerful brain may fall without a suspicion of his own
folly and failure.   The fourth German Chancellor was
not responsible for the sleepless hostility of France,

though he did nothing to diminish it ; yet, forgetting Bismarck's principle of limited liability and shuddering horror of coalitions, he and his master simultaneously antagonised Great Britain by challenging our naval supremacy and Russia by a forward policy in Turkey. He claims credit for his attempts at the end of his tenure of office to reach a naval agreement with Great Britain, without realising, or at any rate without confessing, that the harm had been done and that the effort came too late. There is no ground for the belief that William II or any of his Chancellors planned or desired a world war ; but they pursued a policy which made it almost certain that if it came it would be fought under the most disadvantageous conditions. If diplomacy is the art of adjusting our aims to our resources, Bismarck is the greatest of its practitioners, and Bülow, for all his glitter, a short-sighted bungler.

I have indicated some of the paths which the student of foreign affairs would do well to pursue ; but I have left one of the most important to the last. Nothing is more difficult and nothing is more necessary than to discover the factors and currents of public opinion in the leading States ; for though a ruler or a minister may at times strike out a line of his own, it is public opinion which, as a rule, shapes their course in the larger issues of national policy. We have, in a word, to study the Press, to measure the weight of authority behind every journal of importance, to discover its sources of information, its degree of independence, its *clientèle*. The rise of the syndicated Press in England, the United States and Germany is a new and alarming factor in the life of democratic communities, particularly dangerous in the sphere of foreign affairs, where the reader is least on his guard. ' As long as his newspapers pay,' writes Professor Graham Wallas in *Our Social Heritage*, ' and the telephone from his house to the editorial offices is in working order, the owner of a group of papers has more absolute irresponsibility in the use of great power than any other living man.'

The *Times* has been the greatest paper in the world for almost a century.   Our student will be well advised not only to read it every day of his life but to familiarise himself with its history.   Sir Edward Cook's study of Delane will introduce him to the greatest of its editors, and the autobiographies of Sir Valentine Chirol and Mr. Wickham Steed display two of its experts at work. Its foreign correspondents indeed, from Blowitz to Bourchier, have often made history as well as recorded it.   That the *Times* always expresses the policy of the Foreign Office is as untrue as that it has never been employed for official purposes.   But the world beyond our shores has learned to regard it as the voice of England, and will doubtless continue to do so as long as it endures. Other journals have enjoyed their seasons of influence and authority in the field of foreign affairs owing to the personal relations of their editors to the holders of high office, such as the *Standard* under Salisbury and the *Westminster Gazette* during the Campbell-Bannerman and Asquith Ministries.   In his delightful autobiography *Life, Politics and Journalism* Mr. Spender explains that Lord Grey never asked him to take a particular line, and that his paper was in no sense a Government organ ; yet his close friendship and frequent intercourse with the Foreign Secretary enabled him to understand not only the line that was taken in every issue that arose, but the temperament, outlook and methods of the Minister himself.   The circulation of the *Westminster* was small and even at the height of its fame it failed to pay its way ; but for a crowded decade its leaders were eagerly scanned in the newspaper offices, embassies and chancelleries of the world as authoritative interpretations and anticipations of the mind of the Liberal Government.

In France the *Temps* has long been recognised as the mouthpiece of the Quai d'Orsay, and its editorials are deserving of study irrespective of the personality of their writers ; but from time to time, as for instance during the decade before the war when André Tardieu was in control, they are of exceptional interest. Next in importance were the daily pronouncements of Auguste Gauvain, Foreign Editor of the *Journal des Débats*, of which their author thought so well that he republished them in a shelf of volumes. Since the war all eyes have turned to the *Echo de Paris*, in which ' Pertinax ' proclaims the undiluted gospel of French nationalism. In Tsarist Russia the liberty of the press was narrowly limited, but there was more independence in the treatment of foreign than of domestic affairs. The momentous re-orientation of Russian policy in the later eighties which led to the Dual Alliance was initiated by Katkoff, the most famous of Russian journalists, whose Germanophobe and Francophil leaders in the *Moscow Gazette* were the daily food of Alexander III. When Katkoff passed away in 1887, the *Novoye Vremya*, founded by Suvorin in the seventies and controlled by his imperious hand for a generation, took its place as the leading exponent of Russian opinion.

Imperial Germany possessed in the *Norddeutsche Allgemeine Zeitung* a semi-official organ in which declarations of policy were constantly inserted ; but the Republic has dispensed with such an instrument of publicity. Germany has never boasted a predominant paper, and its federal structure has encouraged regional journalism. Bismarck once described the *Kölnische Zeitung* as worth an army corps on the Rhine ; but after his fall his confidences were reserved for the *Hamburger Nachrichten*, whose editorial office was in convenient proximity to Friedrichsruh. During the last years of peace the Berlin correspondents of the *Kölnische Zeitung* and the *Frankfurter Zeitung* were in the closest touch with the Wilhelmstrasse ; but no organ approached the *Berliner Tageblatt*, under the editorship of Theodor Wolff, for independence of comment on foreign affairs. Professor Schiemann's weekly survey of a kaleidoscopic world in the Conservative *Kreuz-Zeitung*, reprinted in an imposing array of volumes, derived interest from his knowledge of Russia and his intimacy with William II ;

and for thirty years the pen of Maximilian Harden, sharp as a stiletto, made his little weekly, *Die Zukunft*, a power in the land. Imperial Austria, like Imperial Germany, possessed a Foreign Office organ in the *Fremdenblatt*, but, unlike Germany, could also point to a journal of undisputed pre-eminence. It used to be said of Benedikt, the proprietor and editor of the *Neue Freie Presse*, half in joke, half in earnest, that 'next to him Francis Joseph was the most important man in the country.' In Italy the virile voice of the famous Milanese organ, the *Corriere de la Sera*, the only daily paper in the peninsula of European rank, has been silenced by the Fascist dictatorship. Among the journals of the minor European states none is better worth study than the *Journal de Genève*, in which M. William Martin surveys the world from China to Peru. As the Atlantic has become narrower and contacts multiply we may add to the list of papers on which to keep an eye the *New York Times*.

When issues of importance arise we shall be wise to follow the discussion in the Press of the protagonists so far as our knowledge of languages allows. But just because we must as a rule depend on the extracts and summaries provided by British correspondents on the spot, we should know something of the standing and colour of the papers from which the extracts are culled. For in attempting to estimate the strength and direction of public opinion in a foreign country, voices must be weighed rather than counted. The difficulty of differentiation may be illustrated by the varying significance attached to the Anglophobe utterances of the German provincial Press at the opening of the present century by the *Times* Correspondent in Berlin and the Wilhelmstrasse. Mr. Saunders argued that the less important papers were the most truly representative of popular opinion, because the least likely to be influenced by official prompting, while the latter complained that provincial prattle ought not to be mistaken for the voice of a great nation. It was equally difficult for onlookers to be sure how much significance attached to the Press of the Pan-Germans, whose numbers were small but whose tones were loud. The revelations of Busch had sown suspicions not easily obliterated, and only the initiates of the Press Department of the Wilhelmstrasse could tell to what extent the elaborate system of inspiration and manipulation invented by Bismarck had survived his departure. For the flying of a kite, for instance, the provincial Press offered the obvious advantage that it was easier to repudiate in case of need.

No aspect of the problem of the Press in relation to foreign affairs is more difficult than that of its financial independence. It is easy to talk of its venality in this or that country or capital ; but where such guilty secrets exist they are as a rule jealously guarded. A paper may feed from the hand of its own Government, or of an embassy of a foreign Power, or from armament firms at home and abroad. It may receive a regular subsidy or a special payment for temporary services. There are numberless ways in which honourable independence may be compromised and lost. But it is rarely that chapter and verse can be quoted, and circumstantial evidence is never satisfactory. All the more important is the unimpeachable evidence supplied in the correspondence of Izvolsky during his tenure of the Russian Embassy at Paris in the last four years of peace, first published in René Marchand's translation as *Un Livre Noir*. In these tell-tale pages we may read the Ambassador's demands during the Balkan wars for sums adequate to the needs of the occasion and to the standard set by the expenditure of other Embassies in the French capital.

To discuss the influence of the Press in moments of international tension would take us too far afield, for the subject is as controversial as it is extensive. In a few instances its driving force is for all to witness, such as the stampeding of President McKinley into an undesired and needless conflict with Spain when the *Maine* was blown up at Havana. It is only in recent years that the work of the Press in relation to the making and waging of war has begun to be seriously studied. In *The Triumph of Lord Palmerston* Mr. Kingsley Martin has vividly described the Press campaign which helped to launch Great Britain into the Crimean war ; in his *Five Weeks* Dr. Jonathan Scott has reconstructed the evolution of opinion as mirrored in the Press of the Great Powers from the Serajevo murders to the rush of the avalanche ; and in *England's Holy War* Miss Irene Cooper Willis has analysed the mentality of the Liberal Press throughout the long struggle. The power of the Press in foreign affairs is at its maximum when a conflict has broken out, not only because information is rationed and doctored, but because the critical instinct of the reader is dulled by the emotions of mass psychology.

I have sketched out an opulent programme for the serious student of foreign affairs ; but, if he is to complete the training which we suppose him to desire, he should supplement histories and biographies, Blue-books and newspapers by travel and by personal intercourse with men of other lands, official and unofficial. He should visit the capitals of the Powers, choosing September for his sojourn in Geneva. Despite the growing standardisation in civilised countries, subtle atmospheric differences remain which it is as difficult as it is essential to understand. Innumerable writers have tried their hands at the institutions and psychology of other countries ; but if many are called few are chosen. The survey of the United States before and after the Civil War by Tocqueville and Bryce, the massive studies of Russia after the emancipation of the serfs by Mackenzie Wallace and Anatole Leroy-Beaulieu, and Bodley's penetrating interpretation of France in the nineties, though of course they date like a play or a novel, still repay attention ; for many of the landmarks remain. In our own day Professor Madariaga's portrait of Spain, which combines the knowledge of the native with the detachment of foreign residence, takes high rank among national interpretations ; and Benedetto Croce has furnished a panorama of the life and mind of United Italy such as he alone could paint. It is also desirable for us to know how our own country looks through the spectacles of skilled foreign observers. In the last year or two we have received the high compliment of having our portrait painted by Professor Dibelius of Berlin, by Professor Kantorowicz of Kiel, by Émile Cammaerts, the distinguished Belgian poet who has made his home among us, and most recently by André Siegfried, the wittiest of French publicists ; and the briefer sketch provided in Professor Madariaga's *Spaniards, Frenchmen, Englishmen* should not be overlooked. The World War has dispelled the legend that England was enslaved by sport ; but other notions, true or false, persist and it is instructive to learn what they are. For the study of foreign affairs demands much more than a knowledge of governments and diplomacy. The opinions which nations form of one another, however unfair and incomplete, are counters in the great calculation as real and significant as the statistics of population, armaments and wealth.

In addition to our studies of the history, the diplomacy and the Press of individual countries, we must strive to master the forces and tendencies which transcend national boundaries. The historian of the future, knowing the later fortunes of experiments and conflicts now in progress, will be in a better position to assess their significance. But we can already recognise some of the broad features of the age in which we live—the growing interdependence of States, the ebbing of the doctrine of national sovereignty, the fusing of politics with economics, the arrival of organised labour, the emergence of women, the re-awakening of Asia, the challenge to ordered liberty from Fascism and Bolshevism, the weakening of tradition in the sphere of morals and belief. Above all we are witnessing the first attempt in the history of man to organise the world as a whole as we have succeeded in organising our several communities. Today the student of foreign affairs has no more imperious duty than to acquaint himself with the story of the creation, the principles, the structure and the functioning of the League of Nations and its satellites, the Permanent Court of International Justice and the International Labour Organisation. He will be wise to consult such works as Dr. Isaiah Bowman's *The New World*, Mr. Buell's *International Relations*, Mr. Woolf's *International Government*. Mr. Brailsford's *Olives of Endless Age*, and *Ten Years of World Co-operation*, with a Preface by Sir Eric Drummond. He can never know too much, and his life is an unending apprenticeship. Whether he is called to take part in governing his country or instructing his fellow-citizens, the disinterested expert, which our student in the fullness of time may aspire to become, should be recognised as one of the assets of a democracy that has come of age.

HISTORICAL NOVELS

THE purpose of this address is not to discuss how historical novels ought to be written, nor in what proportions the ingredients of truth and poetry should be mixed, but to review the main achievements in a fascinating field of literature, and to indicate how much knowledge and understanding may be acquired if we take the trouble to read the right books. The historical novel, as succinctly defined by Lord Ernle,[1] is the imaginative re-creation of the life of the past. No historian would admit that fiction, however conscientious and erudite, could provide a substitute for genuine historical study. If, however, we bear continually in mind that we are only in the outer courts of the temple of truth, that it is the privilege and indeed the duty of the author to give rein to his imagination, and that his object is rather to stimulate interest than to solve problems, there is no reason why we should not take advantage of the feast which historical novelists all over the world provide for us in rich profusion.

In a striking little book published in 1924 Mr. Butterfield offers a vigorous and convincing defence of the historical novel.[2] That there is a place for it, he argues,

---

[1] Lord Ernle, *The Light Reading of our Ancestors*, ch. 16.
[2] H. Butterfield, *The Historical Novel*. Cp. A. T. Sheppard, *The Art and Practice of Historical Fiction*, 1930; Jonathan Nield, *A Guide to the Best Historical Novels and Tales*, 5th edition, 1929; Sir Charles Firth, *Historical Novels*; and Professor Temperley, *Foreign Historical Novels*. The two latter are leaflets of the Historical Association. *Scenes from Modern History*, selected and annotated by Professor Temperley, contains extracts from Merejkowski, Jensen, Jokai, Tolstoi, and others.

is due to a certain inadequacy in history itself. The chart must be turned into a picture if we are to recover the life of the past. The imagination of the historian may perform this transmutation for himself as he broods over his materials. But scholars are relatively few, and scholars with creative imagination still fewer ; and what they see they cannot always transmit to their readers. Moreover, even the expert knows only what his sources can tell him. Our knowledge of the past remains eternally incomplete, for the dead carry most of their secrets with them to the grave. Thus the historian and the novelist work on parallel lines which never meet, the former telling us what happened and the latter helping us to see it happen. The mind of a great historical novelist is full of the past, as the mind of a musician is full of melodies, and he sets history to fiction as the composer sets words to music. The irrecoverable personal things are recalled, and the past lives again before our eyes. In a word, historical fiction is a supplement to history, not a rival, a twin-brother, to use the phrase of Scheffel, not a usurper.

Before the historical novel could be successfully launched the novel itself had to develop ; and the practitioners of the nineteenth century owe to the early masters the fashioning of the tools which they were to employ for purposes of their own. From the Elizabethan era onwards writers often staged their story in an earlier time, and introduced famous personages of a vanished world. But the retrospect was incidental, and no serious effort was made to recapture the colour and the atmosphere. Not until the Romantic Movement, suggestively defined by Professor Herford as the renascence of wonder, substituted a zealous if uncritical admiration of the Middle Ages for the supercilious indifference of the generation of Hume, Gibbon and Voltaire was the soil prepared in which the historical novel could grow. The technique of fiction had been perfected by Bunyan and Defoe, Richardson and Fielding in England, by the Abbé Prévost, Marivaux and Bernardin

de St. Pierre in France.   In the closing decades of the
eighteenth century the current in Western and Central
Europe set strongly towards poetry and romance ; and an
army of writers hastened to catch the flowing tide.

Lord Ernle assures us that the anonymous *Longsword,
Earl of Salisbury*, published in 1762, was the first historical novel ; but it aroused little interest and exerted
no influence.   It was indeed rather an attempt to warm
up the romances of chivalry than to clothe the bones of
the past with flesh and blood.   Two years later Horace
Walpole wrote the first historical novel which is still read.
The Castle of Otranto, a tale of Italy in the time of the
Crusades, was partly a burlesque of the extravagances
with which the public taste was beginning to be fed ;
but the ingredients of his art—supernatural portents and
spectres, dungeons and tortures—became the bread and
meat of the ' novel of terror,' and were partially adopted
by historical novelists hungering for emotional thrills.
The success of his *jeu d'esprit* indicated that the *saeculum
rationalisticum*, the reign of ' common sense,' was nearing
its end, and that imagination was coming into its own.

There were brave men before Agamemnon, and there
were plenty of historical novelists before Scott.   About
fifty historical novels made their appearance in England
while the Wizard of the North was growing to manhood.
But for practical purposes we may say that he was the
first as well as the greatest of the tribe, and that *Waverley*
burst upon the world like Minerva from the head of
Zeus.   The young Scottish laird was a born antiquarian,
and the past laid its spell on him while he was still in the
school-room.   At the age of thirteen he forgot his dinner
over Percy's *Reliques of Ancient English Poetry*.   Madame
de Staël said that she would not open her window
to look at the Bay of Naples, but would travel leagues to
hear a clever man talk.   Scott would have gone leagues
to see a ruined castle or explore an historic site.   He
loved the romantic story of his own country, and studied
it till its scenes lived again before his eyes.   In 1805,
the year of *The Lay of the Last Minstrel*, his first long

poem, he began his first novel.   But the poetic mood was strong upon him, and *Waverley* lay forgotten in a drawer till it was discovered by accident in 1814.   He once declared that he gave up poetry because Byron beat him.   He now revised his tale, added two-thirds and published it on July 7.   Its instantaneous success determined how he should spend the remainder of his life.

Though some of Scott's most celebrated books are staged in England and France, Germany and the East, it is broadly speaking true that his tread is surest north of the Tweed, or when he follows a Scottish hero or heroine across the Border or the sea.   With unerring instinct he laid down the lines which the best historical novelists have followed ever since.   In his hands history becomes the kernel of the book, while the love story and the adventures form the embroidery.   It is seldom that he makes real personages his protagonists ; yet no one has ever surpassed him in his power of bringing the illustrious dead to life.   To read of the revels at Kenilworth is to visualise Queen Elizabeth in all her masculine strength and feminine weakness.   In *The Abbot* we hold our breath as Mary Queen of Scots escapes from Lochleven.   What reader of *The Fortunes of Nigel* can ever banish the picture of James I, the wisest fool in Europe ?   *The Talisman* stamps King Richard and Saladin on our minds, and Louis XI peers grimly forth from the pages of *Quentin Durward*.   The Young Pretender lives in *Waverley*, and no picture of Queen Caroline brings her so close to us as her interview with Jeannie Deans.   It is idle to discuss once again which is the greatest of the masterpieces which poured forth with the rapidity of a mountain torrent ; for the question involves a combination of literary and historical judgments.   If *Ivanhoe* be admitted the favourite of the crowd, the expert takes offence at the exaggeration of the antagonism of Norman and Saxon.   The student of history and human nature may perhaps argue that *Old Mortality* was never surpassed, if indeed it was ever equalled.   Scott was no more impartial than other

mortals, and *Woodstock* is the measure of his inability
to understand English Puritanism. But *Old Mortality*
presents us with a Claverhouse, the Royalist chief, as
real and convincing as Morton, the iron leader of the
Covenanters.

The great magician has most fully explained and
defended his method in the Dedicatory Epistle to
Ivanhoe, which Professor Trevelyan hails as the first
attempt to envisage our distant ancestors as human
beings. ' The severer antiquary,' he writes, ' may think
that by intermingling fiction with truth, I am polluting
the well of history with modern inventions, and impress-
ing on the rising generation false ideas of the age I
describe. It is true that I neither can nor do pretend
to the observation of complete accuracy, even in matters
of outward costume, much less in the more important
points of language and manners. It is necessary for
exciting interest of any kind that the subject should be,
as it were, translated into the manners as well as the
language in which we live. And this is still more
applicable to sentiments. The sources from which the
passions must spring are generally the same in all ranks
and conditions, all countries and ages ; and it follows
that the opinions, habits of thinking and actions, however influenced by the peculiar state of society, must
still upon the whole bear a strong resemblance to each
other. Our ancestors were not more distinct from us,
surely, than Jews are from Christians. To take an
illustration from a sister art, the antiquarian details may
be said to represent the peculiar features of a landscape
under delineation of the pencil. His feudal tower must
arise in due majesty ; his figures must have the costume
and character of their age. His general colouring too
must be copied from nature. So far the painter is
bound down to the rules of his art ; but it is not required
that he should represent with absolute exactness the
very herbs, flowers and trees with which the spot is
decorated. These, as well as all the more minute points
of light and shadow, are subject to the artist's disposal as

his taste or pleasure may dictate.' Scott made his own rules, and his practice has been followed with varying success by the great army of disciples in every country in Europe for the last century. It is his proud achievement not only to have dowered the world with a crop of imperishable masterpieces but to have created a *genre* which at its best is capable of rendering equal service to history and to literature. In the considered opinion of Professor Trevelyan Scott did more for history than any professed historian of modern times.[1]

Scott took the world by storm, and nowhere was his welcome more enthusiastic than in France. The Romantic Movement had been inaugurated by Rousseau, Bernardin de St. Pierre and Chateaubriand ; but it only reached its full stride during the years which witnessed the appearance of the Waverley Novels. In his admirable volume on Scott's influence in France [2] Maigron describes the rapturous excitement in literary circles in Paris, the hasty translations, the crude dramatisations, the unending discussions in the *salons* and the Press. Classicism was dead and realism was unborn. The public thirsted for diversion, and every young writer of talent felt his pulse quicken to the call of romance. The literature of the Empire had been dry and colourless, subdued to ' good taste ' and the imitation of classical models. There were plenty of historical novels, but none of them possessed the breath of life. With the coming of Scott winter seemed to melt into spring, and the flood-gates of sentiment and imagination were unlocked.

When Scott visited Paris in 1826 Alfred de Vigny was presented to him and offered him *Cinq-Mars*, his first and last historical novel. The young conspirator lacks flesh and blood, and Richelieu as an impossible monster fails to impress ; but the atmosphere of the France of Louis XIII is skilfully reproduced, and many

---

[1] ' History and Fiction,' in *Clio, A Muse*.
[2] *Le Roman Historique à l'Époque Romantique. Essai sur l'influence de Walter Scott*. Cp. Saintsbury, *History of the French Novel*, Vol. II.

of the scenes and characters are instinct with life.
' L'histoire est un roman,' he declared, 'dont le peuple est
l'auteur.' A greater success was scored by Mérimée
with his *Charles IX*, the fruit of assiduous study of the
memoirs and characters of the Wars of Religion.
Superior to both in human interest and technical skill
must be reckoned *Les Chouans*, in which Balzac paints
the civil wars of the French Revolution against the
background of the dark forests and fanatical peasantry
of the West. But neither de Vigny, Mérimée nor
Balzac continued to work the rich vein they had opened
up, and the championship of the historical novel passed
into other hands.

Victor Hugo's star began to pale as romanticism
gave place to realism in the third quarter of the nineteenth century ; but his genius is too dazzling to be
obscured even by his colossal faults, and for the young
at least his place among the Immortals is secure. *Cinq-
Mars*, *Charles IX* and *Les Chouans* were at any rate for
a time cast into the shade by *Notre Dame*, published in
1831. It was an inspiration to make the cathedral the
pivot of the story, the soul and symbol of the great city,
around which surges the life of the France of Louis XI
and with which the fortunes of the actors are mysteri-
ously linked. If we are forced to admit that Paris is
more real than any of its citizens, and if the critical
reader is often aware of the slender historical equipment
of the author, we must pay our tribute to the opulent
colouring, the breathless emotions, the stir and throb
of multiform life. And when the great magician
returned in old age to the arena in which he had out-
paced his youthful contemporaries, *Quatre-Vingt-Treize*
was to reveal that his right hand had not lost its cunning,
and that he could evoke the spirit of the French Revolution in its mingling of savagery and idealism with no less
power than the fifteenth century.

The most popular of French historical novelists was
not Victor Hugo, who only made occasional incursions
into the territory, but Dumas. The French Scott

possessed none of the scholarly instincts and nothing of the moral elevation which radiates from the Waverley novels.   He described himself as a *vulgarisateur*, and no great artist ever carried out his mission with less conscious effort.   His strength lay not in the delineation of character or the subtle reproduction of atmosphere but in the inexhaustible invention of picturesque incident. He poured out romance as Mozart and Schubert poured out melody.   No historical novelist has such an array of wares in his shop-window, for he had Maquet and other ' devils ' to help him ; and it was inevitable that a man who laid all history under contribution from Nero to Marie Antoinette should often stumble and fall.   Yet only a pedant will deny him a place among the supreme masters of his craft.   Mr. Saintsbury, in his delightful *History of the French Novel*, has truly remarked that he was at his best from the second half of the sixteenth century to the end of the eighteenth.   His masterpieces are *Queen Margot* and *The Three Musketeers*.   While the all-round greatness of Scott can only be appreciated by a full-grown mind, the appeal of Dumas is above all to the young ; and human nature will have to change a good deal before the dashing d'Artagnan and his three gallant comrades cease to charm and to enthral.

It is sometimes said that Dumas ruined the historical novel in France by turning it into melodrama, and by seeking in the quarry of history nothing but the picturesque.   Whatever the cause, no French writer of the first rank during the second half of the nineteenth century devoted his full strength to this department of literature.   Théophile Gautier's *Capitaine Fracasse* attempts to revive the age of Louis XIII, but without much success.   George Sand painted a charming picture of eighteenth century Venice, of Vienna under Maria Theresa, and of Berlin under Frederick the Great, in *Consuelo* and its weaker sequel *La Comtesse de Rudolstadt*.   Flaubert endeavoured to resuscitate the glittering savagery of Carthaginian civilisation in *Salammbo*, the most celebrated attempt by a French writer at *le roman savant*, but crushed much of the life out of his book under a load of erudition. Erckmann and Chatrian collaborated in a series of Napleonic studies which for a generation enjoyed immense popularity. Anatole France, the master of delicate irony, recalled the early struggles of Christianity and paganism in *Thaïs*, and the hectic fever of the French Revolution in *Les Dieux ont Soif*. Zola's *La Débacle*, the greatest of war novels, contains almost as much history as fiction, and towers above the volumes in which the brothers Margueritte describe the same fierce struggles. But it is broadly true to say that when the immediate impress of Scott had passed away, the French novel reverted to its earlier traditions and sought its themes rather in the tangled problems of contemporary life than in the distant vistas of the past.

The influence of Scott was felt no less strongly in the Romantic Movement of Italy ; and when Manzoni announced himself as a disciple to the master while passing through Milan he received the flattering reply, ' In that case *I Promessi Sposi* is my best work.' *The Betrothed*, published in 1825, is the first and remains by far the greatest of Italian historical novels. Despite its length it is easy to read ; for it is suffused with the serene humanity of its kindly author, and its perfect fidelity to life wins our confidence from the outset. ' It satisfies us,' remarked Goethe on its appearance, ' like perfectly ripe fruit.' If some critics, Goethe among them, complain that the historical element is too prominent, and that we hear too much of the war, the famine and the plague which afflicted the Milanese under Spanish rule in the first half of the seventeenth century, others will argue that the balance between truth and poetry, between the historical setting and the personal drama, can be justified by precedents from Scott. The success of *The Betrothed* never tempted the modest author to try his hand again ; and though Grossi, D'Azeglio and Cesare Cantú carried on the tradition, their twentieth-century readers echo the exclamation of one of them, 'How far we are behind Manzoni!' Perhaps the best of the Epigoni was D'Azeglio, whose *Ettore Fieramosca* [1] describes the crowded stage on which Bayard, Caesar Borgia and Gonsalvo played their part, and in which the hero, a forerunner of the Risorgimento in an age of Franco-Spanish rivalry, is for 'Italy.'

Almost every country in Europe has played its part in working the rich vein opened up by Scott; but in some cases the leaven worked slowly. The creator of the modern Spanish novel, Perez Galdos, narrated the troubled fortunes of his country from Trafalgar to the expulsion of Queen Isabella in two score volumes, which may be seen in the window of every bookshop in the peninsula. [2] They have taught countless Spaniards, who are not a nation of readers, all that they know of the Napoleonic invasion, the odious Ferdinand, the fierce futilities of the Carlist wars, the Republic, and the Restoration of 1874. Galdos was a democrat and anti-clerical; but he was above all a patriot, and men of every school enjoy his lively survey of the sufferings and achievements of their sorely tried country.

A generation later a second attempt was made, though on a smaller scale, to describe the events of a century ago in a cycle of historical novels. The imposing work of Pio Baroja, *The Memoirs of a Man of Action*, began with *The Conspirator's Apprentice*, the Prologue of which explains the origin of the series. [3] Among the family papers in his Basque home he found the records of a great-uncle, Aviraneta, who had fought in the Peninsular War, supported every Liberal and Constitutional movement, and was said to have been with Byron at Missolonghi. The discovery led Baroja to the records of the time, which were to bear fruit in a dozen volumes partially intended to rectify what he regarded as the unjust treat-

---

[1] Translated as *The Challenge of Barletta*.

[2] It is regrettable that L. B. Walton, in his excellent book on Perez Galdos, devotes so little attention to his historical novels.

[3] There is a good account of Baroja in Trend, *Alfonso the Sage and other Spanish Essays*.

ment of his ancestor's career. The latter portion of
The Conspirator's Apprentice describes the hero's childhood
and education at Madrid, and draws a dark picture of
Spain on the eve of the French invasion. The subsequent
volumes portray Aviraneta in a band of *guerrilleros* during
the Peninsular War, his adventures during the reign of
Ferdinand VII, the episode of Missolonghi, and the
devilry of the Carlist wars. Baroja, like his ancestor, is
always on the side of the Liberals. But his blood is cool,
and he makes no attempt to surround his hero with the
glamour of romance.

The first critical Portuguese historian, Herculano da
Carvalho, was a poet and a novelist as well as a scholar,
and his name deserves mention among the practitioners,
though not among the masters, of historical fiction. His
story of the Arab invasion, *Eurich the Priest*, written in
1843, was translated into German by Heine, and may
also be read in a French translation published long afterwards. *Eurich* describes the collapse of the degenerate
Visigoths before the Moorish attack, and the retreat
of the unconquered Pelagius to the mountains of the
north. These dramatic events are linked with the life
of the hero who, having become a priest in the despair
of frustrated love, re-emerges as ' the Black Knight ' to
perform prodigies of valour, and rescues his beloved
from dishonour in the tent of the conqueror. When,
however, all outward obstacles to their union are removed,
the vow of celibacy remains ; and the story ends with
the voluntary death of Eurich and the madness of the
broken-hearted Hermengard. Herculano was a man
of independent mind ; and the attack on sacerdotal
celibacy reflects the same distaste for clericalism as
his *History of the Establishment of the Inquisition in
Portugal*.

The separation of Belgium from Holland in 1830,
and the attainment of an independence which her people
had never known, gave an impetus to research and prepared the soil for the historical novel. The opportunity
was seized by Hendrik Conscience, a Fleming who

wrote in his own tongue, but who nevertheless gave both of the racial sections of his countrymen the patriotic nourishment that they craved. *The Lion of Flanders*, published in 1838, extols the miracle of deliverance wrought at the battle of Courtrai in 1302, when Philip the Fair was flung back and his proud knights left their golden spurs on the field. The writer keeps close to the chronicles; but his ship carries sails as well as cargo, and the contrast between the haughty chivalry of France and the opulent solidity of the burghers of Bruges is finely drawn. Though he found promising material in other periods, above all that of the Arteveldts, Conscience never recaptured the inspiration of his early flight.

The Romantic Movement had run its course all over Europe before Scandinavian literature rose to its full stature in the closing decades of the nineteenth century, and there was no suppressed nationality sentiment craving expression in the imaginative reconstruction of the past.[1] Strindberg might have created a masterpiece had he not chosen the drama instead of the novel to bring the heroes of the Vasa dynasty back to life. The outstanding contribution of Sweden comes from Verner von Heidenstam, whose glowing patriotism and wide knowledge found utterance in the cycle of stories illustrating the meteoric career of Charles XII, entitled *The Charles Men*.[2] It is an epic of the fall of the Swedish empire, of which the real hero is rather the Swedish people than the warrior king. For though his bravery and steadfastness are fully recognised, there is no glorification of war, and the last scene at Fredrickshall comes as a relief to an intolerable strain. There is a certain monotony in the record of so many battles and struggles, and many readers will prefer his narrative of Sweden from the stone age onwards in a series of *tableaux* designed for the use of schools, entitled, *The Swedes and their Chieftains*,[3] in which the figures of Gustavus Vasa and

---

[1] Kotas, *Skandinavische Literatur seit 1870*, is a useful survey.
[2] Translated in the American series of Scandinavian Classics.
[3] Translated in the same series.

Gustavus Adolphus, Charles XII and Gustavus III stand out in bold relief.

Norway is represented by *Christin Lavrandstatter*, a vast panorama of the fourteenth century which won Sigrid Undset the Nobel prize and instantaneous renown. The unflinching delineation of elemental passions reminds us that we are in the tumultuous surge of the Middle Ages ; but the emphasis throughout is on character rather than incident, and the heroine herself is essentially timeless, the eternal woman.

Denmark adds two names to our list without claiming one of the higher prizes. Jacobsen's *Marie Grubbe*,[1] a picture of the second half of the seventeenth century, rests on patient research in the Copenhagen archives. All the leading personages are historical, including the heroine, who married an illegitimate son of King Frederick III. But Marie and her three husbands are not figures of compelling interest, and the value of the book lies rather in its careful workmanship than in the delineation of the actors. His masterpiece *Niels Lyhne* was to show that Jacobsen was more successful in the invention of character than in raising the dead from the grave. In our own generation Johannes Jensen has written a suggestive trilogy of the human adventure entitled *The Long Journey*.[2] The first volume, *Fire and Ice*, depicts early man struggling heroically with the elements for his life. The second, *The Cimbrian*, opens with the stone age, and closes with the mowing down of the northern hordes by the sword of Marius. The third, *Columbus*, accompanies the explorer across the Atlantic, and completes the ' long journey ' which began in the inhospitable regions of the north. For the great captain is introduced as a Lombard, a descendant of the Northmen, with the migratory instinct strong in his blood. The connecting links of the series are as slender as with Merejkowsky ; but the ascent of man in his conflict with nature to mastery

---

[1] Translated in the Scandinavian Classics.

[2] Jensen receives high praise in Professor Temperley's brochure, *Foreign Historical Novels*.

over himself gives the trilogy at any rate a philosophical unity. Columbus, on the prow of his ship, surrounded by a timorous and mutinous mob, is magnificently drawn ; and with the discovery of the new world we may imagine Jensen whispering to himself that there are no bounds to the march of the human spirit.

The Romantic Movement and the *Ritterromane* which floated like froth on its surface had prepared the soil of Germany when the name and fame of Scott were borne across the North Sea.[1] The appetite for the Waverley Novels was insatiable, and many a young author was fired with the ambition to light his torch at the glowing flame. The most successful attempt to mix the colours of history and romance was made by Hauff, a precocious young Swabian, whose *Lichtenstein*, which he described as a romantic saga from Württemberg history, may claim to be the first real German historical novel. No author of any nationality reproduced the master's touch in his lifetime with greater fidelity ; and an American Professor solemnly assures us that he has found no less than 748 analogies with the Waverley novels.[2] Hauff follows the favourite plan of inventing his hero and launching him into the stream of historical events. Georg Sturmfeder, a young soldier of fortune, joins the army of the Swabian League, which desires to prevent Ulrich of Württemberg from regaining his throne. He quickly changes sides, for the father of his sweetheart, Marie von Lichtenstein, is a leading supporter of the Duke. The varying fortunes of the antagonists in the early days of the Reformation form the background for the adventures and the love story of the hero. Hauff's portrait of the Duke is a little softer than the original, but he was convinced that he had been maligned. Had he not died at twenty-five, Hauff might have realised

---

[1] The best introduction to the study of the historical novel in Germany is Mielke-Homann, *Der deutsche Roman*. Cp. Du Moulin Eckart, *Der historische Roman in Deutschland*, and Pineau, *L'Evolution du roman en Allemagne au dix-neuvième siècle*.

[2] Garrett W. Thompson, *Hauff's Specific Relation to Scott*, in Publications of the Modern Language Association of America, 1911, pp. 549–591.

his dream of earning the proud title of the German Scott.

The vacancy was partially filled by Häring, who wrote under the name of Willibald Alexis.[1] Volunteering at seventeen for the Waterloo campaign, he reached the front too late to join in the fray, but the gesture was an emblem of the ardent patriotism which inspired his life. His first novel *Walladmor* is at once a curiosity of literature and a tribute to the spell of Scott. Written as a parody of what he regarded as the master's failings, the story, which was described as a translation, was universally believed to be a new work by the author of *Waverley*. Sailing under a false flag it won instantaneous success in Germany, and was translated into English and several other languages. Scott described it as the boldest hoax of the age, a description welcomed by the author as the highest praise. The success of his *jeu d'esprit*, however, was of little assistance to the author's literary career, and in later years he complained that his only victory had been won under the patronage of a greater name.

The triumph of *Walladmor* decided its author's destiny, and he found the material for his art in the Mark of Brandenburg. Etienne, the hero of *Cabanis*, published in 1832, is brought up in Berlin ; but when war breaks out in 1740 his sympathies are with Maria Theresa, and he enters an Austrian military academy. Moreover, the eccentric and mysterious Marquis de Cabanis, who turns out to be his father, detests Frederick the Great. When, however, at the height of the Seven Years' War Etienne learns that the life of the King is threatened by treachery, his Prussian sentiment revives. He deserts, and receives the Order *Pour le Mérite* from the King whom he saves. We only catch fleeting glimpses of Frederick, but his spirit broods over the whole scene.

The second excursion into Prussian history, *Der Roland von Berlin*, was a far better book, and despite its

[1] The best account is by Otto Tschirch, ' Willibald Alexis als vaterländischer Dichter und Patriot,' in *Forschungen zur Brandenburgischen und Preussischen Geschichte*, Vol. XII (1899).

prolixity the interest never flags.[1]   The stone figure of
Roland outside the Town Hall of cities which possessed
the exclusive rights of judicature was the symbol of
dignity and independence ; but the conflict of Berlin
with the second Hohenzollern is presented with a decided
leaning to the wise and virtuous Margrave. For
Frederick II strives to regain some of the power which
had been lost to the towns during his father's struggle
with the nobility. ' You are lord of the land, but not
of our town,' argues Rathenow, the old Burgomaster,
after the victory of the Margrave ; ' we were defending
our ancient privileges.' ' My right is to see that justice
is done to all,' rejoins the ruler. The Roland is broken
to pieces in token of the loss of justiciary rights, and the
Burgomaster, broken but unbent, goes into voluntary
exile. The picture of the turbulent life of a fifteenth
century city, proud of its privileges but weakened by
class distinctions and the fickleness of the crowd, is the
high-water mark of the author's talent. His later works
describe the coming of the Reformation in Brandenburg
and the Napoleonic era in Prussia.

The passion of Willibald Alexis for the core of the
Prussian State was shared by Fontane, whose *Wander-
ungen durch die Mark Brandenburg* is a popular classic.
Vor dem Sturm, a story of 1812–13, claims a place in the
short list of first-class German historical novels. Fontane,
whose strength is in character and atmosphere rather than
incident, makes no attempt to hurry over his tale, and the
length of the book is a burden to impatient readers. We
find ourselves in the Oderland, where the memories of
Frederick the Great and his desperate struggles are still
fresh, and where men are bracing themselves for the
reckoning with Napoleon. The invasion of Russia has
failed, and hope has dawned in northern Germany that the
galling fetters may at length be broken. But the French
garrisons are still strong, and the narrative closes with
a premature attack by the little group whose lives and
thoughts we have shared. Fontane was wise in leaving

[1] Translated as *The Burgomaster of Berlin* in 1843.

the drums and trumpets of the War of Liberation to others, and in confining himself to a study of the people who were to rise against the aggressor. The picture of another portion of Germany at the same critical moment was painted by Fritz Reuter in his *platt-deutsch* story *In the Year 13*, which, though it enjoyed a good deal of popularity on its appearance in 1860, does not compare in power or interest with the work of Fontane. For the author's Mecklenburg village is a very limited stage, and we miss the deeper notes of anger and exaltation that made the War of Liberation a possibility and a success.

While Willibald Alexis and Fontane wrote on Prussia for the Prussians, a greater man recalled the long story of the German people in symbolic form to the citizens of the new-born Empire. In his Autobiography Gustav Freytag [1] relates how the campaign of 1870, in which he accompanied the Crown Prince Frederick to the front, gave rise to visions which were one day to be embodied in the cycle collectively described as *The Ancestors*. The whole history of the race seemed to unroll itself before his eyes like a map. ' I was always deeply interested in the connection of man with his ancestors,' he wrote, ' in their mysterious influence on body and soul. What science cannot fathom the poet may attempt.' He formed a plan by which a single family should take part in the decisive events of German history. The first volume dealt with the Roman invasion, the second with the Slavonic inroads and the coming of Boniface. The third and fourth depicted the rise and fall of chivalry. The fifth brings us to the Reformation, mirrored in the career of a merchant of Thorn living under Polish rule but German in feeling. The sixth portrays the Thirty Years' War, the seventh the reign of Frederick William I, the last the Wars of Liberation. Freytag described his work as a symphony in eight parts. Though the pearls are strung on an almost invisible thread, the series possesses a certain unity in its atmosphere of national sentiment. Read with avidity during

[1] See Gooch, *History and Historians in the Nineteenth Century*, 577–80.

the years succeeding the wars of unification, *The Ancestors* helped to make the citizens of every part of the new Empire conscious of their kinship. The series took its place as an imaginative rendering of the author's earlier volumes *Pictures from Germany's Past*, as Schiller's *Wallenstein* dramas grew out of his *History of the Thirty Years' War*. Freytag's novels did more to interest German men and women all over the world in their own history than the writings of any other man of his generation. But despite their scholarly character and their author's apprenticeship in pure fiction, none of them belong to the first or even the second rank ; for his characters are too symbolic to have much vitality of their own.

Two other writers of the middle of the century found their inspiration in widely different periods of German history. Fresh from the resounding triumph of *Der Trompeter von Säckingen* Scheffel cast his net once more into the storied waters of the upper Rhine. The novel, like the poem, went straight to the heart of the German people, and *Ekkehard* may claim to have been the most popular work of German historical fiction in the nineteenth century. The tale of the monastic chronicler of St. Gall was suggested by studies of South German law in the tenth century undertaken in hopes of an academic appointment. Scheffel assures his readers that there is little in his tale that is unsupported by the *Monumenta Germaniae*. The book breathes a gentle charm. The beautiful landscape of Lake Constance is lovingly reproduced, and the raid of the Huns is told with a good deal of spirit. The figures of Ekkehard, the handsome young monk, and the imperious Duchess of Swabia are cleverly sketched. But the work lacks muscle, and a certain conventionality of treatment renders it impossible for modern readers to recapture the enthusiasm of 1855. Very different in character is *The Amber Witch*, in which Meinhold, a Pomeranian pastor, mercilessly exposes the superstition and savagery of north Germany during the Thirty Years' War. The grim strength of this unadorned tale grips the reader, and Professor York Powell used to maintain that there had been nothing like it since Marlowe and the Elizabethans.[1] But the subject is repulsive, and neither it nor its still more repellent successor *Sidonia* has ever been a popular favourite at home or abroad.

While Freytag was employing the historical novel to stimulate patriotism, two German Professors were engaged in creating a type which the French describe as *Le Roman Savant*, the direct purpose of which is to arouse interest and to impart information. Felix Dahn devoted his long and laborious life to the *Völkerwanderung*, the period of the migration of the peoples which separated the fall of the Roman Empire from Charlemagne. His massive historical works are known only to scholars, but the novels in which he has presented the same materials in popular form have carried his name all over the German-speaking world. He relates in his voluminous Autobiography [2] how the conflict of the Ostrogoths with Belisarius fired his imagination, how as a young man of twenty-five he wrote the first part of his most celebrated work, how he put it aside for many years in doubt as to its value, how he resumed his task in middle life, how he soaked himself in the atmosphere of Ravenna, ' the city of the great dead,' and how *The Struggle for Rome* finally appeared in 1876. The book took Germany by storm. Readers of Hodgkin's *Italy and her Invaders* do not need to be reminded of the fascinating story of the Gothic Kingdom at Ravenna, the internal collapse after the death of Theodoric, the landing of Belisarius and his gallant defence of Rome, the triumph of Justinian's arms in the capture of Ravenna, the final flicker of Gothic fortunes with the radiant figure of Totila, the disgrace of Belisarius, and the defeat and death of Teias, the last of the Goths, at the hand of Narses, the eunuch. Closely following the inexhaustible Procopius, on whom he had published an admirable monograph some years before,

[1] Elton, *Frederick York Powell*, II. 302–9.
[2] *Erinnerungen*, Vol. III. and IV.

Dahn leads us from Ravenna to Naples, from Naples to Rome, from the Tiber to the Bosphorus. Scherer complained that Cethegus, the fictitious protagonist, was an impossible monster, others that the Empress Theodora is painted too black ; but, whatever reserves may be made on minor points, no student of the period can fail to admire the author's grasp of its problems, and no lover of literature can be blind to the power of the work. The popularity of *The Struggle for Rome* led Dahn to write a long series of successors of which *Attila* and *Felicitas* are among the best ; but he never found another subject worthy of his powers. It is his distinction to have been the only considerable historian who has produced historical fiction of the first class. A somewhat similar field was cultivated by the distinguished authority on the early Christian Church, Adolf Hausrath, who, writing as George Taylor, sketched the reign of Hadrian in *Antinous*, the best of his stories.

While Dahn interpreted the centuries of the *Völkerwanderung* to his countrymen, Ebers selected Ancient Egypt for his province, and cultivated the territory with no less distinction. He began his studies when Lepsius was giving to the world the twelve gigantic volumes on the results of his first historic journey to the valley of the Nile, and it was to Lepsius that he took the manuscript of his first novel with a timid request for his verdict.[1] The great Egyptologist opened the pages with reluctance, fearing that his beloved science was about to be vulgarised ; but he was gripped from the start, and returned the book with warm words of congratulation. *The Egyptian Princess*, like *The Struggle for Rome*, was an instantaneous success, and its pictures of the Court of Cambyses and the Persian monarch's invasion of Egypt are as fresh today as when they were painted. It is a curious fact that though the author was to make repeated visits to the land of his dreams, and though he produced a long series of novels embodying his learning in popular form, he never repeated the triumph of the

[1] See Ebers, *Geschichte meines Lebens.*

young enthusiast who knew the gorgeous East from books alone.

When the generation which had welcomed Freytag was passing away and the glamour of Dahn and Ebers had begun to pale, the historical novel lost its vogue in Germany for a couple of decades. Ricarda Huch's pictures of the *Risorgimento*, translated as *Garibaldi and the New Italy*, the first describing the defence of Rome, the second the conquest of Sicily, keep almost too close to history, and read more like a record than a reconstruction. The World War, the defeat and the revolution turned the thoughts of young and old to the trials, the glories and the lessons of the past, and in recent years no country can boast of a larger output. The revival was inaugurated by Walter von Molo, whose full-length portrait of Schiller appeared between 1912 and 1916. Though begun before the catastrophe the atmosphere in which it was conceived was already electric, and the vivid picture of the poet-patriot was warmly welcomed in the last years of peace and the first years of war ; but the volumes enjoyed their greatest popularity as a work of edification in the dark era which followed the collapse. Scarcely less successful was the trilogy which carries us from Frederick the Great to the War of Liberation. *Fredericus*, begun before the war and published in 1918, exhibits the King in the concluding crisis of the Seven Years' War, when dreams of victory had vanished and his utmost hope was to save Prussia from annihilation. The picture of Frederick amid the tense horrors of the battle-field is finely drawn, and the curtain falls on the sensational announcement that with the death of the Tsarina Elizabeth Russia is ready for peace. The second volume, *Luise*, describes the struggle at the Court of the helpless Frederick William III, on the eve of the Jena campaign, between the Haugwitz party of peace and the party of action led by Prince Louis Ferdinand, Stein and the radiant Queen. The third volume, *Das Volk wacht auf*, sketches the beginnings of the War of Liberation, and displays Scharnhorst, Blücher and Gneisenau at work.

A later effort, *Brother Luther*, the narrative of a single day, revives the Diet of Worms, vividly portraying Charles V, the Elector of Saxony and other German princes, and the arrogant Aleander. Though Luther is the hero of the book, his figure is perhaps the least convincing of the actors on the crowded stage.[1]

The most sensational triumph of German historical fiction since the war has been scored by Feuchtwanger, whose *Jew Süss*, a study of princely misrule in eighteenth-century Württemberg, owes as much of its world-wide acclaim to its unflinching realism as to its narrative power. His second venture, *The Ugly Duchess*, an episode of the fourteenth century, added little to his fame. A third best-seller is *The Deuce*,[2] by Alfred Neumann, who dared to enter into competition with Scott and Hugo by resuscitating Louis XI and his merry men as they live in history and legend. A smaller but more discriminating public was charmed by Bruno Frank's *Days of the King*, a series of three vignettes of Frederick the Great of exquisite literary workmanship.

The writings of Conrad Ferdinand Meyer, the Swiss novelist and poet, have won the admiration of connoisseurs rather than the plaudits of the crowd ; but his masterpiece, *Jürg Jenatsch*, published in 1874, is among the half dozen classics of historical fiction in the German language. He describes it as 'neither history nor biography nor even a psychological novel, but a sort of fresco.' He chooses an episode of the Thirty Years' War, the liberation of Graubünden from the Spanish yoke, and keeps unusually close to his authorities, though the hero is painted in slightly less repulsive colours than in the pages of history. It is a tragedy born of the conflict between ambition and patriotism, in which his countrymen are finally compelled to free themselves from their liberator. In striking contrast to Jenatsch, a Nietzschean superman ' beyond good and evil,' stands

[1] Molo describes his methods in his volume of essays and addresses, *Zwischen Tag und Traum*.
[2] *Der Teufel*.

the stainless figure of Rohan, the Christian Knight who trusted and was betrayed.

There is no better illustration of the mixture of history, patriotism and romance than the Hungarian Scott. During the dark years that lay between the capitulation of Vilagos and the *Ausgleich* of 1867 Jokai kept the flame alight by the historical novels which he poured forth with a rapidity only excelled by Dumas. He had taught himself English in order to read *Ivanhoe*, and he evaded the perils of the Austrian censorship by choosing for his earliest flights the period of Turkish rule. In writing of the Turkish rule he had Austria in mind, and his readers knew it. His message to his fellow-countrymen was that they had outlived worse tyrannies than the yoke of Schwarzenberg and Bach. Elected to the Diet in 1861 and a member of the Hungarian Parliament for thirty years after the Compromise of 1867, Jokai gloried in the resurrection of the country he had striven so manfully to serve. In the annals of resurgent nationalism Jokai and Sienkiewicz stand supreme among novelists.

Jokai, like Scott, is at his best in his own country, where knowledge of the land and the people held his exuberant imagination under partial control. *The Strange Story of Rab Raby* is an excellent specimen of his art. The hero, a high-minded and well-educated young man, is appalled by the incompetence and corruption of the administration, and attempts to reform it. Finding the task beyond his unaided strength he seeks the help of Joseph II, whose moral standards are as lofty as his own. But the patronage of the Emperor proves a hindrance not a help, and the whole countryside rallies to the defence of Magyar officials and Magyar abuses. The authority of Joseph is openly flouted in Budapest, and the hero, tormented and vilified by the people he is labouring to serve, has to fight for his life. The story ends with the withdrawal of the reforming Emperor's centralising edicts just in time to save Raby from death. We meet Joseph II at fleeting intervals in the Hofburg and in his

Hungarian capital, but he scarcely emerges as a man of flesh and blood. Jokai had no talent for the delineation of character ; but his sketches of Hungarian history help us to understand the meaning and the strength of Magyar nationalism.

Jokai, though not a man of learning, cast his net wide, and some of his most popular stories carry us to distant centuries and climes. *A Christian but a Roman* handles the familiar theme of the persecutions, and the story ends with the death of the dissolute Carinus at the hands of the hero in revenge for the enforced suicide of his beloved. A far better novel is *Halil the Pedlar*, a stirring tale of rebellion in Constantinople in 1730, when the Janissaries, led by the hero, an Albanian sailor, dethrone the nerveless Sultan. Halil rules Constantinople for six weeks, as the more famous Masaniello had ruled Naples, till he is murdered by the order of the new Sultan whom he had enthroned. A third story familiar to lovers of historical fiction is *The Lion of Jannina*, a vivid tale of Ali Pasha, the old Albanian chief whose ferocity is still a living tradition in the Near East. Jokai's books are never too long, and the interest which is aroused on the first page is held to the end by exciting incidents following one another in breathless succession. The pace, however, is too hot and the colours are too crude to allow him a place among the immortals. The multiplication of thrills becomes monotonous, like an exhibition of fireworks which lasts too long ; and he is most enjoyable when swallowed in small doses.

Among the outstanding features of the intellectual history of the last half century has been the discovery by Central and Western Europe of the literary and artistic treasures of the Slavonic world. Pushkin, the father of Russian literature, tried his hand at the historical novel in *The Captain's Daughter*, a tale of the rebellion of Pugatcheff, and Gogol recalled the savage Cossack wars of the seventeenth century in *Taras Bulba* ; but their best work lay in other fields. Tolstoi's *War and Peace*, on the other hand, ranks among the great novels of the world, and it has often been maintained that no other writer has so fully succeeded in conveying the confused delirium of battle as in his picture of Borodino. Yet, though the background of the story is the national saga of the invasion of 1812, with Alexander and Kutusoff, Napoleon and Murat marching across the stage, his main interest lay in the children of his fancy ; and his masterpiece, as Percy Lubbock has argued at length, belongs more to literature than to history.[1] Merejkowsky, on the other hand, has produced a series of studies in which fiction is rather the sauce than the joint. *The Emperor Julian* portrays the last struggle of the Pagan Empire against the flowing tide of Christianity. *The Forerunner* resuscitates the fascinating superman Leonardo, to whom art was only one of the competing interests of the intellectual life. *Peter and Alexis*, the most impressive of the series, recalls the foundation of Petrograd, and paints a convincing picture of the greatest figure in Russian history. A fourth volume, inferior in power and interest, *The Decembrists*, depicts the abortive attempt of a few unpractical talkers to seize power during the days of confusion which followed the death of Alexander I.

During the dark years of partition and persecution the vestal fire of Polish patriotism was tended by pious hands. Kraszewski, the father of the Polish novel, grew to manhood while Scott was still alive.[2] Banished on the eve of the insurrection of 1863 for his political and journalistic activities, he settled in Dresden where he discovered in the archives rich material for the history of his country during the period when two Electors of Saxony were also Kings of Poland. Augustus the Strong lives again in *The Countess Cosel*, a realistic picture of the Dresden Court and of the rise and fall of one of the innumerable favourites of the most dissolute ruler in Europe. Scarcely less vivid is the description

[1] *The Craft of Fiction*, ch. 3. He argues that the book suffers from a confusion of two designs which are never completely blended.
[2] See Krzyzanowski, *Polish Romantic Literature*, 242–56.

of the Court of his successor Augustus III in *Count Bruhl*, the smiling and cunning page who grew to be the real ruler of the land and one of the makers of modern Dresden. At sixty-four Kraszewski began to recount ten centuries of Polish history, and in a single decade scores of volumes saw the light. The pace was too fast and the series was a failure ; but at his best he is a very competent story-teller and his patriotism always burns with a steady flame.

Kraszewski's passionate devotion to his country was shared to the full by his younger contemporary Sienkie-wicz, who took more time over his books and produced work of more enduring worth.[1] The insurrection of 1863 broke out when he was seventeen, and the immense disappointment at its failure inspired him, as it had inspired Kraszewski, to seek consolation in the past. The greatest of Polish novelists chose his main themes from the history of his race, illustrating the fierce medieval struggles of Teuton and Slav in his *Knights of the Cross*, and depicting the terrible conflicts of the seventeenth century in his trilogy *With Fire and Sword*, *The Deluge* and *Pan Michael*. These stories of almost unbearable horrors made their appeal above all to his fellow-countrymen, and helped to keep the soul of Poland alive till a body could be created in which it might dwell ; but in *Quo Vadis ?* he addresses himself to the world. Since *The Egyptian Princess* no historical novel has enjoyed such world-wide popularity as this incomparable picture of Neronian Rome, in which the scholar and the artist play their allotted parts, and where the champions of dying paganism and nascent Christianity meet and grapple in deadly embrace. No grander drama offers itself to the creative artist ; and, though it has tempted many pens, Sienkiewicz alone possessed the alchemy to transform the rich ore into a nugget of shining gold. The novels of Jirasek, the Scott of Bohemia, which describe the fortunes of the Czech people from the Hussite Wars and the Counter-Reformation to the

[1] See Monica Gardner's excellent monograph, *Henryk Sienkiewicz*.

renaissance of the nineteenth century, are too little known in Western Europe ; but numberless Czechs have learned most of what they know of their national history from his pages. More fortunate than Sienkiewicz, Jirasek lived long enough to witness the resurrection and consolidation of an independent State.

Our journey across Europe ends in the Near East, where Greece contributes a little masterpiece to our list. *Loukis Laras*, by Demetrius Bikelas, translated into excellent English by Gennadius, late Greek Minister in London, is a simple but poignant study of the Greek war of independence in the form of reminiscences by an old merchant of Chios long after the terrible experiences which he recalls. The story was adapted as a reading-book in the schools of Greece, where it has fed the patriotism of the race with memories of the great deliverance. Less perfect in form but more thrilling in treatment is Vazoff's *Under the Yoke*, in which the first and greatest of Bulgarian novelists describes with passionate sympathy the revolt of his countrymen against the abominations of Turkish misrule.

The notable contributions of America are comparatively few in number. The Waverley Novels were welcomed with exultant enthusiasm, and America's earliest novelist modestly described himself as nothing more than a chip from Scott's block. For a generation the fame of Fenimore Cooper, both in the New and the Old World, was second to that of Scott alone. With the publication in 1821 of *The Spy*, a tale of the War of Independence, he woke up to find himself famous ; and *The Pilot*, a study of the adventurous career of Paul Jones, earned the commendation of Scott himself. Though Cooper lives in literature above all as the interpreter of Red Indian character, his later stories merely confirmed the fame he had won as the romantic historian of the white man. Of far higher quality are Hawthorne's subtle studies of the atmosphere of Puritan New England in *The Scarlet Letter* and *The House of the Seven Gables*, the most exquisite products of American fiction, even if they cannot be described as historical novels in the narrower sense. Not till our own day has America made further important additions to the world's store. Winston Churchill has painted a stirring picture of the Colonial era and the War of Independence in *Richard Carvell*, and in *The Crisis* he has brought vividly before our eyes the struggle of North and South, with the almost divine figure of Abraham Lincoln dominating the stage. A no less life-like portrait of Alexander Hamilton, the most dazzling figure in American history, was painted by Gertrude Atherton in *The Conqueror*, which, though it contains more history and less fiction than any of its rivals, is as readable as a work of pure romance, and is perhaps the finest historical novel that has sprung from the soil of the New World.

After this rapid survey of the achievements of Scott's spiritual progeny on the Continent and in the New World we return to our own shores, where the spell of the wizard was no less binding on readers and writers. Almost every writer of fiction of the Victorian era tried his hand at the game, and historical novels beyond counting poured from the press. Lytton scored the first resounding success with *The Last Days of Pompeii*, the best of his many ventures, Kingsley with *Westward Ho !*, Charles Reade with *The Cloister and the Hearth*. George Eliot entered the lists with *Romola*, Thackeray with *Esmond* and *The Virginians*, Dickens with *The Tale of Two Cities*, Meredith with *Vittoria*, Blackmore with *Lorna Doone*, to say nothing of the more facile triumphs of Charlotte Yonge, Harrison Ainsworth and the legion of caterers for the appetite of schoolboys. Pressing the historical novel into the service of his church, Cardinal Wiseman painted in *Fabiola* a picture of the persecutions that was deservedly admired throughout the Catholic world ; and Newman sketched the sufferings of Christian converts in Roman Africa in his rather lifeless story *Callista*.

The best historical novels have been written because their authors were in love with their subject, and were

attracted to the period by affinities of taste or temperament. When Kingsley sat down to write *Hypatia* he
was an Anglican parson in his surplice ; but when
Westward Ho ! was on the anvil he was transformed
into an Elizabethan, filled with Protestant fury against
the Popish dogs of Spain, his pulse tingling with the
vitality of the virile age of Raleigh and Drake. But
Kingsley's star, which shone so brightly in the mid-
Victorian heavens, has been sadly dimmed, and a good
deal even of *Westward Ho !* has lost its relish. Thackeray had steeped himself in the literature of the age of
Queen Anne in like manner, and felt equally at home
in the company of Addison and Steele ; but his art is
of far higher quality, and *Esmond* is perhaps our greatest
historical novel since the death of Scott. *The Virginians*
possesses some good scenes, but the book suffers from
prolixity, and illustrates anew the relative failure of
sequels. It is the fashion nowadays to argue that
Romola lacks life and atmosphere ; but for many readers
it remains a treasured picture of the Florence of Lorenzo
and Savonarola and of the great reformer himself. *The
Cloister and the Hearth* is in some degree marred by its
didactic purpose. *The Last Days of Pompeii* survives
by its theme and its author's dazzling abilities ; but
even in his best efforts Lytton, like Kingsley, was a
slipshod and unequal writer. No one would reckon
The Tale of Two Cities or *Barnaby Rudge* among the
masterpieces of Dickens, though the picture of the
Gordon riots in the latter is finely drawn.

At the end of the century we may note Stevenson's
unfinished *Weir of Hermiston* and Stanley Weyman's
Under the Red Robe, the finest of his evocations of French
history. The stories of Marjorie Bowen may be read
with pleasure, and Naomi Mitchison's scholarly pictures
of Greek and Roman life deserve their reputation.
Maurice Hewlett's *Richard Yea and Nea* possesses a distinction of style all its own, and E. F. Benson's *The
Vintage* presents a picture of the early stages of the
Greek War of Independence full of knowledge and

local colour. George Moore's *Héloïse and Abélard*
revives one of the great love stories of the world.
Mrs. Steel recalls the horrors of the Indian Mutiny in
On the Face of the Waters, and Mrs. Woods brings Swift
and his ladies to life in *Esther Vanhomrigh*. If *Marius
the Epicurean* is to be numbered among historical novels,
it must claim high rank ; but Pater's elaborate analysis
of Roman life and thought in the second century, with
its shadowy figures, is perhaps more correctly classified
as a philosophical romance. Father Hugh Benson's
Come Rack Come Rope, a study of the Elizabethan
martyrs, is a work of passionate but powerful propaganda.
In *The Flight of the Eagle*, presented by its author ' not
as a romance but an actual historical episode,' Standish
O'Grady painted a picture of Elizabethan Ireland based
on careful study of the sources. George Gissing's
Veranilda, unfortunately never completed, revives the
age of St. Benedict and the Gothic kingdom in its decline.

No English historical novel, old or new, has been
subjected to such minute critical analysis as *John Inglesant*, which for countless readers made the life of
seventeenth century England and Italy strangely real.
The mellow charm of the book was irresistible ; and
the religious and political issues with which it dealt
claimed the attention of serious minds which cared
nothing for the noise of drums and trumpets. But it
exposed a wide surface to attack, and Gardiner promptly
detected some of the mistakes in the field he had made
his own. Acton told Mary Gladstone that he had read
nothing more thoughtful and suggestive since *Middle-
march*, but he added a formidable list of errors and
contradictions, particularly in the Italian portion, which
reduced the author's academic claims to very modest
dimensions.[1] A later Catholic critic, Baron von Hügel,[2]
attributed its fascination to its author's ' all-penetrating
sense of the massiveness, the awful reality, of the life
within the Roman Catholic Church.' This was its only

[1] *Letters to Mary Gladstone*, ed. 1913, 108–19.
[2] *Selected Letters*, 291–2.

HISTORICAL NOVELS 383

merit, he added, though a great one, to set against its misleading portrait of Molinos and other faults. Later still an article in the *Quarterly Review* [1] revealed the fact, which its learned critics had overlooked, that many passages had been lifted from well-known seventeenth century writers with scarcely the change of a word. The discovery, while confirming its veracity as a picture of certain aspects of English life, stamps the work as a skilful mosaic, a literary curiosity unique in the annals of historical fiction.

At the close of this birdseye view of an enormous territory we may permit ourselves a few words of reflection and recapitulation. Firstly, the historical novel is the child of the Romantic Movement. Secondly, in the whole field of the nineteenth century literature no influence compares in world-wide significance with that of Scott. In the third place the masterpieces of the new genre have added treasures to the spiritual heritage of mankind. Fourthly, a mass of fruitful knowledge has been assimilated by millions who have neither time nor inclination for the effort involved in serious historical study. If it be objected that the fictitious element may implant false ideas, the answer is that readers of professedly historical works have also to be on their guard against prejudice and inaccuracy, and that the danger in the latter case is all the greater since the author professes to be a purveyor of nothing but the truth. Fifthly, historical novels have repeatedly given an impetus to scientific study by awakening youthful interest in a period or a movement, a country or an individual, and evoking the desire in the reader to discover for himself what relation the story bears to the real character of actors and events. In one of the precious fragments dictated in his old age Ranke declared that his discovery of the difference in the portraits of Louis XI and Charles the Bold in *Quentin Durward* and Commines constituted an epoch in his life. ' I found by comparison that

---

[1] 'Some Truths about *John Inglesant*,' by W. K. Fleming, *Quarterly Review,* 1925.

the truth was more interesting and beautiful than the romance. I turned away from it and resolved to avoid all invention and imagination in my works and to stick to facts.' Thus the greatest of historical novelists had his share in the making of the greatest of modern historians. Finally, historical fiction has played an active part in reviving and sustaining the sentiment of nationality, which has grown from strength to strength and has changed the face of Europe in the nineteenth and twentieth centuries.